Contentious Belonging

The **ANU Indonesia Project**, a leading international centre of research and graduate training on the Indonesian economy and society, is housed in the **Crawford School of Public Policy's Arndt-Corden Department of Economics**. The Crawford School is part of **ANU College of Asia and the Pacific** at **The Australian National University (ANU)**. Established in 1965 in response to profound changes in the Indonesian economic and political landscapes, the ANU Indonesia Project has grown from a small group of Indonesia-focused economists into an interdisciplinary research centre well known and respected across the world. Funded by ANU and the Australian Department of Foreign Affairs and Trade, the ANU Indonesia Project monitors and analyses recent developments in Indonesia; informs the Australian and Indonesian governments, business and the wider community about those developments and about future prospects; stimulates research on the Indonesian economy; and publishes the respected *Bulletin of Indonesian Economic Studies*.

ANU College of Asia and the Pacific's **Department of Political and Social Change** focuses on domestic politics, social processes and state–society relationships in Asia and the Pacific, and has a long-established interest in Indonesia.

Together with the Department of Political and Social Change, the ANU Indonesia Project holds the annual Indonesia Update conference, which offers an overview of recent economic and political developments and devotes attention to a significant theme in Indonesia's development. The *Bulletin of Indonesian Economic Studies* publishes the conference's economic and political overviews, while the edited papers related to the conference theme are published in the Indonesia Update Series.

The **ISEAS – Yusof Ishak Institute** (formerly Institute of Southeast Asian Studies) is an autonomous organization established in 1968. It is a regional centre dedicated to the study of socio-political, security, and economic trends and developments in Southeast Asia and its wider geostrategic and economic environment. The Institute's research programmes are grouped under Regional Economic Studies (RES), Regional Strategic and Political Studies (RSPS), and Regional Social and Cultural Studies (RSCS). The Institute is also home to the ASEAN Studies Centre (ASC), the Nalanda-Sriwijaya Centre (NSC) and the Singapore APEC Study Centre.

ISEAS Publishing, an established academic press, has issued more than 2,000 books and journals. It is the largest scholarly publisher of research about Southeast Asia from within the region. ISEAS Publishing works with many other academic and trade publishers and distributors to disseminate important research and analyses from and about Southeast Asia to the rest of the world.

Indonesia Update Series

Contentious Belonging

The Place of Minorities in Indonesia

EDITED BY

GREG FEALY • RONIT RICCI

ISEAS YUSOF ISHAK
INSTITUTE

First published in Singapore in 2019 by
ISEAS Publishing
30 Heng Mui Keng Terrace
Singapore 119614

E-mail: publish@iseas.edu.sg
Website: http://bookshop.iseas.edu.sg

The responsibility for facts and opinions in this publication rests exclusively with the authors and their interpretations do not necessarily reflect the views or the policy of the Institute or its supporters.

ISEAS Library Cataloguing-in-Publication Data

Contentious Belonging : The Place of Minorities in Indonesia / edited by Greg
    Fealy and Ronit Ricci.
    "... an outcome of the Indonesia Update Conference held in Canberra on
    14–15 September 2018."
    1.   Minorities – Indonesia.
    2.   Minorities – Civil rights – Indonesia.
    3.   Indonesia – Social conditions.
    4.   Indonesia – Ethnic relations.
    5.   Minorities – Indonesia – Public opinion.
    6.   People with disabilities – Indonesia.
    7.   Sexual minorities – Indonesia.
    8.   Religious tolerance – Indonesia.
    I.   Fealy, Greg, editor.
    II. Ricci, Ronit, editor.
    III. Indonesia Update Conference (36th : 2018 : Australian National
       University)
DS644.4 I41 2018   2019

ISBN 978-981-4843-46-1 (soft cover)
ISBN 978-981-4843-49-2 (hard cover)
ISBN 978-981-4843-47-8 (ebook, PDF)

Cover photo: Wayang puppets on sale at an antiques market in Jakarta
Photo by Peter Adams Photography Pte Ltd / Alamy Stock Photo

Edited and typeset by Beth Thomson, Japan Online, Canberra
Indexed by Angela Grant, Sydney

Contents

Tables and figures

Contributors

Dina Afrianty, Research Fellow, La Trobe Law School, Melbourne

Ihsan Ali-Fauzi, Director, PUSAD Paramadina, Jakarta

Simon Butt, Professor of Indonesian Law and Director, Centre for Asian and Pacific Law, University of Sydney, Sydney

Robert Cribb, Professor of Asian History, Department of Political and Social Change, Coral Bell School of Asia Pacific Affairs, College of Asia and the Pacific, Australian National University, Canberra

Thushara Dibley, Deputy Director, Sydney Southeast Asia Centre (SSEAC), University of Sydney, Sydney

Greg Fealy, Associate Professor, Department of Political and Social Change, Coral Bell School of Asia Pacific Affairs, College of Asia and the Pacific, Australian National University, Canberra

Sidney Jones, Director, Institute for Policy Analysis of Conflict (IPAC), Jakarta

Tim Lindsey, Malcolm Smith Professor of Asian Law, Redmond Barry Distinguished Professor, and Director of the Centre for Indonesian Law, Islam and Society at Melbourne Law School, University of Melbourne, Melbourne

Butet Manurung, Director, Sokola Institute

Marcus Mietzner, Associate Professor, Coral Bell School of Asia Pacific Affairs, College of Asia and the Pacific, Australian National University, Canberra; and Visiting Research Scholar, Center for Southeast Asian Studies, Kyoto University, Kyoto

Burhanuddin Muhtadi, Senior Lecturer in Political Science, Faculty of Social and Political Sciences, Syarif Hidayatullah State Islamic University, Jakarta; Executive Director, Indikator Politik Indonesia, Jakarta; and Director of Public Affairs, Lembaga Survei Indonesia (LSI), Jakarta

Maria Myutel, School of Culture, History and Language, College of Asia and the Pacific, Australian National University, Canberra

Ronit Ricci, Sternberg-Tamir Chair in Comparative Cultures and Associate Professor, Departments of Asian Studies and Religion, Hebrew University of Jerusalem, Jerusalem; and Associate Professor, School of Culture, History and Language, College of Asia and the Pacific, Australian National University, Canberra

Charlotte Setijadi, Assistant Professor of Humanities, School of Social Sciences, Singapore Management University, Singapore

Antoni Tsaputra, PhD Candidate, Faculty of Arts and Social Sciences (FASS), University of New South Wales (UNSW), Sydney

Saskia E. Wieringa, Chair, Women's Same-Sex Relations Crossculturally, Amsterdam Institute for Social Science Research (AISSR), University of Amsterdam, Amsterdam

Hendri Yulius Wijaya, Writer

Acknowledgments

The papers in this volume were presented during the thirty-sixth Indonesia Update Conference at the Australian National University (ANU), Canberra, on 14–15 September 2018. Our greatest thanks go to the authors, without whom this book would not exist.

The Indonesia Update Conference is organised jointly by the Indonesia Project and the Department of Political and Social Change at the ANU, and has been conducted annually since 1983. In preparing for the 2018 conference, we were greatly supported by Blane Lewis, the head of the ANU Indonesia Project, and we thank him for his guidance. We also acknowledge the helpful suggestions and feedback from all Indonesianists at the ANU.

We thank the core team of the 2018 Indonesia Update Conference for making the conference run smoothly: Kate McLinton, Lydia Napitupulu, Nurkemala Muliani, Ruth Nikijuluw, Maxine McArthur and Thuy Thu Pham. We would also like to thank Rus'an Nasrudin, Wishnu Mahraddika, Joseph Marshan and all the student volunteers for their assistance during the conference, and the speakers, chairs and discussants for their valuable contributions. Perhimpunan Pelajar Indonesia Australia (PPIA) ACT, the Australia–Indonesia Youth Association (AIYA) ACT and the ANU ASEAN Society also assisted with preparations for and logistical support during the conference. We are grateful to Liam Gammon and his team at *New Mandala* for helping to promote the event.

We acknowledge the continuing support of the ANU College of Asia and the Pacific. The Australian Department of Foreign Affairs and Trade (DFAT), through its grant to the ANU Indonesia Project, has been a long-term supporter of the Update conferences and the associated series of books. We thank Virginia Hooker for her welcoming remarks at the conference, and Julie Heckscher, the Director of DFAT's Southeast Asia Division, for formally opening the conference. After the Update we held two follow-up events in Sydney and Melbourne (the 'Mini Updates'). For these, we thank Aaron Connelly and his colleagues at the Lowy Institute for International Policy in Sydney and Tim Lindsey at the Centre for Indonesian Law, Islam and Society at the University of Melbourne.

The Indonesia Update series of books has been published annually since 1989. Once again, we would like to thank our publisher, the ISEAS – Yusof Ishak Institute, especially Ng Kok Kiong and Rahilah Yusuf, for their excellent work. We are indebted to Beth Thomson for her superb editorial work; she has been involved in the Update book series since 1994. We also thank Angela Grant for assistance with indexing.

Greg Fealy and Ronit Ricci
Canberra, April 2019

Glossary

adat	custom or tradition; customary law, traditional law
agama	religion
Ahok	Basuki Tjahaja Purnama (former governor of Jakarta)
AILA	Aliansi Cinta Keluarga (Family Love Alliance)
aliran kepercayaan	'stream of beliefs'; term for traditional religious beliefs that do not belong to one of the six officially recognised religions
AMAN	Aliansi Masyarakat Adat Nusantara (Alliance of Archipelagic Indigenous Peoples)
ANBTI	Aliansi Nasional Bhinneka Tunggal Ika (Unity in Diversity National Alliance)
asas kekeluargaan	family principle, family values
asas tunggal	sole basic principle
asli	authentic, indigenous, native
banci	transgender person
Bappenas	Badan Perencanaan Pembangunan Nasional (Ministry of National Development Planning)
Bhaiband	'Brothers'; a subcaste of Hindu Sindhis
Bhinneka Tunggal Ika	'Out of Many, One', 'Unity in Diversity', 'The Many Are One'
bissu	a gender category among the Bugis (South Sulawesi)
BJP	Bharatiya Janata Party
BKS Gereja	Badan Kerjasama Seluruh Gereja (All Churches Cooperation Agency)
BKSDA	Balai Konservasi Sumber Daya Alam (Natural Resource Conservation Agency)
BMA	Bombay Merchant Association
BPS	Badan Pusat Statistik (Statistics Indonesia), the central statistics agency
BRWA	Badan Registrasi Wilayah Adat (Ancestral Domain Registration Agency)

Budi Utomo	the first Indonesian nationalist organisation, founded in 1908
cacat	defect, deformity
camat	subdistrict head
CAPPA Foundation	Ecological Justice for People Foundation
CRPD	Convention on the Rights of Persons with Disabilities
dakwah	religious outreach, Islamic proselytising
Darul Islam	Islamist insurgent movement that rebelled against the Republic of Indonesia between 1948 and 1962 and declared Indonesia to be an Islamic state in 1949
desa adat	customary village
difabel	'diffability'; differently abled
disabilitas	disability
DPR	Dewan Perwakilan Rakyat (People's Representative Council), also known as 'House of Representatives' and as 'parliament'
DPRD	Dewan Perwakilan Rakyat Daerah (Regional People's Representative Council)
dukun godong	shaman in an Orang Rimba community
e-KTP	*kartu tanda penduduk elektronik* (electronic identity card)
FBR	Forum Betawi Rempug (Betawi Brotherhood Forum)
fiqh	Islamic jurisprudence or legal prescriptions
FJI	Front Jihad Islam (Islamic Jihad Front)
FKUB	Forum Kerukunan Umat Beragama (Interreligious Harmony Forum)
FLNKS	Front de Libération Nationale Kanak et Socialiste (Kanak and Socialist National Liberation Front)
FPI	Front Pembela Islam (Islamic Defenders Front)
FTM	female-to-male
Gerindra	Gerakan Indonesia Raya (Great Indonesia Movement)
Gerwani	Gerakan Wanita Indonesia (Indonesian Women's Movement)
GMIS	Gandhi Memorial International School
GMIT	Gereja Masehi Injili di Timor (Christian Evangelical Church in Timor)
GMS	Gandhi Memorial School
Golkar	Golongan Karya (the state political party under the New Order, and a major post-New Order party)
GPdI	Gereja Pantekosta di Indonesia (Pentecostal Church of Indonesia)
Guided Democracy	political system in place from 1957 to 1966 under President Sukarno

Hadith	report or account of the words and deeds of the Prophet Muhammad transmitted through a chain of narrators
hajj	the annual pilgrimage to Mecca
Hanura	Partai Hati Nurani Rakyat (People's Conscience Party)
HTI	Hizbut Tahrir Indonesia
IAIN	Institut Agama Islam Negeri (State Islamic Institute)
ICMI	Ikatan Cendekiawan Muslimin Indonesia (Indonesian Association of Muslim Intellectuals)
Indo	Indonesian of European descent
IPT 1965	International People's Tribunal on 1965 Crimes Against Humanity in Indonesia
jilbab	headscarf worn by Muslim women
Jokowi	(President) Joko Widodo
kafir	infidel
kampung	urban village
kartu keluarga	family card
KBM 1969	Surat Keputusan Bersama 1969 (Joint Decree 1969)
kepercayaan	'beliefs'; term for traditional religious beliefs that do not belong to one of the six officially recognised religions
Kesbangpol	Badan Kesatuan Bangsa dan Politik (Agency for the Protection of National Unity and Politics)
Ketuhanan Yang Maha Esa	Almighty God
kitab kuning	'yellow books' (a reference to the colour of the pages); commentaries on the Qur'an and Islamic law used as teaching texts in *pesantren*
KKI Warsi	Komunitas Konservasi Indonesia Warsi (Indonesian Conservation Community Warsi)
Koalisi Masyarakat 'Tolak PP Sapu Jagat'	People's Coalition to 'Reject the One-Size-Fits-All Government Regulation'
Komnas HAM	Komisi Nasional Hak Asasi Manusia (National Commission for Human Rights)
Kompak	Komunitas Peace Maker Kupang (Kupang Peacemaker Community)
Kopkamtib	Komando Operasi Pemulihan Keamanan dan Ketertiban (Operational Command for the Restoration of Security and Order)
KPI	Koalisi Perempuan Indonesia (Indonesian Women's Coalition)
KSP	Kantor Staf Presiden Republik Indonesia (Executive Office of the President of the Republic of Indonesia)
KTP	*kartu tanda penduduk* (identity card)
KUHP	Kitab Undang-Undang Pidana (Criminal Code)

Laksusda	Pelaksana Khusus Daerah (Special Territorial Administrator)
LBH	Lembaga Bantuan Hukum (Legal Aid Office)
LEKRA	Lembaga Kebudayaan Rakyat (People's Cultural Institute)
Lemhannas	Lembaga Ketahanan Nasional Republik Indonesia (National Resilience Institute)
LGBT	lesbian, gay, bisexual and transgender
LGBTQI	lesbian, gay, bisexual, transgender, queer and intersex
LSI	Lembaga Survei Indonesia (Indonesian Survey Institute)
madrasah	Islamic school
masyarakat adat	'traditional' or 'customary' community
masyarakat hukum adat	customary law community
masyarakat terasing	isolated community
masyarakat tertinggal	'left-behind community'; underdeveloped or isolated community
Melindo	Melanesia Indonesia
MGS	Mahatma Gandhi School
MPR	Majelis Permusyawaratan Rakyat (People's Consultative Assembly), Indonesia's upper house
MSG	Melanesian Spearhead Group
MSM	men who have sex with men
MTF	male-to-female
MUI	Majelis Ulama Indonesia (Indonesian Council of Religious Scholars), founded in 1975
NasDem	Nasional Demokrat (National Democrats)
Nawacita	Nine Development Goals
negara hukum	rule of law
New Order	political system in place from 1966 to 1998 under President Suharto
NGO	non-government organisation
NKRI	Negara Kesatuan Republik Indonesia (Unitary State of the Republic of Indonesia)
non-pribumi	non-indigenous Indonesian
orang	person
Orang Rimba	People of the Jungle; Forest People
Pancasila	the five guiding principles of the Indonesian state: belief in God, humanitarianism, nationalism, democracy and social justice; or, in another formulation: belief in one supreme God, just and civilised humanity, national unity, democracy led by wisdom and prudence through consultation and representation, and social justice

PBM 2006	Peraturan Bersama Menteri 2006 (Joint Ministerial Regulation 2006)
PDI-P	Partai Demokrasi Indonesia-Perjuangan (Indonesian Democratic Party of Struggle)
pemekaran	'blossoming'; the subdivision of administrative regions to create new provinces, districts and subdistricts
penghayat kepercayaan	believer in an indigenous religion
Peranakan	Chinese Indonesians who have adopted local customs and assimilated into local communities
peraturan	regulation
perda	*peraturan daerah* (regional government regulation)
pesantren	Islamic boarding school
PKB	Partai Kebangkitan Bangsa (National Awakening Party)
PKH	Program Keluarga Harapan (Family Hope Program)
PKI	Partai Komunis Indonesia (Indonesian Communist Party)
PKMT	Pemukiman Kembali Masyarakat Terasing (Resettlement of Isolated Peoples)
PKS	Partai Keadilan Sejahtera (Prosperous Justice Party)
Pokja	Kelompok Kerja Undang-Undang Disabilitas (Working Group on the Disability Law)
pornoaksi	pornographic action/activities
PP	*peraturan pemerintah* (government decree or regulation)
PPP	Partai Persatuan Pembangunan (United Development Party)
PRC	People's Republic of China
pribumi	indigenous, native
Pribumi Party	Partai Priboemi
priyayi	traditional Javanese upper-class elite
punakawan	attendant to a main character in the Indic Mahabharata story
PUSAD Paramadina	Pusat Studi Agama dan Demokrasi (Center for the Study of Religion and Democracy in the Paramadina Foundation)
QUANGO	quasi-autonomous non-government organisation
Ramadan	ninth month of the Islamic calendar during which fasting is required
reformasi	'reform'; name for the post-Suharto period (since 1998)
Riskesdas	Riset Kesehatan Dasar (Basic Health Research)
rombongan	Orang Rimba clan
rumah ibadat	house of worship

SAD	Suku Anak Dalam (Tribes of the Interior; People from the Deep Jungle)
SARA	*suku, agama, ras dan antar golongan* (ethnicity, religion, race and intergroup)
SBKRI	Surat Bukti Kewarganegaraan Republik Indonesia (Proof of Indonesian Citizenship Document)
sinetron	commercial soap opera
SLB	*sekolah luar biasa* (special school)
Sobat KBB	Solidaritas Korban Pelanggaran Kebebasan Beragama dan Berkeyakinan (Solidarity of Victims of Violations of Religious Freedom and Belief)
SOGIE	sexual orientation, gender identity and gender expression
Suku Anak Dalam	Tribes of the Interior; People from the Deep Jungle
Susenas	Survei Sosio-Ekonomi Nasional (National Socio-Economic Survey)
Totok	China-born or Chinese residents in Indonesia who have not assimilated or only partially assimilated into local society
Tuhan Yang Maha Esa	Almighty God
tumenggung	chief of an Orang Rimba community
UIN	Universitas Islam Negeri (State Islamic University)
ulama	'learned'; Islamic scholar(s)
ULMWP	United Liberation Movement for West Papua
umrah	pilgrimage to Mecca that can be undertaken at any time of the year
UN	United Nations
UNDP	United Nations Development Programme
US	United States
USAID	United States Agency for International Development
VOC	Vereenigde Oost-Indische Compagnie (United East India Company; Dutch East India Company)
wadam	*wanita Adam* (transgender person), from *wanita* and *Adam* and no longer common
wandu	(Javanese) transgender person
Wantimpres	Dewan Pertimbangan Presiden (Presidential Advisory Council)
waria	*wanita–pria* (woman–man), inadequately translated as 'transgender women'
Warsi	*see* KKI Warsi

Currencies

$	US dollar
Rp	Indonesian rupiah

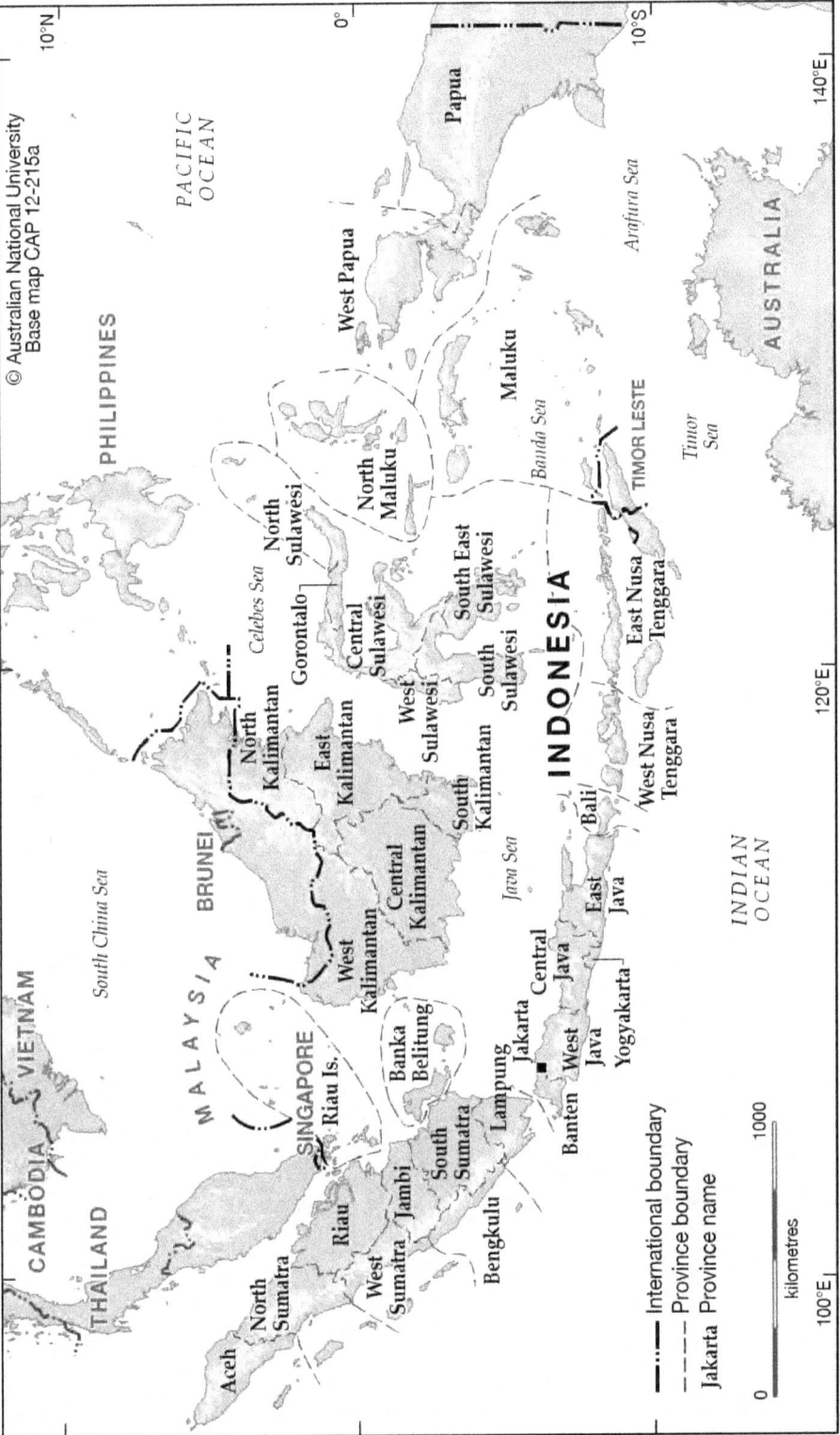

© Australian National University
Base map CAP 12-215a

1 Diversity and its discontents: an overview of minority–majority relations in Indonesia

Greg Fealy and Ronit Ricci

Indonesia has always perceived itself as being a tolerant, diverse and pluralist nation. As one of the most ethnically, religiously and culturally complex societies on earth, Indonesia has cast acceptance of difference and equality of rights and opportunities as a cornerstone of its exist-ence. The nation's motto is *Bhinneka Tunggal Ika*, an Old Javanese phrase typically translated as 'Unity in Diversity' but perhaps more accurately rendered as 'Out of Many, One'. The motto implies that Indonesia not only embraces but also celebrates diversity. Founding president Sukarno set the tone in a speech in 1955 when he declared: 'This country, the Republic of Indonesia, does not belong to any group, nor to any religion, nor to any ethnic group, nor to any group with particular customs and traditions, but is the property of all of us from Sabang to Merauke! [i.e., from the further-most northwestern to southeastern points of the archi-pelago]' (quoted in Vatikiotis 2017: 157). In essence, he was claiming that all who lived within Indonesia's borders were owed the same rights and no single group had preference. More recently, presidents Susilo Bambang Yudhoyono (2004–14) and Joko Widodo (2014–) have made terms such as 'moderation', 'tolerance' and 'multiculturalism' central to their nation's international diplomacy. Yudhoyono, for example, declared at a Harvard address in 2009 that Indonesia was a 'bastion of freedom, tolerance and harmony' (Yudhoyono 2009) and stated at a high-level event in New York in 2013 that '[Indonesia] will always protect our minorities and ensure that no one suffers from discrimination' (Parlina and Aritonang 2013). In addition, and reflecting a broad sentiment, public opinion surveys have repeatedly shown that an overwhelming majority of Indonesians believe their country to be tolerant and respectful of the rights of minorities (Fealy 2016: 120; Mietzner and Muhtadi in Chapter 9 of this volume).

But is this self-perception justified? In recent years Indonesia's reputation for tolerance and inclusivity has come under growing scrutiny from domestic and overseas civil society and human rights groups, the international media and the diplomatic community. Much of this scrutiny relates to the treatment of religious and ethnic minorities and of the country's lesbian, gay, bisexual and transgender (LGBT) communities. They have variously been subject to condemnation or denigration by other sections of society and political leaders, and in some cases have been the target of violent attack.

Sectarian incidents have been rising since the mid-2000s, drawing international media coverage. The most high-profile targets have been the minority Muslim sects, Ahmadiyah and Shi'a. Ahmadi mosques, schools and residences have been attacked and sometimes destroyed by opponents, often with tardy or reluctant intervention by law enforcement officials. The most serious attack occurred in Cikeusik in Banten province in 2011, when three Ahmadis were killed as police looked on. Videos of the attack went viral on social media and the incident was widely reported internationally. In other instances, many hundreds of Ahmadis have been harassed and displaced from their homes, with little effective government action to resolve their predicament. On a lesser scale, Shi'as have also been targets of intimidation and violence from groups within the Sunni majority. One Shi'a died in 2012 during an attack on his village in Sampang, East Java, and some 220 fellow Shi'a villagers were evacuated, with only those who agreed to 'convert' to Sunni Islam being repatriated to their village. Major Muslim organisations have called for both the Ahmadiyah and Shi'a sects to be banned, but so far the government has only restricted Ahmadi outreach activities.

Non-Muslim religious minorities such as Christians and Buddhists have also reported an elevated number of breaches of religious freedoms over the past decade and a half, a claim supported by human rights groups. Many dozens of minority houses of worship, most commonly churches but sometimes also temples, have been denied permits for construction or renovation by local authorities on questionable grounds or have been attacked by vigilantes from the local majority religion (see Chapter 10 of this volume by Ali-Fauzi). Moreover, numerous provincial and district administrations have sought to restrict the activities of minority faith congregations and local Ministry of Religious Affairs officials have pressured heterodox religious groups to become 'orthodox' in order to avoid problems in gaining identity cards and receiving related welfare and educational support.

National laws and regulations also affect the rights of religious minorities. Only six religions are recognised by the state: Islam, Catholicism, Protestantism, Hinduism, Buddhism and Confucianism. All other faiths are excluded from receiving state support and typically cannot be listed on official documentation. Thus, Indonesia's small number of Jewish and Baha'i citizens are often forced to choose one of the six official religions for listing on their identity documents. Near-insurmountable obstacles are also placed in the path of those seeking interfaith marriages. This is especially the case if someone from a minority faith is seeking to marry a Muslim. Although civil registration of such marriages is possible, the Ministry of Religious Affairs usually refuses to recognise marriages between Muslims and non-Muslims. Non-Muslims and heterodox Muslims have also fallen victim to the draconian 1965 Blasphemy Law, which has a broad and vaguely worded definition of the offence of insulting religion and religious authorities. This law has been the basis of an unprecedented number of prosecutions in the past decade and a half. Since 2004, more than 100 convictions have been recorded, with no defendant being acquitted (see Chapter 3 by Lindsey).

The most controversial blasphemy case was that involving Basuki Tjahaja Purnama (commonly known as Ahok), the governor of Jakarta. During that city's gubernatorial election campaign in late 2016 and early 2017, Ahok, a Chinese Christian, was accused of insulting the Qur'an and Islamic scholars (*ulama*) when he told a rally that Muslims could elect a non-Muslim leader despite some *ulama* stating that the Qur'an forbade this. His remarks drew widespread condemnation not only from Islamist groups, which had long objected to his governorship, but also from many mainstream Muslims. This led to unprecedented public protests, including one in early December 2016 that was estimated to have brought more than half a million demonstrators onto Jakarta's streets. The protests were accompanied by a massive social media campaign demanding that the governor be charged with, and jailed for, blasphemy.

A major feature of the anti-Ahok protests was their explicit anti-Chinese and anti-Christian tone. Senior Islamic leaders made frequent reference to Ahok's race and religion and some called for laws preventing members of a religious minority from holding executive positions in a majority-Muslim community, such as Jakarta. Vilification of Chinese Christians was especially virulent on social media platforms. The sheer intensity and spread of the outpouring against Ahok forced a reluctant government to prosecute him and to expedite his trial. Most of the trial proceedings were conducted during the election campaign. Ahok lost the election and shortly afterwards was found guilty of blasphemy and jailed for two years.

The impact of the Ahok case both within and outside Indonesia was significant. Many politicians from minorities, especially Chinese and Christians, worried that their own careers in public life were now far less certain as they too might be vulnerable to similar forms of attack. In addition, the events had a chilling effect on up-and-coming members of minority groups contemplating entry into politics. Foreign media also carried extensive reporting on the protests and the trial, with many journalists stating openly that the Ahok case was proof of growing racial and sectarian intolerance in Indonesia, driven particularly by the politics of rising Islamic conservativism (see Chapter 9 by Mietzner and Muhtadi and Chapter 11 by Setijadi).

The other major 'intolerance' issue that attracted global attention was the sharp rise of anti-homosexual and anti-transgender discourses from 2015 (see Chapter 7 by Wieringa and Chapter 8 by Wijaya). Beginning with a campaign by conservative Muslims to ban LGBT awareness and rights programs on campuses, the issue was taken up in early 2016 by a wide range of leaders from across the political and religious spectrums. Ministers and community figures denounced 'sexual deviancy' and advocated rehabilitation programs; universities began asking incoming students to sign declarations that they were not homosexual; and the Indonesian Psychiatrists Association classified homosexuality as a mental disorder, drawing objections from Western psychiatric organisations. Local authorities also began to arrest men for alleged homosexual activities, with two men in Aceh publicly caned after being found guilty of indecent behaviour by a sharia court.

The international response to these cases of intolerance towards religious, ethnic and sexual minorities has been increasingly critical. In early 2018, the UN high commissioner for human rights, Zeid Ra'ad al-Hussein, warned that he saw 'strains of intolerance seemingly alien to Indonesian culture that have made inroads here [in Indonesia]. The extremist views playing out in the political arena are deeply worrying, accompanied as they are by rising levels of incitement to discrimination, hatred or violence in various parts of the country' (OHCHR 2018).

Major human rights organisations such as Amnesty International and Human Rights Watch have also written damning reports on what they perceive to be Indonesia's worsening record on minority rights (Amnesty International 2018; Human Rights Watch 2018).

For all these reasons, it is timely to make a closer examination of minorities in Indonesia—their lives, struggles and aspirations, and the ways in which they may feel a sense of belonging, or not belonging, within Indonesian society. To explore this theme we consider the position and status of different minorities within the Indonesian state both across time and in the present day. Thinking about the place of minorities in Indonesia today involves thinking about religion and ethnicity; about the gap between creating laws and implementing them; about how ideas and movements that have emerged far from Indonesia affect Indonesian perceptions; about Indonesia's place among the nations in comparative perspective; about the power of discourses to shape politics and everyday life; and more. This book discusses the complex historical and contemporary dimensions of Indonesia's minorities from a range of perspectives, including historical, legal, political, cultural, discursive and social. While much of the current commentary on Indonesia's treatment of minorities is highly critical, our purpose here is to provide a balanced, nuanced and rigorous assessment. Although there clearly are particular minorities that experience discrimination and persecution, this is not true of all minorities, or even for the entirety of a given minority community. In other words, Indonesia's treatment of minorities is neither uniform nor monolithic. Why is it that a certain minority in a particular location incurs the wrath of state officials or surrounding communities when other groups within the same minority are undisturbed or even embraced by the majority? And why might the standing of a particular minority change dramatically over a short span of time? What role do discourses about minorities, and especially shifting nomenclatures that refer to particular groups, play in their plight? These are some of the questions that the contributors to this book seek to answer.

The overarching theme of the volume is that of contentious belonging. Itself an ambiguous and hotly debated term, 'belonging' here encompasses not only citizenship and legal rights but also a more subtle sense of attachment, loyalty and community within a national framework that is more difficult to define and quantify. How strongly do members of minority groups feel that they belong to and occupy a place within Indonesia? To consider this theme we examine the ways in which Indonesia has conceived of the place of minorities within the nation and how it has dealt with its minorities in practice. As noted in the opening paragraph, Indonesia prides itself on being a nation that acknowledges and accommodates diversity. But as recent cases of intolerance make clear, there can be a large gap between aspiration and reality. Indeed, from the earliest days of discussing the idea of 'Indonesia' in the 1920s, the issue of who or what should be part of the independent post-colonial state has divided opinion. The emergent nationalist movement in the Dutch East Indies discussed at length how inclusive or exclusive the proposed nation should be. Should preference be given to or limits imposed upon particular religious or ethnic groups, or certain political ideologies or cultural orientations? Should Indonesia be a nation in which the rights and wishes of the majority take precedence over those of minorities, or should all who reside within its borders have equal rights? Consensus on such issues proved elusive, whether for the nationalists of the colonial period or the political and community leaders who have shaped public debate since Indonesia's independence in 1945. In fact, for the best part of a century, debates about which minorities 'belong' in Indonesia and what position in society, law and politics they should be accorded have been ever-present.

IDENTIFYING MINORITIES

Determining who or what is a minority is far from straightforward. At one level, it can seem a simple matter of numbers and proportions. Dictionary definitions usually refer to minorities as being the 'smaller number or part, representing less than half of the whole' (Oxford English Dictionary) or as 'the smaller in number of two groups constituting a whole' (Merriam-Webster). Such numerical definitions appear to render minority status a clear-cut matter, but they fail to capture the complexity of lived experience and relations between groups of different sizes and power dynamics within a society. For this reason, many scholars have focused on such matters as the relative disadvantage borne by one category of people compared to the dominant group. This emphasis raises questions of equality of rights and opportunities and, more broadly, differential treatment and access to power within communities. For example, in apartheid-era South Africa, blacks were a numerical majority but manifestly subordinate to the much-smaller ruling white minority.

There is a large literature, especially in sociology and law, that attempts to provide more nuanced definitions of minorities. Much emphasis is given both to the qualities that a particular group may have that give rise to a self-perception of being a minority or to being classed as such by other groups, as well as to the nature of the relations between groups. Sociologists commonly define a minority as a group with observable characteristics or practices based on such things as gender or sexual orientation, religion, ethnicity or disability. For example, Wirth (1945: 347) defined a minority as

> any group of people who, because of their physical or cultural characteristics, are singled out from the others in the society in which they live for differential and unequal treatment.

Membership of a minority group may be ascribed objectively by society or applied subjectively by members of a particular group. According to this view, minority identity is socially constructed. Perhaps the definition that comes closest to combining the numerical with the qualitative is that of the UN official and scholar Francesco Capotorti (1977: 96):

a group numerically inferior to the rest of the population of a State, in a non-dominant position, whose members—being nationals of the State—possess ethnic, religious or linguistic characteristics differing from those of the rest of the population and show, if only implicitly, a sense of solidarity, directed towards preserving their culture, traditions, religion or language.

Capotorti's focus was on religious and ethnic minorities but sexuality and disability could easily be added to his definition without undermining its cogency.

Such discussions about minority status have emerged repeatedly in an Indonesian context, arousing much dispute about the categorisation and characterisation of minorities. For example, although Ahmadiyah regards itself as part of the Islamic community and indeed has this legal status in Indonesia, a large majority of Indonesian Muslims—up to 78 per cent according to one opinion poll—believe Ahmadis are not Muslims (Fealy 2016: 119). Ahmadi leaders have strenuously opposed attempts by some religious affairs ministers to reclassify them as non-Muslims or to shift Ahmadiyah from the religion (*agama*) category to the lower status of a belief (*kepercayaan*). For Ahmadiyah, being a subgroup within the Muslim majority is theologically valid as well as legally preferable to being a stand-alone minority, much less a minority without an officially recognised religion. Conservative Islamist groups also declare Shi'a to lie outside the faith, although this is not a position held by major Islamic organisations.

A quite different inflection on the majority–minority discourse was apparent during the repressive years of Suharto's New Order regime (1966–98), when some Islamic leaders were wont to declare that the Muslim community was a majority with minority mentality—repeating a statement first made in 1980 by the Dutch sociologist W.F. Wertheim (see Chapter 2 by Cribb). In effect they were observing that, despite its vast numerical superiority, the Muslim community was marginalised by the regime and behaved as if it were a small part of the nation. In a similar vein, numerous feminist writers have argued that despite comprising about half of Indonesia's population, women are effectively a minority, such is their lack of political, economic and cultural power. Gay activists also contend that excessive focus on their sexual orientation casts them into the status of a small and often-reviled minority, thereby overlooking their role as full citizens and contributors to mainstream society.

The position with ethnic minorities is even more complicated, as their sense of belonging and allegiance may be diffuse. The Chinese, Arab, Euro-Indonesian (usually known as Indo) and Indian communities are all examples of minorities that have experienced major internal differences over relations with majority communities and the degree of identification with the nation. Each of these communities contains elements that identify

primarily, even exclusively, with Indonesia and regard themselves une-
quivocally as Indonesian citizens. But each also possesses groups that
retain strong loyalties to and connections with their homelands, whether
real or imagined. For instance, a majority of the Chinese minority (known
as Peranakan) are thoroughly Indonesian-ised, linguistically, culturally and in terms of national allegiance, whereas many other Chinese
Indonesians remain strongly oriented towards mainland China. Arab
communities also contain groups who maintain close ties with Yemen,
whence many of their forebears came. Until the recent conflict in Yemen,
many Arab families sent their sons to study in Yemeni schools and col-
leges, and prominent Yemeni *ulama* are revered within Indonesian Arab
circles. As Maria Myutel makes clear in Chapter 12 of this book, many
Sindhis living in Indonesia continue to visit India regularly and retain
substantial economic, kinship and cultural links there.

Perhaps most complex of all is the position of 'indigenous' Indonesians,
a varied array of minorities, estimated to number in the millions, who
regard themselves as being the original inhabitants of a region or as
having much longer ties of settlement to and affinity with a locality than
the majority communities. Some of these communities seek to remain
isolated from mainstream communities. For example, the Orang Rimba
(Forest People) of Jambi and Riau continue to preserve centuries-old practices of living deep within the forest and having minimal contact with
outsiders rather than integrate into Indonesian society (see Chapter 13 by
Manurung). Relatively few Orang Rimba know about Indonesia's national
history or its legal and political structures—matters regarded as obligatory for other citizens. Their awareness and primary identity are largely
directed inward, not towards the nation. The Orang Rimba do perceive
themselves to be part of Indonesia but nonetheless seek to maintain a
high degree of separation from the state.

Hence, the sense of 'belonging' in Indonesia takes markedly different forms within different minority groups. This can heavily influence
majority attitudes to particular minorities. In general, those minority
communities that display a high degree of cultural assimilation and conform to majority notions of loyalty to the Indonesian nation tend to be
better received and less likely to attract suspicion and denigration. By
contrast, those that maintain very distinctive cultural patterns or remain
separate from the mainstream are more likely to be regarded with suspicion, resentment or condescension. Peranakan Chinese tend to be better
received than Totok Chinese, who do not speak Indonesian or demonstrate cultural integration. Smaller, less conspicuous minorities, such as
the Indians, are largely absent from national debates about belonging.
Indigenous groups such as the Orang Rimba generate paternalistic sentiment as governments at the national and local levels seek to 'modernise'

these communities and integrate them more fully into national life. And so it is that relations between the majority and minorities can vary substantially, making the task of generalisation hazardous.

A GUIDE TO THE STRUCTURE OF THE BOOK

This volume is divided into five parts: history and law; disability; sexuality; religion and ethnicity; and a final set of reflections. In the following 13 chapters, the contributors explore diverse aspects of minority life in Indonesia. Taken together, the articles expand and deepen our understanding of Indonesia by highlighting and engaging critically with core themes of Indonesian life through the 'minority lens': the role of civil society, the stakes of political struggles, past and present discourses in the public sphere, integration versus separateness, justice and democracy, the malleability of collective categories and more.

Part 1 opens with a broad survey of the history of minorities in Indonesia by Robert Cribb. Although at present we tend to think of minorities as living under threat, the author suggests that minority status has at times carried advantages and even privilege. Above all, Cribb argues, minority status in Indonesia needs to be considered as a product of complex social and political forces that have shifted over time. He shows this by focusing on three groups: the Indo-Europeans, the Chinese, and the Islamists who have rejected the idea of a secular Indonesia. The latter's growing self-confidence during the New Order's later years, and especially after Suharto's fall, has propelled them to centre stage in Indonesian society and politics. Cribb argues that, with this shift and the accompanying rise in intolerance towards various 'others' (with the Ahok case signalling a watershed moment), a new tendency towards cantonisation based on religious and ethnic identity has emerged. This poses a threat to the unity of the state and its historical embracing of plurality, as well as creating challenges for what Cribb terms the 'new minorities' (for example, indigenous groups, women, people with disabilities) that cannot readily be cantonised.

In Chapter 3, Tim Lindsey provides an overview of aspects of the complex legal framework regulating the treatment of minorities in Indonesia. Although the post-Suharto era began with aspirational and often impressive constitutional reform between 1999 and 2002, followed by policy debates (typically led by civil society) that produced sophisticated reform models based on global standards, the laws and regulations eventually produced by the government or the national legislature tend to be flawed or incomplete. Further complicating things has been a lack of compliance measures and sanctions as well as multiple enforcement challenges. All this, plus a growing culture of intolerant Muslim majoritarianism, means that there is in fact no coherent framework for the protection of minorities, leaving them vulnerable to discrimination and abuse. To demonstrate this point, Lindsey surveys key laws and regulations relating to the treatment of disabled Indonesians, lesbian, gay, bisexual, transgender, queer and intersex (LGBTQI) Indonesians, religious minorities, customary (*adat*) communities and the ethnic Chinese. Lindsey concludes that the shortcomings of minority-related laws create major challenges for minorities, ensuring that 'their "belonging" remains contentious legally as well as in other ways'.

In Chapter 4, Simon Butt examines Indonesia's Constitutional Court, established in 2003, as an arena in which minorities can pursue their interests. To exemplify the workings of the court, he focuses on two cases handed down in 2017. The first touched on the interests of some of Indonesia's LGBTQI community. Had the applicants, members of a conservative Muslim group, won, the court would effectively have outlawed consensual gay sex. Although the applicants did not win the case, Butt writes that the court's very narrow decision (five judges rejected the application while four supported it) 'does not bode well for the future of Indonesian pluralism'. The second case concerned the constitutional recognition of indigenous beliefs (*kepercayaan*), the followers of which have often suffered marginalisation and discrimination. The court's decision to change the provisions of a statute that required the followers of indigenous religions to leave the religion column in their state-issued identity cards blank may be a step towards greater state recognition and support of indigenous minority religions. The decision represents an advance for religious freedom in Indonesia but nevertheless needs to be viewed with caution because its actual implications are far from clear. In his analysis of both cases Butt shows that, despite the Constitutional Court's image as a protector of human rights and democracy, its work leaves much to be desired: its review powers are narrow, it has no formal powers of enforcement and its rulings are not retrospective. In addition, its decision-making process is far from transparent and its often-crude methods of balancing minority and majority rights 'will rarely, if ever, permit acceptable levels of constitutional protection for minorities'.

Part 2 of the book, consisting of two chapters, focuses on disability. In Chapter 5, Thushara Dibley and Antoni Tsaputra begin by positing that being disabled in Indonesia has traditionally been seen as an impediment, a source of pity and a driver of acts of charity. Influenced by shifts in attitudes taking place elsewhere, Indonesian activists began to campaign for this 'welfare' approach to disability to be replaced with a 'social model' that prioritised the social structures that make it difficult for people with disability to participate in society. Ensuring that the principles of the social model are put into practice in Indonesia, the authors argue, lies at the heart of why disability activists have remained so persistent in their pursuit of legislative and policy change. In their exploration of activists' role in bringing about change, Dibley and Tsaputra focus in particular on how activists have maintained pressure on the government since the passing of Law No. 8/2016 on People with Disabilities. While activists are deeply committed to ensuring that the ministerial and other regulations required to implement the Disability Law reflect the changing international norms, there has been considerable resistance from policymakers to applying these ideas. Pragmatism and the notion of people with disability as requiring charitable assistance have prevailed throughout the process of implementing the Disability Law. Another impediment to implementing the law is the fact that, unlike other (sexual, ethnic, religious) minority groups, people with disability are advocating for an issue that is 'morally appealing but politically neutral', giving policy-makers little incentive to follow through on their promises. A final obstacle is the significant gap in access to disability services and information between Jakarta and other parts of the country.

In Chapter 6, Dina Afrianty analyses efforts to integrate people with disability into Indonesia's education system, especially the Islamic sector. Indonesians with disabilities continue to face significant difficulties in gaining entrance to the higher education sector due to barriers in the form of policy, funding and—above all—attitudes within the administration of higher education institutions. In recent years, however, gradual improvements have been evident. Beginning with the premise that cultural and religious beliefs play a role in shaping perceptions of people with disabilities and citing research showing that certain religious interpretations have contributed to discriminatory treatment, Afrianty argues that there is potential, nonetheless, for religious teachings to become a major source of social change. The intersection of faith-based cultural views and social practices, she suggests, could ultimately contribute to a dialogue about faith as a source of inclusive and pluralist beliefs and practices more broadly.

The two chapters that make up Part 3 of the book discuss the problems faced by sexual minorities in Indonesia. Saskia Wieringa argues in Chapter 7 that despite the widespread perception that Indonesia is relatively tolerant towards sexual minorities, heteronormativity has in fact always been the dominant regime. After querying how 'tolerant' in relation to same-sex practices the Indonesian archipelago actually was in the past, Wieringa provides examples of the homophobic campaign sweeping the country since 2015. Coming in the footsteps of a period in which LGBT issues gradually became more visible and sexual rights were discussed more openly in Indonesia after the fall of Suharto's military dictatorship in 1998, this homophobic campaign, Wieringa says, constitutes the second sexual moral panic in Indonesia's modern history. The first, motivated by political interests, started in 1965 following an army-orchestrated campaign of sexual slander, epitomised by the accusations of sexual deviancy and violence directed against the members of the prominent socialist women's organisation, Gerwani. The present-day sexual moral panic builds on the earlier one and has been spurred by the rise of conservative Muslim militias. Although homophobia has taken different manifestations in Indonesia, it has been persistent; the brief post-*reformasi* lull in its expression was more of an anomaly than a long-held conviction.

Chapter 8 by Hendri Yulius Wijaya focuses on the multiple strategies of Indonesia's queer activisms and the ways these have shifted over time, with the term 'queer activisms' referring to the articulation of Indonesian queer activists' efforts to eradicate stigma and discrimination through diverse forms of advocacy. Drawing on discourse analysis of historical archives and his own personal engagement with local queer activisms, Wijaya traces the emergence of diverse sexual and gender identities in Indonesia, from gay, to LGBT, to more nuanced understandings of sexual orientation, gender identity and gender expression (SOGIE). He suggests that the adoption and refashioning of those identities reveal the activisms' strategies and encounters with transnational discourses, localised in an Indonesian context. Wijaya claims that LGBT and, later, SOGIE discourses are inextricably linked to claims of national belonging, and are deployed to forge a sense of community and political allegiance among Indonesian sexual minorities in their resistance of heteronormativity.

Part 4 of the book, consisting of five chapters, discusses various religious and ethnic minorities. The opening chapter in this section, by Marcus Mietzner and Burhanuddin Muhtadi, analyses Muslims' attitudes towards religious and ethnic minorities using quantitative data gained primarily from surveys conducted in 2018 but also drawing on other polling going back to 2010. The authors ask if the mass mobilisation against Ahok in 2016–17 represented deeply held discriminatory views or was triggered by exclusivist Islamist sentiment. They also seek to establish whether the protests led to an increase in intolerance that persisted well after the tumult of the gubernatorial election had receded. The authors find that about a third of Muslims hold strongly intolerant views towards both non-Muslims and Chinese, and that the level of intolerance actually increased after the election campaign, something they believe is due to the role of conservative religio-political entrepreneurs in building on existing community dislike of those minorities. Moreover, their data suggest that while well-to-do and well-educated urban Muslims drove much of the anti-Ahok mobilisation, the swelling numbers of protestors on the streets of Jakarta were drawn mainly from lower-class Muslims, many of whom have maintained their activism since Ahok's defeat and jailing. Mietzner and Muhtadi conclude that anti-minority thinking is penetrating more deeply into mainstream politics and, as such, undermines Indonesia's standing as a democracy that upholds principles of religious and ethnic pluralism.

In Chapter 10, Ihsan Ali-Fauzi explores the dynamics of religious conflict in Indonesia by focusing on the role of the state-mandated Interreligious Harmony Forums (Forum Kerukunan Umat Beragama, FKUBs) in resolving community tensions over houses of worship. He uses two contrasting case studies—one of a disputed mosque construction in the majority-Christian city of Kupang in eastern Indonesia and the other of a contentious church development in a largely Muslim area of Gunung Kidul in Java—to examine how local FKUBs, officials and civil society organisations serve either to facilitate or to obstruct the resolution of religious disagreements. Ali-Fauzi shows that in the Kupang case, the local FKUB contributed to the escalation of the mosque dispute by incorrectly issuing a construction permit and that it was interfaith community groups that eventually succeeded in negotiating a compromise solution and bringing the disputing parties together. In Gunung Kidul, too, the local FKUB was of limited effectiveness, but a resourceful and astute local official managed to broker a lasting and peaceful agreement between Muslim groups and the Christian congregation. Ali-Fauzi uses these case studies to show that the Interreligious Harmony Forums have the potential to resolve religious conflicts but lack the resources, training and local government support to fulfil their mandate.

Charlotte Setijadi in Chapter 11 investigates xenophobic discourses about the Chinese community during the 2016–17 Jakarta gubernatorial election, paying particular attention to the return of the term *pribumi* (indigenous or native) to the rhetorical vocabulary of political and community leaders who were pursuing anti-Chinese agendas. She traces the long historical precedents for counterposing *pribumi* and Chinese in a way that consigned the latter to being conspicuous outsiders or 'others' in Indonesian society. In such a context, *pribumi* denotes a sense of 'nativeness', marking a racial boundary between those who are seen as belonging to Indonesia and those who are not. After Ahok's defeat, various Muslim political leaders used the term *pribumi* to signal the grievances of 'indigenous' Indonesians against economic inequality and dispossession by foreigners, especially the Chinese. Setijadi further argues that, despite its apparent restoration of Chinese rights that were withdrawn during the Suharto era, the *reformasi* period has in fact seen a continuation of powerful anti-Chinese views and activism. Long before the anti-Ahok mobilisation, vilification of Chinese and conspiracy theories surrounding the Chinese were commonplace in politics. Unlike Mietzner and Muhtadi, she contends that anti-Chinese sentiment declined following the Jakarta election but she points to the 2019 general elections as providing an indicator of whether Chinese have lessened their political participation as a result of the Ahok case.

In Chapter 12, Maria Myutel opens a window to the little-known Sindhi minority in Indonesia. Although numerically miniscule (numbering approximately 10,000 out of Indonesia's 260 million inhabitants), this minority has played a significant role in the country's economy and in cultural production in particular. Myutel argues that, contrary to conventional narratives that view minorities as always occupying a disadvantaged position and/or resisting the state, the case of the Sindhis shows that minority status can signal an advantage, even privilege, over a majority of the country's population. Their case, she suggests, shows how an overall disregard of state power, often in the form of disregarding both obligations and rights, can be an effective way of preserving a distinct identity. She claims that the mostly neutral relations between the Sindhis and the state, with very few points of interaction, have only rarely led to pressure or antagonism. Thus, overall, the relations between the Sindhi minority and the Indonesian state do not fit into the commonly used frameworks of forced assimilation or targeted discrimination and marginalisation, offering an alternative paradigm for considering minority status in Indonesia.

Butet Manurung examines the position of the Orang Rimba, a largely forest-dwelling indigenous community in Jambi, in Chapter 13. Drawing on her extensive experience of working among the Orang Rimba as an educator and human rights activist, she describes in detail the culture, values and lifestyle of the community and its increasingly complex relations with the Indonesian state and local government and society. For more than 50 years, Manurung says, state policies have progressively marginalised and disempowered the Orang Rimba. During the Suharto period, developmentalist priorities meant that forest areas in which the Orang Rimba lived were cleared for lumber, mining and plantations, with subsequent displacement and disruption of traditional lifestyles. *Reformasi* period policies on the creation of national parks and environmental sustainability have also impacted negatively on forest peoples by impinging on their traditional zones of habitation, cultivation and religious activities as well as limiting the free movement of Orang Rimba within the jungle. The national and local governments have sought to integrate the Orang Rimba by encouraging conversion to mainstream religions and participation in the national education system, despite many indigenes regarding these as irrelevant to and destructive of their customary way of life.

In a final chapter reflecting on the main theme of this book, contentious belonging, Sidney Jones suggests that we need to shift the focus away from the national to the local level, and from Java to the Outer Islands, in order to identify several additional dimensions of minority status. One such dimension is the tension between indigenous and migrant communities: in many areas of Indonesia outside Java the line between the two is constantly changing, at times leading to animosity and violence. The process of subdividing administrative regions (*pemekaran*) provides another example of constantly changing minority–majority status at the local level, because an ethnic minority can be transformed into an ethnic majority by redrawing the boundaries so that a particular ethnic group dominates at the district level. A third additional dimension of minority status explored in the chapter is racial identity, especially along Melanesian versus Malay lines. The diverse examples of these phenomena discussed by Jones underscore how the concept of 'ethnic minority' in Indonesia is 'both politically charged and infinitely malleable'. Jones concludes by returning to the growing spectre of Muslim majoritarianism in Indonesia, a concern that informed the analysis in many of the preceding chapters. She closes the volume with the apt observation that 'a fundamental principle of democracies is political equality and justice for all—and that means equal rights regardless of race, religion, ethnicity or sexual orientation. It does not mean simply that the majority can dictate the rules'.

REFERENCES

Amnesty International (2018) 'Indonesia: crackdowns on LGBTI people hit alarming levels', Amnesty International, 6 November. https://www.amnesty.org/en/latest/news/2018/11/indonesia-crackdowns-lgbti-people-hit-alarming-level/

Capotorti, F. (1977) *The International Protection of Persons Belonging to Ethnic, Religious and Linguistic Minorities since 1919*, United Nations Economic and Social Council, New York NY.

Fealy, G. (2016) 'The politics of religious intolerance in Indonesia', in T. Lindsey and H. Pausacker (eds) *Religion, Law and Intolerance in Indonesia*, Routledge, London and New York, 115–31.

Human Rights Watch (2018) 'Indonesia: failure to confront intolerance', Human Rights Watch, 18 January. https://www.hrw.org/news/2018/01/18/indonesia-failure-confront-intolerance

OHCHR (Office of the High Commissioner for Human Rights) (2018) 'UN human rights chief ends visit to Indonesia', OHCHR, Geneva, 7 February. https://www.ohchr.org/en/NewsEvents/Pages/DisplayNews.aspx?NewsID=22637&LangID=E

Parlina, I., and M.S. Aritonang (2013) 'SBY vows to address religious intolerance upon receiving international award', *Jakarta Post*, 1 June.

Vatikiotis, M. (2017) *Blood and Silk: Power and Conflict in Modern Southeast Asia*, Weidenfeld & Nicholson, London.

Wirth, L. (1945) 'The problem of minority groups', in R. Linton (ed.) *The Science of Man in the World Crisis*, Columbia University Press, New York NY.

Yudhoyono, S.B. (2009) 'Towards harmony among civilizations', speech delivered to John F. Kennedy School of Government, Harvard University, Cambridge MA, 29 September. http://indonesia-oslo.no/towards-harmony-among-civilizations-speech-at-the-john-f-kennedy-school-of-government-harvard-university/

PART 1

History and Law

2   Minorities in Indonesian history: from ambiguous advantage to cantonisation

Robert Cribb

Minorities have been a volatile phenomenon in Indonesia's social and political history for centuries. Over time, minority identity has been shaped by the imperatives of trade, by ideas of ritual purity and power, by ethnicity, by national allegiance, by religious affiliation and by lack of access to the full privileges of citizenship. Older forms of identity have existed alongside, and have sometimes intersected with, newer forms.

In today's world, we are accustomed to seeing minorities as disadvantaged. To belong to a minority is to have less than full acceptance as a citizen in the state where one belongs. It is to be treated, at least in some respects, as being alien in one's own country. The consequences of minority status range from neglect, social marginalisation and legal discrimination to forced assimilation, exclusion, expulsion and even extermination. In understanding minorities as communities under siege by their host societies, we quite correctly invoke the language of human rights and we propose remedies underpinned by law and education. If we are to chart a way forward, however, we need to understand that, historically, minority status has sometimes delivered advantage to the minorities themselves and to the host community. Minority status in Indonesia has been the product of complex social and political forces that have shifted over time. Minorities change character and sometimes disappear as historical circumstances change. We are now in the midst of a major change in the configuration of Indonesia's minorities.

Two categories of minority—trading minorities and ritual minorities (that is, minorities defined by perceived ritual 'impurity')—were known in the Indonesian archipelago in early times. The more important were the foreign trading minorities. Living as small communities in the trading cities and towns of the archipelago, they prospered above all when their shared identity provided a basis for trust within the community and among similar communities elsewhere, permitting the exchange of credit and information that was crucial to commercial success (Cohen 1971). Social distance from the host community, and consequent immunity from broader social obligations, was also important. Max Weber, focusing on the example of the Jews in Europe, called such minorities 'pariahs', implying that they were driven into commerce by hatred and contempt on the part of host communities, but more recent research has highlighted the positive consequences of ethnic solidarity, not only in commerce but also in other occupations (Dobbin 1996; Light and Karageorgis 2005). It is likely that at any one time hundreds of ethnic minority communities defined by occupation existed in the Indonesian archipelago, some of them focused on trade, others providing services ranging from medicine to armed protection or engaged in specialist manufacture. Such communities were not necessarily 'foreign' according to contemporary political configurations. Traders, for instance, from the island of Bawean in the Java Sea, now firmly part of Indonesia, constituted a trading minority in Java (Dobbin 1991). Many communities of this kind may have been short-lived, arising in the special circumstances where there was an economic niche they could occupy as well as sustained communication with a homeland or with a large diaspora that could keep the community replenished with marriage partners, and then disappearing as circumstances changed. The fate of most minorities appears to have been that their menfolk married locally and that the community was gradually absorbed into indigenous society.

The young people in contemporary Indonesia who marry across ethnic lines (as long as they are not religious lines as well) are only the most recent enthusiasts for exogamy; the Indonesian gene pool is full of inheritance from outsiders who arrived, settled down and found partners in the indigenous population (Utomo and McDonald 2016). Anecdotal evidence from Indonesians who have undertaken personal genetic tests suggests the unsurprising conclusion that a great many Indonesians who see themselves as local can trace some of their ancestry to outside the archipelago, a conclusion that appears to be confirmed by genetic research (Karafet et al. 2005). Indonesian genes in turn are scattered all along the coasts of the Indian Ocean and the Western Pacific. Communities such as the Sindhis (analysed by Myutel in Chapter 12 of this volume), the Arabs (Mandal 2018; Van der Kroef 1953) and the Jews (Hadler 2004; Ricci 2010) had complex relationships with local societies in which antagonism was subdued but social distance was often pronounced. Remarkably, there is no evidence to suggest ethnically motivated violence between trading minorities and local people before the twentieth century.[1] On the contrary, Southeast Asian societies sometimes looked to outsiders even for political leadership in the institution of the 'stranger king' (Henley 2004; Sahlins 2008).

Evidence for the existence of ritual minorities in Indonesia is sparse, but some records from seventeenth-century Java note the existence of a community called the Kalang. They were peripatetic; that is, they had no known home place but instead moved about the island plying a variety of trades, including carpentry, leatherwork, transport of goods and musical entertainment. They were also associated with the harvesting of wood from forests. Although they were Muslim, they were described as accursed outcastes, whose ancestral story included a pig, a dog and a touch of incest. At times, Javanese rulers forced some of them to settle down, but they retained a social stigma as pariahs (Wieringa 1998). Their position in Javanese society thus corresponded with aspects of the position of the itinerant Sinti and Roma in Europe, the outcaste Cagot in France and Eta (Burakumin) in Japan, and the so-called 'untouchables' (now Dalit) in India. The causes of outcaste status in all these cases are still poorly understood, yet by the early twentieth century some Kalang were able to parlay their community solidarity into a strong position as a trading minority (Guillot 1988).

There is intriguing evidence, too, that some disabled people formed communities in Indonesia in early times. In Batavia in the seventeenth century, the Dutch physician Jacobus Bontius may have seen a group of cretins, that is, sufferers from endemic iodine deficiency, a condition that has historically been common in the mountain regions of Java (Goslings et al. 1977; Kochupillai, Ramalingasawmi and Stanbury 1980). They were naked, could not speak and were dismissed by Bontius's informants as *orang utan* (people of the forest) who were the products of liaisons between women and apes. Like similarly affected people in the Himalayas, they may have lived in distinct communities (Miles 1998: 50), and were apparently present in Batavia as a group. These people were evidently despised, yet cretinism may also be a basis of the *wayang kulit* character Bagong, one of the *punakawan* or attendants to the main characters of the Indic Mahabharata story. The *punakawan* have traditionally been interpreted as being both comically irreverent and secretly powerful. Bagong, who is a companion of the leading *punakawan*, Semar, in the West Java and western Central Java forms of the Mahabharata, shows some of the distinctive features of endemic cretinism: impenetrable stupidity, short

---

1 In 1740, Dutch troops in Batavia massacred Chinese residents after clashes in which Dutch troops had been killed (Ricklefs 2001: 120–21). In this massacre, however, the main perpetrators were Dutch troops, not local people.

stature, waddling gait, prominent belly and buttocks, and protuberant lips (Anderson 1965: 44; Pausacker 2004). For the most part, however, disabled people appear to have lived often-difficult lives as individuals, rather than as communities. According to the Dutch anthropologist G.A. Wilken, the people of Nias believed albinos to be the offspring of demons and often killed them; Javanese rulers, by contrast, kept albinos, dwarves and hunchbacks at court because they were believed to have been conceived by powerful spirits (Wilken 1890).

Many elements of the pre-colonial pattern of trading minorities were left intact after the arrival of Europeans in the archipelago in the sixteenth century. European records offer more detailed information on the tendency of minorities to emerge in specific circumstances and then to disappear as those circumstances changed. A significant number of Japanese were resident in the archipelago in the early seventeenth century, working especially as mercenaries. This community disappeared after the Tokugawa authorities restricted travel to and from Japan. Under the Dutch East India Company (Vereenigde Oost-Indische Compagnie, VOC), Mardijkers emerged as a minority community of Catholic, Portuguese-speaking descendants of freed slaves, especially in the Batavia region. They persisted as a distinct but dwindling community until the early twentieth century (Bosma and Raben 2008: 46–51). Nonetheless, the arrival of large numbers of Chinese, not only as traders but also as labourers, changed the dynamics of the process of minority formation. For the first time, Chinese formed communities so large that they constituted local majorities, both in cities such as the VOC capital of Batavia and in mining regions such as west Borneo (Blussé 1986; Somers Heidhues 2003). Even with a significant degree of intermarriage with local people, and even after absorbing many aspects of local culture, including the language, some of these large communities had the critical mass to endure as self-sustaining minorities.

In two other respects, moreover, the Dutch presence began to change the character of minority status in the archipelago. First, the VOC made systematic use of Chinese as managers of tax franchises, known as tax or revenue farms. Under this arrangement, a Chinese entrepreneur would pay a substantial fee to the company in exchange for the right to collect a particular kind of revenue, such as road tolls, or to sell a commodity, such as opium. The company received payment upfront and the entrepreneur bore the cost of collecting from the populace. This arrangement bound prominent Chinese to the sometimes-unpopular political authority of the company (Butcher and Dick 1993; Rush 1990).

Second, the VOC imposed a rudimentary system of ethno-religious classification. This classification was manifest especially in the formal recognition as European of the offspring of marriages between company employees and local Christian women. Under Dutch rules privileging religion and patriarchy over skin colour, these children were considered legally to be European as long as they remained Christian (Taylor 1983). The classification was also expressed in an explicit system of indirect rule and legal pluralism, under which the company endeavoured to ensure that every person in the archipelago was ruled by the laws of his or her own ethnic group. Half the territory of the archipelago was under the rule of so-called *zelfbesturen*, self-governing native states headed by local rulers; even in regions of direct rule, colonial government rested on indigenous aristocracies, most notably the *priyayi* in Java. Dutch legal scholars identified 19 'traditional law realms' (*adatrechtskringen*) across the archipelago. Colonial policy-makers and jurists applied different family and property law, and sometimes even different criminal law, to local people depending on the ethnic group to which they belonged. In many respects, each person carried a personal legal status that interacted in complex ways with the varying laws of the land (Cribb 2010; Von Benda-Beckmann and Von Benda-Beckmann–Drooglever Fortuijn 1980). Unless some direct economic interest was at stake, colonial intervention in remote regions was limited to the basics of collecting tax and suppressing local warfare. In colonial cities and towns, too, the Dutch authorities used a form of indirect rule. Indigenous *kampung* were largely left to govern themselves while the larger migrant communities were ruled through so-called officers, generally with the titular rank of captain or major. We should not imagine colonial Indonesia was a multicultural paradise: indigenous rulers were obliged to govern in the interest of the colonial endeavour; many were self-indulgent and even oppressive in their own right; and Dutch authorities used ethnic diversity as a tool of domination, posting Javanese soldiers of the colonial army to keep order in the outer islands and using Ambonese, Manadonese and Timorese units in Java. Dutch colonial policy went to great lengths to preserve as much as possible of the fabric of pre-colonial society, not out of any respect for other cultural values but because this was the cheapest and least obtrusive way to govern the colony. Nonetheless, this structure ensured that there was no majority community with the power to discriminate against minorities within its territory.

After the fall of the VOC and the installation of direct colonial rule, the Dutch system of ethno-religious classification was formalised. The population of the archipelago was classified into two categories, European and Native (Inlander). A large majority of the Europeans were of mixed descent and were known as 'Indo-Europeans', a designation that gave rise to the later term 'Indo'. Christians, regardless of ethnicity, were equated with Europeans, whereas 'Foreign Orientals', including Chinese, Japanese and Arabs, were equated with Natives. Subsequent changes in this classification had a profound effect on the position of minorities when Indonesia became independent.

Even in VOC times, there had been tensions between Indo-Europeans, whose ties were mainly within the archipelago, and senior VOC officials, who saw themselves only as sojourners in the Indies (Horton 2003). These tensions increased in the nineteenth century as Indo-Europeans questioned Article 4 of the 1854 colonial basic law (Regeringsreglement), which specified baldly that the Netherlands Indies was a *wingewest* or 'region for making profit' (Jongmans 1921: 31). Unmistakable expressions of archipelagic nationalism appeared in the 1880s, when Indo-European journalists in Java proposed radically that the Indo community should disengage from the colonial enterprise and place itself at the head of a nationalist movement encompassing all who lived in the Indies. In *Het jong Indië* (The young Indies, 1884), A.M. Voorneman explicitly evoked Young Italy and Young Ireland, nationalist movements in Europe that portrayed themselves as representing youth and the future of colonised nations. The goal of the movement, he said, was that 'justice be done, regardless of person, consequently without distinction for race, color or religion' (cited in Van der Veur 1955: 80; see also Bosma and Oonk 1998: 37). Voorneman was explicit in urging settlers of mixed descent to recognise their shared identity with the Natives as children of the archipelago. Especially after Filipinos, the *mestizo* counterparts of the Indo-Europeans in the Philippines, joined forces with the indigenous Indios to launch the Philippine Revolution in 1896, the colonial authorities saw the assertiveness of the Indo-European community as a serious threat.

Under the so-called Ethical Policy, which commenced in 1901, the colonial authorities launched a three-pronged assault on the ambitions of the Indo-Europeans. They exiled and suppressed the writings of the leaders of the Indische Partij, which campaigned on a platform of an Indies for all who made their home there. They sought to persuade the emerging indigenous elite that Indo-European privilege was the greatest barrier to their advancement and they endeavoured to persuade the Indo-Europeans themselves that their only hope for the future lay in throwing in their lot with colonial rule. These endeavours succeeded to a significant extent. The history of archipelagic nationalism is conventionally written to commence with the founding in 1908 of Budi Utomo, a conservative association of Javanese bureaucrats and aristocrats that aimed to uplift native people within the colonial order. The earlier, more radical, history of Indo-European-led nationalism was erased, and bitter hostility to Indo-Europeans became commonplace in the nationalist movement that identified 'Indonesia' as its goal (Coté 2008: 373). Indo identity came to be represented most strongly by the conservative Indo-Europeesch Verbond (Indo-European Alliance).

Parallel processes marginalised Chinese living in the archipelago. There were three important elements in the rift. First was the influence on the Native (by then self-consciously 'Indonesian') side of new macro-economic ideas, some of them Marxist, some mercantilist, that saw the economic activity of Chinese elites as a structural part of colonial exploitation. Although the structure of revenue farms had largely been dismantled in the late nineteenth and early twentieth centuries, Chinese entrepreneurs largely controlled rural credit, sometimes imposing exorbitant rates, and were often the most important buyers of the produce of Indonesian smallholders. Dutch proponents of the Ethical Policy who portrayed Indo-Europeans as the enemy of Indonesian elites, also portrayed Chinese as a malevolent social influence (Shiraishi 1997: 187–8). Many nationalists found it easy to believe that Indonesia could only become prosperous if it excluded the economic power of both Dutch and Chinese. R.E. Elson quotes an exchange—perhaps apocryphal—that encapsulates the contradictory perceptions: 'Wherever there are Chinese, there is prosperity', said a Chinese Indonesian speaker at a student conference in Leiden in 1917; 'Wherever there is prosperity, there are the Chinese', responded an Indonesian (Elson 2005: 154).

Second, on the Chinese side, there were no counterparts to the inclusivist Voorneman.[2] Much of the political activity by Chinese in colonial Indonesia in the nineteenth and twentieth centuries was focused on enhancing the status of the Chinese as a distinct group within the colony. Chinese leaders consistently advocated the separation of Chinese from the Native category in the colonial constitution and their 'equation' with Europeans. One of the most important events to galvanise Chinese political activism was an amendment of the basic law of the Netherlands Indies in 1899 to give Japanese in the Indies the same legal status as Europeans. This amendment, a consequence of the renegotiation of the 'unequal' Netherlands–Japan Treaty of 1856, infuriated Chinese in the Indies. Chinese organisations launched a sustained campaign, calling on the help of the Chinese republican government after 1911, to have their status raised to that of the Japanese, and emphasising the inappropriateness, in Chinese eyes, of being consigned to Native status. Conceding European status to Chinese residents proved too much of a stretch, but the Dutch authorities made several other concessions that had the effect of separating Chinese interests from those of the Natives. Controls on Chinese travel and residence were removed, and Chinese were given representation on elected councils, separate from and on a far more generous basis than Indonesians (Shiraishi 1997: 188). In 1925, the colonial basic

---

2   For a valiant attempt to identify Chinese activists who aligned with the Indonesian nationalist movement, see Suryadinata (1971).

law was amended to create a category of Foreign Orientals that formally distinguished Chinese from Europeans and Natives and that provided the framework for greater practical, though not symbolic, assimilation of Chinese to European status (Fasseur 1994; Tjiook-Liem 2009). In focusing on their own status, many Chinese became detached from, and even antagonistic to, the central concerns of what had become the mainstream nationalist movement.

The third element in the rift between the Chinese in colonial Indonesia and the mainstream nationalist movement arose from the engagement of Chinese with the politics and identity of China. The main opposition within Chinese society to equation with Europeans came from those who wanted to emphasise their status as Chinese subjects. On the whole, the radical stream within Chinese politics in the archipelago engaged enthusiastically with Chinese politics before and after the 1911 Chinese Revolution, and were thus simply not part of the growing Indonesian movement.

When Indonesian nationalists declared independence in 1945, both Indo-Europeans and Chinese paid a heavy price for their detachment from the Indonesia movement. There was widespread violence against Indo-Europeans in which thousands were killed (Cribb 2008; Frederick 2012). Chinese were murdered in smaller numbers (Tan 2008: 239–40). Article 6(1) of the new Indonesian Constitution, moreover, specified that the president must be *asli*, or native. It remains unclear whether this clause was symbolic or was seen as a serious precaution against some new form of stranger king. Nonetheless, it marked the formal relegation of both Indo-Europeans and Chinese to second-class status. For some years after the independence war was over, both Indo-Europeans and Chinese continued to experience difficulties. They experienced the pain of losing all trace of colonial-era privilege and faced routine harassment in daily life, difficulty in getting citizenship confirmed and expulsion from the country as non-citizens. Indo-Europeans faced deep discrimination also as proxies for the continued Dutch state, which had retained control of western New Guinea, against the wishes of the Indonesian republic. In the late 1950s, those who had not taken Indonesian citizenship were deported. But thereafter Indo-Europeans sank into the broader pattern of ethnic diversity within Indonesia. They were no longer numerous enough or economically powerful enough to constitute a political force and they had no significant ties with the Netherlands. The natural forces of cultural fusion went to work and the boundaries between Indo-Europeans and Indonesian Christians became increasingly blurred (Hewett 2017).

At the end of the 1950s, the formerly parallel trajectories of the Indo-European and Chinese communities began to diverge. A 1959 presidential decree prohibiting foreign businesses from operating in the Indonesian countryside was implemented to block rural trade by both citizens and non-citizens of Chinese descent. Under Suharto, Chinese-language schools were closed, public displays of Chinese culture were prohibited, the importation of Chinese-language printed material was banned, the public celebration of Chinese festivals was prohibited and Indonesians with Chinese names were encouraged to adopt 'indigenous' ones for public purposes (Coppel 1983: 52–72, 82–5). There were also repeated outbreaks of violence in which the property of Chinese Indonesians was looted or destroyed (Purdey 2006).

The conventional explanation for the continuing minority status of Chinese Indonesians is pervasive indigenous Indonesian racism (Siegel 2001: 101, 105, 121). This view, however, is problematic. It is based partly on circular reasoning that says that repeated outbreaks of violence are caused by deep racism, which is demonstrated by those repeated outbreaks of violence. Moreover, prejudice against Chinese is greater, but not dramatically greater, than prejudice among indigenous Indonesian ethnic groups that have not been treated as minorities in the same way. The little research that has been done on interethnic prejudice indicates that Chinese are indeed the most pronounced target of ethnic prejudice, but that strong prejudices flow in every direction (Jaspars and Warnaen 1982: 343–51). In the broader global literature on interethnic relations, however, the contours of indigenous Indonesian prejudice against Chinese Indonesians do not register as deep enough to explain violence. More important, anti-Chinese violence coincides largely with the four decades of military dominance in Indonesian politics from the 1960s until the end of the century. There is significant evidence that anti-Chinese outbreaks were prompted and managed by security forces, both to divert attention from other issues and as a pretext for extracting vast amounts of protection money from Chinese businesses and property owners (Panggabean and Smith 2011).

Following the fall of Suharto in 1998 and the end of Indonesian military dominance, the position of Chinese Indonesians appeared to return to the trajectory that had integrated Indo-Europeans into the fabric of Indonesian diversity after about 1960. Constitutional and most legal discrimination was abolished. Official use of the derogatory term *Cina* to refer to the Chinese was ended. Numerous Chinese Indonesian ministers have sat in cabinet, the lion dance is performed in public, Confucianism is a recognised religion, Chinese New Year is a public holiday and it is more than a decade since any mass violence that could plausibly be characterised as anti-Chinese has occurred (Coppel 2008: 120–21). Of course, there is still crude anti-Chinese prejudice (as discussed by Setijadi in Chapter 11 of this volume), alongside Chinese Indonesian prejudice towards *pribumi* (indigenous) Indonesians wrapped in a narrative of exaggerated Chinese victimhood (Ang 2001; Callahan 2004).

In 2017, however, the governor of Jakarta, Basuki Tjahaja Purnama (Ahok), who was both Christian and Chinese, was defeated in a bitter election campaign in which he was accused of committing blasphemy by criticising Muslim scholars for citing a passage of the Qur'an, known as Al-Ma'idah 51, to argue that a non-Muslim could not be ruler of a Muslim society. Ahok had previously been elected deputy governor to Joko Widodo when he was the governor of Jakarta and became governor automatically when Jokowi resigned to become Indonesia's president. Ahok went on trial for blasphemy during the campaign and was found guilty and sentenced to two years' imprisonment soon after his defeat (Power 2018). Several factors contributed to Ahok's defeat: anti-Chinese prejudice; anti-Christian sentiment; Ahok's style of government, which, although clean and efficient, was seen as ruthless in displacing slum dwellers; and the blasphemy accusation. Whereas the first three elements had conspicuously failed to mobilise large groups against Ahok, the blasphemy accusation led to mass rallies and an acute sense of indignation.

To understand the significance of the blasphemy accusation, it is useful to understand that the Indonesian Constitution of 1945 created a third 'minority' alongside Indo-Europeans and Chinese. That minority comprised the Islamic community, and especially those Muslims who believed that the state should formally acknowledge Islamic principles. For the insight that Muslims, in reality a majority in Indonesia, could functionally be a minority, I am indebted to the Dutch sociologist W.F. Wertheim (1980), who described them in 1980 as a 'majority with minority mentality'. Ironically, this minority mentality was a consequence of the remarkable success of the idea of Indonesia in encompassing diversity. Even though they worked to marginalise Indo-Europeans and Chinese, Indonesia's colonial-era nationalists were inspired in creating an idea of Indonesia to which all of Indonesia's many indigenous ethnic and religious groups could subscribe. The five guiding principles incorporated into the preamble to the 1945 Constitution, known collectively as the Pancasila, were the culmination of a remarkable ideological effort over two or three decades to create a civic nationalism based on progressive aspirations, rather than just ethnic identity. The national motto, 'Unity in Diversity' (*Bhinneka Tunggal Ika*), expressed the same intention. This civic nationalism was a riposte to the belief that true nations can be constituted only on the basis of ethnicity, a belief that is implicit in every characterisation of Indonesia as an improbable nation. The specific target of this civic nationalism was the risk of fragmentation, more specifically the entrenched authority of traditional elites under the colonial system of indirect rule and the late-colonial policy of the Dutch authorities to present themselves as the only force capable of keeping Indonesians from each other's throats (Elson 2009).

Civic nationalism, however, came at the cost of marginalising Islam, the religion of a substantial majority of the population. The 1945 Constitution did not include clauses that had been agreed in the drafting stage requiring the president to be a Muslim and requiring Muslims to follow Islamic law. These clauses, if they had been included, would have marked the followers of other religions unambiguously as minorities. Failing to include them, however, marked the Constitution and the Indonesian state as something less than fully inclusive for large numbers of Muslims. Ironically, the Islamist component of Indonesia's Muslim majority had more reason than most communities to feel dissatisfied with the fruits of the independence struggle. Neither the Darul Islam rebellion of the 1950s and 1960s nor the Constituent Assembly of the late 1950s delivered Islamists any of their aspirations (Formichi 2012; Nasution 1992). Instead, they had to make do with the consolation of having a ministry of religion to look after their specific interests.[3] Under Sukarno's Guided Democracy, Islam was forced into an unpalatable political *ménage à trois* with nationalism and communism. During the first decades of Suharto's New Order, the regime appeared to marginalise Islam definitively, culminating in a decree that all social organisations, including religious bodies, had to adopt the Pancasila as their sole basic principle or *asas tunggal* (Assyaukanie 2009: 104–5). Indonesia's Islamists had much to be disappointed with in independent Indonesia.

During the second half of Suharto's long rule, however, the tide began to turn. Islam became an increasingly prominent part of public life. Suharto himself undertook the *hajj* and adopted the Islamic given name Muhammad. Crucially, Islamic leaders, realising that their aspirations had been defeated by Islamic heterodoxy, undertook a sustained and patient program of teaching that nudged Muslims in the direction of orthodoxy. By the time Suharto fell from power in 1998, Indonesia's religious landscape had been transformed. The number of followers of so-called *aliran kepercayaan*, comprising a variety of non-standard traditional religious beliefs, had shrunk enormously.

After the fall of Suharto, the consequence of this shift was not a headlong rush into Islamism but a new and growing confidence, on the part of orthodox Muslims, in the centrality of Islam to Indonesian life and politics. This confidence in turn has underpinned a broadening expectation that public life will conform to Islamic practice. The diversity of orthodox Islamic views means that there is no consensus on what that practice is. Like other religions elsewhere, Islam in Indonesia is not a single coherent belief, but rather a changing set of doctrines, each of which is invoked in the name of the religion without necessarily articulating intellectually

---

3 This narrative is presented elegantly and at length in Sidel (2006).

with other doctrines. Thus, Indonesia has experienced an irregular, even experimental, Islamist grappling with the possibility of setting up new standards of sobriety and morality, with the possibility of enforcing doctrinal orthodoxy within the Muslim community, with the possibility of shifting some political authority into the hands of religious scholars (*ulama*) and with the possibility of limiting public signs of the observance of other religions. Emblematic of this experimental approach was the 2016 proposal by the Muslim United Development Party (Partai Persatuan Pembangunan, PPP) to restore Article 6(1) to the Constitution so that the presidency would be restricted once more to indigenous Indonesians (Fachrudin 2016).

The campaign against Ahok was a touchstone for the transition between the minority politics of the twentieth and the twenty-first centuries. The campaign against his re-election as governor of Jakarta conjured up the fading ethnic politics of the twentieth century, but its underlying agenda was Islamist. *Ulama* who participated in the campaign to oust Ahok invoked two doctrines. First, they ruled that Muslims were not permitted to vote for a non-Muslim, while making clear that they did not object doctrinally to being governed by a non-Muslim if that person was properly elected. Second, they identified Ahok as a blasphemer. It was the invocation of this doctrine that proved decisive. Ahok's injudicious comments were an affront to Islamic authority, even before rumour and manipulation amplified the offence caused by them. The claims of non-Muslims that they could show that the comments were not blasphemous only added to the offence. Ahok's defeat was a portent of future Muslim assertiveness more than it was a relic of twentieth-century racism, although both elements were present and, as Mietzner and Muhtadi show in Chapter 9 of this book, the different manifestations of prejudice tended to reinforce each other. For religious groups regarded by some as heretical—Shi'a, Gafatar, Ahmadi (Fachrudin 2015; Kine 2017; Sidiq 2017)—the outlook is bleak, as it is for adherents of other religions who inadvertently offend Islamic belief.

Islam's movement towards centrality in Indonesian politics creates a new set of criteria for the definition of minorities. For the first time, a discourse of majority–minority relations has become commonplace in Indonesian public life (see, for instance, Liswijayanti 2017). Most salient has been the growing restriction on followers of a religion from establishing places of worship in any district where it is not in a majority (see Chapter 10 of this volume by Ali-Fauzi). This trend coincides with an increased salience in Indonesian politics of discourses referring to *putra daerah* (children of the region). In their mildest expression, these discourses have insisted that local leaders and representatives should be native to the district in which they seek office. More serious have been the occasional outbreaks of violence by locals against migrants, as in Sampit in West Kalimantan in 2000 (De Jonge and Nooteboom 2006; Wilson 2013). Sidney Jones discusses more such discrimination in the final chapter of this volume.

One potential outcome of this process is a de-integration of Indonesia into subnational cantons, each defined by a specific religion and/or ethnic group. The proliferation of local government districts that took place after the fall of Suharto, in a process known as *pemekaran*, established the administrative framework within which cantonisation can take place (Fitrani, Hofman and Kaiser 2005). Such segregation was accelerated in Ambon as a result of the conflict there (Colombijn 2018). This trajectory presents a grim prospect for Indonesia as a fluid and flexible society in which people can move freely to make their fortunes as they have done in the past. The strength of the tradition of social fluidity and population mobility in Indonesia, however, may mean that the experiment with cantonisation is relatively short-lived.

Cantonisation—for as long as it persists—presents a different kind of challenge for minorities that cannot readily be cantonised, specifically the 'new' minorities identified in international declarations in the second half of the twentieth century: women, children, the disabled, refugees, indigenous peoples, LGBT people—and even great apes. The human groups have come to be classified as minorities because global activists and policy-makers came to recognise that the 1948 Universal Declaration of Human Rights did not always specify universal rights in a form that made them clearly applicable to people who were not adult, able, male, heterosexual citizens of recognised countries. For the most part, the declarations that identity specific rights associated with each of these groups are conceived of as clarifying, rather than adding to, the 1948 Universal Declaration of Human Rights.

In practice, recognition of these specific manifestations of universal human rights has been strongest when they are seen as elements of international law that apply within national jurisdictions. Cantonisation, however, functions above all to shield local communities from national jurisdiction. By virtue of their small size, cantons are generally ill-equipped to develop and maintain complex legal regimes. There is a significant risk, therefore, that cantonisation will work against the interests of the new minorities.

REFERENCES

Anderson, B.R.O'G. (1965) *Mythology and the Tolerance of the Javanese*, Cornell University Modern Indonesia Project, Ithaca NY.

Ang, I. (2001) 'Trapped in ambivalence: Chinese Indonesians, victimhood and the debris of history', in M. Morris and B. de Bary (eds) *'Race' Panic and the Memory of Migration*, Hong Kong University Press, Hong Kong: 21–47.

Assyaukanie, L. (2009) *Islam and the Secular State in Indonesia*, ISEAS, Singapore.

Blussé, L. (1986) *Strange Company: Chinese Settlers, Mestizo Women, and the Dutch in VOC Batavia*, Foris, Dordrecht.

Bosma, U., and G. Oonk (1998) 'Bombay Batavia: Parsi and Eurasian variations on the middleman theme', in N. Randeraad (ed.) *Mediators between State and Society*, Verloren, Hilversum: 17–40.

Bosma, U., and R. Raben (2008) *Being 'Dutch' in the Indies: A History of Creolisation and Empire, 1500–1920*, National University of Singapore Press, Singapore.

Butcher, J., and H. Dick (eds) (1993) *The Rise and Fall of Revenue Farming: Business Elites and the Emergence of the Modern State in Southeast Asia*, St. Martin's Press, New York NY.

Callahan, W.A. (2004) 'National insecurities: humiliation, salvation, and Chinese nationalism', *Alternatives* 29: 199–218.

Cohen, A. (1971) 'Cultural strategies in the organization of trading diasporas', in C. Meillassoux (ed.) *The Development of Indigenous Trade and Markets in West Africa*, Oxford University Press, London: 266–81.

Colombijn, F. (2018) 'The production of urban space by violence and its aftermath in Jakarta and Kota Ambon, Indonesia', *Ethnos* 83(1): 58–79.

Coppel, C.A. (1983) *Indonesian Chinese in Crisis*, Oxford University Press, Kuala Lumpur.

Coppel, C.A. (2008) 'Anti-Chinese violence in Indonesia after Soeharto', in L. Suryadinata (ed.) *Ethnic Chinese in Contemporary Indonesia*, Chinese Heritage Centre and ISEAS, Singapore: 117–36.

Coté, J. (ed.) (2008) *Realizing the Dream of R.A. Kartini: Her Sisters' Letters from Colonial Java*, Ohio University Press, Athens, OH.

Cribb, R. (2008) 'The brief genocide of the Eurasians in Indonesia, 1945/1946', in A. Dirk Moses (ed.) *Empire, Colony, Genocide: Conquest, Occupation, and Subaltern Resistance in World History*, Berghahn, New York NY: 424–39.

Cribb, R. (2010) 'Legal pluralism and criminal law in the Dutch colonial order', *Indonesia* 90: 47–66.

De Jonge, H., and G. Nooteboom (2006) 'Why the Madurese? Ethnic conflicts in West and East Kalimantan compared', *Asian Journal of Social Science* 34(3): 456–74.

Dobbin, C. (1991) 'The importance of minority characteristics in the formation of business elites on Java: the Baweanese example, c. 1870–c. 1940', *Archipel* 41: 117–27.

Dobbin, C. (1996) *Asian Entrepreneurial Minorities: Conjoint Communities in the Making of the World-Economy, 1570–1940*, Curzon, Richmond.

Elson, R.E. (2005) 'Constructing the nation: ethnicity, race, modernity and citizenship in early Indonesian thought', *Asian Ethnicity* 6(3): 145–60.

Elson, R.E. (2009) *The Idea of Indonesia: A History*, Cambridge University Press, Cambridge.

Fachrudin, A.A. (2015) 'Endless Sunni–Shia sectarianism in Indonesia', *Jakarta Post*, 11 March. http://www.thejakartapost.com/news/2015/03/11/endless-sunni-shia-sectarianism-indonesia.html

Fachrudin, F. (2016) 'PPP usul amandemen UUD 1945 kembalikan frasa "presiden ialah orang Indonesia asli"', *Kompas*, 4 April. https://nasional.kompas.com/read/2016/10/04/06472651/ppp.usul.amandemen.uud.1945.kembalikan.frasa. presiden.ialah.orang.indonesia.asli

Fasseur, C. (1994) 'Cornerstone and stumbling block: racial classification and the late colonial state in Indonesia', in R. Cribb (ed.) *The Late Colonial State in Indonesia: Political and Economic Foundations of the Netherlands Indies, 1880–1942*, KITLV, Leiden: 31–56.

Fitrani, F., B. Hofman and K. Kaiser (2005) 'Unity in diversity? The creation of new local governments in a decentralising Indonesia', *Bulletin of Indonesian Economic Studies* 41(1): 57–79.

Formichi, C. (2012) *Islam and the Making of the Nation: Kartosuwiryo and Political Islam in 20th Century Indonesia*, KITLV, Leiden.

Frederick, W.H. (2012) 'The killing of Dutch and Eurasians in Indonesia's national revolution (1945–49): a "brief genocide" reconsidered', *Journal of Genocide Research* 14(3–4): 359–80.

Goslings, B.M., R. Djokomoeljanto, R. Docter, C. van Harteveld, G. Hennemann, D. Smeenk and A. Querido (1977) 'Hypothyroidism in an area of endemic goiter and cretinism in central Java, Indonesia', *Journal of Clinical Endocrinology and Metabolism* 44: 481–90.

Guillot, G. (1988) 'Les Kalang de Java: rouliers et preteurs d'argent', in D. Lombard and J. Aubin (eds) *Marchands et hommes d'affaires asiatiques dans l'Océan Indien et la Mer de Chine 13e-20e siècles*, L'Ecole des hautes etudes en sciences sociales, Paris: 267–77.

Hadler, J. (2004) 'Translations of antisemitism: Jews, the Chinese, and violence in colonial and post-colonial Indonesia', *Indonesia and the Malay World* 32(94): 291–313.

Henley, D. (2004) 'Conflict, justice, and the stranger-king: indigenous roots of colonial rule in Indonesia and elsewhere', *Modern Asian Studies* 38(1): 85–144.

Hewett, R. (2017) 'Indo (Eurasian) communities in postcolonial Indonesia', PhD thesis, Australian National University, Canberra.

Horton, W.B. (2003) 'Pieter Elberveld: the modern adventure of an eighteenth-century Indonesian hero', *Indonesia* 76: 147–98.

Jaspars, J.M.F., and S. Warnaen (1982) 'Intergroup relations, ethnic identity and self-evaluation in Indonesia', in H. Tajfel (ed.) *Social Identity and Intergroup Relations*, Cambridge University Press, Cambridge: 335–66.

Jongmans, P.H.C. (1921) *De exorbitante rechten van den gouverneur-generaal in de praktijk*, J.H. de Bussy, Amsterdam.

Karafet, T.M., J.S. Lansing, A.J. Redd, S. Reznikova, J.C. Watkins, S.P.K. Surata, W.A. Arthawiguna, L. Mayer, M. Bamshad, L.B. Jorde and M.F. Hammer (2005) 'Balinese Y-chromosome perspective on the peopling of Indonesia: genetic contributions from pre-Neolithic hunter-gatherers, Austronesian farmers, and Indian traders', *Human Biology* 77(1): 93–114.

Kine, P. (2017) 'Indonesia's anti-Gafatar campaign ends in blasphemy convictions: religious community leaders get up to 5 years for "deviant" beliefs', *Human Rights Watch*, 7 March. https://www.hrw.org/news/2017/03/07/indonesias-anti-gafatar-campaign-ends-blasphemy-convictions

Kochupillai, N., V. Ramalingasawmi and J.B. Stanbury (1980) 'Southeast Asia', in J.B. Stanbury and B.S. Hetzel (eds) *Endemic Goiter and Endemic Cretinism: Iodine Nutrition in Health and Disease*, John Wiley, New York NY.

Light, I., and S. Karageorgis (2005) 'The ethnic economy', in N. Smelser and R. Swedberg (eds) *The Handbook of Economic Sociology*, Princeton University Press, Princeton NJ: 650–77.

Liswijayanti, F. (2017) 'Ini cara melebur perbedaan antara kaum minoritas dan mayoritas', *Femina*, 4 August. http://www.femina.co.id/trending-topic/ini-cara-melebur-perbedaan-antara-kaum-minoritas-dan-mayoritas

Mandal, S.K. (2018) *Becoming Arab: Creole Histories and Modern Identity in the Malay World*, Cambridge University Press, Cambridge.

Miles, M. (1998) 'Goitre, cretinism and iodine in South Asia: historical perspectives on a continuing scourge', *Medical History*, 42: 47–67.

Nasution, A.B. (1992) *The Aspiration for Constitutional Government in Indonesia: A Socio-legal Study of the Indonesian Konstituante, 1956–1959*, Pustaka Sinar Harapan, Jakarta.

Panggabean, S.R., and B. Smith (2011) 'Explaining anti-Chinese riots in late 20th century Indonesia', *World Development* 39(2): 231–42.

Pausacker, H. (2004) 'Presidents as *punakawan*: portrayal of national leaders as clown-servants in Central Javanese *wayang*', *Journal of Southeast Asian Studies* 35(2): 213–33.

Power, T.P. (2018) 'Jokowi's authoritarian turn and Indonesia's democratic decline', *Bulletin of Indonesian Economic Studies* 54(3): 307–38.

Purdey, J. (2006) *Anti-Chinese Violence in Indonesia, 1996–99*, University of Hawai'i Press, Honolulu.

Ricci, R. (2010) 'Jews in Indonesia: perceptions and histories', *Indonesia and the Malay World* 38(112): 325–7.

Ricklefs, M.C. (2001) *A History of Modern Indonesia since c. 1200*, third edition, Palgrave, Houndmills.

Rush, J.R. (1990) *Opium to Java: Revenue Farming and Chinese Enterprise in Colonial Indonesia, 1860–1910*, Cornell University Press, Ithaca NY.

Sahlins, M. (2008) 'The stranger king', *Indonesia and the Malay World* 36(105): 177–99.

Shiraishi, T. (1997) 'Anti-Sinicism in Java's New Order', in D. Chirot and A. Reid (eds) *Essential Outsiders: Chinese and Jews in the Modern Transformation of Southeast Asia and Central Europe*, University of Washington Press, Seattle OR: 187–207.

Sidel, J.T. (2006) *Riots, Pogroms, Jihad: Religious Violence in Indonesia*, Cornell University Press, Ithaca NY.

Sidiq, F. (2017) 'Indonesian hard-liners again turn up heat on Ahmadis', *Jakarta Post*, 25 February. http://www.thejakartapost.com/news/2017/02/25/indonesian-hard-liners-again-turn-up-heat-on-ahmadis.html

Siegel, J.T. (2001) 'Thoughts on the violence of May 13 and 14, 1998, in Jakarta', in B.R.O'G. Anderson (ed.) *Violence and the State in Suharto's Indonesia*, Cornell University Southeast Asia Program, Ithaca NY: 90–123.

Somers Heidhues, M.F. (2003) *Golddiggers, Farmers and Traders in the Chinese Districts of West Kalimantan, Indonesia*, Cornell University Southeast Asia Program, Ithaca NY.

Suryadinata, L. (1971) 'Pre-war Indonesian nationalism and the Peranakan Chinese', *Indonesia* 11: 83–94.

Tan, M.G. (2008) *Etnis Tionghoa di Indonesia*, Yayasan Obor, Jakarta.

Taylor, J.G. (1983) *The Social World of Batavia: European and Asian in Dutch Asia*, University of Wisconsin Press, Madison WI.

Tjiook-Liem, P. (2009) *De Rechtspositie der Chinezen in Nederlands-Indie 1848–1942: Wetgevingsbeleid Tussen Beginsel en Belang*, Leiden University Press, Leiden.

Utomo, A., and P. McDonald (2016) 'Who marries whom? Ethnicity and marriage pairing patterns in Indonesia', *Asian Population Studies* 12(1): 28–49.

Van der Kroef, J.M. (1953) 'The Arabs in Indonesia', *Middle East Journal* 7(3): 300–23.

Van der Veur, P. (1955) 'A social political study of the Eurasians of Indonesia', PhD thesis, Cornell University, Ithaca NY.

Von Benda-Beckmann, F., and K. von Benda-Beckmann–Drooglever Fortuijn (1980) 'Rechtspraak: traditionele en westerse waarden in historisch perspectief', in R.N.J. Kamerling (ed.) *Indonesië toen en nu*, Intermediaire, Amsterdam: 127–45.

Wertheim, W.F. (1980) *Moslems in Indonesia: Majority with Minority Mentality*, South East Asian Studies Committee, James Cook University, Townsville.

Wieringa, E. (1998) 'Who are the Kalang? An unknown minority group on Java and their so-called myth of origin', *Anthropos* 93(1/3): 19–30.

Wilken, G.A. (1890) 'Albino's in den Indischen archipel', *Bijdragen tot de Taal-, Land- en Volkenkunde van Nederlandsch Indië* 39: 105–20.

Wilson, C. (2013) '"Ethnic outbidding" for patronage: the 2010 riots in Tarakan, Indonesia', *South East Asia Research* 21(1): 105–29.

3   Minorities and discrimination in Indonesia: the legal framework

Tim Lindsey

'They are indeed different, but they are of the same kind, as there is no duality in truth.'
– Mpu Tantular[1]

This chapter aims to provide a brief overview of aspects of the complex legal framework regulating the treatment of minorities in Indonesia.[2] It shows that there is, in fact, no coherent framework for the protection of minorities. Instead, a range of laws apply different rules to different groups, sometimes conferring rights, sometimes denying them. Coverage is patchy and some minorities are ignored. Some of these laws are very new, some far too old. Overlap and inconsistency between them is common, and most minorities are left vulnerable to discriminatory treatment and abuse.

In fact, overall, the law regulating minorities reflects an all-too-common pattern of post-Suharto law reform. This began with aspirational, and often impressive, constitutional reform between 1999 and 2002, drawing on international conventions and norms. That was followed by detailed, and often heated, policy debate, usually led by civil society, which produced models for reform. These were often sophisticated, and in many cases were based on global standards. However, the laws and regulations eventually produced by the government or by the national legislature,

---

1   Santoso's (1975: 578) translation of the last line of canto 139, stanza 5, of Mpu Tantular's fourteenth-century *Kakawin Sutasoma*, which is the source of the Indonesian state motto, *Bhinneka Tunggal Ika* ('The Many Are One').

2   This chapter draws on some material in Butt and Lindsey (2018), Lindsey (2012) and Lindsey and Pausacker (2005).

the People's Representative Council (Dewan Perwakilan Rakyat, DPR), were typically flawed or incomplete. They were often characterised by a lack of compliance measures and sanctions, and the key institutions given responsibility to administer the schemes created by the new laws were frequently weak.

The enforcement of these laws was then made still more problematic by a wicked mix of factors, including poor socialisation by the government of new laws and institutions, which too often left intact widespread ignorance and apathy about the law; covert (sometimes overt) resistance by parts of government and the bureaucracy to the policies that underpinned the new laws; absent, inadequate or fiercely contested budgets; incompetent or uninformed police, prosecutors and judges; and, of course, outright rent-seeking by government officials charged with implementing the new laws, across all levels of central and regional government.

In recent years, a growing culture of intolerant Muslim majoritarianism has created further problems, especially because of the hugely increased influence of the Indonesian Council of Religious Scholars (Majelis Ulama Indonesia, MUI).[3] Although a quasi-autonomous non-government organisation (QUANGO), MUI now behaves like a branch of government, and is openly hostile to many religious, ethnic and social minorities.[4]

As a result of this pattern, most minority rights remain largely aspirational. This does not mean, however, that the laws relating to minorities in Indonesia are irrelevant. In fact, their shortcomings create major challenges for minorities, and ensure that their 'belonging' remains contentious legally as well as in other ways.

To demonstrate this, I next offer a short account of domestic and international laws relevant in Indonesia to rights against discrimination in general. Key laws and regulations relating to the treatment of disabled Indonesians, lesbian, gay, bisexual, transgender, queer and intersex (LGBTQI) Indonesians, religious minorities, *adat* communities and the ethnic Chinese are then surveyed in more detail, with a focus on problematic provisions and areas where reform is needed.

---

3 MUI was established as an independent NGO by a charter signed by Muslim religious scholars (*ulama*) on 26 July 1975 and is not formally a state organisation or a branch of government. However, it receives funding from government, has significant statutory roles and is widely seen as the official voice of orthodox Sunni Islam in Indonesia (Lindsey 2012: 128). In 2014 MUI was declared the 'government's partner' in Islamic affairs (Presidential Regulation No. 154/2012).

4 On MUI's attitude towards minorities, see Lindsey and Pausacker (2016), especially the chapters by Stewart Fenwick and Syafiq Hasyim. See also Fenwick (2017: 78–110).

DISCRIMINATION AND HUMAN RIGHTS

Although Indonesia has been a member of the United Nations since 1950,[5] and was therefore theoretically bound by the Universal Declaration of Human Rights (Eldridge 2002: 127),[6] the New Order explicitly 'rejected the universalism of human rights as an innately Western concept that was alien to East Asia' (Lindsey 2004: 286).[7] After 1998, a strong desire to break from the repressive Suharto years spurred a radical change of approach. Within just a few years, Indonesia had adopted key international human rights instruments[8] and introduced major legislative reforms relating to human rights.

The most significant of these reforms were constitutional, with an extensive Charter of Human Rights inserted into a new Chapter XA of the Constitution in 2000. This was modelled closely on the Universal Declaration of Human Rights and included a range of provisions that protected minorities from discrimination. These have been the fountainhead of many of the post-Suharto legislative reforms intended to improve minority rights. Among these rights is an array of provisions that, in principle, protect minorities from discrimination, guarantee their rights to citizenship and protect them from discriminatory treatment. For example:

- Article 26, paragraph 1: Indonesian citizens are native Indonesian persons and persons of other countries who have acquired the legal status of citizens.

---

5   Indonesia withdrew from the United Nations on 1 January 1965 and rejoined in September 1966. The United Nations treated this as a break in cooperation rather than a withdrawal.

6   Although the declaration is not legally binding, it is considered to inform the human rights provisions in the UN Charter, which is binding on states, including Indonesia.

7   The Indonesian state under Suharto did accede to two key human rights instruments—the Convention on the Elimination of All Forms of Discrimination Against Women, and the Convention on the Rights of the Child—but because Indonesia had not ratified other international human rights instruments, and has never submitted to the jurisdiction of the International Court of Justice, the impact of these conventions was limited.

8   In 1998, Indonesia ratified the Convention Against Torture and Other Cruel, Inhuman or Degrading Treatment or Punishment, and the International Labour Organization's Convention on Freedom of Association and Protection of the Right to Organise. In late 2005, Indonesia passed laws to ratify the International Covenant on Civil and Political Rights and the International Covenant on Economic, Social and Cultural Rights, and acceded to both covenants in early 2006.

- Article 27, paragraph 1: All citizens have equal status before the law and the government, and are obliged to abide by the law and the government without any exception.
- Article 28D, paragraph 1: Every person has the right to the recognition, security, protection and certainty of just laws, as well as equal treatment before the law.
- Article 28D, paragraph 4: Every person has the right to citizenship status.
- Article 28E, paragraph 1: Every person is free to profess their religion and worship in accordance with their religion, to choose their education and training, to choose their occupation, to choose their citizenship, to choose their place of domicile within the territory of the State, and to leave it as well as return to it.
- Article 28I, paragraph 2: Every person has the right to be free from discriminatory treatment on any grounds and has the right to obtain protection from such discriminatory treatment.

I now turn to two of the more sophisticated efforts to implement these principles, the 2008 Anti-discrimination Law and the 2016 Law on People with Disabilities.

THE 2008 ANTI-DISCRIMINATION LAW

In 1999, Indonesia ratified the Convention on the Elimination of All Forms of Racial Discrimination and nine years later it enacted Law No. 40/2008 on the Elimination of Racial and Ethnic Discrimination. Article 12 of Law No. 40/2008 limits its application to race and ethnicity, but the ambit of ethnicity is very wide. 'Race' is defined as a group of people distinguished by physical characteristics and lineage (Article 1(2) and (3)), while 'ethnicity' is a grouping based on belief, values, habits, traditions, norms, language, history, geography and kinship (Article 1(1) and (4)).

The most important provisions for the purposes of this chapter are Articles 15, 16 and 17, which impose criminal sanctions for acts of racial and ethnic discrimination resulting in human rights or equality being limited or revoked. 'Discriminatory behaviour' includes race- or ethnicity-based hate expressed through, for example: publicly displayed text, images or clothing; public speeches; and murder, assault, rape, abuse, violent robbery or deprivation of liberty based on racial and ethnic discrimination (Article 4). Perpetrators of acts of racial and ethnic discrimination that result in human rights or equality being limited or revoked face penalties of up to one year's imprisonment and/or a Rp 100 million fine (Article 15). If hatred or hostility is involved, then five years' imprisonment and/or a

Rp 500 million fine can be imposed (Article 16). And if intentional deprivation of life, assault, rape, abuse, robbery or deprivation of liberty results
from the discrimination, then the penalties for those offences under other
legislation, such as the Criminal Code, increase by one-third (Article 17).

In other words, Law No. 40/2008 is, to a large extent, about hate speech,
which is an area already covered by Indonesian criminal law. In fact,
Articles 15, 16 and 17 replicate much of Article 156 of the so-called Blasphemy Law (discussed below) and, like Article 156, are rarely used to
defend minorities. Rather, police and prosecutors tend to see them more
as a revival of the New Order 'SARA' prohibitions on discussing the so-
called sensitive topics of ethnicity (*suku*), religion (*agama*), race (*ras*) and
other intergroup differences.[9]

THE 2016 LAW ON PEOPLE WITH DISABLIITIES

Of all Indonesia's new legislative schemes intended to prevent discrimination against minorities, that relating to the disabled is the most
sophisticated. There are now three domestic statutes that deal specifically
with the rights of the disabled. The first is Law No. 39/1999 on Human
Rights, which grants certain rights specifically to disabled persons, mainly
in relation to facilities, treatment, education and training (Articles 41, 42
and 54).

The second relevant statute is Law No. 35/2014 on Child Protection
(amending a 2002 statute on child protection), introduced to enable Indonesia to meet its obligations under the United Nations Convention on the
Rights of the Child, which Indonesia ratified in 1990. Law No. 35/2014
grants rights to rehabilitation, social assistance, social welfare, education
and 'special protection' for disabled children (Articles 12 and 51).

The most important part of the new legislative scheme for the disabled, however, is Law No. 8/2016 on People with Disabilities, again

---

9   An example of this is the case of Bambang Tri Mulyono, author of *Jokowi Under-
    cover*, a controversial book distributed through social media that accused
    President Joko Widodo of being the son of a Communist Party member and
    of having falsified his biography. Mulyono was charged with breaches of
    Articles 4 and 16 of Law No. 40/2008 on the Elimination of Racial and Ethnic
    Discrimination, Article 2 of Law No. 19/2016 on Electronic Information and
    Transactions and Article 207 of the Criminal Code. He was sentenced to
    three years' imprisonment in 2017 for 'giving rise to ethnic, religious, race or
    intergroup (SARA) disunity and enmity between individuals and/or certain
    social groups', although only under the latter two laws (Blora District Court
    Decision No. 47/Pid. Sus/2017/PN, 29 May 2017). For more on this case, see
    Suherdjoko (2017) and Syaefudin (2017).

introduced to allow Indonesia to meet its obligations under an international convention: the United Nations Convention on the Rights of Persons with Disabilities, ratified by Law No. 19/2011.

Law No. 8/2016 is sophisticated and detailed legislation, based on a far more modern understanding of disability than the previous statute, Law No. 4/1997, which had long been criticised by Indonesian civil society for treating people with disabilities as objects of charity. That law defined disabled or 'crippled' people (*penyandang cacat*) as suffering from mental or physical abnormalities that impeded their ability to do things as they should (Article 1(1)). Law No. 8/2016 changed this. It introduced a social model of disability—that is, the understanding that disability is not an inherent flaw but rather is caused by societal barriers that prevent the full interaction of people living with physical, sensory, intellectual or psychological limitations (Article 1(1)).

Law No. 8/2016 is discussed in detail by Dibley and Tsaputra in Chapter 5 of this volume but, in brief, it contains a large catalogue of 'on-paper' rights for people with disability that tracks the convention, and includes specific additional rights for women with disability. It strengthens the rights of people with disabilities to education[10] and their rights to, and at, work, and reiterates their political rights and rights to religious freedom. It also requires governments to guarantee and protect the rights of people with disability, to provide social rehabilitation, welfare and protection, and to improve accessibility (see Articles 5–26, 40–44, 48, 53, 75–82, 91–95 and 105–108).

These fine reforms are, however, yet to be fully implemented. Law No. 8/2016 provides for the establishment of an independent National Disability Commission (Article 131) to monitor and evaluate the government's efforts in respecting, protecting, fulfilling and advocating for the rights of people with disabilities (Article 133). This is the keystone of the new legal scheme for the protection of the disabled, but little detail is provided and no deadline set for the commission's establishment. Instead, the work, functions and selection of members of the putative commission are left to be determined in a presidential regulation, a familiar and often fatal formula in Indonesian laws (Article 134).

At the time of writing, the National Disability Commission had not been established, much to the ire of disability activists (Prabowo 2017). As a result, people with disabilities do not, in practice, enjoy the full catalogue of rights in Law No. 8/2016 , which are, in fact, rarely enforced. In other words, despite their significance, the convention and the statute together remain largely irrelevant for many disabled Indonesians.

---

10   The impact of Law No. 8/2016 on rights to education for the disabled is discussed in more detail in Chapter 6 of this volume by Afrianty.

LGBTQI INDONESIANS

Homosexuality is not illegal in Indonesia, except in the province of Aceh, where it is a criminal offence. Sodomy (*liwath*) and lesbian sex (*musahaqah*) are specifically prohibited under Aceh's sharia criminal code, the Qanun Jinayat. Punishments for violations include up to 100 lashes with a cane, a fine of 1,000 grams of gold or 100 months in prison (Articles 63 and 64).

However, there is no legislation in Indonesia that grants protection against discrimination or other rights specifically to LGBTQI Indonesians, and there are a number of laws of general application that enable discrimination against them. The result, as Wijaya shows in Chapter 8 of this book, is that LGBTQI Indonesians are a highly vulnerable minority.

For example, LGBTQI Indonesians everywhere in Indonesia face the possibility of prosecution under Law No. 44/2008 on Pornography. This is because the Pornography Law is not limited to pornographic publications but extends to catch almost any form of public eroticism, seen by law enforcers as 'pornographic action' (*pornoaksi*).

This concept was the subject of much controversy when the bill for this law was being debated in the DPR, and in fact the term *pornoaksi* was eventually deleted before Law No. 44/2008 was enacted (Lindsey 2012: 464–6). It is not widely understood, however, that the concept was nonetheless retained in Article 1. The definition of 'pornography' there is very broad. It includes:

> [...] pictures, sketches, illustrations, photos, writing, voice, sound, moving pictures, animation, cartoons, *conversations, movements of the body* or other forms through a variety of communication media and/or *performances in public that contain obscenity or sexual exploitation that violates the moral norms in society* [emphasis added].

This provision is so vague that it can be used by police to harass almost any person involved in almost any form of sexual or erotic behaviour; as Wieringa points out in Chapter 7 of this volume, it is often used to target LGBTQI Indonesians socialising in public venues such as bars or clubs.

Another provision often deployed against LGBTQI Indonesians is the specific prohibition on 'nakedness', 'giving an impression of nakedness' or 'displaying the genitals' (Article 4(1)(d) and (e)). The elucidation (explanatory memorandum) to Article 4(1)(d) explains that 'giving the impression of nakedness' means using a covering over the body that still allows the sexual organs to be seen in an explicit fashion. This provision has also been used to prosecute LGBTQI people, for example, gay men arrested in gyms and saunas.

Another statute of general application that is of concern to LGBTQI people in Indonesia is Indonesia's Criminal Code (Kitab Undang-Undang

Pidana, KUHP). According to Article 292, adults who engage in 'indecent activities' with a minor of the same gender face up to seven years' imprisonment.

This provision of the Criminal Code, along with Article 284 on adultery and Article 285 on rape, was challenged before the Constitutional Court, which handed down its decision in late 2017.[11] The applicants—among them a conservative Muslim group called the Family Love Alliance (Aliansi Cinta Keluarga, AILA)—asked the court to reinterpret Article 292 in ways that went far beyond its plain words. They said the court should declare that it prohibited 'indecent acts' between any people of the same gender, regardless of their age. A narrow five-to-four majority rejected this request, holding that the court did not have jurisdiction to create criminal offences, because this was a matter for the legislature. In Chapter 4 of this volume, Butt discusses this decision in more detail and suggests that a future Constitutional Court bench might well take a different view.

In fact, a bill to significantly revise the Criminal Code along the lines sought by AILA has been under consideration by the DPR for some time and has been the subject of much debate. Article 495 of this bill, the so-called LGBT article, has been one of its most controversial provisions. As a result, it has undergone many changes during drafting but the most recent version I have seen would make it a criminal offence to perform any 'indecent act' (*perbuatan cabul*) with any person of the same sex in public, punishable by 18 months' imprisonment or a Category II fine (Article 495(1)(a)).[12]

If the bill is passed in this form, the criminalisation of public indecency in Article 495(1)(a) could probably be used to target almost any kind of display of affection between LGBTQI people, which, in the current climate of morally conservative Islamist majoritarian intolerance, might well be deemed to be inherently 'immoral'.

---

11 Constitutional Court Decision No. 46/PUU-XIV/2016.
12 Heavier punishments would apply where the offences are aggravated. For example, 'indecent acts' with a person of the same sex that involve force, violence or the threat of violence, or that are published in the form of pornography, would be punishable by nine years' imprisonment or a Category III fine (Article 495(1)(b) and (c)), regardless of whether performed in public or not. Likewise, if the 'indecent act' is done with a person who was known, or should have been known, to be under the age of 18, it would be punishable by 12 years' imprisonment or a Category IV fine (Article 495(2)), or, if accompanied by violence or the threat of violence, by 15 years' imprisonment or a Category V fine (Article 495(3)), again regardless of whether performed in public or not (Erdianto 2017).

RELIGIOUS MINORITIES

Unlike LGBTQI Indonesians, religious minorities do enjoy specific legal protection, but it is deeply flawed, and they have become increasingly vulnerable to discriminatory criminal prosecution as Muslim intolerance rises.

Indonesia's state ideology, the Pancasila, which is the 'basis of the state' (*dasar negara*) and 'the source of all sources of law' (Article 2, Law No. 12/2011 on Law-making), appears in the preamble to the Indonesian Constitution. The first of its five principles is 'Belief in Almighty God' (*Ketuhanan Yang Maha Esa*). This has been held by the Constitutional Court to be the 'yardstick' to measure the ambit of religious freedom in Indonesia, and is the basis for its finding that Indonesia is neither a 'religious state' (*negara agama*) nor an atheist or secular one, but a 'Godly' (*berTuhan*) 'country that is religious' (*negara beragama*).[13] In other words, the right to religious belief is seen as part of the fundamental identity of Indonesia.

Article 28E of the Constitution further provides that:

1. Each person is free to profess their religion and to worship in accordance with their religion [...]
2. Each person has the freedom to possess convictions and beliefs, and to express their thoughts and attitudes in accordance with their conscience.

This is reiterated in Article 29:

1. The State shall be based upon belief in Almighty God.
2. The State guarantees all persons the freedom of worship, each according to their own beliefs.

Despite these plain words, the freedom guaranteed by the provisions is, in reality, an extremely limited one.

This is for two reasons. First, Article 28J(2) of the Constitution allows the restriction of rights granted elsewhere in the Constitution. It provides:

In carrying out his or her rights and freedom, *every citizen has the responsibility to abide by the restrictions set out by laws* with the sole aim to guarantee consideration and respect for the rights and freedoms of other citizens and *to fulfil the requirements of justice in accordance with moral considerations, religious values,* security and public order in a democratic society [emphasis added].

The Constitutional Court has relied on this provision to allow the government to legislate almost as it chooses to limit citizens' freedom to follow their religious beliefs (Lindsey and Butt 2016: 20–26). In 2010, for example, it upheld the so-called Blasphemy Law, discussed below, which

---

13   Constitutional Court Decision No. 140/PUU-VII/2009.

is routinely used to criminalise the behaviour of members of minority religious groups and so-called 'deviant' sects (*aliran sesat*).[14] It held that the Blasphemy Law was a legitimate mechanism by which the government could protect 'religious values', as determined by orthodox religious 'parent organisations', such as MUI (Lindsey and Butt 2016: 24–6).

The second major limitation arises from the distinction between 'religions' (*agama*) and 'beliefs' (*kepercayaan*). In short, the religious freedoms in Articles 28E and 29 have been read down by a political interpretation of the 'belief in Almighty God' so that they are usually available only to followers of officially recognised and protected religions (and even then only to the extent the state decides). After much political and legal manoeuvring, the New Order came to accept just five religions as monotheistic and thus 'protected' by the Pancasila: Islam, Roman Catholic Christianity (*Katolik*), Protestant Christianity (*Kristen*), Hinduism and Buddhism. A sixth religion, Confucianism (*Khonghucu*), lost recognition in 1978 but was recognised again in 2000.[15] These six remain the only officially recognised and protected religions (*agama*) in Indonesia today.

As the Blasphemy Law suggests in its elucidation, religions other than the official six are 'not prohibited' but are designated mere 'beliefs' (*kepercayaan*). They do not receive the same level of recognition by, and support from, the state as religions. For example, they are not supported by the bureaucratic apparatus of the Ministry of Religion, which has five directorates-general for the official religions (except Confucianism) but none for 'beliefs'. Instead, responsibility for 'beliefs' is left in the hands of the Ministry of Education and Culture. This ministry has a substantially reduced budget for these duties and shows little interest in supporting belief communities. It no longer requires them even to register, as was once the case (Howell 2004: 6). This may be seen as freeing these communities from state supervision, but it also denies them recognition and support.

---

14   Constitutional Court Decision No. 140/PUU-VII/2009.

15   Confucianism was first officially recognised as a religion in 1965 in the elucidation to Article 1 of Sukarno's Blasphemy Law. It continued to be a state religion under the New Order until it was derecognised in 1978 by a circular (*surat edaran*) of the Ministry of Home Affairs (No. 477/74054), confirmed in 1979 by a cabinet decision of the Suharto government—although whether the circular or the decision could overrule the provisions of the Blasphemy Law's elucidation is debatable. In any case, in 2000 President Abdurrahman Wahid issued a statement reinstating Confucianism as a recognised religion, and the Ministry of Home Affairs issued Instruction No. 477/805/Sj repealing the 1978 circular. In the same year, the Supreme Court reversed earlier jurisprudence to hold that Confucianism was a state religion for the purposes of marriage registration (Decision No. 178K/TUN/1997 of 26 June 2000). See generally Lindsey (2005).

'Beliefs' are, however, still officially recognised—on paper at least—as falling within the 'belief in Almighty God' principle. They are therefore not illegal per se. In theory, a citizen could argue membership of a *keper-cayaan* (belief) to justify state protection for beliefs that orthodox religious groups label 'deviant'. In practice, however, these 'beliefs' attract little protection—or respect—from the state. In the past, for example, 'beliefs' could not be listed in the section on an Indonesian identity card (*kartu tanda penduduk*, KTP) where the holder's religion was identified. Instead, followers of beliefs were forced to adopt a nominal religion or, much less commonly, to leave this part of the card blank, exposing them to the risk of persecution as a godless atheist or communist.[16]

A recent Constitutional Court Decision[17] has changed this, allowing a person to opt for either one of the six religions or 'belief in Almighty God' to be included on his or her KTP. However, as Butt explains in Chapter 4 of this book, this has not fully resolved the problems faced by followers of beliefs, who are still vulnerable to discrimination for not accepting an official religion.

The second-class status of 'beliefs' is also demonstrated by the risk their followers run of being prosecuted under the Criminal Code for offences under the Blasphemy Law. This typically happens for two reasons. First, similarities between the beliefs or practices of followers of a 'belief' and those of one of the recognised religions can be construed as an inherently deviant form of that religion, and therefore a slur on it, and thus blasphemous. An example is the well-known case of sect leader Lia Eden, who was convicted of blasphemy against Islam because she believed she had communicated with the angel Gabriel, who is, for Muslims and Christians, the messenger of God (Lindsey 2012: 412–14).

Second, certain statements or behaviour of a person who is not a member of a particular recognised religion (for example, a follower of a 'belief') can be construed as denigrating that religion. This can also apply to followers of a recognised religion, as in the high-profile case of the former governor of Jakarta, Basuki Tjahaja Purnama, known as Ahok, a Christian-Chinese Indonesian convicted of blasphemy and jailed for two years in May 2017 for calling on Muslims not to be fooled by *ulama* advocating a particular interpretation of a Qur'anic verse (Peterson 2018). A recent case in which Meiliana, a Buddhist-Chinese Indonesian, was convicted of blasphemy in the district court of Medan and jailed for 18 months for complaining that a mosque's loudspeakers were too noisy, is another good example of this (Tehusijarana and Gunawan 2018).

---

16 On the legal standing of atheists in Indonesia, and the persecution they face, see Hasani (2016).

17 Constitutional Court Decision No. 97/PUU-XIV/2016.

This wide interpretation of what constitutes blasphemy is made possible by the loose wording of the Blasphemy Law. This 'Law', in fact, comprises just five provisions in Section V of the Criminal Code, 'Crimes against public order', that deal with crimes against religion or 'groups', including through hate speech.[18] The most controversial of these provisions is Article 156(a), which dates back to the last full year of Sukarno's rule.[19] It states that anyone who intentionally and in public expresses sentiments or carries out acts that:

1. are principally of a nature of enmity towards, misuse of or dishonouring of a religion adhered to in Indonesia;

2. are intended to stop a person believing in any religion that is based on Belief in Almighty God (*Ketuhanan Yang Maha Esa*)

will be liable to imprisonment for a maximum of five years.

One obvious difficulty created by these provisions is that they provide no definition of many of the key terms on which they rely, in particular the word 'dishonouring' (*penodaan*). This leaves law enforcement officials to decide for themselves what religious practices are prohibited by Article 156(a) for the purposes of decisions to arrest or prosecute. For this reason, police and prosecutors usually look to MUI for guidance.

---

18 The relevant provisions other than Article 156(a) are as follows. Article 156 provides that anyone who in public expresses sentiments of 'enmity, hate or humiliation' (*permusuhan, kebencian atau penghinaan*) directed at a 'group of the Indonesian population' will be liable to a maximum sentence of four years or a maximum fine of Rp 4,500. 'Group' is defined broadly to mean 'race, country of origin, religion, place of origin, ethnic descent, ethnicity or position'. Article 157 prohibits writing or pictures that (as in Article 156) express 'enmity, hate or humiliation' towards a 'group of the Indonesian population'. While 'group' is not defined, the definition is assumed to be the same as in Article 156, which includes religious groups. Article 175 provides that anyone who, by violence or threats of violence, obstructs a public and non-prohibited religious gathering, religious ceremony or funeral will be liable for a maximum prison sentence of one year and four months. Article 176 provides that anyone who intentionally disrupts a public and non-prohibited religious gathering, religious ceremony or funeral, causing confusion or a commotion, will be sentenced to a maximum term of one month and two weeks in prison or a maximum fine of Rp 1,800. Article 177 provides that anyone who ridicules (*menghina*) a religious official who is carrying out a permitted task or anyone who ridicules objects used for religious ceremonies in a place where a religious ceremony is being carried out or when a religious ceremony is in progress will be sentenced to a maximum term of four months and two weeks in prison or a maximum fine of Rp 1,800.

19 It was Article 4 of Presidential Decision No. 1/PNPS/1965 on the Prevention of the Abuse and/or Dishonouring of a Religion, which was upgraded to become a statute by Law No. 5/1969 Declaring Several Decisions and Regulations of the President to Be Laws. See Lindsey (2012: 402).

MUI has exploited this to exercise a quasi-judicial function. Its *fatwa* are now usually decisive on questions of blasphemy and—despite having no actual legal authority—are routinely applied by courts, to the great disadvantage of religious minorities. This has meant that the number of prosecutions under these provisions has increased hugely in recent years as MUI's attitude towards unorthodox religious groups it considers 'deviant' (*sesat*) has toughened (Fenwick 2018; Lindsey 2012: 408–9: Peterson 2018: 86–8).

ETHNIC MINORITIES: *ADAT* COMMUNITIES

I now turn to the legal position of, first, *adat* communities and then Chinese Indonesians, minorities identified by ethnicity. Both have, in theory, benefited from post-Suharto law reforms that purport to strengthen their rights, but in reality these reforms have delivered only limited change.

Adat is commonly translated as 'customary law' or 'traditional law'. It is highly diverse and varies significantly from place to place—even across relatively short distances. It is mostly followed in rural areas where the reach of the modern state and its laws is still limited. The Orang Rimba of Sumatra, described by Manurung in Chapter 13 of this book, are a good example of a remote community that applies *adat*.

The good news is that the Constitution was amended in 2000 to recognise the rights of minority communities that continue to apply their traditional *adat*, and that the Constitutional Court has been enthusiastic in defending and articulating these rights—even invalidating some legislation that ignored the rights of communities that followed *adat*.[20]

Article 18B(2) of the Constitution states that:

> The state recognises and respects *adat* law communities and their traditional rights provided that they remain in existence, accord with community developments and [accord with] the principle of the Unitary State of the Republic of Indonesia, which is regulated by statute.

Article 28I(3) adds that:

> The cultural identity and rights of traditional communities are respected in line with the development of the times and civilisation.

---

20 See, for example, Constitutional Court Decision No. 3/PUU-VII/2010 (reviewing the 2007 Coastal Areas and Small Island Management Law); and Constitutional Court Decision No. 35/PUU-X/2012 (reviewing the 1999 Forestry Law). This discussion of *adat* rights draws on Butt and Lindsey (2018: 136–41).

As a result of these new provisions and the norms that drove their adoption in the Constitution, *adat* rights have been mentioned in various statutes concerning natural resources enacted from 1999 onward. These include Law No. 41/1999 on Forestry (Article 67(1)), Law No. 31/2004 on Fisheries (Article 6), Law No. 18/2004 on Plantations (Article 9), Law No. 7/2004 on Water Resources (Article 6(2)), Law No. 32/2009 on Environmental Protection and Management (Article 62(1–3)) and Law No. 27/2007 on the Management of Coastal Areas and Small Islands (Articles 21(4)(a) and (c), 61 and 62).

Although they have received a great deal of public applause, the new *adat* community rights are in many cases a legal mirage, chiefly because the statutes provide only conditional protection. Most, for example, require that *adat* rights be consistent with the national interest and prosperity, or the vaguely stated idea of 'community development'. These are Suharto-era concepts that allow *adat* rights to be displaced with relative ease, should powerful interests so desire.

Most of the relevant statutes also require that the *adat* principle 'remain in existence' (*masih hidup*)—after all, an *adat* principle should not be enforced in an *adat* community if that principle is not followed there. In practice, however, this restriction means that the *adat* community that follows the *adat* principle must be formally recognised by state law—for example, by a regional regulation (*peraturan daerah*, or *perda*)—for its *adat* principles to be recognised or protected. This is a significant impediment found in many statutes that mention *adat*.[21] A few communities have won this recognition, but for most, the legal and political steps necessary to win such recognition, and the costs involved, make this requirement an insuperable obstacle.

In addition, most of these provisions do not provide sanctions if, for example, the government or another party violates *adat* rights. As any lawyer will argue, a rule without a sanction is not a rule at all. Despite the 'on-paper' protection these statutes confer, traditional rights therefore remain highly vulnerable to expropriation with inadequate or no compensation.

ETHNIC MINORITIES: CHINESE INDONESIAN COMMUNITIES

At the time of Indonesia's accession to the International Convention on the Elimination of All Forms of Racial Discrimination in 1999, many of

---

21   See, for example, Article 1(43) of Law No. 23/2014 on Regional Autonomy and Articles 97 and 103, in particular, of Law No. 6/2014 on Villages.

the country's laws discriminated against Chinese Indonesians. Presidential Decision No. 240/1967, for example, required Chinese Indonesians to adopt Indonesian-sounding names, and Presidential Instruction No. 14/1967 banned the celebration of Chinese culture and the use of Chinese characters.

Presidential Instruction No. 26/1998 was issued by President Habibie to mark a shift in policy. It banned the use of the contentious terms *pribumi* (indigenous) and *non-pribumi* (non-indigenous, commonly understood to refer to ethnic Chinese Indonesians) in all government documentation. Ministers and all other office-holders were instructed to end the use of these words in public policy formulation and implementation. They were also ordered to treat all citizens equally, regardless of ethnicity, race or religion. Other symbolic reforms continued under President Wahid and his successor, Megawati Sukarnoputri, with the ban on Chinese cultural celebrations removed by Presidential Decree No. 6/2000, Confucianism reinstated as a state religion in the same year (as discussed above), and Chinese New Year becoming an official national holiday through Presidential Decision No. 19/2002.

Reflecting the thrust of the reforms just described, an amended citizenship law—Law No. 12/2006 on Citizenship—was introduced in 2006 to redefine 'citizen' and 'citizenship' and end the classification of Indonesia-born citizens into 'authentic' (*asli*) Indonesians and Indonesians of 'foreign descent'. Ethnic Chinese born in Indonesia were now to be considered *asli*, as was made clear in the elucidation to Article 2:

> A 'native Indonesian' is an Indonesian who became a citizen of Indonesia at the moment of birth and who has never held another citizenship of [his/her] own volition.

The general elucidation to the 2006 Citizenship Law declared that non-discrimination was one of the 'specific principles' (*asas khusus*) on which Law No. 12/2006 and its new approach to citizenship was based:

> The non-discrimination principle (*asas nondiskriminatif*) is a principle that does not differentiate in all matters of implementation relating to citizenship on the grounds of ethnicity, race, religion, group, sex and gender.

Despite these reforms, many regulations that discriminate against Chinese Indonesians remain, and the new laws are often ignored. As Setijadi shows in Chapter 11 of this book, even the terms *pribumi* and *non-pribumi* have begun to make a come-back, as was obvious in the rhetoric deployed against the Christian-Chinese former governor of Jakarta, Ahok. The best example of the way in which reforms intended to prevent discrimination against Chinese Indonesians have been stymied is the persistence of the oppressive Proof of Indonesian Citizenship Document, the Surat Bukti Kewarganegaraan Republik Indonesia (SBKRI).

The SBKRI derives from an earlier iteration of the Citizenship Law, Law No. 62/1958, which recognised a category of locally born alien:

> An alien who was born and resides in the territory of the Republic of Indonesia, whose father or mother—if he or she had no familial relationship with the father—was also born in the territory of the Republic of Indonesia, may submit an application to the Minister of Justice to acquire Indonesian citizenship [...][22]

Law No. 62/1958 did not make specific mention of the ethnic Chinese but in practice the concept of the locally born alien was usually applied only to Indonesian citizens of Chinese descent. The SBKRI thus became essential evidence of citizenship for most ethnic-Chinese Indonesians, and necessary to access state services, such as education. To make matters worse, in 1992 the Ministry of Justice introduced a requirement for Chinese Indonesians to undergo a periodic SBKRI re-registration process, forcing even those already recognised as citizens to go through the arduous process again and again.[23] This system was intrusive, discriminatory, complex and repressive—and intentionally so.

In fact, the SBKRI system became notorious as a source of illegal rents for the bureaucracy, and its obvious injustice eventually led to the issuing by Suharto of Presidential Decision No. 56/1996. This announced that the SBKRI would no longer be required to obtain Indonesian citizenship for the wives, children under the age of 18 and unmarried adult daughters of male naturalised citizens, as well as the children under the age of 18 of unmarried female citizens. In place of the SBKRI, applicants for a passport would be able to use their birth certificates and KTPs or their family cards.

However, this left many poor non-SBKRI families—who could no more afford to extract birth certificates and KTPs or family cards from the bureaucracy than they could SBKRIs—no better off. It also did not make matters all that much easier for most 'stateless' Chinese women. For example, an adult ethnic-Chinese woman who was married but did not have an SBKRI would have to produce her husband's SBKRI if she wanted to obtain official documentation such as a passport, or perform any act requiring Indonesian citizenship. If she was single but did not possess an SBKRI, then she would have to produce evidence of her father's SBKRI, including if she wanted to marry. The process of collecting documentation such as birth certificates, KTPs and SBKRIs for themselves or family

---

22 Article IV(1); and see Presidential Decision No. 52/1977. It was also possible to obtain an SBKRI by application to the court (Article 14 of the Citizenship Law) or to the local subdistrict head (*camat*) (Presidential Decisions No. 2 and No. 13 of 1980).

23 Ministerial Decision No. 02-HL.04/10/1992 on Proof of Indonesian Citizenship Status for Children of Indonesian Citizenship Holders of Foreign Descent.

members was slow and costly, with many opportunities for corruption on the part of officials. As Chan (2017) argues, the SBKRI system thus discriminated against Chinese women twice, for their ethnicity and for their gender. Of course, those who were not Muslim were also vulnerable to a third form of discrimination, based on their religion, as explained earlier.

Presidential Instruction No. 4/1999 Implementing Presidential Decision No. 56/1996 on the SBKRI was another regulation issued by Habibie as part of wider post-Suharto efforts to end discrimination against the ethnic Chinese. However, it was ineffective because, as its name suggests, it essentially just reiterated the problematic formula in Suharto's 1996 decision. It therefore did little to halt the many instances in which officials required Indonesian Chinese to produce an SBKRI in order to access state services (Purdey 2005: 22).

In practice, even if the SBKRI appears to have been made redundant by the 2006 Citizenship Law, it continues to survive in the bureaucratic system in some parts of the country—where it still restricts access to education for some poor Chinese—due to ignorance, prejudice, simple rent-seeking or a combination of these. It thus continues to function as an effective barrier to entry across a whole range of sectors for many ethnic Chinese (Chan 2017; Purdey 2005).

CONCLUSION: REFORM, INTERRUPTED

Overall, the picture presented by this brief survey of laws relevant to the protection of the rights of minorities is not impressive. In fact, these laws are, in the main, deeply inadequate and have failed to live up to the reformist aspirations embodied in the constitutional amendments passed between 1999 and 2002.

For convenience of analysis, the laws relevant to minorities in Indonesia can be grouped into four categories. The first comprises sophisticated new laws that were intended to prevent discrimination against minorities but which are not properly enforced. They therefore remain largely aspirational, often because of weaknesses in the new regimes they introduce. An example of this is Law No. 8/2016 on People with Disabilities; another is the new laws that purport to strengthen the rights of *adat* communities but in many cases do not achieve much. The second category is made up of new laws that were intended, in part at least, for discriminatory purposes, such as Aceh's Qanun Jinayat, the 2008 Pornography Law or the proposed 'LGBT article' of the Criminal Code. The third category consists of old laws that enable discrimination and are enforced regularly and, in some cases, even more than in the past, such as the Blasphemy Law. The fourth category is reserved for highly discriminatory legal regimes that many believe no longer apply but which in fact continue to be enforced to the disadvantage of minorities, such as the SBKRI system.

The reasons for this disappointing situation are many and complex, and are explored in more detail in other chapters in this book, but they are, in simple terms, the 'usual suspects' that are so often rightly blamed for legal dysfunction in Indonesia. They include, among others, poor drafting and legislative horse-trading that subverts policy formation; bureaucratic inertia or outright resistance to new laws; widespread ignorance of laws that is not remedied by adequate 'socialisation' within government or among the public; weak enforcement by police and prosecutors; flawed judicial decisions; routine elite intervention to protect vested interests; and, of course, simple corruption and abuse of power, which are widespread.

These problems point to a wider failure of Indonesia's political and legal institutions to live up to the expectations of the Indonesian public, or at least the expectations of the civil society reformers who advocated for better protection for minorities during the decade and half from 1998 when so many of the new laws described above were introduced. They also raise wider questions about the faltering trajectory of *reformasi* in Indonesia.

REFERENCES

Butt, S., and T. Lindsey (2018) *Indonesian Law*, Oxford University Press, Oxford.

Chan, F.Y.-W. (2017) 'Citizenship vs. alienage and the intersectionality of law, race and gender', *Vida! Blog of the Australian Women's History Network*, 19 February. http://www.auswhn.org.au/blog/citizenship-vs-alienage/

Eldridge, P. (2002) 'Human rights in post-Suharto Indonesia', *Brown Journal of World Affairs* 9(1): 127–39.

Erdianto, K. (2017) 'DPR-pemerintah belum sepakat, pasal LGBT dalam RKUHP ditunda', *Kompas.com*, 5 February.

Fenwick, S. (2016) 'Faith and freedom in Indonesian law: liberal pluralism, religion and the democratic state', in T. Lindsey and H. Pausacker (eds) *Religion, Law and Intolerance in Indonesia*, Routledge, London and New York: 68–94.

Fenwick, S. (2017) *Blasphemy, Islam and the State: Pluralism and Liberalism in Indonesia*, Routledge, London and New York.

Fenwick, S. (2018) 'Eat, pray, regulate: the Indonesian Ulama Council and the management of Islamic affairs', *Journal of Law and Religion* 33(2): 1–20.

Hasani, I. (2016) 'The decreasing space for non-religious expression in Indonesia', in T. Lindsey and H. Pausacker (eds) *Religion, Law and Intolerance in Indonesia*, Routledge, London and New York: 197–210.

Hasyim, S. (2016) 'The Council of Indonesian Ulama (MUI) and *aqida*-based intolerance: a critical analysis of its fatwa on Ahmadiyah and "Sepilis"', in T. Lindsey and H. Pausacker (eds) *Religion, Law and Intolerance in Indonesia*, Routledge, London and New York: 211–33.

Howell, J.D. (2004) '"Spirituality" vs "religion" Indonesian style: framing and re-framing experiential religiosity in contemporary Indonesian Islam', paper presented to the 15th Biennial Conference of the Asian Studies Association of Australia, Canberra, 29 June – 2 July (paper on file with the author).

Lindsey, T. (2004) 'Indonesia: devaluing Asian values, rewriting the rule of law', in R.P. Peerenboom (ed.) *Asian Discourses of Rule of Law*, Routledge Curzon, London and New York: 286–323.

Lindsey, T. (2005) 'Reconstituting the ethnic Chinese in post-Soeharto Indonesia: law, racial discrimination, and reform', in T. Lindsey and H. Pausacker (eds) *Chinese Indonesians: Remembering, Distorting and Forgetting*, ISEAS and Monash Asia Institute, Singapore and Clayton.

Lindsey, T. (2012) *Islam, Law and the State in Southeast Asia. Volume I: Indonesia*, IB Tauris, London and New York.

Lindsey, T., and S. Butt (2016) 'State power to restrict religious freedom: an overview of the legal framework', in T. Lindsey and H. Pausacker (eds) *Religion, Law and Intolerance in Indonesia*, Routledge, London and New York: 19–41.

Lindsey, T., and H. Pausacker (2005) *Chinese Indonesians: Remembering, Distorting and Forgetting*, ISEAS and Monash Asia Institute, Singapore and Clayton.

Lindsey, T., and H. Pausacker (eds) (2016) *Religion, Law and Intolerance in Indonesia*, Routledge, London and New York.

Peterson, D. (2018) 'Blasphemy, human rights, and the case of Ahok', in J. Rehman and A. Shahid (eds) *The Asian Yearbook of Human Rights and Humanitarian Law*, Volume 2, Brill: 52–94.

Prabowo, D. (2017) 'Pemerintah diminta segera realisasikan Komisi Nasional Disabilitas', *Kompas*, 17 February.

Purdey, J. (2005) 'Anti-Chinese violence and transitions in Indonesia: June 1998–October 1999', in T. Lindsey and H. Pausacker (eds) *Chinese Indonesians: Remembering, Distorting and Forgetting*, ISEAS and Monash Asia Institute, Singapore and Clayton: 14–40.

Santoso, S. (ed.) (1975) *Sutasoma: A Study in Old Javanese Wajrayana*, International Academy of Indian Culture, New Delhi.

Suherdjoko (2017) '"Jokowi Undercover" author sentenced to three years in prison', *Jakarta Post*, 29 May.

Syaefudin, A. (2017) 'Divonis 3 tahun penjara, penulis buku "Jokowi Undercover" banding', *detikNews*, 29 May.

Tehusijarana, K., and A. Gunawan (2018) 'The Meiliana case: how a noise complaint resulted in an 18-month sentence', *Jakarta Post*, 23 August.

4 The Constitutional Court and minority rights: analysing the recent homosexual sex and indigenous belief cases

Simon Butt

Since its establishment 15 years ago, Indonesia's Constitutional Court has become a forum in which various minorities have been able to pursue their interests, often in the face of subjugation by larger groups and even the state itself. These minorities include customary law (*adat*) communities, whose dependence on natural resources such as forests and coastal areas has brought them into conflict with the interests of the state and businesses, who often claim a legal entitlement to those resources. They also include adherents of so-called 'deviant' sects—that is, those who call themselves believers of a religion officially recognised in Indonesia, but believe in a 'version' of that religion that, at least in the view of some religious authorities, diverges from the orthodox tenets of the religion. The cases involving these two minority groups have drawn significant controversy and been the subject of much academic writing (Budiwanti 2009; Butt 2014; Crouch 2011, 2012; Fenwick 2017; Lindsey 2012: 20; Lindsey and Pausacker 2016; Lindsey in this volume).

The court's constitutional review function potentially offers minority groups an avenue to use the court as both a 'sword' and a 'shield'. As a 'sword', the court enables these groups to actively push for legal change in the face of legislation that appears to discriminate against them or to disregard their constitutional rights. As a 'shield', the court has allowed them to seek to protect themselves from legislation that violates their constitutional rights.

This chapter focuses on two Constitutional Court cases handed down in late 2017 involving two other broad minority groups, upon whose interests the Constitutional Court had not previously adjudicated. These cases drew significant public attention and controversy but very little has yet been written about them. The first of these cases touched upon the interests of some of Indonesia's lesbian, gay, bisexual, transgender, queer and intersex (LGBTQI) community, which has suffered increasing intolerance in recent years (Firdaus 2018; see also Chapter 7 by Wieringa and Chapter 8 by Wijaya in this book). In December 2017 the court handed down its decision in a case brought by members of a conservative Muslim group, the Family Love Alliance (Aliansi Cinta Keluarga, AILA). Among other things, they challenged Article 292 of the Criminal Code, which prohibits 'indecent activities' (*perbuatan cabul*) with a minor of the same gender as the perpetrator. Although Article 292 does not refer to homosexual or other types of non-heterosexual sexual activity, most Indonesian legal commentators accept that it covers non-heterosexual activity, among other things.

The applicants asked the court to change Article 292 so that it applied to indecent acts between people of the same gender, regardless of their age. By the narrowest of margins, a five-judge majority decided that the court lacked the power to amend the Criminal Code, but nevertheless appeared to support the conservative sentiment behind the application. The four-judge minority agreed with the applicants, and would have outlawed consensual gay sex if its opinion had carried the day.

The second case concerned the constitutional recognition of indigenous beliefs, which are referred to variously in Indonesia as *aliran kepercayaan*, *kepercayaan, keyakinan* and *kebatinan*. In this chapter, I refer to them simply as 'beliefs' (*kepercayaan*) to distinguish them from recognised 'religions' (*agama*). Indonesia has six state-recognised religions—Islam, Catholicism, Protestantism, Hinduism, Buddhism and Confucianism—all of which fall under the authority of the Ministry of Religious Affairs. By contrast, beliefs are neither state-recognised, nor necessarily blasphemous 'deviations' of recognised religions. Some of them pre-date the reception into Indonesia of the officially recognised religions; others more readily fall into the category of 'new age' spiritual movements. Responsibility for beliefs rests with the Ministry of Education and Culture. The number of those adhering to such beliefs is not certain; however, the ministry estimates that there are 12 million followers spread across 187 groups in 13 provinces (Nadlir 2017; Voanews 2018).[1]

---

1   By contrast, Hefner (2017: 211) puts the number of adherents of indigenous religions at between 200,000 and 300,000, with a similar number of people involved in new religious movements; another author puts the number of native faith groups at 12,000 (Heriyanto 2017).

For many years, some minority-belief groups, and their supporters, have asked the state to treat their beliefs as equal to the official religions. While the government has in fact recognised them during some periods (Hosen 2014: 338–40; Lindsey 2012: 59–62), they have not received the same level of financial or institutional support as official religions and, on the whole, have been marginalised, ignored or even discriminated against.

In November 2017, the Constitutional Court issued a decision that may clear a path for greater state recognition and support of indigenous minority religions. In the decision, the court unanimously decided to change the provisions of a statute that had required those following an indigenous religion to leave the religious column or entry in their state-issued family card and identity card blank. The court decided that this was discriminatory and that *penghayat kepercayaan* (believer in an indigenous religion) could appear instead.

THE CONSTITUTIONAL COURT AND HUMAN RIGHTS

Before discussing these cases in detail, I shall make some observations about the court's function in cases involving minority rights. On the one hand, the Constitutional Court portrays itself as a protector of human rights, primarily through exercise of its constitutional review function. Using this power, the court can invalidate national legislation that it thinks violates the charter of human rights contained in the Constitution, which includes a bundle of rights that appear directed towards 'minorities'. There is, for example, a provision that guarantees the rights of customary law communities. This has been used to justify the court's decision that the state must recognise community forests and allow community access to forest resources, for instance.

On the other hand, it is easy to overstate the utility of bringing a claim before the Constitutional Court, for various reasons related to the court's institutional design. For example, despite their importance, the court's review powers are narrow: the court cannot review government regulations and decisions that violate constitutional rights, but rather can only consider whether national statutes violate them. This is unfortunate, because many of these regulatory instruments are thought to violate constitutional rights, including those of minority groups. Also, the Constitutional Court has no formal powers of enforcement, relying almost entirely on its reputation and public support to push the government to comply with its decisions. Despite some examples of government defiance, the court's decisions are usually followed. However, it bears noting that, beyond media reportage and potential political fallout, there are few consequences for the government if it ignores the court's decisions.

The utility of Constitutional Court proceedings is brought further into question by some of the practices the court has chosen to employ, which seem to preclude applicants from getting any benefit from winning a case. Two of these practices are of relevance here. The first is that the court has continually refused to review the constitutionality of the way statutes are implemented, or the practical effect they have. According to the court, its reviews are limited to assessing the words or norms in statutes, rather than how they are interpreted or applied in practice. It is for other courts in Indonesia's judicial hierarchy to determine whether the implementation of a law corresponds with its norms. Nevertheless, the court sometimes makes exceptions to these practices, and such an exception appears to have been made in the *Beliefs* case, discussed below.

The court also limits its decisions by giving most of them prospective effect. In other words, if the court decides that a statute breaches the Constitution and declares it to be invalid, that statute will only be invalid from the moment the court finishes reading its decision. Any action taken under the statute between its enactment and its invalidation is not affected by the declaration of invalidity and therefore remains legal.[2] As the court commonly explains, it has taken this approach because it is concerned with the constitutionality of statutory norms that apply generally to all cases, rather than to actual or 'concrete' cases. Of course, this approach significantly undermines the utility of bringing an application before the Constitutional Court. Even if the applicant wins, he or she can obtain no redress for damage to constitutional rights already suffered. For most applicants, then, the most they can hope for is a moral victory; applicants can only expect to prevent future constitutional damage to themselves or others by having the court remove the offending statute from the books.

HOMOSEXUAL SEX CASE[3]

As mentioned, in this case, brought in April 2016, members of AILA, represented by a team of 36 lawyers calling themselves the Advocacy Team for a Civilised Indonesia, challenged various provisions of the Criminal Code. These included Article 292, which prohibited 'indecent acts' between people of the same gender, but only if one of them was a minor, which under Indonesian law is defined as someone under 21 years of age.

---

2   For statements to this effect, see Constitutional Court Decision No. 3/PUU-VII/2010, reviewing Law No. 27 of 2007 on the Management of Coastal Areas and Small Islands, para. 3.15.13; and Constitutional Court Decision No. 36/PUU-X/2012, reviewing Law No. 22 of 2001 on Oil and Natural Gas, para. 3.21.

3   The description and analysis of this decision that follows draws on Butt (2018).

The applicants also complained about Article 284, which defined adultery as unfaithfulness to one's marriage partner rather than prohibiting all sex outside marriage.

The applicants argued that the provisions violated the Constitution, including its religion-related rights and protections, and Indonesia's national philosophy, the Pancasila, the first principle of which is 'Belief in Almighty God'. They also claimed that the provisions threatened the 'integrity of the family' and religious values, both of which were 'very important in developing the people and the nation'.[4] They said, for example, that the adultery provision's limited application—that is, to unfaithfulness to one's marriage partner, rather than to prohibit any sex outside marriage—was 'dangerous to family culture in Indonesia and [...] the structure of the community'.[5] Accordingly, the impugned provisions did not merely touch upon domestic issues, but rather were of great national importance. This was, the applicants argued, also made clear by the constitutional inclusion of the rights to form and have a family (Articles 28B(1) and 28G(1)) and of the various religion-related rights mentioned above. The applicants claimed that:

> Indonesia was not established by its founders as 'religion neutral' or a 'secular state'. The Pancasila and the Preamble to the Constitution are laden with religious values as the basis of the establishment of the State of Indonesia. With this philosophical basis, the need to base all laws on moral foundations based on Almighty God is a non-negotiable certainty. Religions in Indonesia fundamentally prohibit adultery, rape by anyone, and same-sex relations.[6]

The applicants also criticised the Criminal Code as being a product of Dutch colonialism. Enacted by the Dutch for the colony in 1886, the code has remained largely unamended ever since, despite efforts to update or replace it since 1963. For the applicants, not only was the code old; it also did not suit Indonesian cultural or religious beliefs. The applicants cited serious 'flare-ups' in the community, which, they claimed, were caused by a 'lack of legal clarity about morality, particularly in respect of adultery [...] and same sex immorality'.[7]

A majority of the court turned down the applicants because they had asked the court for a decision it lacked jurisdiction to provide. The applicants had not asked the court to broadly interpret the provisions—a

---

4 Constitutional Court Decision No. 46/PUU-XIV/2016, p. 427. In Indonesia, dates used in case references generally indicate the year in which the relevant case was lodged with the court, rather than the year in which the case was decided.

5 Constitutional Court Decision No. 46/PUU-XIV/2016, p. 428.

6 Constitutional Court Decision No. 46/PUU-XIV/2016, p. 428.

7 Constitutional Court Decision No. 46/PUU-XIV/2016, p. 428.

request to which the court could have acceded. Rather, they had asked it to create new criminal norms and apply them to new classes of people.[8] But according to the court, only the legislature could 'criminalise or decriminalise'; the court was a negative legislator, not a positive one,[9] so it could not act as a 'mini parliament'.[10] The court also expressed scepticism that amendments to the Criminal Code's provisions along the lines suggested by the applicants would result in any changes to behaviour.[11]

Nevertheless, the majority rejected neither the fundamental religious premise upon which the application was based, nor the specific arguments of the applicants, accepting, in the case of adultery, that:

> It is very possible that one reason for the destruction of social and family systems and structures is that the broader concept of adultery has not been criminalised under Indonesian law [...][12]

As mentioned, four dissenting judges would have granted the applicants' requests.[13] They emphasised that the Pancasila was 'the source of all sources of law' and that, therefore, all laws must not contradict its values.[14] Indeed, the minority declared 'Belief in Almighty God' to be the 'highest' principle of the Pancasila because it was first on the list of five. The first principle was therefore 'absolute' and the source of 'all values of goodness',[15] and even underlay the Pancasila's four remaining principles.[16] The minority also pointed to the constitutional provisions providing freedom of religion and freedom to worship in accordance with

---

8   Constitutional Court Decision No. 46/PUU-XIV/2016, p. 431. The court explained in some detail how the amendments proposed by the applicants would change the nature of the offences, at pp. 433–41.

9   Constitutional Court Decision No. 46/PUU-XIV/2016, p. 441.

10   Constitutional Court Decision No. 46/PUU-XIV/2016, p. 444.

11   Constitutional Court Decision No. 46/PUU-XIV/2016, pp. 445–6.

12   Constitutional Court Decision No. 46/PUU-XIV/2016, p. 448.

13   The judges were Chief Justice Arief Hidayat, Deputy Chief Justice Anwar Usman and Constitutional Justices Wahiduddin Adams and Aswanto.

14   The Pancasila has long been 'the source of all sources of law'. This is not controversial in Indonesia, despite the Pancasila being a particularly vague philosophy that is difficult to apply, and even though it has almost never been judicially interpreted (Butt 2007).

15   As the minority put it, 'An act is said to be good if it does not violate the values, norms and law of God': Constitutional Court Decision No. 46/PUU-XIV/2016, p. 454.

16   Constitutional Court Decision No. 46/PUU-XIV/2016, p. 454. As the minority put it (at p. 455), Indonesia's founding fathers had established the Pancasila as a principle of life for a nation with a variety of religions, in order to help the nation to stay together. To my knowledge this was the first time the norms of the Pancasila had been formally ranked by a judicial institution.

that religion, and requiring respect for customary law (or 'living law' as the minority called it).

For the minority, the first Pancasila principle, and these constitutional rights, meant that no law would be valid if it violated religious law or 'living law'. The Pancasila and these rights also affected the interpretation of *other* constitutional rights. For example, Article 28D(1) grants the constitutional right to a 'just legal certainty'. For the minority,

> [T]his is not mere legal certainty. If there is legal certainty in the form of a norm of a Statute that reduces, narrows, invades or violates the [first principle] or religious values or living law [...] then that legal certainty is not a just legal certainty [...] [Such a statute] must be declared to violate the Constitution and to no longer have any binding force, and certainty cannot be left to the *open legal policy* of lawmakers [emphasis in original].[17]

The minority, therefore, appeared to consider that a 'just law' in Article 28D(1) was a law that did not violate religious values. This is an important conclusion, not least because the court uses 'legal certainty' perhaps more often as a constitutional ground to invalidate legislation than any other.

The minority also pointed to Article 28J(2), which reads:

> In exercising his or her rights and freedom, every person must be subject to the restrictions stipulated in laws and regulations with the intention of guaranteeing the recognition of and respect for the rights and freedoms of other people and to fulfil fair demands in accordance with the considerations of moral and religious values, security and public order in a democratic society.

The minority emphasised that Article 28J(2) mentions religious norms as a ground upon which the legislature can justify overriding the constitutional rights of some to protect the constitutional rights of others. This meant that the Constitution was a 'godly constitution'; accordingly, statutes that reduced or limited religious values needed to be amended so that they did not violate those values and religious teachings.[18]

The minority continued:

> If the status quo is maintained, then constitutional supremacy and the authority of the law in Indonesia will be severely threatened, because a statute that contains the phrase 'by the grace of Almighty God' will in fact contain legal norms that contradict or at least narrow and reduce the scope of culpability of an act that has clearly been established by the law of God. The same goes

---

17   This reference to 'open legal policy' refers to the scope the legislature has to enact laws within the confines imposed by the Constitution. Within those confines, the legislature may have numerous choices, all of which may be constitutional. For discussion of this concept, see Butt (2015).

18   Constitutional Court Decision No. 46/PUU-XIV/2016, p. 456.

for judicial decisions that include in the headnote the words 'In the name of Justice based on Almighty God'. These decisions must acquit perpetrators who have clearly been validly and convincingly proven to have performed an act that is strictly prohibited according to the law of God, just because the elements of the crime were not fulfilled, even though the act was clearly prohibited and was extremely culpable according to religious values and divine enlightenment.[19]

While the minority accepted that the Constitutional Court should generally exercise judicial restraint and not function as a positive legislator, an exception could be justified here for three reasons. First, the impugned provisions clearly reduced or even violated religious values.[20] Second, a draft of Indonesia's proposed new Criminal Code, which included a broader definition of the offence, in line with what the applicants sought, was before parliament.[21] And third, the minority said that its decision did not in fact expand the concept of adultery. Instead, it simply reverted to the concept of adultery as it was originally understood in Indonesia, before being narrowed by the Criminal Code, which had been enacted by the Dutch during their colonisation of Indonesia.[22] Specifically with regard to Article 292, the minority labelled it a 'victory' for members of the Dutch parliament when the code was enacted because, according to the minority, they were

> indeed affirmative with respect to homosexual practices, even though homosexual practices clearly were sexual behaviours that were intrinsically [...] and universally reprehensible according to religious law and divine enlightenment, and living law.[23]

The minority concluded with the following statement:

> The incidence of people 'taking the law into their own hands', which the community is doing against perpetrators of prohibited sexual relations (whether in the form of adultery, rape or homosexuality), happens because the religious values and living law of the community in Indonesia do not have a place that is proportional in Indonesia's criminal law system. If there is a modification of legal norms concerning this issue, then it is hoped that the legal structure and legal culture of the Indonesian community in facing these acts can also change for the better.[24]

---

19 Constitutional Court Decision No. 46/PUU-XIV/2016, p. 460.
20 Constitutional Court Decision No. 46/PUU-XIV/2016, p. 461.
21 Constitutional Court Decision No. 46/PUU-XIV/2016, p. 459.
22 Constitutional Court Decision No. 46/PUU-XIV/2016, p. 462.
23 Constitutional Court Decision No. 46/PUU-XIV/2016, p. 465.
24 Constitutional Court Decision No. 46/PUU-XIV/2016, p. 466.

Discussion

This decision has been described as a 'win' by moderates against conservatives (Hawley 2017). This appears to be true in respect of some LGBTQI groups. The draft Criminal Code before parliament resembles the current code in that it only prohibits consensual same-sex intercourse with a minor.[25] Of course, the code may be amended before enactment to prohibit other same-sex activities, but if it is not, or if the code is not enacted at all,[26] then the decision represents a significant setback for conservatives.

That this decision was so close does not bode well for the future of Indonesian pluralism. It appears to have teetered on a knife's edge for almost a year, with early rumours suggesting that the court had decided in favour of AILA in a six-to-three majority. As it turns out, the result might have been different had former Constitutional Court judge Patrialis Akbar not been removed from office when he was. In early 2017 Akbar was arrested for taking bribes to fix the outcome of an unrelated constitutional review case. He was removed from office soon thereafter and prosecuted and convicted in September 2017. He had not yet been arrested when *Homosexual sex* was being argued, and is said to have displayed a preference for the minority position during the proceedings (Hutton 2017). If he had remained on the bench, the minority view may well have carried the day. In the event, his replacement, Professor Saldi Isra, voted with the majority. This almost-equal division within the court suggests that the minority's thinking could one day be adopted by a majority, particularly if one or two judges with more conservative views are appointed to replace retirees in coming years.

This is certainly possible. The appointment system for Constitutional Court judges—under which the national parliament, the executive and the Supreme Court are each responsible for filling three positions on the nine-judge bench—appears initially to have been designed to encourage 'moderate' appointments. This 'cooperative' appointment model is adopted in other countries and is intended to discourage arms of government from making appointments clearly sympathetic to their own interests, for fear that one of the other arms might do the same (Ginsburg 2003: 45). Cooperating institutions can, therefore, be effective checks on

---

25 This sits in stark contrast with the adultery offence. The draft broadly defines adultery to include all extramarital intercourse. If the code is enacted, then the adultery-related legal changes the applicants wanted will materialise in any event, so any victory for the moderates would only be temporary.

26 It is by no means certain that the draft will be enacted, amidst significant controversy, including about many aspects that are not related to these morality offences. To pick just one example, over a decade ago, debate focused on whether witchcraft should be criminalised (Butt 2003).

each other's choices under this model. However, if more than one arm supports a conservative appointment then these checks will no longer operate. This could happen in Indonesia if, for example, the executive and legislature both made such an appointment, perhaps in response to perceived conservative public sentiment. Worse, nominating institutions appear to have absolute discretion to appoint who they please, provided that appointees meet the technical requirements to occupy judicial office, and are notoriously opaque about how they choose and vet their candidates.

Perhaps most significant is that the decision indicates further judicial acceptance of the use of religious norms—particularly Islamic norms—in constitutional interpretation. Of course, this observation applies most particularly to the minority decision. However, it also bears emphasising that the majority expressly indicated that its rejection of the application was not a rejection of legal change along the lines the applicants suggested. Indeed, the court responded to claims that its decision was 'pro-LGBT' by holding a press conference at which its spokespersons declared that the court was indeed worried by the 'social phenomena' about which the applicants complained (Sahbani 2017). Importantly, the majority did not criticise the way the minority had used religious norms as a new yardstick for constitutional review; rather, it was simply unwilling to reformulate criminal norms on *any* basis.

A serious shortcoming of both the majority and minority decisions was that they accepted assumptions and propositions about the norms of religions practised in Indonesia, without providing supporting evidence—or even specific references to religious texts or expert opinions adduced during proceedings. Instead, the court presumed that all religions and beliefs in Indonesia, and the 'living law', prohibited these acts. But there is certainly no consensus on this, at least beyond groups of more conservative Muslims, much less a consensus on whether the state should intervene in such cases (Fachrudin 2017; Pisani 2014: 2). It bears noting, too, that while the court mentioned Indonesia's various religions and beliefs, it referred specifically only to the Qur'an, ignoring the sources of the prescripts of other widely practised religions in Indonesia, such as Christianity, Hinduism and Buddhism.

Likewise, both the majority and the minority seemed to accept that homosexual sex and adultery posed a threat to families and the nation, apparently because they would destroy the social fabric of society. Yet evidence was provided neither to support this conclusion nor to explain precisely how such damage could be defined, caused or quantified. Also concerning was that, while the majority questioned the appropriateness and utility of using law to affect the behaviour to which the applicants objected, the minority appeared to explain 'vigilante justice' as a failure of national laws to incorporate religious norms. Though the minority certainly did not endorse violence against those accused of adultery or homosexual practices, it also did not condemn it. The minority appeared to portray it as an understandable response to perceived immoral behaviour.

BELIEFS CASE

The *Beliefs* case was brought in late September 2016 by four citizens—a farmer, a student and two small business operators—who followed indigenous beliefs rather than a state-recognised religion. These beliefs were called Marapu (East Sumba), Parmalin (North Sumatra), Ugamo Bangsa Batak (North Sumatra) and Sapto Dharmo (East Java). The applicants complained about two provisions of Law No. 23/2006 on Population Administration. The first was Article 61, which covers the information a family card (*kartu keluarga*) must contain, including a citizen's religion. Article 61(1) states that family cards must mention the religion of the family. Article 61(2) states that those who do not adhere to a recognised religion, or who are adherents of an indigenous religion (*penghayat kepercayaan*), should not have any religion listed, but should nevertheless be 'given services' and 'recorded in the population database'. Article 64 deals with electronic identity cards (*kartu tanda penduduk elektronik*, or e-KTP) and, like Article 61, requires that a citizen's religion be noted on the card (Article 64(1)). It states that those who adhere to an unofficial religion or belief are to have the 'religion' section on the card left blank, but should nevertheless receive services and be recorded in the population database (Article 64(2)).

The applicants had encountered difficulties in obtaining an ID card, even though Article 64(2) required that they 'receive services' if they left the religion column blank. Some of them even admitted to lying on the official form—by listing a recognised religion, even though they did not follow it—just so that they could obtain a card.[27] Without having a religion listed on their cards, others had trouble getting marriage certificates[28] and birth certificates for their children; obtaining employment, particularly in the public service, and social security rights; enrolling their children in school; accessing financial services; and even organising burial in a public cemetery.[29]

---

27 Constitutional Court Decision No. 97/PUU-XIV/2016, p. 132.
28 This difficulty is created by Government Regulation No. 37/2007, which requires marriages to be endorsed by an elder of a registered organisation (Hukumonline 2016).
29 Constitutional Court Decision No. 97/PUU-XIV/2016, p. 133. Groups with non-mainstream religious beliefs have long encountered such administrative impediments (Bagir 2017: 286; Hosen 2014: 339).

The applicants were represented by a group of 18 lawyers who argued that Articles 61 and 64 violated the applicants' constitutional rights, even though the articles required that the applicants be 'given services' if they left the religion column blank on their identity cards.[30] Their main argument was that the provisions were discriminatory because they referred only to a citizen's 'religion' and did not accommodate a 'belief', even though a 'belief' had the same constitutional status as a 'religion'. They argued, too, that this violated the 'rule of law' (*negara hukum*), and asked the court to declare these provisions invalid, unless 'religion' was interpreted to encompass 'belief'.

The national executive and the national legislature submitted separate responses to the application to the court. Neither put forward particularly strong arguments to defend the impugned provisions. The executive's representatives in particular appeared almost sympathetic to the applicants' arguments, accepting that the current system sometimes forced citizens to put down a religion they did not follow or simply to do without a KTP.[31] It did not even ask the court to reject the application, but rather to provide a constitutional interpretation and decision that was 'as just as possible'.[32]

The applicants won this case. In a unanimous decision, the court declared that the provisions of the Population Administration Law were invalid for three main constitutional reasons. First, they were discriminatory. The court dedicated significant space to discussing whether the Constitution distinguished between religion and belief, or whether they formed part of the same concept. This discussion was confusing, and the court appeared to reach different conclusions in different parts of its judgment. Nevertheless, it seems clear that the court's decision was predicated on the assumption that religions and beliefs are both constitutionally protected, and have the same status, even if they are not part of the same concept. Accordingly, because the provisions of the Population Administration Law treated those with a recognised 'religion' (who were able to list their religion) differently from those with a 'belief' (who had to leave the religion column blank), they were discriminatory.[33]

This form of discrimination was prohibited by the Population Administration Law itself,[34] by the Constitution and by various international

---

30 Constitutional Court Decision No. 97/PUU-XIV/2016, p. 135.
31 Constitutional Court Decision No. 97/PUU-XIV/2016, pp. 107–8.
32 Constitutional Court Decision No. 97/PUU-XIV/2016, p. 109.
33 The court concluded that these provisions violated the 'rule of law' (*negara hukum*), though it did not really explain why.
34 Article 4 prohibits discrimination based on religion, ethnicity, socioeconomic status and the like in the compilation of the population database.

conventions Indonesia had signed and ratified. It was also at odds with the court's own jurisprudence, which had held that discrimination occurred when one 'thing' (*hal*), which presumably includes a group, was treated differently to another, without there being a reasonable ground to make the distinction; or where different 'things' were treated the same, leading to injustice.[35] Applied to this case, discrimination would not have occurred if, in Articles 61(1) and 64(1), the word 'religion' had encompassed indigenous beliefs. However, Articles 61(2) and 64(2) made it clear that 'religion' was intended to refer only to a recognised religion, because they set out rules and procedures that applied to belief-holders, which excluded those beliefs from the operation of Articles 61(1) and 64(1). The rules and procedures contained in the articles would not have been necessary if 'religion' was intended to encompass those beliefs.

Second, because the law had confined its definition of 'religion' to recognised religions, the state had failed to meet its obligation to guarantee or respect the rights of adherents of beliefs. The court said:

> This is not in line with the spirit of the 1945 Constitution, which clearly guarantees that every citizen is free to embrace a religion and belief and to worship in accordance with that belief.[36]

Even though the law entitled citizens who did not list their religion to receive services, this was not in furtherance of the religion-related rights of those citizens, but rather the state's obligation to provide public services and administer the population database.[37] The court also criticised the provisions for 'implicitly constructing the formulation of the right to adhere to a religion or belief as something given by the state', when in fact that right attaches to every person as a natural right.[38]

Third, the court concluded that the provisions violated the constitutional principle of legal certainty, primarily because followers of beliefs found it difficult to obtain a family card and an identity card and, if they obtained one with a blank religion column, to secure the public

---

35 Constitutional Court Decision No. 97/PUU-XIV/2016, p. 146, citing Constitutional Court Decision No. 070/PUU-II/2004 and No. 27/PUU-V/2007.

36 Constitutional Court Decision No. 97/PUU-XIV/2016, p. 149.

37 Constitutional Court Decision No. 97/PUU-XIV/2016, p. 149. On this point, the court said that Law No. 25/2009 on Public Services required the state to provide public administration services—among other things by obtaining the data it needed to run various government programs effectively. The very purpose of compiling the database would be undermined if important facts about citizens were left out (as Articles 61(2) and 64(2) seemed to require), or if citizens were 'forced' to provide incorrect data (such as by choosing a religion they did not follow in order to access public services): Constitutional Court Decision No. 97/PUU-XIV/2016, p. 147.

38 Constitutional Court Decision No. 97/PUU-XIV/2016, p. 150.

services to which they were entitled. For the court, this was 'constitutional damage' that 'should not be permitted to happen'.[39] This was quite a strange conclusion. After all, there was nothing unclear about the provisions themselves or their operation. Also, this decision sits uncomfortably alongside the court's refusal in other cases, mentioned above, to consider how statutes are implemented or their consequences. The court unconvincingly attempted to distinguish this case from these earlier decisions, holding that the problems the applicants had experienced in obtaining employment and the like were not related to the implementation of a norm, but were rather the logical consequence of the understanding of 'religion' in the law.[40]

The court's final holding was that the word 'religion' in Articles 61(1) and 64(1) was unconstitutional unless taken to include 'belief'. However, it also declared that 'to create order in population administration', and considering the number and variety of indigenous beliefs, it would be sufficient simply to note *penghayat kepercayaan* (adherent of a belief) on these cards, without detailing the particular belief adhered to.[41]

Discussion

This case clearly marks an advance for religious freedom in Indonesia—particularly for those who hold indigenous beliefs. Some appear to have taken the decision as wholesale state recognition of indigenous beliefs for all purposes, and as a basis to undo decades of discrimination and even repression. However, the extent of the advance this case really represents is far from clear. Indeed, the precise scope and implications of the decision were unclear to the minister of religious affairs, who, soon after the decision was handed down, said that religion and belief did not have the same status and that he would be meeting with the court to obtain further clarification (Marsyaf 2017).[42]

The decision, and its potential ramifications, needs to be viewed with caution, for a variety of reasons. First, the decision does not extend constitutional acknowledgment to all 'beliefs' practised in Indonesia today. The court was very careful to confine the application of its decision to beliefs in *Ketuhanan Yang Maha Esa* (Almighty God). This is not particularly

---

39 Constitutional Court Decision No. 97/PUU-XIV/2016, p. 151.
40 Constitutional Court Decision No. 97/PUU-XIV/2016, p. 152.
41 Constitutional Court Decision No. 97/PUU-XIV/2016, para 3.13.5.
42 The minister pointed to MPR Decision No. IV/MPR/1978 on Broad Outlines of State Policy, which says that *aliran kepercayaan terhadap Tuhan Yang Maha Esa* (streams of belief in Almighty God) are not *agama* (religions) (Marsyaf 2017).

controversial in constitutional terms, given that both the preamble and Article 29(1) of the Constitution declare that Indonesia is a state based on this principle.[43] Although it is beyond the scope of this chapter to discuss the variety of contested translations of *Ketuhanan Yang Maha Esa*, it is currently taken to imply monotheism (Bagir 2017). This means that poly-theistic or other religions are unlikely to be taken to fall within its scope, and followers of those religions may continue to face the same problems as had the applicants, unless they can somehow reconstruct their beliefs to fit within the accepted parameters, as Buddhists and Hindus have long been forced to do (Bagir 2017: 287).

The decision also does not appear to lend any legitimacy to the so-called 'deviant' sects (*aliran sesat*)—that is, groups of people claim-ing to follow one of Indonesia's recognised religions, but whose beliefs, according to religious orthodoxy, deviate from the main tenets of those religions. It does not, for example, assist Indonesia's Ahmadis, who have been declared 'deviant' by the Indonesian Council of Religious Scholars (Majelis Ulama Indonesia, MUI), who are subject to state restrictions on their outreach activities and who often have problems obtaining a KTP (Suroyo 2017), quite apart from other discrimination and violence.

Second, the court's suggested solution of allowing adherents to list *penghayat kepercayaan* on their ID cards, instead of the specific name of their belief, is questionable. Of course, given the large numbers of 'beliefs' in Indonesia, listing them individually might cause complications and confusion, particularly for the development of a population database. Nevertheless, full constitutional recognition appears to require citizens to be able to list their specific beliefs—not just that they have a belief that falls outside the recognised religions. The court's solution is equivalent to allowing adherents of recognised religions to list *agama* in the reli-gion column, rather than their specific religion, whether that be Islam, Christianity or one of the other state-recognised religions. No doubt the established religions would reject this.

Third, it is by no means clear that the decision will be implemented uniformly across the archipelago. Soon after the decision was handed down, MUI criticised it at a national meeting in November 2017 for treat-ing religions and beliefs as having the same status. MUI called for special identity cards to be issued without a religion column for those with indig-enous beliefs. The government appears to have followed this suggestion.

---

43 The court did not highlight this point in its decision. It does, however, bring into question the court's claim that Indonesian law and international human law concerning religious freedoms are broadly similar, given that the main human rights conventions contain no such limitation in order to recognise a religion.

In June 2018, the Ministry of Home Affairs issued a regulation and a circular containing information about the new types of family cards that are needed to implement the Constitutional Court's decision.[44] Rather than having a 'religion' column, these cards will have a 'beliefs' (*kepercayaan*) column in which *Kepercayaan Terhadap Tuhan Yang Maha Esa* (Belief in Almighty God) will appear, not *penghayat kepercayaan* (adherent of a belief) as the court suggested. However, progress in issuing the new KTPs has been slow (Cochrane 2018). At the time of writing, the cards were available in some parts of Indonesia, but not others (Jawa Pos 2018; Liputan6 2018).

Finally, being able to indicate a 'belief' on an identity document, rather than leaving the religion column blank, may do little to end the discrimination, in practice, facing those who do not adhere to one of the recognised religions. There are many areas of life in Indonesia where not following a recognised religion—particularly Islam—is a disadvantage, regardless of what religion is listed on one's identify card. Discrimination will likely continue in the workplace—particularly in the public sector—and perhaps in politics. Children may still find it difficult to progress in school if religious education is mandatory but their particular religion is not taught. It may still prove difficult to obtain a marriage certificate if the marriage ceremony is not officiated by a religious figure who has been registered with the Ministry of Education and Culture.[45] In this context it is significant that MUI has rejected the Constitutional Court's decision, arguing that religion and belief are separate, and suggesting that believers of indigenous religions should be given a different type of identity card. MUI's view is likely to be influential, at least in more conservative circles, including within the government.

CONCLUDING OBSERVATIONS

The Constitutional Court often portrays itself as the 'guardian' of democracy and human rights. In a formal sense this is undoubtedly true: one of its main functions is to defend Indonesia's constitutional bill of rights from legislative interference. Of course, many of these constitutional rights are designed to protect minorities. However, constitutional rights cases are rarely straightforward, and the Indonesian Constitutional Court, like courts the world over, is often asked to make decisions when the rights of different groups of citizens seem to conflict with each other. Many of the world's courts have developed quite sophisticated legal tests

---

44 Minister of Home Affairs Regulation No. 118/2017 on Family Card Forms; and Circular Letter No. 471.14/10666/DUKCAPIL.

45 See Article 81 of Government Regulation No. 37/2007.

to work out which of these rights should trump any others. These tests are differently formulated from place to place, but will generally require a court to identify a legitimate goal that interfering with the right must seek to attain; to determine whether the interference with that right is a suitable means of achieving the goal; to examine any less intrusive alternatives; and to decide whether the burden placed on right-holders is proportionate to the goal (Möller 2012).

The Indonesian Constitution appears to have a basic test for this: Article 28J(2) of the Constitution, set out above. However, while the Constitutional Court has used Article 28J(2) countless times to justify a refusal to protect the rights of applicants, it has not explained in its decisions how it applies this article. (Of course, the application of Article 28J(2) may be quite clear behind closed doors, but such discussions are confidential.) In particular, the court does not explain how it balances rights, and whether interfering with those rights is necessary to meet the purpose of the legislation. This leads to a lot of legal head-scratching about how the court reaches its decisions.

The *Homosexual sex* and *Beliefs* cases are different to many human rights cases the Constitutional Court has heard in that the court was not directly called upon to consider competing rights claims. Unlike in the 2009 *Blasphemy Law* case, for example, in *Beliefs* the government and the parliament did not put forward strong arguments against the application, and no religious organisations, such as MUI, appeared as a 'related party'. Accordingly, they were not able to argue before the court that, for example, recognising indigenous faiths might affect the religion-related constitutional rights of adherents of Islam or other recognised religions. There was therefore no pressure on the court to consider whether the decision compromised or jeopardised the rights of others; it sufficed for the court simply to mention that the rights of others would not be affected by recognising indigenous faiths, without being more specific. In *Homosexual sex*, too, the majority was able to throw out the application on jurisdictional grounds without having to consider competing rights. The minority did not attempt to balance any rights against Article 28J(2), although it did mention Article 28J(2) to support its conclusion that the Constitution was a 'godly constitution', meaning that the validity of legislation could be determined by reference to religious norms.

While the outcomes in both cases may be positive for minority groups, one is not left with an impression of consistency in decision-making, or confidence that the legitimate rights and interests of minorities will be upheld in future cases, when the balancing of rights may be necessary. In previous cases in which the court has refused to uphold the rights of minority groups, it appears that the court has used Article 28J(2) simply to justify what it considers to be the interest of majority groups—presumably on the grounds that the rights of large numbers of people will always outweigh the rights of smaller numbers. This type of thinking appears to have been behind the court's decision in the 2009 *Blasphemy Law* case, for example, where the court held that the feelings of believers of the ortho-dox religion, apparently adhered to by a majority, trumped the rights of a religious minority to express their religious beliefs.[46] Clearly, this crude method of balancing rights will rarely, if ever, permit acceptable levels of constitutional protection for minorities when their interests do not cor-respond with those of larger groups.

REFERENCES

Bagir, Z.A. (2017) 'The politics and law of religous governance', in R. Hefner (ed.) *Routledge Handbook of Indonesia*, Routledge, London: 284–95.

Budiwanti, E. (2009) *Pluralism Collapses: A Study of the Jama'ah Ahmadiyah Indonesia and Its Persecution*, Asia Research Institute, National University of Singapore, Singapore.

Butt, S. (2003) 'Indonesia's draft Criminal Code: can legal diversity exist within a single national law?', *Alternative Law Journal* 28(6): 306–8.

Butt, S. (2007) 'Judicial review in Indonesia: between civil law and accountability? A study of Constitutional Court decisions 2003–2005', PhD thesis, Law Faculty, Melbourne University, Melbourne.

Butt, S. (2014) 'Traditional land rights before the Indonesian Constitutional Court', *Law, Environment and Development Journal* 10(1): 57–73.

Butt, S. (2015) *The Constitutional Court and Democracy in Indonesia*, Brill, Leiden.

Butt, S. (2018) 'Religious conservatism, Islamic criminal law and the judiciary in Indonesia: a tale of three courts', *Journal of Legal Pluralism and Unofficial Law*. https://www.tandfonline.com/doi/full/10.1080/07329113.2018.1532025?af=R

Cochrane, J. (2018) 'In Indonesia, feeling like outcasts over ancient beliefs', *Philadelphia Tribune*, 20 April.

Crouch, M. (2011) 'Asia Pacific. Ahmadiyah in Indonesia: a history of religious tolerance under threat?', *Alternative Law Journal* 36(1): 56–7.

Crouch, M. (2012) 'Judicial review and religious freedom: the case of Indonesian Ahmadis', *Sydney Law Review* 34(3): 545–72.

Fachrudin, A.A. (2017) '"Religion" and "belief" in Indonesia: what's the differ-ence?', *New Mandala*, 20 December.

Fenwick, S. (2017) *Blasphemy, Islam and the State: Pluralism and Liberalism in Indonesia*, Routledge, Abingdon and New York.

Firdaus, F. (2018) 'Indonesia's LGBT crackdown', *The Interpreter*, 8 June.

Ginsburg, T. (2003) *Judicial Review in New Democracies: Constitutional Courts in Asian Cases*, Cambridge University Press, Cambridge.

Hawley, S. (2017) 'Gay and extramarital sex remains legal in Indonesia after court hearing', *ABC News*, 14 December.

---

46 Quite apart from this, the court did not explain how the religious practices of one very small group could affect the 'right to have a religion and to worship in accordance with that religion' of the Muslim majority.

Hefner, R. (2017) 'The religious field: plural legacies and contemporary contestations', in R. Hefner (ed.) *Routledge Handbook of Indonesia*, Routledge, London: 211–25.

Heriyanto, D. (2017) 'Q&A: Indonesia's native faiths and religions', *Jakarta Post*, 14 November.

Hosen, N. (2014) 'Promoting democracy and finding the right direction: a review of major constitutional developments in Indonesia', in A.H.Y. Chen (ed.) *Constitutionalism in Asia in the Early Twenty-first Century*, Cambridge University Press, Cambridge: 322–42.

Hukumonline (2016) 'Ini catatan Komnas HAM terhadap pemenuhan hak kelompok minoritas', *Hukumonline*, 1 June.

Hutton, J. (2017) 'Indonesian Constitutional Court declines to ban sex outside marriage', *New York Times*, 15 December.

Jawa Pos (2018) 'Kolom penghayat kepercayaan terganjal aplikasi', *Jawa Pos: Radar Solo*, 18 October.

Lindsey, T. (2012) *Islam, Law and the State in Southeast Asia. Volume I: Indonesia*, IB Tauris, London and New York.

Lindsey, T., and H. Pausacker (eds) (2016) *Religion, Law and Intolerance in Indonesia*, Routledge, London and New York.

Liputan6 (2018) 'Layanan e-KTP bagi penghayat kepercayaan mulai tersedia di Yogyakarta', *Liputan6*, 11 August.

Marsyaf, M.I. (2017) 'Kemenag: putusan MK tak berarti agama dan kepercayaan sama', *Sindonews.com*, 8 November.

Möller, K. (2012) 'Proportionality: challenging the critics', *International Journal of Constitutional Law* 10(3): 709–31.

Nadlir, M. (2017) 'Ada 187 kelompok penghayat kepercayaan yang terdaftar di pemerintah', *Kompas*, 9 November.

Pisani, E. (2014) *Indonesia etc.: Exploring the Improbable Nation*, Godown Lontar, Jakarta.

Sahbani, A. (2017) 'MK tegaskan tak bisa kriminalisasi delik kesusilaan', *Hukumonline*, 19 December.

Suroyo, G. (2017) 'Indonesian Islamic sect say they're "denied state IDs" over their beliefs', *Reuters*, 21 June.

Voanews (2018) 'Penghayat kepercayaan: setelah putusan MK dan kolom KTP', *Voanews*, 10 April.

PART 2

Disability

5 Changing laws, changing attitudes: the place of people with disability in Indonesia

Thushara Dibley and Antoni Tsaputra

'My parents never treated me any differently to my brothers and sisters. I was given the same responsibilities as my siblings and the same opportunities [...] And [being brought up like that] was so useful for my sense of independence. As I became an adult, I was able to do things on my own without having to bother anyone else.'
– Dewi

Dewi was born with a physical impairment and raised by a family who believed she was able to participate fully in the day-to-day activities of the family and the community. With the encouragement and support of her family, Dewi completed her education and is now the leader of the local branch of the Indonesian Association of Women with Disabilities, where she campaigns for the rights of other Indonesians with disability. By creating the conditions for Dewi to be educated and by supporting and encouraging her independence, her family challenged how most Indonesians think of people with disability—as being highly dependent, to be pitied and needing charity.

Stories like Dewi's are part of the reason that disability activists in Indonesia have campaigned so energetically for changes to how disability is conceptualised, legislated and funded by government organisations. For decades, being disabled in Indonesia, as in many other parts of the world, was seen as an impediment, a source of pity and a driver of acts of charity. This 'welfare' approach to disability was premised on the understanding that the source of the problem faced by people with disability was their impairments, and that support for people with disability was best delivered in the form of rehabilitation to 'fix' their impairments or through payments or other forms of charity. Over the course of the 1990s, the work of disability activists in the global north contributed to a significant shift in how disability was conceptualised, and therefore how support for people with disability was best delivered. The social model of disability, which places the onus of the problem not on the individual living with disability but rather on the social structures that make it difficult for those with disability to participate in society, has become the foundation for how disability is understood globally and, in turn, for how policy related to people with disability is formulated. Ensuring that the principles of the social model are put into practice in Indonesia lies at the heart of why disability activists have remained so persistent in their pursuit of legislative and policy change.

Their efforts have not been in vain. Over the last two decades, people living with disability in Indonesia have witnessed a significant shift in how disability is discussed and positioned within public debate. At the most fundamental level, the vocabulary available to talk about people with disability has changed. The word *cacat*—literally meaning 'deformity' or 'defect'—is no longer accepted, being replaced with *disabilitas* or *difabel*—'disability' or 'diffability' (Suharto, Kuipers and Dorsett 2016). From a policy perspective, the government has signed and ratified the United Nations Convention on the Rights of Persons with Disabilities (CRPD) and it has passed a new national law on disability based on this convention, Law No. 8/2016 on People with Disabilities. Eleven provincial governments have passed regulations on disability based on the UN convention and at least seven cities and districts have done the same. Overall, Indonesia has introduced a wide range of frameworks, protocols and laws at the national and local levels that affect people with disability.

The changes to disability policy in Indonesia are the result of a combination of changing norms and expectations at the transnational level, together with successful lobbying at the local level. Much progress has depended upon the ability of domestic actors within Indonesia to make a case to the Indonesian state that aligning itself with the normative international shift in favour of disabled persons' rights is important and valuable. Norms are widely defined as a standard of behaviour for states that share a particular identity (Katzenstein 1996). Norms about the treatment and place of people with disability have experienced a major shift over the last two decades. Beginning with the campaign for the development of the CRPD, through to the signing and ratification of this convention by over 150 countries, the ways in which disability are defined and the opportunities available for people with disability to make a case for their rights have changed markedly. This process of change has been felt worldwide, including in Indonesia, which signed the convention in 2007 and ratified it in 2011.

In this chapter, we examine the role of activists in bringing about these changes, with a particular focus on how activists have maintained pressure on the government since the passing of the Disability Law. We demonstrate that while activists have been deeply committed to ensuring that the national legislation related to disability reflects the changing international norms, policy-makers have shown considerable resistance to applying these ideas. Pragmatism and the notion that people with disability require welfare and charitable assistance have prevailed throughout the process of implementing the Disability Law, despite the concerted efforts of activists to challenge these ideas.

THE CHANGING PLACE OF DISABILITY IN INDONESIA

People living with disability in Indonesia face a range of unique challenges. Despite the absence of a single reliable source of data (Kusumastuti, Pradanasari and Ratnawati 2014; Priebe and Howell 2014), reports indicate that the prevalence of disability in Indonesia is between 10 and 15 per cent, which is in line with the global disability rate according to the World Health Organization's 2011 'World report on disability' (Adioetomo, Mont and Irwanto 2014).[1] People with disability are less likely to attend school due to physical and attitudinal barriers and the problematic implementation of the principles of inclusive education. They face more challenges in accessing employment because employers are either unwilling or unable to accommodate their needs. As discussed by Afrianty in Chapter 6 of this volume, people with disability also face challenges in participating fully in family and community life due to prevailing stereotypes and social stigmatisation. The lack of accessible infrastructure is another major impediment to their full participation in society (Adioetomo, Mont and Irwanto 2014). Nevertheless, there have been significant changes over the last two decades in how disability is conceptualised, how activism for disability is organised and, in turn, how the position of people with disability is reflected in government policy in Indonesia. These changes have happened at a slow but steady pace, and demonstrate how shifts in international conceptualisations of, funding for and commitment to disability have translated in the Indonesian context.

The language used to describe people with disability reflects contemporary understandings of the place of people with disability within a

---

1   The rate varies depending on the institution. For example, the 2010 census reported that the disability prevalence rate in Indonesia was 4.2 per cent of the total population, whereas the national Basic Health Research (Riset Kesehatan Dasar, Riskesdas) conducted by the Ministry of Health in 2007 indicated that the overall rate was 11.1 per cent (Priebe and Howell 2014).

given social context. Scholars of disability have long made the case for thinking critically about the kind of language that is used to describe people with disability, arguing that inappropriate language choices contribute to their marginalisation (Bolt 2005; Corbett 2013). In Indonesia, similar debates have occurred within activist and policy-making circles, contributing to an evolution of the language used to describe disability.[2] In the early days of independence, the word *cacat*, or 'defect', was used to describe disability, reflecting a social belief that people with disabilities were worth less as humans (Suharto, Kuipers and Dorsett 2016; Thohari 2012). During Sukarno's presidency (1945–67), a more common phrase was 'people with a physical or mental deficit' (*orang yang dalam kekurangan jasmani atau rohani*), reflecting a tendency for that regime to use euphemisms to soften the meanings of a range of different words (Suharto, Kuipers and Dorsett 2016). Suharto's New Order (1966–98) saw the proliferation of euphemisms to describe disability, including the use of the prefix *tuna* (*tuna netra* for 'blind', *tuna rungu* for 'deaf' and so on), *terganggu* (disturbed), *penderita cacat* (suffering from a deformity) and *penyandang cacat* (person with a deformity). These terms were used widely in various policy documents and laws but were not accepted by many disability activists (Suharto, Kuipers and Dorsett 2016).

The end of the New Order was a time for renewed debate on the terminology relating to disability. This period aligned with shifts in conceptualisations of disability globally. The growing popularity of the social model of disability—the idea that disability is a consequence of social structures and infrastructure that cannot accommodate people unless they are able-bodied—was reflected in a push to use the term *difabel*. Derived from the English phrase 'differently abled', this term was meant to reflect the range of capabilities that people living with disability possessed (Suharto, Kuipers and Dorsett 2016; Irwanto and Thohari 2017). *Difabel* became increasingly popular among activists in Yogyakarta and other parts of central Java, but among the network of disability advocates and policy-makers based in Jakarta, the more commonly used term was *penyandang disabilitas* (people with disabilities), which was introduced when the government of Indonesia ratified the CRPD through Law No. 19/2011 (Priebe and Howell 2014).

The difference in views about terminology between the activists based in central Java and the disability advocates in Jakarta reflected broader

---

2 Debates about language and terminology are also important to other Indonesian social movements. In this volume, see Chapter 11 by Setijadi for a discussion of the term *pribumi*, Chapter 7 by Wieringa and Chapter 8 by Wijaya for commentary on LGBT terms, and Chapter 13 by Manurung for a discussion on how to talk about the Orang Rimba.

trends in disability activism that were emerging at this time. During the New Order, the key organisations involved in disability activism were Jakarta-based peak bodies established by the regime (Dibley, forthcoming). Other kinds of organisations that existed during this period were rehabilitation centres and religious groups (Irwanto and Thohari 2017). The primary focus of these organisations was on meeting the welfare needs of people with disability. For the peak disability bodies, this meant seeking funding from the government for people with disability. Similarly, rehabilitation and religious organisations were focused on treatment, housing and other welfare issues (Irwanto and Thohari 2017).

Much like the transnational activism that contributed to changing perspectives towards lesbian, gay, bisexual and transgender (LGBT) communities in Indonesia (see Chapter 8 by Wijaya, this volume), changing international ideas about disability contributed to reshaping attitudes towards disability. In the late 1990s, the global disability movement itself began to change focus, shifting to a more rights-based approach to thinking about disability grounded in the social model (Kanter 2003; Kayess and French 2008). The global shift towards the social model of disability meant there was greater scope to think about people with disability as individuals with rights that needed to be fulfilled, rather than as individuals with problems who needed to be helped. This global change slowly began to influence disability activism in Indonesia.[3] The formation of Dria Manunggal in Yogyakarta, a non-government organisation influenced by the global discourse on disability, and the ideas and approaches used by NGOs and activists in other sectors, was a pivotal point in the development of a more rights-based approach to the treatment of disability issues in Indonesia. Volunteers at Dria Manunggal went on to develop a range of other disability NGOs in Yogyakarta and other parts of central Java in the early post-authoritarian years. These organisations focused on such themes as employment, access to justice and women's issues, and used approaches that were more in line with the international discourse and agendas on disability rights (Dibley, forthcoming).

This broad shift in focus from welfare to rights was reflected in changes to policy. In 1997, at around the time the disability movement in Indonesia was moving towards a more rights-based approach, the New Order government agreed to the formation of its first national disability law, Law No. 4/1997 on People with Defects (*Penyandang Cacat*). Prior to the passing of this law, there was no single law dealing solely with disability. The rights of people with disability were broadly addressed in the 1945

---

3 See Chapter 6 of this volume by Afrianty for a discussion of how these changes influenced ideas about disability specifically within the framework of Islamic education.

Constitution, which ascribed rights to all citizens to establish a family, to have their basic needs met and to have access to education, employment, health and social protection. A series of laws enacted in 1992 (Laws 13, 14, 15 and 21) addressed accessibility issues for people with disability across all modes of transport. In addition, a ministerial decree passed in 1986, a Ministry of Education circular letter passed in 1989 and a government regulation passed in 1991 addressed how the education system was to accommodate children with disability (Priebe and Howell 2014). In this context, the passing of the 1997 law was a significant step forward, despite its charity-based focus in which the fulfilment of disability rights was limited to social welfare such as social security and rehabilitation.

As the debates within the international domain evolved, this law quickly became outdated. In December 2006, the UN General Assembly adopted the CRPD, which formally grounded the social model of disability in international law and created an international platform for the campaign for disability rights (Kanter 2003; Kayess and French 2008; Palacios 2015). Indonesia signed the convention in 2007 and ratified it in 2011. As a signatory to the convention, the government of Indonesia was then in a position where it had to adjust its policies related to disability, many of which directly contradicted the central tenets of the CRPD. As Edwards (2014: 4) has pointed out, the terminology used in Law No. 4/1997 continued to portray people with disability as needing support and assistance, as opposed to being entitled to 'actionable rights'. As a further example, in the domain of education, the 1997 law reinforced 'the kind of segregated education that is discouraged under the CRPD' (Edwards 2014: 5). These inconsistencies provided the foundation for a lengthy campaign by disability activists for the government to develop a law in line with the international convention.

The campaign for a new disability law was driven primarily by activists based in Jakarta. A network called the Working Group on the Disability Law (Kelompok Kerja Undang-Undang Disabilitas, more commonly referred to as Pokja) was instrumental in driving the campaign for this law. Members of Pokja worked with the National Commission for Human Rights to develop a draft law based on the CRPD. Supported by activists around the country, the campaign lasted for four years and culminated in the passing of a new national disability law, Law No. 8/2016 on People with Disabilities, in May 2016.

IMPLEMENTING THE LAW

Disability activists have played an important role in driving the Indonesian government's adoption of international disability norms. During the process of drafting and campaigning for a new disability law, activists were able to benefit from the government's lack of knowledge about disability to push strongly for the elements they thought were important. Fajri Nursyamsi, a member of Pokja, explained that because most policymakers had very little understanding of disability issues, activists were able to have a significant influence on the content of the law (interview, 28 February 2018). This same lack of knowledge on the part of government officials, however, had proved to be more of an impediment during the process of implementing the law. This comes as no surprise because, as Lindsey observes in Chapter 3 of this book, human rights laws in Indonesia are often aspirational in character.

In the case of the Disability Law, a lack of understanding of some of the key principles of the CRPD and a preference for expediency over accuracy on the part of the government have generated significant obstacles in the implementation of the law to date. Activists continue to hold the government accountable to the commitments it has made, but they have faced an uphill battle to overturn policy-makers' assumptions about how disability-related issues should be funded and who should be responsible for overseeing them. These difficulties are illustrated by the challenges faced in three areas: persuading the government to embrace a multi-sectoral approach to the implementation of the Disability Law; implementing the disability card proposed in the national law; and campaigning to implement the law outside Jakarta.

A multi-sectoral approach

A key illustration of the challenges activists have faced so far is the protracted process of developing the implementing regulations for the 2016 Disability Law. In Indonesia, a law requires subsidiary regulations, introduced at the ministerial level, in order for its various parts to be fully implemented. These regulations are linked to the relevant ministry's budget, which is an integral part of enacting the law. Implementing regulations also have a timeframe during which they have to be enacted. In the case of the Disability Law, the activists involved in the drafting of the law (the members of Pokja) believed that to properly implement the law, 18 implementing regulations were required: 15 government regulations (*peraturan pemerintah*, PP), two presidential regulations and one ministerial regulation (Nugrahenyantara 2016). The 15 government regulations involved 10 ministries: the Ministry of National Development Planning (Bappenas), the Ministry of Law and Human Rights, the Ministry of Research, Technology and Higher Education, the Ministry of Education and Culture, the Ministry of Manpower and Transmigration, the Ministry of Administrative and Bureaucratic Reform, the Ministry of Tourism, the Ministry of Social Affairs, the Ministry of Public Works and Public Housing and the Ministry of Finance. One of the presidential regulations concerned the development of the National Disability Commission and the other related to government departments offering incentives to provide public facilities that met the needs of people with disabilities.

The law itself did not specify which ministries were to be involved in the implementation of the law, but a key goal for disability activists was to ensure that the new law would create a framework that addressed disability as a multi-sectoral issue. Throughout Indonesia's history, disability issues have been within the domain of the Ministry of Social Affairs, which has been responsible for providing rehabilitation services and social protection programs for people with disability. In order to reflect the key principles of the CRPD, activists campaigned hard for the new disability law to provide a framework that would make it possible for a much broader range of ministries to be involved in the management of disability-related issues. For example, Pokja opposed the final draft of the disability law prepared by Commission VIII of the House of Representatives (Dewan Perwakilan Rakyat, DPR), in which the Ministry of Social Affairs was again positioned as the single focal point for disability. Pokja saw this as a step back from approaching disability as a multi-sectoral issue (Soekanwo et al. 2015).

The activists' efforts were not reflected in the final wording of the law, which named only the Ministry of Social Affairs. They responded to this development by closely analysing the final version of the law, and attributing a relevant ministry any time 'the government' was referenced as being responsible for some element of implementing the law. After going through this process, the activists were able to identify what they considered to be the 18 implementing regulations required to fully enact the law (interview, Fajri Nursyamsi, 28 February 2018). Table 5.1 provides an overview of these implementing regulations. As is evident from the table, the law's scope extends far beyond the traditional responsibilities of the Ministry of Social Affairs, and involves a range of different ministries.

In late July 2017 the government announced that it would enact a single government regulation to cover the implementation of the law and that this regulation would be managed by the Ministry of Social Affairs (Nursyamsi 2017a). Government officials provided three reasons for their decision. First, the decision to streamline the number of regulations was in line with President Joko Widodo's more general 'deregulation' policy, which sought to simplify government processes and reduce red tape. Second, the other ministries identified as being responsible for the regulations had limited budgets. Finally, the bureaucrats argued that passing a single regulation would be quicker and more efficient than passing 18 regulations.

Table 5.1 Overview of implementing regulations for Law No. 8/2018 on People with Disabilities

Type & focus of implementing regulation	Proposed ministry
Government regulation (*peraturan pemerintah*, PP)	
1 Planning, implementation & evaluation	Bappenas
2 Suitable accommodation for people with disabilities in judicial processes	Ministry of Law & Human Rights
3 Mechanism for administrative sanctions for higher-education institutions that do not establish a disability service unit	Ministry of Research, Technology & Higher Education
4 Suitable accommodation for students with disability	Ministry of Education & Culture
5 Mechanism for administrative sanctions for schools & education providers that do not provide suitable accommodation for students with disability	Ministry of Education & Culture
6 National & local government incentives for private enterprises that employ people with disability	Ministry of Manpower & Transmigration
7 Disability Service Units	Ministry of Admin. & Bureaucratic Reform
8 National & local government incentives for hospitality & tourism industries that provide disability-friendly & accessible travel services	Ministry of Tourism
9 Social rehabilitation, social security, social empowerment & social protection	Ministry of Social Affairs
10 Accessible housing for people with disability	Ministry of Public Works & Public Housing
11 Accessible public services for people with disability	Ministry of Public Works & Public Housing
12 Management & participation of people with disability in disaster risk reduction	Ministry of Public Works & Public Housing
13 Habilitation & rehabilitation services	Ministry of Social Affairs
14 Concessions for people with disability	Ministry of Finance
15 Provision of incentives by national & local governments to private enterprises that provide concessions for people with disability	Ministry of Finance
Presidential regulation (*peraturan presiden*)	
16 Organisation, structure & membership of National Disability Commission (Komisi Nasional Disabilitas)	Office of the President
17 National & local government incentives for providers of public facilities & utilities that meet the needs of people with disability	Office of the President
Ministerial regulation (*peraturan menteri*)	
18 Production of disability cards (*kartu penyandang disabilitas*)	Ministry of Social Affairs

Source: Kelompok Kerja Undang-Undang Disabilitas (Pokja).

The Pokja activists interpreted the government's decision differently. They argued that the underlying reason for this approach was that the other ministries still did not understand the relevance and importance of a multi-sectoral approach to addressing disability, and had not taken ownership of the government regulations related to their ministerial functions. The ministries named in the list of 15 government regulations had made no effort to budget for their allocated tasks, with the exception of the Ministry of Social Affairs. Under these circumstances, and with increasing pressure to begin implementing the law, the most expedient path for the government was to pass just a single government regulation that related to the ministry that most policy-makers knew had traditionally been responsible for disability issues (interview, Fajri Nursyamsi, 28 February 2018).

Disability advocates responded strongly to this decision, mobilising quickly to reject what they called the 'one-size-fits-all government regulation' (*PP sapu jagat*). In August 2017, they established the People's Coalition to 'Reject the One-Size-Fits-All Government Regulation' (Koalisi Masyarakat 'Tolak PP Sapu Jagat') and held a press conference at which they voiced their opposition to the decision. Their key argument was that rolling what should have been 18 government regulations into a single regulation went against the 'spirit of the formation of the Disability Law, which was firm in its commitment to include a range of government sectors' (Nursyamsi 2017b). Fajri Nursyamsi outlined the position of the Pokja activists in a blog post in which he argued that political will rather than budgeting issues was the real obstacle for most ministries. He also disputed the claim that passing a single government regulation would be quicker, on the grounds that the Ministry of Social Affairs would not necessarily be able to improve the awareness or understanding of other ministries about the roles they would inevitably have to play to implement the law as it was written (Nursyamsi 2017b). He also claimed that by stepping away from the commitment to multi-sectorality, the government was breaking a promise it had made during Jokowi's election campaign to reframe disability issues as a human rights issue (Dibley 2014, 2016; Nursyamsi 2017b).

Building on the ideas presented in Nursyamsi's blog post, Bappenas proposed an alternative that involved having eight government regulations. Due to the unofficial coordinating role played by Bappenas in pushing for this idea, four ministries (in addition to the Ministry of Social Affairs) confirmed their readiness to prepare government regulations in their respective domains. These were Bappenas, the Ministry of Education and Culture, the Ministry of Law and Human Rights and the Ministry of Public Works and Public Housing. The Ministry of Finance and the Ministry of Manpower and Transmigration remained silent on their position

(Gerak Inklusi 2018). In early 2018, activists were optimistic that, although the three-year deadline for implementing the law was rapidly approaching, this development would soon lead to some concrete changes.

Much to the disappointment of disability activists, the government's lack of awareness of and commitment to the principles underlying the CRPD became apparent yet again in mid-2018. On 3 May 2018, President Joko Widodo issued Presidential Decree No. 9/2018 on the Government Regulations Formulation Program, which approved 43 draft government regulations for processing and enactment within a year of the decree. In this decree, only four of the eight draft government regulations on disability were included, and of these, two were the responsibility of the Ministry of Social Affairs. The other four draft government regulations, which according to activists were more likely to contribute to positive change for people with disability, were not included. Pokja criticised the government's decision and demanded a revision to the decree to include all eight draft government regulations, and their enactment as quickly as possible. They also demanded more active participation of people with disability in the formulation of future government regulations related to the Disability Law (Solider 2018).

The challenges that activists have faced in convincing policy-makers to adopt a multi-sectoral approach to dealing with disability reflect both the slow pace at which new ideas come to be deeply understood and the political place of disability in the Indonesian context. It is clear that although policy-makers were willing to enact a law based on the principles in the CRPD, there were considerable limits to their understanding of what those principles meant in practice. Activists have consistently tried to translate these international norms for policy-makers, but in the absence of a broader culture of seeing people with disability as having rights (rather than needing assistance) and in the context of a government having to spread its energy across a range of different issues, policy-makers continue to fall back on the default position of treating disability as an issue of rehabilitation and welfare.

Another important factor limiting the government's willingness to put the more complex and potentially expensive elements of the law into practice is the limited political value of doing so. Disability, unlike many other social issues in Indonesia, is not a highly politically contentious issue. Although people with disability can be found across Indonesia, unlike many of the other minority groups discussed in this book, they have historically been hidden from public view and considered to be the responsibility of their families. As such, for the general population, the issue of disability is a low priority and the changes that disability activists demand do not challenge any mainstream religious or political practices. Consequently there are limited benefits to policy-makers and politicians in investing time and resources in making significant change in this domain.

Disability card

The persistence of the welfare approach to thinking about disability among government officials is also reflected in the implementation of the disability card mandated by the Disability Law. Article 22 of the law stipulates that the Ministry of Social Affairs is to issue a card to people with a disability after undertaking a national data-collection process. To date, this card is yet to be officially issued (anonymous interview, Ministry of Social Affairs official, August 2018). Progress has stalled in part because the card itself is controversial, with some in the activist community believing it to be a tool for empowerment and others seeing it as a mechanism for further discrimination. Adding further complexity to the situation is the fact that other types of disability cards have recently been released by the Ministry of Social Affairs and by a number of local governments. The conflicting views among activists about the suitability of the disability card, coupled with the enthusiasm that policy-makers have for such a concept, indicate that there is a lack of consensus around the norms underpinning this idea.

The Disability Law itself provides very limited information about the disability card and how it is to be implemented. Beyond stating that the card is to be linked to a national data-collection process, the law provides no further details, with much of the information about eligibility and the function of the card being set out in Ministerial Regulation No. 21/2017 on the Production of Disability Cards (Jogloabang 2017). The release of this ministerial regulation in November 2017 was met with criticism and demands for its revision by Pokja activists due to inconsistencies that made it difficult for people with disability to access the card (Rakyatku News 2018). For example, Article 7 of the ministerial regulation requires people with disability to register at their local Social Affairs offices, which are mainly located in the district capitals. This makes it difficult for people living outside the capital to register without spending considerable money on transportation (Solider 2018). The Ministry of Social Affairs continues to deliberate on its response to these criticisms (anonymous interview, Ministry of Social Affairs official, August 2018).

These criticisms aside, the concept of the disability card itself has been a source of controversy among disability activists. The key point of contention relates to whether the card is a form of discrimination or rather a pathway to access resources that can potentially empower people with disabilities. While neither the law nor the ministerial regulation indicates that the card would be linked to the provision of welfare benefits, some disability activists believe this should be an important element of the card. Others believe the whole concept of the card is flawed, whether or not it includes provision for welfare payments. Bahrul Fuad, for example, has argued that a card used exclusively to identify citizens with disability goes against the principles of the social model and the CRPD. The deliberate differentiation of people with disability from other citizens contributes to what he calls the 'legalisation of stigma', while the provision of welfare payments will contribute to a sense of jealousy among those who do not have a disability (Fuad 2015).[4] Other activists argue that while the differentiation of people with disability may be problematic, so few mechanisms are in place for people with disability to participate in society that any kind of support is welcome (interview, Risna Utami, 26 March 2018).

The Pokja activists' view was that the inclusion of the card in the law was an important part of ensuring that better data on disability were collected. Consistent data about disability in Indonesia are difficult to source, with different government bodies using different tools and measures to collate information about the rates, distributions and types of disability that exist in Indonesia (Cameron and Suarez 2017; Adioetomo, Mont and Irwanto 2014). Those involved in drafting the law thought that the disability card would provide an incentive for the government to undertake a more comprehensive national disability data-collection process (interview, Maulani Rotinsulu, 26 February 2018).

The situation has been made more complicated by the introduction of other forms of disability cards by both the Ministry of Social Affairs and district governments. In 2016, Khofifah Parawansa, the former minister of social affairs, launched a disability-inclusive card related to the ministry's conditional cash transfer scheme, the Family Hope Program (Program Keluarga Harapan, PKH). At the launch, the minister claimed that the PKH card was being introduced as part of the implementation of the new Disability Law and announced that 125,000 cards would be issued over the course of the following year (Tribunnews 2016). The PKH card in fact had no links to the Disability Law. It was conceived of before the law was drafted, and was launched before the ministerial regulation related to the

---

4   This concern about having one's minority status formally classified is consistent with the difficulties encountered by other minorities discussed in this book. See Chapter 4 of this book by Butt for a discussion of the classification difficulties faced by followers of a faith other than one of the five main religions, Chapter 11 by Setijadi for the difficulties faced by people who are singled out as being *pribumi* or *non-pribumi*, and Chapter 7 by Wieringa for the problems experienced by descendants of members of the Indonesian Communist Party (Partai Komunis Indonesia, PKI).

Disability Law card was formulated. The minister's reference to a connection between the PKH card and the Disability Law is best explained as an attempt to make it appear that the Ministry of Social Affairs was taking action related to the Disability Law.

Meanwhile, governments at the district level have also been developing disability cards. The Social Affairs offices in the districts of Sukoharjo and Banyuwangi, for example, created their own versions of the disability card and distributed them to people with disability in the local area (Fanani 2018; Jawa Pos 2018). They did this even though there are no provisions in the law or in the ministerial regulation that stipulate that local governments need to develop their own version of the card. The decisions by both the Ministry of Social Affairs and its counterparts at the district level to launch separate disability cards indicate that, even though the idea is controversial among activists, there is something appealing to policy-makers about the development of such a card.

Disability activism beyond Jakarta

The Disability Law has little bearing on the day-to-day lives of activists outside Jakarta. Their ability to contribute to the debates related to the implementation of the law is limited by their geographic distance from Jakarta, where the vast majority of the decisions are made. Nevertheless, the passing of the law has provided activists with a tool to leverage changes at the local level.

Each article in the law outlining a particular action that needs to be taken by a government body indicates that both the central government and local governments are responsible. However, regulations at the local level, called *peraturan daerah* (*perda*), need to be in place for the provisions of the law to be implemented. The focus of disability activists in Jakarta has been on the government, presidential and ministerial regulations, leaving the work of campaigning for provincial and district regulations to their counterparts around the country. In some provinces activists have lobbied for provincial regulations related to disability to be put in place, but in others these regulations were enacted *before* the Disability Law was passed, meaning that they may need to be amended to align with the national law. A few of these regulations even still refer to and use the terminology in the former disability law, such as Provincial Regulation of Kepulauan Bangka Belitung No. 10/2010 on Protection and Social Welfare Services for People with Defects.

For activists outside Jakarta, the enactment of the Disability Law has provided what one person described as a 'weapon for advocacy' (focus group discussion, January 2018). The existence of a national law stipulating that local governments have an obligation to make changes in support of people with disability offers activists a platform to lobby for change within their local areas, which many activists have taken up. The challenge, however, is considerable depending on the area. In some places, activists report that their local leaders are not even aware that a new national disability law has been enacted, which provides some indication of the level of work that will be required to ensure that the relevant local regulations are passed.

CONCLUSION: LAW, ACTIVISM AND DISABILITY IN INDONESIA

The implementation of the 2016 Disability Law has happened slowly, and while this is frustrating for disability advocates, it is neither surprising nor unusual in the Indonesian context. Observers of Indonesian law-making, and politics in general, are well aware that it is often much easier to pass a law than to implement it. Laws like the Disability Law that are driven by activists who are pushing for the implementation of international norms in domestic policy, can take an extended period of time to be fully implemented, and even then may not be implemented perfectly (Butt 2013).

One of the key challenges for disability activists has been to challenge policy-makers' view of disability as primarily a welfare issue. Activists have had to consistently make the case that, for Indonesia's treatment of people with disability to align with international norms, namely the CRPD and the social model, disability must become the responsibility of a range of different actors, which would all be required to make it easier for people with disability to participate actively in society. In the case of government regulations, there has been push and pull between activists and policy-makers around this key tension. The government's latest decision to implement just four regulations, two of which are the responsibility of the Ministry of Social Affairs, reinforces the idea that disability remains a welfare, rather than a rights, issue for the government.

The difficulties that activists have encountered in maintaining policy-makers' commitment to the principles underpinning the Disability Law also speak to the 'politics' of disability in Indonesia. Unlike other minority groups, such as groups representing the LGBT community or religious minorities, people with disability are advocating for an issue that is morally appealing but politically neutral. This contributed to the ease with which disability advocates were able to convince policy-makers to integrate key elements underpinning the CRPD into the Disability Law. But that same politically neutral position also means that as the implementation phase of the law begins, there are limited incentives for policy-makers to follow through on their promises.

The other major challenge ahead in the implementation of the Disability Law is the need for continuing political action at the local level all around the country. For the law to be fully implemented, provincial and district governments will have to pass their own regulations. As has been demonstrated at the national level, local activists will most likely need to play a central role in ensuring that these regulations are passed, and that they accurately reflect the principles of the law. The problem is that the ability of people with disability to advocate on their own behalf varies so greatly across the country. The skills and contacts that advocates at the national level have developed through their engagement with the national law do not necessarily translate into benefits for their counterparts outside Jakarta, and national disability organisations do not have the resources or skills to empower members in the branches. Therefore, what is likely to occur is an uneven distribution of change around the country, with no clear agenda by the government or activists to ensure that the rights of people with disability are met equally across the country.

REFERENCES

Adioetomo, S.M., D. Mont and Irwanto (2014) 'Persons with disabilities: empirical facts and implications for social protection policies', Demographic Institute, Faculty of Economics, University of Indonesia, and Tim Nasional Percepatan Penanggulangan Kemiskinan (TNP2K), Jakarta.

Bolt, D. (2005) 'From blindness to visual impairment: terminological typology and the social model of disability', *Disability & Society* 20(5): 539–52.

Butt, S. (2013) 'Freedom of information law and its application in Indonesia: a preliminary assessment', *Asian Journal of Comparative Law* 8: 1–42.

Cameron, L., and D.C. Suarez (2017) 'Disability in Indonesia: what can we learn from the data?', Australia Indonesia Partnership for Economic Governance, Monash University, Melbourne.

Corbett, J. (2013) *Bad Mouthing: The Language of Special Needs*, Routledge, London.

Dibley, T. (2014) 'Able to choose', *Inside Indonesia* 117, 8 July.

Dibley, T. (2016) 'Keeping promises', *Inside Indonesia* 123, 27 January.

Dibley, T. (forthcoming) 'Democratization and disability activism in Indonesia', in M. Ford and T. Dibley (eds) *Activists in Transition*, Cornell University Press, Ithaca NY.

Edwards, N.J. (2014) 'Disability rights in Indonesia? Problems with ratification of the United Nations Convention on the Rights of Persons with Disabilities', *Australian Journal of Asian Law* 15(1). https://ssrn.com/abstract=2459818

Fanani, A. (2018) 'Penyandang disabilitas di Banyuwangi dimanjakan dengan kartu gandrung', *detikNews*, 1 March. https://news.detik.com/berita-jawa-timur/d-3892951/penyandang-disabilitas-di-banyuwangi-dimanjakan-dengan-kartu-gandrung

Fuad, B. (2015) 'Legalisasi stigma', *Kompas*, 22 September.

Gerak Inklusi (2018) 'Sahkan PP implementasi UU penyandang disabilitas, segera!', *Gerak Inklusi*, 4 March. https://www.gerakinklusi.id/133-sahkan-pp-implementasi-uu-penyandang-disabilitas-segera

Irwanto, and S. Thohari (2017) 'Understanding national implementation of the CRPD in Indonesia', in D.L. Cogburn and T. Kempin Reuter (eds) *Making Disability Rights Real in Southeast Asia: Implementing the UN Convention on the Rights of Persons with Disabilities in ASEAN*, Lexington Books, Lanham MD.

Jawa Pos (2018) 'Belum semua penyandang disabilitas terima kartu difabel', *Jawa Pos*, 16 February. https://radarsolo.jawapos.com/read/2018/02/16/49789/belum-semua-penyandang-disabilitas-terima-kartu-difabel

Jogloabang (2017) 'Permensos 21 Tahun 2017 tentang Kartu Penyandang Disabilitas', *Jogloabang*, 23 December. https://www.jogloabang.com/pustaka/permensos-21-tahun-2017-tentang-kartu-penyandang-disabilitas

Kanter, A.S. (2003) 'The globalization of disability rights law', *Syracuse Journal of International Law and Commerce* 30: 241–69.

Katzenstein, P. (1996) 'Introduction: alternative perspectives on national security', in P. Katzenstein (ed.) *The Culture of National Security: Norms and Identity in World Politics*, Columbia University Press, New York NY: 1–32.

Kayess, R., and P. French (2008) 'Out of darkness into light? Introducing the Convention on the Rights of Persons with Disabilities', *Human Rights Law Review* 8(1): 1–34.

Kusumastuti, P., R. Pradanasari and A. Ratnawati (2014) 'The problems of people with disability in Indonesia and what is being learned from the World Report on Disability', *American Journal of Physical Medicine and Rehabilitation* 93(1, Supplement 1): S63–7. http://www.ncbi.nlm.nih.gov/pubmed/24356085

Nugrahenyantara, D.E. (2016) 'Tuntaskan PP disabilitas', *Republika*, 26 October. http://www.republika.co.id/berita/koran/halaman-1/16/10/26/ofn7g639-tuntaskan-pp-disabilitas

Nursyamsi, F. (2017a) 'Masyarakat penyandang disabilitas menolak PP "sapu jagat"', Pusat Studi Hukum dan Kebijakan Indonesia (PSHK), 28 July. http://www.pshk.or.id/id/berita/aktivitas/masyarakat-penyandang-disabilitas-menolak-pp-sapu-jagat/

Nursyamsi, F. (2017b) 'Meninjau kembali PP "sapu jagat" implementasi UU penyandang disabilitas', *Hukum Online*, 3 August. http://www.hukumonline.com/berita/baca/lt5982cf6388274/meninjau-kembali-pp-sapu-jagat-implementasi-uu-penyandang-disabilitas-oleh--fajri-nursyamsi

Palacios, A. (2015) 'The social model in the international Convention on the Rights of Persons with Disabilities', *Age of Human Rights Journal* 4 (June): 91–110.

Priebe, J., and F. Howell (2014) 'A guide to disability rights laws in Indonesia', TNP2K Working Paper 13, Tim Nasional Percepatan Penanggulangan Kemiskinan (TNP2K), Jakarta.

Rakyatku News (2018) 'Penyandang disabilitas desak pemerintah sahkan PP soal UU No 8 Tahun 2016', *Rakyatku News*, 26 April. http://news.rakyatku.com/read/98571/2018/04/26/penyandang-disabilitas-desak-pemerintah-sahkan-pp-soal-uu-no-8-tahun-2016

Soekanwo, A., A. Indrawati, Y.R. Damayanti, M. Rotinsulu, M. Fasa, T. Hutapea and F. Nursyamsi (2015) 'RUU penyandang disabilitas versi Panja Komisi VIII tidak aspiratif', Lembaga Bantuan Hukum Jakarta (LBH Jakarta), Jakarta.

Solider (2018) 'Kepres Nomor 9 Tahun 2018 ciderai hak difabel', *Solider*, 15 May. https://www.solider.id/baca/4491-kepres-nomor-9-2018-ciderai-hak-difabel

Suharto, S., P. Kuipers and P. Dorsett (2016) 'Disability terminology and the emergence of "diffability" in Indonesia', *Disability & Society* 31(5): 693–712.

Thohari, S. (2012) 'Habis sakti, terbitlah sakit: berbagai macam konsepsi difabel di Jawa', discussion paper, Komunitas Salihara, Jakarta, 12 July.

Tribunnews (2016) 'Sambangi Jember, Mensos Khofifah luncurkan kartu khusus penyandang disabilitas', *Tribunnews.com*, 3 December. http://www.tribunnews.com/nasional/2016/12/03/sambangi-jember-mensos-khofifah-luncurkan-kartu-khusus-penyandang-disabilitas

6 Disability inclusion in Indonesia: the role of Islamic schools and universities in inclusive education reform

Dina Afrianty

Indonesia's ratification of the United Nations Convention on the Rights of Persons with Disabilities in 2011 and the introduction of Law No. 8/2016 on People with Disabilities in 2016 require the government to shift its policy on people with disabilities from a medical- and charity-based approach to a rights-based approach. Among the many rights that are guaranteed by the Disability Law is the right for people with disabilities to receive an education (Article 5(1) and Article 10). The law requires the national government and local governments to provide accessible and inclusive education for all students from the primary through to the tertiary level. Three years after the adoption of the Disability Law, however, the education sector still awaited passage of the crucial government regulations (*peraturan pemerintah*) needed to guide its implementation. At the time of writing, the government had given no clear timeline for introducing those regulations.

In this chapter I will discuss Indonesia's efforts to include people with disabilities in education. I will focus in particular on the Islamic education sector, which constitutes about 30 per cent of the total education sector. Among other things, I will examine practices of inclusion, how Islamic higher-education institutions are working to increase participation for people with disabilities and how Muslims are exploring their faith to promote inclusion.

I began this research in 2015, looking at societal attitudes and processes of disability inclusion in Muslim communities. This research was prompted by the realisation that in a society where discrimination and exclusion are deeply entrenched, it is important to understand people's views on disability, because these can be a significant barrier to inclusive policies. A study by Miles (2002), for example, found that religious teachings can contribute to negative societal attitudes towards people with disabilities and be an impediment to inclusion. Research on disability inclusion in Islamic educational institutions may help us to identify the areas in need of improvement and to gain insights that can transform societal attitudes towards disability. The aim is to explore religious thought as a source of inspiration for societal change.

Looking at the efforts and level of enthusiasm of faith-based educational institutions to include people with disabilities allows us not only to understand policy development but also to learn about social change. While there have been improvements in disability services and inclusion in the education sector, surveys of the attitudes of policy-makers, parents, students and members of the Muslim community show there is still room for improvement. This chapter therefore discusses both the policies that have been put in place in relation to disability and the societal attitudes and implementation problems standing in the way of full inclusion in Islamic education of people with disabilities.

Islamic educational institutions are required by law to provide equal access to education for persons with disabilities. The role of the Islamic education sector in promoting the rights of persons with disabilities is important for two main reasons. First, in a society such as Indonesia's where religious adherence is high, Islamic schools and tertiary institutions can help to break down the societal barriers and stigma towards disability emanating from religious and cultural beliefs. Second, most Islamic educational institutions, such as schools (*madrasah*) and traditional boarding schools (*pesantren*), are located in rural areas, which is also where the majority of people with disabilities live. It is therefore particularly important for rural Islamic educational institutions to develop and implement policies to include students with disabilities.

The chapter begins with a discussion of perceptions of disability among religious communities, looking at the link between cultural beliefs and the shaping of societal perceptions and how these in turn have influenced policy on disability inclusion. I then discuss the Indonesian government's efforts to strengthen the rights of people with disabilities in education by legislating the right to equal participation and inclusive education for persons with disabilities. I describe some inclusive practices initiated by the Islamic tertiary sector, including the attempts of some Islamic higher-education institutions to provide better access for students with disabilities, and give some examples of how Islamic values have been used to promote inclusion.

PERCEPTIONS OF DISABILITY IN THE MUSLIM COMMUNITY

The intersection of disability and religion has been the subject of research for at least three decades (Schumm and Stoltzfus 2011). Although most of the literature on religion and disability is based on Christian traditions and perspectives, there have also been several major studies looking at disability from a Muslim standpoint (Al-Aoufi, Al-Zyoud and Shahminan 2012; Bazna and Hatab 2005; Ghaly 2008; Richardson 2012).

According to Miles (2002), studying the teachings of religion on disability helps us not only to understand how society treats people with disability but also to find ways to enlighten the community and encourage its members to embrace a more inclusive perspective based on a better understanding of their faith. In the case of Islam, Al-Aoufi, Al-Zyoud and Shahminan (2012: 217) believe that an investigation of Islamic philosophy on the rights of persons with disabilities, and their relationship to and status within their society and their religion, may inspire a more robust approach to the provision of essential services and support for people with disabilities.

Research shows that Muslim societies view disability in much the same way that other cultures do—as both a blessing and a curse. Mental disabilities, for example, are often associated with supernatural or spiritual powers, while physical disabilities may be seen as a curse resulting from wrongdoing by the parents (Al-Aoufi, Al-Zyoud and Shahminan 2012: 214–15). Based on an examination of the sources of Islamic law, however, Bazna and Hatab (2005) conclude that both the Qur'an and the Hadith regard physical disability or difference as neither a blessing nor a curse. They argue that 'the Qur'an removes any stigma and barrier to full inclusion of people with physical conditions' (p. 24).

Research on inclusive practices in Muslim communities shows that although a mixture of cultural traditions and religious values influences community attitudes towards people with disabilities, negative attitudes are often falsely attributed to religious faith alone (Al-Aoufi, Al-Zyoud and Shahminan 2012: 214). While practices and attitudes may reflect people's understanding of what their religion says about disability, other factors, such as the local culture, a person's socio-economic status and level of education, and cultural differences in the way the religion is practised and understood, also need to be considered.

Some Muslim communities view disability in a more positive light, looking at it as an example of the need to be fatalistic in the acceptance of life's difficulties; Islam requires submission to the will of God so disability can be seen as a test of faith. Bazna and Hatab (2005) have identified teachings from the Qur'an and stories from the Hadith that show that the first generation of Muslims emphasised inclusion and the need to address difference and inequality. They relate a story to demonstrate how the Prophet Muhammad took steps to make Muslim society more inclusive. In this account, the Prophet asked the father and mother of a young woman to marry their daughter to a dwarf who was shunned by society despite being a good Muslim (Bazna and Hatab 2005: 20). Although the concept of disability, in the modern sense, cannot be found in the Qur'an or the Hadith, they do frame disability within the notion of 'disadvantage'. This disadvantage is created and perpetuated by society. Therefore, the Qur'an places responsibility on every Muslim to rectify this inequality (Bazna and Hatab 2005: 24).

In Indonesia, some elements within the Muslim community continue to see disability as a manifestation of sin, as a source of embarrassment and as a burden on the family and the community (Husna 2018). In 2013 in the city of Makassar, for example, a well-known local preacher told his congregation that leprosy, which is quite prevalent in the province, was a punishment from God for one's sins (Arsyam 2013). This comment sparked outrage among disability activists at the provincial and national levels. Nevertheless, such views are not uncommon. Many parents in villages across South Sulawesi hide children with disabilities or keep them at home because they feel embarrassment or shame. This has resulted in widespread shackling of people with mental illness, even though the Indonesian government banned this practice in 1977 (Diatri 2016).

Maola (2017) looked at the way disability is treated in the literature widely used in Indonesian *pesantren* in order to better understand what has shaped Muslim perceptions of disability in Central Java. He focused on the use of the *Qurrat al-Uyun*, a book written by Syekh Imam Abu Muhammad to guide students through the pitfalls of marriage and sexual relations. It is one of the classical religious texts known as *kitab kuning* (yellow books) taught at *pesantren*. The book contains information on how Muslim couples should perform their conjugal duties and offers guidelines on how to avoid having children with disabilities. It warns against marrying a relative (incest), having sex while the wife is menstruating, kissing the wife's eyes during sex, talking during sex, having sex at particular times (the night of Eid al-Adha, the first, middle and last days of the month, Fridays), looking at and touching the genitals, and failing to precede sexual intercourse with foreplay. The consequences of failing to follow these guidelines include having offspring born with various types of disability, including deafness, blindness, leprosy and mental illness. Based on interviews with *pesantren* students and the community in Central Java, Maola argues that the teachings in the *Qurrat al-Uyun* have contributed to the stigmatising view that disability is a punishment from God.

At an international conference on Islam and disability held at Sunan Kalijaga State Islamic University (Universitas Islam Negeri, UIN) in

Yogyakarta in May 2015, students with disabilities described how the discrimination and stigma they had experienced had prevented them from participating fully in public life. One of the consequences was that were often unable to perform basic religious obligations such as praying in a mosque or performing the *hajj*. Despite being taught that Islam teaches compassion, equality and respect, their lived experiences said otherwise. Those who had a physical impairment said that it was almost impossible for them to enter a mosque to pray and those who were deaf said they struggled to follow the prayers and understand sermons. Those in wheelchairs were prevented from entering mosques because the wheels were believed to be dirty (*mengandung najis*) and would make the mosque 'impure'. This was in addition to the fact that most of the mosques were wheelchair-inaccessible in the first place.

A leading disability activist at the conference, Cucu Saidah, said that she and her husband had been told that because of their disabilities—both of them use wheelchairs—it would be impossible for them to travel to the holy cities of Mecca and Medina to participate in religious rituals there. She asked the director-general of Islamic higher education at the Ministry of Religious Affairs, Professor Amsal Bahtiar, why the ministry had not done anything to address this matter. She observed that foreign television coverage often showed Muslims in wheelchairs who were from other countries performing religious rituals in Mecca and Medina, so why not from Indonesia? She stressed that Muslims with disabilities like herself had the exact same religious obligation as other Muslims to travel to Saudi Arabia to perform the *hajj* and *umrah* pilgrimages, to pray in a mosque and to listen to sermons. The director-general admitted that his ministry had much to do to guarantee inclusion, not only in the area of education but also in making sure that people with disabilities had the freedom and independence to practise their religious beliefs.

PROMOTING THE RIGHT OF PEOPLE WITH DISABILITIES TO EDUCATION

Stories of Islamic higher-education institutions rejecting people with disabilities are not uncommon. UIN Syarif Hidayatullah Jakarta, the most prestigious Islamic university in Indonesia, made headlines in 2008 when it prevented a visually impaired high-school graduate from entering its *tarbiya* (education) faculty (Kompas 2008). The student had in fact passed the national entrance exam to study at this university, but when he tried to enrol he was told that university regulations prevented applicants with disabilities from becoming students. In the face of protests from disability and human rights activists, the university justified its decision by claiming that the education faculty lacked the infrastructure and resources to give the student proper access and support. Allowing a blind student to study at the faculty would not be in the interests of the student, the university argued.

UIN Sunan Gunung Jati Bandung in West Java also rejected the application of a visually impaired student who wanted to enrol in its *tarbiya* faculty (Iman 2011). This time, the university said that the purpose of the faculty was to train students to become teachers, and a visually impaired person could not possibly perform that role because they would not be able to interact fully with the students in the classroom (Herdiana 2011). The application of a blind person to study at the *tarbiya* faculty at Alauddin State Islamic Institute (Institut Agama Islam Negeri, IAIN) in Makassar was also knocked back on the grounds of disability (interview, 30 May 2015, Makassar).

These stories about otherwise-suitable applicants being rejected by Islamic higher-education institutions are not intended to demonstrate that discrimination is unique to the Islamic sector. In fact, discrimination against people with disabilities is widespread across both the Islamic and public education sectors, from primary through to tertiary level. In 2014, the Ministry of Education and Culture was threatened with a lawsuit by human rights and disability activists, who alleged that the ministry discriminated against students with disabilities wishing to enrol in public universities. The ministry had allowed several universities to restrict admission to students who were 'healthy' and 'not physically impaired'. It was only after massive protests that the ministry finally agreed that there must be no further discrimination towards people with disabilities (Ferri 2014).

Access to education is crucial to poverty alleviation, including among people with disabilities. The 2011 'World report on disability' found that people with disabilities had lower levels of educational attainment, leading to lower levels of economic participation and higher levels of poverty (WHO and World Bank 2011: 39). While the report identifies education as one of the critical factors in lifting rural communities out of poverty, people with disabilities living in rural areas face even more barriers to education than their able-bodied peers (Grech 2014; WHO and World Bank 2011). Lack of access to good roads and public transport is one of the first challenges parents encounter when they consider sending their children with disabilities to school. A scarcity of school buildings with access ramps and disability toilets and the lack of an inclusive curriculum further prevent children with disabilities from obtaining equal access to education.

In Indonesia only a small percentage of children with disabilities have access to education. Data from the 2012 National Socio-Economic Survey

(Survei Sosio-Ekonomi Nasional, Susenas) show that of the total population of school-aged children with disabilities, 81.81 per cent are in primary
school or not in school at all, 8.75 per cent are in junior secondary school
and 9.44 per cent are in senior secondary school (Ministry of Health 2014:
13). Overall, data from the 2013 Basic Health Research (Riset Kesehatan
Dasar, Riskesdas) conducted by the Ministry of Health show that 11.7
per cent of people with disabilities aged 15 or above are primary school
graduates, 7.6 per cent are junior secondary graduates, 7.0 per cent are
senior secondary graduates and 6.4 per cent have a diploma or bachelor's
degree (Ministry of Health 2014: 13). This means that most Indonesians
with disabilities either have no education at all (29.8 per cent) or did not
finish primary school (18.0 per cent). While data are difficult to find, a
report by the Ministry of Research, Technology and Higher Education in
2017 shows that of the 4,631 tertiary education institutions regulated by
the ministry, only 152 had students with disabilities, and that of a total
of 3.07 million female tertiary students and 2.63 million male tertiary
students, only 401 had a disability (Ministry of Research, Technology
and Higher Education 2017a: 2).[1] Together with the anecdotal evidence
about inadequate policies and facilities, particularly at the tertiary level,
these figures point to significant barriers preventing full participation by
people with disabilities in all levels of education.

Following independence, the Indonesian government introduced special schools (*sekolah luar biasa*, SLB) at the primary and secondary levels
so that children with disabilities would be able to get an education.[2] The
'special school' model segregates students with disabilities from their non-
disabled peers, leaving them ill-prepared to study or work alongside the
non-disabled. This exclusive education system does not provide an environment in which children with disabilities can reach their full potential
and participate equally with their non-disabled counterparts. When they
finish their education at the end of secondary school, the graduates of
special schools must apply to mainstream universities if they wish to

---

1 For further information on the numbers of students in tertiary education
   in Indonesia, see Ministry of Research, Technology and Higher Education
   (2017b).
2 The Dutch were the first to establish special schools (in the form of sheltered
   workshops) for Indonesians with vision or hearing impairments, in the early
   1900s (Tsaputra n.d.). In 1954, the Indonesian government passed Law No.
   12/1954 on Education regulating special education for disabled children,
   with each school designed to accommodate a specific type of disability. By
   the 1980s Indonesia had about 200 special schools at the primary level. They
   focused on educating children with physical impairments; thus, children
   with learning difficulties and mental illnesses were not accommodated by
   the schools.

continue their education. Interviews with disabled activists in Makassar suggest that the special school system makes disabled students feel that they are not ready to attend regular classes or study and mix with their non-disabled peers, and therefore leaves them reluctant to pursue higher education (Afrianty 2015).

The reluctance to pursue higher education also stems from the fact that people with disabilities find it difficult to enter the labour force because employers are reluctant to hire them. This further demotivates them from pursuing higher education and discourages parents from supporting their children's education. A survey conducted by the Ministry of Health in 2013 showed that only 6 per cent of people with disabilities aged 15 or above were employed in the formal sector while 27.2 per cent worked in the informal sector and 14.4 per cent were unemployed (Ministry of Health 2014: 14). These figures suggest that most people with disabilities remain trapped in a cycle of poverty or become dependent on others in adulthood, adding to their family's economic burden.

LEGAL GUARANTEES TO EDUCATION FOR PEOPLE WITH DISABILITIES

Law No. 8/2016 on People with Disabilities reiterates the constitutional and legal obligation of the state to eliminate discriminatory practices and introduce policies and practices that allow people with disabilities to participate in all aspects of life. The law is in line with Indonesia's international obligation to abide by human rights principles as set out in Law No. 39/1999 on Human Rights and Law No. 19/2011 ratifying the Convention on the Rights of Persons with Disabilities. More importantly, it is consistent with the Indonesian Constitution of 1945, which states that every citizen has the right to achieve their full potential in all aspects of life, including education, employment, health care, and social, economic, legal and political participation. By 2015, Indonesia had passed 17 laws containing provisions on the rights of people with disabilities (Liu and Brown 2015). The Disability Law is just the latest, but also the broadest and most comprehensive, commitment to enhancing the rights of people with disabilities.

Article 2 of the Disability Law guarantees the rights of people with disabilities to equal opportunity and access to education, employment, health care, and social, economic, legal and political participation, including the right to participate in religious rituals. The law bans practices that discriminate against, alienate or marginalise people with disabilities and promotes practices that further their protection, empowerment and fulfilment. Consistent with Indonesia's decentralisation policy, some local governments have introduced local regulations to implement the principles of equality and inclusion enshrined in the Disability Law. Among those that have introduced inclusive policies are the provinces of Jakarta, Yogyakarta and South Sulawesi, which have begun this process by building accessible public infrastructure.

Article 10 of the Disability Law states that people with disabilities have the right to a good-quality and inclusive education, to equal opportunity to become educators at every educational level and to infrastructure that allows them to access education services and various forms of learning and teaching assistance.

Before the introduction of the Disability Law, education for persons with disabilities was regulated by Law No. 20/2003 on the National Education System, which guarantees the right of every child to six years of basic education (Article 34). Article 5(1) of this law states that every citizen has the right to receive a good-quality education and Article 5(2) says that people with physical, emotional, mental, intellectual or social deficiencies have the right to a special education. 'Special education' is defined as 'education for students who encounter difficulty in participating in the learning process because of physical, emotional, mental, or social deficiencies and/or who are intellectually gifted and have special talents' (Article 32(1)). The elucidation to Article 15 of the National Education Law emphasises that special education for students with disabilities, or for the intellectually gifted, is to be administered in an 'inclusive' fashion, or in the form of a special education unit, at the primary and secondary levels of schooling.

The provisions of the National Education Law mainly deal with primary and secondary education. In 2014, the Ministry of Education and Culture issued Ministerial Regulation No. 46/2014 on Special Education in Higher Education to clarify the rights of people with disabilities wishing to access higher education. Article 1(1) of the regulation defined special education at the tertiary level as:

> [...] the implementation of education for students who face physical, emotional, intellectual or social barriers and/or those with special intelligence and talent.

This regulation was considered progressive in terms of how it regulated the obligation of tertiary institutions to provide access to students with disabilities; it specified that higher-education institutions must provide assistive devices, accessible infrastructure, practical support such as sign language interpreters for deaf students, and tools and technology to allow all students with disabilities to participate fully and effectively in classroom and other educational activities (Article 1(4)).

Following Indonesia's ratification of the Convention on the Rights of Persons with Disabilities and the passing of Law No. 8/2016 on People with Disabilities, the Ministry of Research, Technology and Higher Education introduced Ministerial Regulation No. 46/2017 on Special Education in Higher Education. This revised version of Ministerial Regulation No. 46/2014 describes the services that must be provided to students with special physical, intellectual, mental and sensory needs, and those with special talents, in order to guarantee equal participation. It requires tertiary education providers to be equipped with accessible infrastructure and to provide assistive devices to give all students the same opportunities to learn. To support inclusive learning processes, higher-education institutions must provide learning tools and resources such as braille textbooks, sign language interpreters, classroom assistants, screen readers with speech output, and inclusive curriculums that have been adapted to offer alternative teaching methods and assessment mechanisms for students with special needs (Article 8). Despite this, it is evident from a report published by the Ministry of Research, Technology and Higher Education (2017a) that only a small number of universities are complying with these requirements.

It appears that the current policy guidelines are sufficient to ensure that educational institutions can provide access to education for persons with disabilities. Sadly, however, many universities still maintain discriminatory policies, such as refusing to admit students with a physical disability or allowing them to enrol only in certain fields (Soleh 2014: 3). Thus, even though disabled students can enrol in university, they are likely to encounter unsuitable facilities and receive inadequate support, circumstances that limit their ability to participate and to succeed.

DISABILITY INCLUSION POLICY AND PRACTICE IN ISLAMIC TERTIARY INSTITUTIONS

In Indonesia, public education is administered by the Ministry of Education and Culture and Islamic education by the Ministry of Religious Affairs (Azra, Afrianty and Hefner 2007). The Islamic sector receives less support from the government than the public sector, resulting in lower-quality teaching and poorer student results. The policy of providing minimal support to the Islamic education sector began in the colonial period and continued throughout the New Order (Jamhari 2009: 247). It was only after the fall of Suharto in 1998 that the Islamic sector began to receive more support from the national government. As a result, the quality of Islamic educational institutions gradually started to improve and enrolments began to increase.

Law No. 20/2003 on the National Education System requires the Islamic education sector to offer 'special education', 'inclusive education' and access to education for children with disabilities. The Ministry of Religious Affairs was supposed to produce a ministerial regulation to guide the implementation of this legislation but at the time this research commenced in 2015, it had not yet done so. A study of inclusive education practices in Islamic primary and secondary schools (*madrasah* and *pesantren*) in 2014 found that while 57 non-Islamic schools (both public and private) in Yogyakarta had introduced inclusive practices, no *madrasah* or *pesantren* had done so (Sholikhah 2016: 4).

Sholikhah's (2016) research revealed that the ministry had no policy on how to provide access for students with disabilities, or any policy guidelines to assist schools to introduce special education. Nevertheless, some *madrasah* had accepted students with disabilities, chiefly because their parents had begged them to do so. The heads of the *madrasah* claimed that they were unable to provide the support students with disabilities needed to participate equally with their peers in class. Lack of resources as well as lack of knowledge about the principles of inclusive education were some of the reasons for this.

It was only in 2015 that the Ministry of Religious Affairs began to actively promote inclusive education for *madrasah* and *pesantren*, following the signing of a memorandum of understanding with the Australian government. Its initial focus was on building physical infrastructure, such as ramps, to make *madrasah* accessible. During a speech to the international conference on Islam and disability held at UIN Sunan Kalijaga in 2015, Amsal Bahtiar, the director-general of Islamic higher education, admitted that the ministry still had not developed a policy on the provision of special and inclusive education in *madrasah* or *pesantren*. There were no 'special *madrasah*' equivalent to the 'special schools' in the public sector. The ministry had no information on how many students with disabilities were enrolled in Islamic primary and secondary schools.

UIN Sunan Kalijaga Yogyakarta is a pioneer among the State Islamic Universities (UIN) in providing access to students with disabilities. It has built accessible infrastructure, such as ramps for students in wheelchairs and braille signs to help visually impaired students move around the campus, and it is one of the few Islamic universities to have an accessible library, mosque, classrooms and cafeteria, as well as other disability-friendly public spaces. In 2007 it established the Center for Disability Services (Pusat Layanan Disabilitas) as part its commitment to become an inclusive university that welcomed people with disabilities. The centre was the initiative of several students with disabilities who were studying at UIN Sunan Kalijaga, supported by student activists and lecturers who shared their motivation to improve the status and experience of students with disabilities. The Center for Disability Services is a non-structural institution within the university, meaning that it is funded by the university rather than the ministry and is accountable to the university for its budget and programs (Soleh 2014: 22).

According to the database of the Center for Disability Services, 55 students with disabilities were enrolled in various faculties at UIN Sunan Kalijaga in 2015. The university provides equipment and assistive devices in classrooms, and trains academics and staff in inclusive practices (Basuki and Jaelani 2015). It provides specially designed monitors, braille translators to change text into braille, braille printers and portable keyboards with braille and speech output. Students with hearing and speech impairments are given electronic notetakers that convert speech into text, to help them understand what is being said in class. Students with physical impairments are offered specially designed desks, chairs and computer keyboards. The Center for Disability Services recruits student volunteers to help disabled students complete their assignments. The centre's director, Maftuhin, told me that the volunteers take lecture notes for deaf students, and observed that 'student volunteers are very committed to supporting their disabled peers' (interview, Yogyakarta, 23 May 2015). He said that the idea of an inclusive university had received strong support from the rector of the university at the time the policy was introduced, Professor Amin Abdullah, who was known for his moderate and progressive views. It had been Abdullah's idea to use the university's internal budget to fund the disability centre, because he realised that reform would take too long if the university waited for approval and funding from the Ministry of Religious Affairs. This demonstrates that having institutional leadership that is committed to disability initiatives is important in bringing about change, particularly in the absence of action at the ministry level.

While UIN Sunan Kalijaga has made efforts to support and provide access for students with disabilities, the head of the Center for Disability Services said that the university still faced serious challenges to full integration of disabled students. In particular, some academics lacked awareness of, or ignored, the needs of students with disabilities, insisting on applying blanket policies to all students and thus making it difficult for those with disabilities to fulfil their academic tasks.

In research conducted at UIN Syarif Hidayatullah Jakarta, the nation's biggest Islamic university, I discovered that similar attitudes were widespread among the academic staff. An official from the Department of Psychology, for example, expressed reluctance to embrace an inclusive academic policy towards students with disabilities. He told me that people with disabilities were born with innate limitations and it was simply fanciful to expect them to have the same capacity as non-disabled students (interview, Ciputat, 4 May 2016). In fact, it was a burden on students with disabilities to ask them to perform tasks that they were incapable of carrying out and he doubted that lecturers could assess the performance of such students genuinely and fairly because they would be swayed by feelings of pity or sympathy. He favoured the creation of a special, segregated system at the tertiary level for students with disabilities.

Another academic at the same institution said that the parents of children with disabilities had to understand that their children had special needs and would never be the same as other children. Those parents should not force their children to study in the same school or classroom as able-bodied students. Some academics referred to religious teachings to justify their view that students with disabilities should be treated differently. They pointed out that people with disabilities were often exempted from performing certain religious duties, such as performing the daily prayers and fasting during the fasting month. This meant they would never be 'the same' as able-bodied Muslims.

Some other Islamic tertiary institutions have followed the example of UIN Sunan Kalijaga and established units within the university to provide services for students with disabilities and to conduct research into disability. Among them are UIN Syarif Hidayatullah Jakarta and UIN Ar-Raniry Banda Aceh, which both established disability centres in 2017.

Indonesia's two largest Islamic social organisations, Muhammadiyah and Nahdlatul Ulama, have also adopted the principles of disability inclusion as part of their rights-based strategies. During its 2015 congress in Makassar, Muhammadiyah agreed to introduce an inclusive disability policy for its educational institutions and health services that would protect and respect the rights of persons with disabilities. Despite social justice being one of the organisation's key principles, Muhammadiyah acknowledged that it had done very little in the past to promote equality and participation for persons with disabilities. It also acknowledged that discrimination against, and the marginalisation of, people with disabilities was a widespread social phenomenon that required urgent policy action. In June 2018, Muhammadiyah announced that it would require all its religious facilities to be accessible to disabled people and that it would explore a new Islamic jurisprudence (*fiqh*) that could guarantee the rights of persons with disabilities.

A similar step has been taken by Nahdlatul Ulama, which recently published *Fiqih Penguatan Penyandang Disabilitas*, a set of regulations on disability inclusion derived from scholarly interpretation of Islamic jurisprudence (Husna 2018). Among other things, *Fiqih Disabilitas* states that mosques must provide access and support for people with disabilities so that they can perform prayers, develop procedures to enable people with physical disabilities to perform ablutions and provide assistance for blind Muslims so that they know in which direction to face when performing their prayers.

CONCLUSION

Cultural and religious beliefs help to shape perceptions towards people with disabilities. Research on this phenomenon has shown that while certain religious interpretations have contributed to discriminatory treatment, there is nonetheless potential for religious teachings to be a force for social change. The intersection of faith-based cultural views and social practices could ultimately contribute to a dialogue about faith as a source of inclusive and pluralist beliefs and practices more broadly.

To date, Indonesians with disabilities have faced significant difficulties in gaining entrance to the higher education sector. The barriers include policies, funding and—above all—attitudes within the administrations of higher education institutions themselves. In recent years improvements have been evident, although change could come far more quickly. Tertiary education is important for providing participants, including disabled participants, with critical leverage in terms of their social and economic advancement. The positive stories outlined in this chapter show that the barriers can be overcome and students can be given the opportunities they seek.

The Islamic higher-education sector is a prominent service provider in the tertiary education sector, and the provider of choice for many Muslim Indonesians. In a highly religious society like Indonesia's, religious faith is believed to have the capacity to enlighten society through its ideas on social justice, compassion, respect and equality. For this reason, religious education institutions have a crucial role to play in transforming society's attitudes towards, and perceptions of, people with disabilities.

REFERENCES

Afrianty, D. (2015) 'People with disability: locked out of learning?', *Indonesia at Melbourne*, 27 July.

Al-Aoufi, H., N. Al-Zyoud and N. Shahminan (2012) 'Islam and the cultural conceptualisation of disability', *International Journal of Adolescence and Youth* 17(4): 205–19.

Arsyam. I. (2013) 'Lecehkan kusta di Trans TV, Ustad Maulana diprotes', *Tribun-Timur.com*, 20 May, http://makassar.tribunnews.com/2013/05/20/lecehkan-kusta-di-trans-tv-ustad-maulana-diprotes

Azra, A., D. Afrianty and R.W. Hefner (2007) '*Pesantren* and *madrasa*: Muslim schools and national ideals in Indonesia', in R.W. Hefner and M.Q. Zaman (eds) *Schooling Islam: The Culture and Politics of Modern Muslim Education*, Princeton University Press, Princeton, NJ: 172–98.

Basuki, U., and A.Q. Jaelani (2015) 'Kajian atas pelaksanaan pemenuhan hak pendidikan tinggi bagi penyandang difabilitas di UIN Sunan Kalijaga melalui pengesahan CRPD sebagai upaya perlindungan hak asasi manusia dalam negara hukum Indonesia', *Jurnal Panggung Hukum* 1(2). http://www.aifis-digilib.org/uploads/1/3/4/6/13465004/01_isi._udiyo-aqj.pdf

Bazna, M., and T. Hatab (2005) 'Disability in the Qur'an', *Journal of Religion, Disability & Health* 9(1): 5–27.

Diatri, H. (2016) 'How can Indonesia free the mentally ill from shackles once and for all?', *The Conversation*, 15 April. https://theconversation.com/how-can-indonesia-free-the-mentally-ill-from-shackles-once-and-for-all-57185

Ferri, O. (2014) 'Tak dibolehkan ikut SNMPTN, penyandang disabilitas protes', *Liputan6*, 29 April. http://news.liputan6.com/read/2043613/tak-dibolehkan-ikut-snmptn-penyandang-disabilitas-protes

Ghaly, M.M. (2008) 'Physical and spiritual treatment of disability in Islam: perspectives of early and modern jurists', *Journal of Religion, Disability & Health* 12(2): 105–43.

Grech, S. (2014) 'Disability, poverty and education: perceived barriers and (dis)connections in rural Guatemala', *Disability and the Global South* 1(1): 128–52.

Herdiana, I. (2011) 'ITMI tuding UIN SG tolak mahasiswa tuna netra', *Okezone. com*, 5 August. https://news.okezone.com/read/2011/08/05/373/488548/itmi-tuding-uin-sgd-tolak-mahasiswa-tuna-netra

Husna, S. (2018) *Fiqih Penguatan Penyandang Disabilitas*, Lembaga Bahtsul Masail PBNU, Jakarta.

Iman, H. (2011) 'ITMI tuding UIN SGD tolak mahasiswa tuna netra', *Okenews*, 5 August. https://news.okezone.com/read/2011/08/05/373/488548/itmi-tuding-uin-sgd-tolak-mahasiswa-tuna-netra

Jamhari (2009) 'New trend of Islamic education in Indonesia', *Studia Islamika* 16(2): 243–90.

Kompas (2008) 'Tunanetra gagal jadi Mahasiswa UIN', *Kompas.com*, 19 July. https://nasional.kompas.com/read/2008/07/19/09100138/tunanetra.gagal.jadi.mahasiswa.uin

Liu, E., and L. Brown (2015) 'Disability data and the development agenda in Indonesia', *Inside Indonesia* 119 (January–March).

Maola, M. (2017) 'Islamic Kamasutra: prevention from giving birth children with disability', *Advances in Social Science, Education and Humanities Research* 153: 142–5.

Miles, M. (2002) 'Disability in an Eastern religious context: historical perspectives', *Journal of Religion, Disability & Health* 6(2–3): 53–76.

Ministry of Health (2014) 'Situasi penyandang disabilitas', Ministry of Health, Jakarta. www.depkes.go.id/download.php?file=download/...disabilitas.pdf

Ministry of Research, Technology and Higher Education (2017a) 'Panduan layanan mahasiswa disabilitas di perguruan tinggi', Ministry of Research, Technology and Higher Education, Jakarta. https://belmawa.ristekdikti.go.id/wp-content/uploads/2018/01/PANDUAN-LAYANAN-MAHASISWA-DISA-BILITAS-DI-PT-Oke.pdf

Ministry of Research, Technology and Higher Education (2017b) 'Statistik pendidikan tinggi 2017', Ministry of Research, Technology and Higher Education, Jakarta. http://kopertis3.or.id/v5/wp-content/uploads/Buku-Statistik-Pendidikan-Tinggi-2017.pdf

Richardson, K. (2012) *Difference and Disability in the Medieval Islamic World*, Edinburgh University Press, Edinburgh.

Schumm, D., and M. Stoltzfus (2011) *Disability and Religious Diversity: Cross-cultural and Interreligious Perspectives*, Palgrave Macmillan, New York NY.

Sholikhah, R.M. (2016) 'Pendidikan inklusif di Kementerian Agama', Master's thesis, UIN Sunan Kalijaga Yogyakarta, Yogyakarta. http://digilib.uin-suka.ac.id/22720/1/1420420023_BAB-I_IV-atau-V_DAFTAR-PUSTAKA.pdf

Soleh, A. (2014) 'Kebijakan perguruan tinggi Negeri Yogyakarta terhadap penyandang disabilitas', *Jurnal Pendidikan Islam* 3(1): 1–30.

Tsaputra, A. (n.d.) 'Inclusive education for children with disabilities in Indonesia: dilemma and suitable framework for Indonesian context'. http://www.australiaawardsindonesia.org/files/arg/ARTICLE%20FOR%20ARG%20BULLETIN-ANTONI.pdf

WHO (World Health Organization) and World Bank (2011) 'World report on disability', WHO and World Bank, Geneva. https://www.who.int/disabilities/world_report/2011/report.pdf

PART 3

Sexuality

7 Is the recent wave of homophobia in Indonesia unexpected?

Saskia E. Wieringa

Indonesia has long been seen as a country that is relatively friendly towards lesbian, gay, bisexual and transgender (LGBT) people.[1] This is due in particular to the public visibility of male-to-female (MTF) trans people, known as *waria* (from *wanita–pria*, woman–man).[2] Until a few years ago, consensual homosexual acts among adults were not criminalised. Since late 2015, however, a campaign of virulent homophobia has shattered the image of Indonesia as an LGBT-tolerant country, and a campaign to criminalise all sex outside marriage is now under way. The people behind this campaign invoke tradition, morality and religion to 'prove' that same-sex relations and transgender practices are alien to the country. This homophobic campaign is interwoven with and strengthened by a 'red scare'. In this chapter, I analyse the sexual moral campaigns deployed in the 'othering' of two minorities, LGBT activists and alleged communists.

I argue that heteronormativity has always been the dominant regime in the country, invisibilising same-sex practices. Its passionate aesthetics[3]

---

1 In this chapter I will use the term 'LGBT' to refer to all people who self-identify as lesbian, gay, bisexual, transgender, queer, intersex and so on. See Chapter 8 of this volume by Wijaya for a discussion of terminology.

2 Other terms used for MTF trans people in Indonesia are *wandu, banci, bencong* and *wadam*. Some of these terms are derogatory or are no longer much used.

3 I define 'passionate aesthetics' as the dynamics, motivations, codes of behaviour and presentation, subjectivities and identities that together make up the complex workings of erotic attraction, sexual relations and partnership patterns. For an in-depth discussion of heteronormativity and passionate aesthetics in Indonesia, see Wieringa (2015a).

have even informed attitudes towards the major exception to invisibility, the *waria*. I first query how 'tolerant' the Indonesian archipelago may actually have been towards same-sex practices. Next, I provide some examples of the homophobic campaign that has swept the country since 2015. I contrast this with the preceding period, in which LGBT issues gradually became more visible and sexual rights could be discussed more openly. A discourse of human and women's rights emerged after the fall of the military dictatorship of President Suharto in 1998 (Wieringa 2015b). In this more open climate, gay and lesbian people attempted to stake a claim in the public sphere and to set up or strengthen various sexual rights groups (Boellstorff 2005; Wieringa 2007).

Indonesia has experienced two major episodes of sexual moral panic in the post-independence period. The first occurred in the mid-1960s in conjunction with an army-orchestrated campaign of sexual slander that helped to incite Indonesians to slaughter their neighbours. The massacre of up to 1 million people, which amounted to a genocide, and other crimes against humanity occurred after a segment of the army murdered six generals and a lieutenant on 1 October 1965 in what was seen as an unsuccessful coup attempt (Robinson 2018; Wieringa, Melvin and Pohlman 2019). The sexual moral panic of the mid-1960s was driven by political interests, especially among those seeking to establish a new military-based regime. The second major sexual moral panic of the present day builds on the original one, and has been spurred by the rise of conservative Islamic forces. In this chapter I argue that homophobia has been a persistent aspect of life in Indonesia, though it has had different manifestations. In that sense the relatively short period of increasing visibility for LGBT persons from around 2000 to 2015 should be considered an anomaly rather than the norm in Indonesian history.

A TOLERANT INDONESIA?

In February 2018 the then United Nations high commissioner for human rights, Zeid Ra'ad al-Hussein, criticised proposals in the Indonesian parliament to criminalise gay and extramarital sex. He expressed concern that legislators were debating revisions to the Criminal Code that would outlaw sex outside marriage, same-sex relations and cohabitation, all of which had previously been unregulated by law, and warned that the proposed amendments could harm the LGBT community. 'Discussions of [revisions] betray strains of intolerance seemingly alien to Indonesian culture that have made inroads here', Al-Hussein said (cited in Smith 2018). How true is this perception? At the same time as Al-Hussein was making his statement, radical Islamic and other homophobic groups were arguing that LGBT rights were part of an insidious Western agenda and were contrary to Indonesian culture and norms (Topsfield 2017). Thus, we must ask which one is alien to Indonesia: tolerance of same-gender/ same-sex practices or homophobia?

Interwoven with homophobia has been a renewed phobia about communism. In the presidential election campaign currently under way, both themes are apparent. In demonstrations, marchers carry banners opposing both LGBT issues and what they call the 'new communist movement'. On 5 September 2018, Neno Warisman, a prominent supporter of a campaign to replace the president, Joko Widodo (Jokowi), called on her supporters to vote against the incumbent in order to prevent their children from 'becoming homosexuals'. Since 2017 President Jokowi has also repeatedly been accused by his opponents of having communist leanings (Allard and Da Costa 2017).

Historically, transgender practices were found across the Southeast Asian archipelago, including Indonesia (Blackwood 2005; Gouda 1995; Peletz 2009; Wieringa 2010). Among the courtly texts, the 12-volume *Serat Centhini* from Java, written in the nineteenth century, depicted homosexual practices in detail. Transgender practices, mostly related to certain ritual and shamanistic traditions, were a theme of both literary texts such as *La Galigo*[4] and the reports of colonial administrators.

Many of these traditions and practices are now in decline. The best-known remnant of such a tradition is the *bissu*—a transgender or intersex group of ritual specialists belonging to the Bugis ethnic group in Sulawesi (Davies 2010; Pelras 1996; Sugianto 2015).[5] However, they have lost much of their traditional power and prestige in recent decades (Davies 2010; Lathief 2004). Various popular art forms featuring transgender practices, such as the Reog dance and the Ludruk and Ketoprak theatrical performances, have waned because the performers were persecuted by anti-communist forces after 1965 on the basis of their alleged communist leanings (Wieringa and Katjasungkana 2018; Wilson 1999). Artists and other members of the People's Cultural Institute (Lembaga Kebudayaan Rakyat, LEKRA) were also singled out for persecution during the 1965–66 massacres because of the organisation's alleged pro-communist,

---

4   *La Galigo* describes the epic creation myth of the Bugis people in South Sulawesi. Based on oral tradition, it was put in manuscript form from the eighteenth century onward and runs to over 6,000 pages.

5   The Bugis adopted a five-gender system, with male/masculine and female/feminine on the outer edges, and male/feminine, female/masculine and *bissu* (intersex or fusing all sex/gender positions) in the middle. *Bissu* were viewed as intermediaries between the world of humans and the world of the gods, and were highly venerated as priests, particularly in the royal courts. They continue to officiate at weddings and other ceremonies.

anti-Islamic orientation. LEKRA was the leading cultural institution on the left during the Sukarno period. It promoted so-called people's art, in which social critique could be incorporated.

In colonial times, transgender or same-sex practices that were part of traditional cultural or religious practices were generally accepted by the Dutch colonial power-holders, but *paederastie* was considered immoral (Gouda 1995). Colonial moral outrage about pederasty was evident in 1938–39, when raids targeting pederasts took place across Indonesia and over 200 men were arrested, including the German painter Walter Spies (Aldrich 2002; Boellstorff 2005). Under the Dutch civil and penal codes in force in the colony, the only type of same-sex act that was criminalised was sex between an adult and a minor. This Dutch-era law remains in force in Indonesia today, although it is a topic of debate, as is discussed below. The prevalence of particular forms of same-sex or same-gender practices in Indonesia during the colonial era does not mean that all forms of such behaviour were accepted or tolerated. It is probable that only particular practices were accepted in certain regions and that recognition was accorded only to the practitioners of certain practices. Heteronormativity was deeply entrenched.

By the 1950s and 1960s, only MTF trans people were still a visible part of the community, though not necessarily an accepted one: *waria* were often forced to make themselves more masculine in order to conform to the dominant norms of masculinity (Hegarty 2017). Female-to-male (FTM) trans people as well as women and men with same-sex desires were mostly invisible during those years (Blackwood 2010; Wieringa 1987). Public acceptance of *waria* began to increase only in the 1970s when the then Jakarta governor, Ali Sadikin, offered them his protection (Boellstorff 2007). Even then, this was only a partial acknowledgement of their existence, applying only to *waria* and to MTF people in certain professions, such as hairdressing and sex work. Most men and women with same-sex desires, particularly the women, lived in isolation, tucked away from society by their families because of their 'immaturity', if they managed to avoid being married off. In rural areas, cross-dressing transgender *wandu* and *banci*—both men and women—somehow managed to make a living within their communities (Boellstorff 2005; Davies 2010; Ediati 2014). Another common location of male–male sexual practices was (and probably still is) Indonesia's all-male Islamic boarding schools (*pesantren*) (Boellstorff 2005: 95; Wieringa 2015a). It is ironic, then, that so many Islamic preachers are among those stirring up anti-homosexual sentiment and that radical Islamist politicians are among the most vocal proponents of anti-LGBT legislation. The practice of religious teachers and older students having sexual relations with a younger student (*mairil*) is well known but is not publicly discussed (Khumaini 2014).

Academic literature from the 1980s onward reported silence, stigma, hatred and various forms of discrimination towards people who identified themselves as *gay* or *lesbi* (Blackwood 2010; Boellstorff 2005, 2007; Wieringa 1987, 2007).[6] Even if *waria* were acknowledged publicly, they were generally seen as 'suffering from a mental condition' (Boellstorff 2005: 31), while societal opinions of *gay* and *lesbi* ranged from 'grudging tolerance to open bigotry' (p. 6). In 1993, when the first stirrings of an LGBT movement became evident, a *lesbi* journal described the image of the *tomboi*—a woman who identifies as and acts like a man—as 'a comedic form that sickens and nauseates' (p. 165).

In the early 1980s the first articles about same-sex relations began to appear in newspapers and magazines. In 1981, a story about the 'marriage' of two young women—Jossie (sporting a masculine white jacket) and Bonnie (dressed in a feminine red gown)—attracted considerable public attention. This was the first public celebration of a female same-sex relationship in Indonesia. It made other people with a same-sex orientation realise that there were other people like themselves, and gave their feelings and sexual acts a name (Boellstorff 2005; Wieringa 1987). In general, however, the print media, especially advice columns in women's magazines such as *Kartini* and *Femina*, counselled *lesbi* on how to become 'normal' again (Blackwood 2010).

From 1997, some television talk shows began to discuss LGBT issues (Boellstorff 2005: 75). The supposedly comic figure of the *bencong/waria* appeared in comedies, with exaggerated feminine mannerisms and speech. Only *Arisan*—a 2003 film focusing on the relationships between a close group of friends—portrayed an apparently healthy and accepted gay relationship (Murtagh 2013). However, the audience for this film was small and the content was so far removed from the everyday lives of ordinary *gay* and *lesbi* that they could scarcely relate to this distant wonderland. Meanwhile, references to homosexuality as being contagious and an illness continued to pop up regularly in the print media and even in interviews with *gay* and *lesbi* individuals themselves, although many said they were 'born that way' and that it was therefore a God-given condition (Boellstorff 2005; Wieringa 2015a).

While Indonesia has always stressed the virtue of traditional heterosexual marriage, the particular form of heteronormative marriage practised in Indonesia today is a product of the authoritarian and repressive New Order period (1966–98). Under the preceding Sukarno regime

---

6 A notable exception was the former tourism minister, Joop Ave, who remained close to the ruling powers despite widespread rumours that he was gay. Although he became the object of a gay scandal in 1995, he always kept silent about his sexual orientation.

(1945–67), members of the powerful, socialist Indonesian Women's Movement (Gerakan Wanita Indonesia, Gerwani) had fought for women's rights in marriage, the economy and politics. Following the murder of six generals and a lieutenant on 1 October 1965, Suharto's forces accused members of Gerwani of having castrated and tortured the generals before killing them. This sexual slander was widely propagated and believed, inciting conservative groups to participate in the massacres that followed. Hundreds of thousands of people were murdered or incarcerated in the months following this vicious campaign of sexual vilification (Robinson 2018; Wieringa 2002).

Suharto used the Gerwani myth to help justify the campaign to wipe out 'amoral' communists and instil a conservative family ideology. In the decades that followed, state control over women's sexuality, and an emphasis on women's docility as wives and mothers, would become the bedrock of the regime (Wieringa 2003). To be a good citizen one had to be married according to the stipulations of Law No. 1/1974 on Marriage, which placed men at the head of the household (Katjasungkana and Wieringa 2003). This was formalised in ideology based on 'family values' (*asas kekeluargaan*). After Suharto stepped down in 1998, a short period of democratisation followed, dubbed the *reformasi* period. But the opening up of society also gave radical Islamic groups greater scope to propagate their views. Nowadays, the pressure on women to be obedient wives is stressed again, overlaid by a religious insistence on women being *sholehah*, that is, pious (Wieringa 2015b). Although very few women wore a *jilbab* to cover their hair in the early 1970s, even in staunchly Muslim areas, now most Muslim women wear this 'traditional' Muslim garb.

Before *reformasi*, heteronormativity was so hegemonic that there was no need for overt expressions of homophobia. In the post-colonial period, and especially after 1965, Indonesia developed amnesia about its past, forgetting about the transgender practices and same-sex acts recorded in the colonial period and reinventing itself as a country that had always been strongly heterosexual (Wieringa 2009). It is relevant to note here that the concepts of *gay* and *lesbi* in Indonesia do not have their origins in local culture; they are foreign-derived terms, emerging during the New Order (see Chapter 8 of this volume by Wijaya).

This short account of the history of same-sex practices may have little direct relevance for *gay* and *lesbi* in the present day, as it does not offer identities or role models that they can immediately emulate. Nevertheless, it does help to disprove the claim that same-sex and transgender practices are a foreign import. Moreover, the realisation that they have a history may help to infuse the lives of *gay* and *lesbi* Indonesians with meaning, as several male-oriented *lesbi* exclaimed when I introduced them to the statues of the half-male, half-female Hindu god Ardhanari in the National

Museum in Jakarta.[7] When they decided to set up their own organisation in 2005, they named it the Ardhanary Institute after this god.

Though homophobia can be considered a legacy of colonialism, Al-Hussein's optimistic remarks about Indonesia's supposedly LGBT-tolerant past cannot be corroborated. Heteronormativity has been dominant for so long that homophobia remained latent in the community. The tales of early Western travellers to Indonesia who observed young men walking hand in hand without attracting disapproval—something that was rare in the West until recently—may have contributed to this optimistic picture of LGBT tolerance. But young men in Indonesia could hold hands without attracting criticism precisely because no one suspected them of same-sex intimacy—let alone suspected that two women might be more than just close friends.

GROWING VISIBILITY: TOWARDS SEXUAL RIGHTS

Before a campaign for sexual rights commenced in the early *reformasi* period, gay men used to hang out in public places, both to meet friends and to find sex partners. In this way they would be less visible, as they would be mixing with both homosexual and heterosexual men. Unmarried women never had that option; they were restricted to their own friendship circles. In Jakarta more men than women could be found in the few discos that opened from the late 1970s (Boellstorff 2005; Wieringa 1987). When malls appeared, middle-class gays, both men and women, began to congregate there. Other common meeting places were the hairdressing salons run by *waria* and the boarding houses (*rumah kos*) where men and women were housed separately in order to avoid mixing of the sexes—which was frowned upon more than same-sex fraternisation. Until the internet became available, most Indonesians were unaware of the global context of same-sex desires and practices. When I first met a group of *lesbi* in Jakarta in 1982, they did not know that there were also lesbians in Amsterdam.

Indonesia's first gay organisation, Lambda Indonesia, was set up in 1982 in Surabaya by Dede Oetomo. Its members published a magazine and organised various LGBT events. Later Lambda Indonesia evolved into the well-known group GAYa Nusantara, which has received substantial HIV/AIDS funding over the years. LGBT organising received a boost

---

7 By 'male-oriented *lesbi'*, I mean persons who may or may not be FTM transgender, but who commonly refer to themselves as 'women with a male soul'. The term includes *butchi* (from the English word 'butch'), *tomboi, cowok* and *sentul*.

from international discourses on sexuality and LGBT rights in 1994 when the International Conference on Population and Development in Cairo emphasised the importance of sexual rights. In 1998 Indonesia's first mass organisation for feminists, the Indonesian Women's Coalition (Koalisi Perempuan Indonesia, KPI), was established. It made room for sexual minorities in spite of strong protests from conservative Muslim women. In 2005, the women advocating on behalf of sexual minorities left KPI to set up their own organisation, the Ardhanary Institute.

When foreign funding to support LGBT issues became available in the early 2000s, various other LGBT organisations were established and a process of professionalisation set in. Activists attended international conferences, set up websites, organised trainings, appeared on talk shows and altogether became more visible and vocal. Their growing presence in the public sphere, coupled with a conservative, illiberal turn in society and the government, ultimately led to a backlash that started in earnest in late 2015. Access to the latest theories on LGBT issues, the formulation of human rights in relation to sexual orientation in the Yogyakarta Principles (in 2007), the revisions to the influential *Diagnostic and Statistical Manual of Mental Disorders* (in 1973) and to the World Health Organization's *International Statistical Classification of Diseases* (in 1990) to declassify homosexuality as a disease—all had apparently not diminished the homophobic biases in society. Activist groups continued to claim the human rights they were entitled to under the Yogyakarta Principles and various other conventions and human rights documents the Indonesian government had signed or ratified. Much of the print media, however, continued to run negative stories on homosexuality that portrayed it as an illness, a crime, a sin or a mental disease, or all of the above.

A 'RED SCARE' AND A HOMOPHOBIC BACKLASH

Indonesia's second sexual moral panic began in late 2015, when conservatives began to whip up fear about communism and homosexuality. Political motivations, and the growing strength of hardline Muslim groups, played a major role in both cases. The attacks peaked in 2017 with aggressive mass demonstrations demanding the jailing of the popular Christian-Chinese governor of Jakarta, Basuki Tjahaja Purnama—better known as Ahok—who was up for re-election. Trumped-up charges of blasphemy saw the governor convicted and jailed for two years; he also lost the gubernatorial election. Whereas the country's first sexual moral panic had used propaganda linking socialist women with acts of heterosexual perversion to incite violence against communists, the present panic has whipped up fear by associating communism with homosexuality. I begin by discussing the background of the first sexual moral panic, that of 1965–66.

In the early hours of 1 October 1965, soldiers taking part in what was alleged to be a coup attempt against President Sukarno abducted six generals and a lieutenant. Three of the generals were killed immediately and the others were murdered in a field near the suburb of Lubang Buaya in Jakarta (Robinson 2018; Roosa 2006). General Suharto quickly crushed the action and then organised a genocide of still-unknown dimensions. His troops imprisoned hundreds of thousands of people and within a year the general had managed to seize power from President Sukarno. The active role of Suharto, his advisors and the military, and the part of the CIA and other intelligence services in helping the army to build a mass base prior to 1965, has been conclusively documented (Melvin 2018; Scott 1985; Simpson 2008; Suroso 2013).

This creeping but very violent and successful takeover of government, resulting in the transfer of power from President Sukarno to General Suharto, was accompanied by a propaganda campaign to incite Muslim, Christian and other conservative mass organisations to participate in the mass killings.[8] Suharto blamed the entire Indonesian Communist Party (Partai Komunis Indonesia, PKI) and its supporters for masterminding the alleged attempted coup, and needed to persuade his fellow Indonesians of their culpability. He claimed, falsely, that PKI and its supporters were opposed to religion and the national philosophy of Pancasila (Herlambang 2013; McGregor 2007; Wieringa and Katjasungkana 2018). Through the media, which he controlled, he also accused young girls of around 13–14 years of age from various PKI-affiliated organisations of seducing the generals by performing, unclothed, a lurid dance, the Fragrant Flower Dance, while singing the 'communist' song *Genjer-Genjer*. The girls had then castrated the generals and gouged out their eyes. This story was concocted to link PKI and progressive, politically active women with unspeakable sexual perversions, and to portray the party and its mass organisations as inhuman, primitive (*biadab*) and evil.

This campaign of absurd lies was so successful that, more than 50 years later, the now-elderly women survivors of the New Order's mass incarceration of PKI members and sympathisers, many of whom suffered repeated sexual abuse as inmates, are still stigmatised. Moreover, the phobia about communism remains so strong that today's younger feminist activists are often accused of being communists, or of being the 'new Gerwani'. In fact, an autopsy proved that the dead generals were not sexually mutilated, although few Indonesians are aware of this (Anderson 1987).

---

8 For details of this media campaign, see Wieringa (2002, 2003).

In 2015, events marking the 50th anniversary of the 1965 genocide set off a new wave of hysteria about communism. The International People's Tribunal on 1965 Crimes Against Humanity in Indonesia (IPT 1965) was held in The Hague in November 2015. The tribunal gave new impetus to efforts to establish the truth about what happened (Wieringa, Melvin and Pohlman 2019). The judges found that Indonesia was guilty of committing crimes against humanity on nine counts after 1 October 1965 and that those crimes fell within the definition of genocide. Their provisional conclusions were not well received by the Indonesian government, however. In April 2016 the then coordinating minister for politics, law and security, Luhut Panjaitan, organised his own symposium on the events of 1965–66, claiming that it was denigrating to Indonesia that such a tribunal had been held in the Netherlands (Gumilang 2016). Conservative generals appearing at the symposium upheld the New Order mantra that PKI had posed, and indeed continued to pose, a threat to national stability.

Coinciding with the rise in anti-communist sentiment, in late 2015 and early 2016 a wave of hostile, anti-LGBT sentiment hit the press, fuelled by homophobic statements issued by high-level political figures that violated the rights of LGBT persons to freedom of expression, privacy and freedom of assembly. This began as a campaign to ban LGBT organisations from Indonesian campuses before turning into broader condemnation of LGBT groups in general. The first university to prohibit a discussion of LGBT rights was Diponegoro University in Semarang, on 13 November 2015 (Sinuko 2015). On 24 January 2016, the rector of the prestigious University of Indonesia denied the Support Group and Resource Center on Gender and Sexuality Studies a presence on campus. The higher-education minister, Muhammad Nasir, approved, opining that 'the presence of an LGBT group on campus harms the morality of the people' (Wijanarko 2016).

Political parties joined the chorus, including the National Awakening Party (Partai Kebangkitan Bangsa, PKB), a moderate Muslim party associated with the late president, Abdurrahman Wahid, who was known for his commitment to diversity and pluralism. The party decided that although the rights of LGBT people as individuals should be protected, this did not extend to allowing same-sex marriage. Based on 'Eastern and religious values', and despite reaffirming its commitment to pluralism, the party agreed that LGBT groups should be banned from universities. This stance was surprising given that Indonesian LGBT groups had never raised the issue of same-sex marriage. It appears, therefore, that PKB's attitude was informed more by the universal struggle for LGBT rights than by anything that was happening in Indonesia (Salim and Parlina 2016). On 24 January 2016, the chair of the People's Consultative Assembly (Majelis Permusyawaratan Rakyat, MPR), Zulkifli Hasan, called for homosexuality to be banned, arguing that it did not 'fit with the culture of

Indonesia'. Interestingly, the minister of religion, Lukman Hakim Saifuddin, took a more conciliatory approach; he called on Indonesians not to expel LGBT people from society, while conceding that homosexuality was an 'illness' (Wijaya 2016).

On 5 February 2016, the National Commission for Human Rights urged public officials to stop making comments that infringed the human rights of, and incited violence towards, the LGBT community. It also called on law enforcement agencies to take action to curb anti-LGBT abuse perpetrated by community organisations and individuals. The commission referred to the need to uphold the Yogyakarta Principles and the provisions of the only two government regulations that protected the rights of LGBT groups: Ministry of Social Affairs Regulation No. 8/2012 on Minority Groups; and Ministry of Home Affairs Regulation No. 27/2014 on Guidelines for Regional Development in 2015, which was inclusive of gays, transsexuals and lesbians (Yosephine 2016). Few people listened. In March 2016 the Indonesian Psychiatrists Association classified homosexuality as a mental illness, defying the broad international scientific consensus rejecting such classification (Sundari 2016). In February 2017, the mental health director at the Ministry of Health declared that LGBT people suffered from psychiatric disorders (Westcott 2018).

The same former generals who had been issuing warnings about a communist threat featured in the anti-LGBT campaign. They included defence minister Ryamizard Ryacudu, who declared in February 2016 that 'the emergence of a pro-LGBT movement among Indonesia's youth poses a larger threat than nuclear warfare' (Tempo 2016). Although this was clearly a preposterous statement, he was not alone in believing that the LGBT community undermined the nation's youth and imperilled national security (Cook 2016).

The minister for social affairs, Khofifah Indar Parawansa, suggested that LGBT people could be 'cured', just as drug users could be, by placing them in water of around 85 degrees Celsius infused with spices, as she had witnessed at a rehabilitation centre in Purbalingga (Rezkisari 2016). Other proposed conversion therapies included the widely touted *ruqyah* method, in which evil spirits (*roh jahat*) were driven out of a person using prayer and other Islamic practices (Tuasikal 2016). In 2016, the government of Aceh announced that anybody belonging to the LGBT community would be caned (Jakarta Post 2016b). In January 2018, 12 transgender women were shaved and stripped during a raid on salons in Aceh (Westcott 2018).

Major donors to the LGBT community, such as the Ford Foundation and the United Nations Development Programme (UNDP), have been forced to halt their LGBT-related programs in Indonesia. At a time when overtly homophobic militias such as the Islamic Defenders Front (Front Pembela Islam, FPI) are riding high after taking a leading role in the anti-Ahok rallies, the future for LGBT people in Indonesia looks bleak. The state, which should defend minorities, has instead turned a blind eye to violations of the basic rights of its LGBT citizens.

The effects have been felt all over the country. In February 2018, the municipality of Depok announced it would set up a taskforce, including police officers and religious leaders, to 'anticipate the spread of LGBT' among young people (Jakarta Post 2018; Smith 2018). In many parts of the country, police have conducted raids on the places where LGBT people congregate or live, targeting *waria* and masculine-identified lesbians in particular, as they are the most visible members of the LGBT community (Topsfield 2017). Another effect of the crackdown has been to prevent LGBT people from expressing themselves openly online and make it difficult for them to conduct seminars or trainings. This has had a dampening effect on their ability to provide information on safe sex, reproductive rights and sexual health to vulnerable communities (Haynes 2018).

CREEPING CRIMINALISATION

The influence of conservative Islamic thought began to rise in the late 1970s and accelerated after *reformasi* (Buehler 2016; Kersten 2015). It has inspired a proliferation of local government regulations since regional autonomy was put into effect in 2001, many of them targeting same-sex practices. Even when these regulations were found to violate articles in the Constitution or in other laws, the responsible national authorities did nothing to force their retraction (Katjasungkana and Wieringa 2016).

Law No. 44/2008 on Pornography was the first national law to contain homophobic provisions; same-sex practices were called 'deviant behaviour' and the community was exhorted to report such behaviour. This process of creeping criminalisation of homosexuality was fanned by the conservative Indonesian Council of Religious Scholars (Majelis Ulama Indonesia, MUI), Indonesia's top clerical body. Though the *fatwa* of this council have no legal standing, some have been considered binding by the courts, as Lindsey argues in Chapter 3 of this volume. On 4 March 2016, MUI issued a *fatwa* stating that same-sex acts were a sin that should be punished by caning or even death. In an apparent contradiction, the *fatwa* also stated that homosexuality was a serious disease that, like most other illnesses, could be cured (Kine 2015).

Political leaders have also used hate speech to press for legal restrictions on same-sex practices. Hidayat Nur Wahid, the deputy speaker of the MPR and a Prosperous Justice Party (Partai Keadilan Sejahtera, PKS) politician, warned that communists and LGBT people threatened to undermine the ideology that was the very basis of the state: the Pancasila

(Riau Daily 2016). On another occasion, he reminded President Jokowi that even Russia, a communist country, had taken steps against LGBT people and organisations. Indonesia, he felt, should do the same, because:

> LGBT people can be classified as waging an asymmetrical war, the kind of war that tries to influence people with the goal of destroying the moral foundation of society [...] It is a low-cost war, and therefore asymmetric. It is not a physical war [...] but when the morality of the people is destroyed, the country will have no morality any more, no vision for the future; its glorious ideals will be destroyed so that the country collapses (Risfil 2016).

In a similar vein, the secretary-general of the People's Conscience Party (Partai Hati Nurani Rakyat, Hanura), Berliana Kartakusumah, told parliament on 4 March 2016 that 'LGBT people must be banned, like we banned communism and drug trafficking' (Jakarta Post 2016a).

The Indonesian Broadcasting Commission announced restrictions on the portrayal of LGBT people on television in March 2016. This immediately affected *waria* TV actors in particular. The practice of *waria* portraying comical characters in several popular TV shows was based on stereotypes but it was also good-humoured and gave *waria* dancers and singers an opportunity to demonstrate their skills to a wide public and to earn a decent income.

In response to groups calling for protection of children who are supposedly at risk, the Ministry of Information is developing a cyber-security bill that will reportedly ban LGBT websites. In this respect, the ministry appears to be drawing inspiration from China, which has imposed strict controls on the cyber-content its population is allowed to access, and from Russia, which has promulgated anti-LGBT legislation. Though communism is reviled in Indonesia and has been banned since 1966, ironically both Russia and China are held up as models for Indonesia to follow in curbing the freedom of expression and organisation of LGBT people.

The content of any proposed anti-LGBT legislation is still unclear. In March 2016, Hanura called for a specific law to curb the presence of members of the LGBT community, and stated that 'the law should provide for sanctions, rehabilitation and restrictions on LGBT activities' (Singgih 2016). The political parties that share this view do not form a majority in parliament, but that does not mean that such statements should not be taken seriously. For all kinds of opportunistic political reasons, other parties could well decide to support an anti-LGBT law if it were put to a vote.

Although the virulent anti-LGBT scare campaign that engulfed Indonesia in early 2016 had died down by the end of May, conservative groups continued to stir up hatred by proposing changes to the Criminal Code that would criminalise homosexuality (see also Chapter 3 by Lindsey, Chapter 4 by Butt and Chapter 8 by Wijaya in this volume). A group of 12 academics from the Family Love Alliance (Aliansi Cinta Keluarga,

AILA) petitioned Indonesia's highest court, the Constitutional Court, to review three articles in the Criminal Code that it claimed violated the Constitution. The article of chief interest here is Article 292, the Dutch-era law criminalising same-sex relations between an adult and a minor (and long since revoked in the Netherlands). The applicants argued that this article violated the religious values that were the moral foundation of the Constitution and the Indonesian state. They proposed that the phrase 'between an adult and a minor' should be deleted to make all forms of homosexuality illegal, regardless of age and consent, and suggested that such an offence should be punishable by up to five years in jail. The applicants also wanted Article 284 of the Criminal Code to be revised to ban all sex outside marriage, not just infidelity to a marriage partner. In December 2017 the court ruled that changes to the Criminal Code were a matter for parliament, which had already begun to discuss revisions to the Criminal Code (see Chapter 3 by Lindsey in this volume). Amidst growing public anxiety about the draconian nature of some of the proposed changes, parliament has sent the draft bill on the Criminal Code back for redrafting. At the time of writing it was unclear when debate in parliament on the criminalisation of homosexuality would resume.

COMPARING THE ANTI-COMMUNIST AND ANTI-LGBT CAMPAIGNS

Whereas communists were some of the most despised people in Indonesia during the New Order, today that unenviable position seems to be occupied by LGBT persons. A survey conducted in April 2016 by the Indonesian Survey Institute (Lembaga Survei Indonesia, LSI) and the Wahid Institute found that the LGBT community was the minority group most disliked by Muslim people in Indonesia. The results showed that 26.1 per cent disliked LGBT people, 16.7 per cent communists and 10.6 per cent Jews (Jong 2016).[9] The last finding is interesting considering that there are very few Jews in Indonesia.

Yenny Wahid, the daughter of former president Abdurrahman Wahid and the director of the Wahid Institute, explained that during the month in which the survey was conducted, 'the LGBT issue went viral on social media; therefore, the respondents were influenced to name LGBT people as the most disliked group'. In 2018 a survey by Saiful Mujani Research and Consulting found that 87.6 per cent of respondents who were aware

9   The survey involved 1,520 respondents across all 34 provinces. All respondents were Muslim, and over the age of 17 and/or married. The survey used a random sampling method with a 2.6 per cent margin of error.

of the term 'LGBT' believed that LGBT people posed a threat to the nation (Coconuts 2018).

As we have seen, hate-mongering against communists inspired the 1965 sexual slander against Gerwani, and this established a pattern in which 'deviant' sexuality came to be viewed as a threat to the nation. To further its own political interests, the New Order regime imposed uniformity on society, including of 'traditional' gender and sexuality norms. The effect of a tyrannical system in which human rights were ignored was to defile the diverse and vibrant culture of Indonesia. After decades of indoctrination and propaganda, and in the gap left by the killing or silencing of thousands of teachers and artists who could be linked to LEKRA, a climate of intellectual apathy took hold, breeding the kind of warped reasoning that still characterises much of the present-day campaigns against communism and homosexuality. From the mid-New Order period onward, and especially during *reformasi*, growing Islamic conservatism has fuelled anti-LGBT views in much of society, including the educated middle class.[10] These conservative, patriarchal, religious ways of thinking have come to dominate the country's academic and religious institutions.

In both the anti-communist and anti-LGBT campaigns, it is apparent that there is a widespread view in society that the nation has to be defended against threats to its integrity and morality, defined as attacks on the Pancasila and Islam. In both cases science is distorted to confuse homosexuality with paedophilia and contagion, and sexual orientation (homosexuality) with behaviour. LGBT people are viewed with a 'pornographic gaze' as being obsessed with anal sex (as if they were the only ones to engage in this practice). Contemporary literature perpetuates the view that a subversive underground communist movement continues to exist in Indonesia, while at the same time ignoring the history of violence of hardline Islamic groups, or absolving them from blame (Wieringa and Katjasungkana 2018). Defenders of human, women's and sexual rights who do not specifically proclaim (mainstream) religious values are seen by conservative Muslims as 'liberals' who do not uphold Islamic values but, instead, spread LGBT propaganda and communist ideas.

Another effect of these parallel and almost simultaneous campaigns has been to strengthen the discrimination experienced by both LGBT groups and victims of the 1965 genocide. As I have explained, the LGBT community has become linked in the public mind with communism, while the victims of the 1965 genocide, already associated with heterosexual perversion, have become tainted with the stigma of homosexuality. Both groups are portrayed as enemies of the nation, treacherously undermining the

---

10 For more on middle-class religious conservatism, see Chapter 9 by Mietzner and Muhtadi in this volume.

state's morality and weakening its vigilance. I have seen banners held aloft during demonstrations that proclaimed that both LGBT and PKI must be 'wiped from the earth' (*dibumihanguskan*). This struggle for the soul of the nation is intended to produce an obedient, religious society from which all 'abnormal' elements have been erased. This is clearly in the interest of the army, which stands to gain both politically and economically from a quiescent society.[11] The simultaneous stirring up of communist phobia and homophobia has produced a toxic mix of Indonesian exceptionalism, in which globally accepted standards of human, women's and sexual rights are ignored, resulting in humiliation, fear, social exclusion and economic distress for countless Indonesian citizens.[12] As in 1965–66, the army has emerged victorious whereas democracy has suffered. Unlike in 1965–66, the victory is shared with hardline Muslim groups.

I maintain that it is not so much the demand for rights that has antagonised the adversaries of the LGBT community. More upsetting to conservatives has been the gradual breakdown of the model of belonging in which same-sex people were expected to blend in with the hetero-normative world, for example by accepting (if temporarily) the obligation to marry or by accepting that they had an inferior status in society. Their accommodation to the tenets of heteronormativity reinforced the contemporary regime of hegemonic heteronormativity. At the same time, the wider circulation of terms like *gay* and *lesbi* drew attention to the isolated *wandu* or *banci* living in the countryside and to the same-sex couples living hitherto-inconspicuous lives in neighbourhoods or boarding houses, leading to their outing and in some cases eviction. Public debates on homosexuality on television, in the print media or on social media gave Islamic clerics and other conservatives a platform to argue that LGBT persons were living an immoral lifestyle. Thus, the increased visibility of LGBT people did not lead to greater acceptance but rather turned public opinion against them.

A similar phenomenon could be observed when the National Commission for Human Rights first exposed the crimes against humanity committed by the state in 1965–66 (in 2012) and the IPT 1965 report then

---

11 Although the army is not as powerful as it was during the New Order, it still stands to receive economic perquisites from its territorial structure, which allows it to exert a strong influence on local governments down to the village level. In addition, the absurd claim that the LGBT community is waging a proxy war on the nation allows the army to pose as the defender of the nation, in the absence of external enemies. This in turn is used as an argument to maintain the army budget.

12 Indonesia is of course not alone in this regard. The debate on so called 'Asian values' is premised on the same line of thinking.

concluded that the massacres of 1965–66 counted as a genocide (in 2016). The increased visibility of the victims and the calls for truth finding and an end to impunity for the perpetrators appear only to have infuriated conservative politicians, generals and religious leaders, rather than causing them to reconsider their positions.

CONCLUSION

The notion that Indonesia has always been relatively tolerant of homosexuality is a misguided one. *Waria* have indeed always been publicly visible, but they have never been accepted as full members of society. Similarly, the phobia in Indonesian politics about communism that emerged after the 1965 genocide has never died down. Indonesia is considered one of the world's most democratic Muslim-majority countries. The country's phobias about communism and homosexuality, however, are not temporary aberrations but rather structural elements of its social and political cultures. At present, human rights defenders are seen as providing cover for both LGBT groups and a revived PKI. Ultimately, the double-edged campaign against them is about how the Indonesian nation imagines itself and whether it is prepared to allow space for LGBT people and their organisations, and for people fighting for social justice.

REFERENCES

Aldrich, R. (2002) *Colonialism and Homosexuality*, Routledge, London.
Allard, T., and A.B. Da Costa (2017) '"Red scare" puts pressure on Indonesian president', *Reuters*, 28 September.
Anderson, B. (1987) 'How did the generals die?', *Indonesia* 43: 109–34.
Blackwood, E. (2005) 'Gender transgression in colonial and post-colonial Indonesia', *Journal of Asian Studies* 64(4): 849–79.
Blackwood, E. (2010) *Falling into the Lesbi World*, University of Hawai'i Press, Honolulu
Boellstorff, T. (2005) *The Gay Archipelago: Sexuality and Nation in Indonesia*, Princeton University Press, Princeton and Oxford.
Boellstorff, T. (2007) 'Warias, national transvestites', in T. Boellstorff, *A Coincidence of Desires*, Duke University Press, Durham: 78–114.
Buehler, M. (2016) *The Politics of Shari'a Law: Islamist Activists and the State in Democratic Indonesia*, Cambridge University Press, Cambridge.
Coconuts (2018) '87.6% of Indonesians see LGBT as a threat, but slim majority say they deserve right to life and protection: survey', *Coconuts*, 25 January.
Cook, E. (2016) 'There's never been a harder time to be gay in Indonesia', *Vice*, 26 April.
Davies, S.G. (2010) *Gender Diversity in Indonesia: Sexuality, Islam and Queer Selves*, Routledge, London and New York.

Ediati, A. (2014) 'Disorders of sex development in Indonesia', PhD thesis, Erasmus University, Rotterdam. https://repub.eur.nl/pub/50331/140115_Ediati-Anna-stasia-BEWERKT.pdf

Gouda, F. (1995) *Dutch Culture Overseas: Colonial Practice in the Netherlands Indies, 1900–1942*, Amsterdam University Press, Amsterdam.

Gumilang, P. (2016) 'Menko Luhut: pengadilan tragedi 1965 di Belanda, memalu-kan!', *CNN Indonesia*, 21 April.

Haynes, S. (2018) 'Indonesia's crackdown on LGBT rights is fueling an HIV epidemic, rights group warns', *Time*, 2 July.

Hegarty, B. (2017) 'Becoming incomplete: the transgender body and national modernity in New Order Indonesia (1967–1998)', PhD thesis, Australian National University, Canberra.

Herlambang, W. (2013) *Kekerasan Budaya Pasca 1965: Bagaimana Orde Baru Melegitimasi Anti-komunisme melalui Sastra dan Film*, Galang Press, Yogyakarta.

Jakarta Post (2016a) 'Poor knowledge leads to prolonged discrimination against LGBT people', *Jakarta Post*, 14 March.

Jakarta Post (2016b) 'Aceh clamps down on LGBT people, threatens caning', *Jakarta Post*, 21 March.

Jakarta Post (2018) 'Anti-LGBT team established in Depok', *Jakarta Post*, 19 February.

Jong, H.N. (2016) 'LGBT community most disliked by Indonesian Muslims: survey', *Jakarta Post*, 1 August.

Katjasungkana, N., and S.E. Wieringa (2003) 'Sexual politics and reproductive rights in Indonesia', *Development* 46(2): 63–7.

Katjasungkana, N. and S.E. Wieringa (2016) *Creeping Criminalisation of Women's and LGBTI Rights*, OutRight, New York NY.

Kersten, C. (2015) *Islam in Indonesia: The Contest for Society, Ideas and Values*, Hurst & Company, London.

Khumaini, A. (2014) 'Di Ponorogo ada gemblak, di pesantren ada mairil', *Merdeka. com*, 11 May.

Kine, P. (2015) 'Dispatches: challenging Indonesia's intolerant Muslim clerics', *Human Rights Watch*, 17 March.

Lathief, H. (2004) *Bissu: Pergulatan dan Peranannya di Masyarakat Bugis*, Desantara, Depok.

McGregor, K. (2007) *History in Uniform: Military Ideology and the Construction of Indonesia's Past*, National University of Singapore Press, Singapore.

Melvin, J. (2018) *The Army and the Indonesian Genocide: Mechanics of Mass Murder*, Routledge, London.

Murtagh, B. (2013) *Genders and Sexualities in Indonesian Cinema: Constructing Gay, Lesbi and Waria Identities on Screen*, Routledge, London.

Peletz, M.G. (2009) *Gender Pluralism: Southeast Asia since Early Modern Times*, Routledge, London.

Pelras C. (1996) *The Bugis*, Blackwell Publishers, Oxford.

Rezkisari, I. (2016) 'Menteri Khofifah klarifikasi soal ingin merebus LGBT', *Republika*, 14 March.

Riau Daily (2016) 'Kata wakil ketua MPR: LGBT langgar sila pertama', *RiauDaily. com*, 23 February.

Risfil, A. (2016) 'MPR: Rusia, negara komunis saja, gerah dengan perilaku LGBT', *Teropongsenayan.com*, 20 March.

Robinson, G. (2018) *The Killing Season: A History of the Indonesian Massacres, 1965–1966*, Princeton University Press, Princeton NJ.

Roosa, J. (2006) *Pretext for Mass Murder: The September 30th Movement & Suharto's Coup d'État in Indonesia*, University of Wisconsin Press, Madison WI.

Salim, T., and I. Parlina (2016) 'NU, PKB take tough stance against LGBT community', *Jakarta Post*, 6 February.

Scott, P.D. (1985) 'The United States and the overthrow of Sukarno, 1967–1967', *Pacific Affairs* 58(2): 239–64.

Simpson, B. (2008) *Economists with Guns: Authoritarian Development and US–Indonesian Relations 1960–1968*, Stanford University Press, Stanford CA.

Singgih, V.P. (2016) 'Hanura calls for law against LGBT people', *Jakarta Post*, 21 March.

Sinuko, D. (2015) 'Universitas Diponegoro tolak diskusi soal gay', *CNN Indonesia*, 13 November.

Smith, N. (2018) 'LGBT "taskforce" in Indonesian city adds to fears of gay rights crackdown', *The Telegraph*, 20 February.

Sugianto, L. (2015) *Eksistensi Calalai dalam Budaya Sulawesi Selatan*, Ardhanary Institute, Jakarta.

Sundari, E.K. (2016) 'Indonesia's obligation to protect the rights of all citizens', *Jakarta Post*, 12 March.

Suroso, S. (2013) *Akar dan Dalang: Pembantaian Manusia tak Berdosa dan Penggulingan Bung Karno*, Ultimus, Bandung.

Tempo (2016) 'Minister: LGBT movement more dangerous than nuclear warfare', *Tempo.co*, 23 February.

Topsfield, J. (2017) 'Suspicion that LGBT rights are "Western agenda" fuels Indonesian crackdown', *Sydney Morning Herald*, 21 October.

Tuasikal, R. (2016) 'Ruqyah LGBT, Arus Pelangi: itu seperti harapan kosong', *KBR*, 15 March.

Westcott, B. (2018) 'Fear and horror among Indonesia's LGBT community as gay sex ban looms', *CNN*, 26 February.

Wieringa, S.E. (1987) *Uw Toegenegen Dora D. Reisbrieven*, Furie, Amsterdam.

Wieringa, S.E. (2002) *Sexual Politics in Indonesia*, Palgrave Macmillan, London.

Wieringa, S.E. (2003) 'The birth of the New Order state in Indonesia: sexual politics and nationalism', *Journal of Women's History* 15(1): 70–92.

Wieringa, S.E. (2007) '"If there is no feeling …" The dilemma between silence and coming out in a working class butch/fem community in Jakarta', in M. Padilla, J. Hirsch, M. Muñoz-Laboy, R.E. Sember and R.G. Parker (eds) *Love and Globalisation: Transformations of Intimacy in the Contemporary World*, Vanderbilt University Press, Nashville TN: 70–93.

Wieringa, S.E. (2009) 'Postcolonial amnesia: sexual moral panics, memory and imperial power', in G. Herdt (ed.) *Moral Panics, Sex Panics: Fear and the Fight over Sexual Rights*, New York University Press, New York NY: 205–34.

Wieringa, S.E. (2010) 'Gender variance in Asia: discursive contestation and legal implications', *Journal of Gender, Technology and Development* 14(2): 143–72.

Wieringa, S.E. (2015a) *Heteronormativity, Passionate Aesthetics and Symbolic Subversion in Asia*, Sussex Academic Publishers, Eastbourne.

Wieringa, S.E. (2015b) 'Gender harmony and the happy family: Islam, gender and sexuality in post-*reformasi* Indonesia', *South East Asia Research* 23(1): 5–27.

Wieringa, S.E. and N. Katjasungkana (2018) *Propaganda and the Genocide in Indonesia: Imagined Evil*, Routledge, London.

Wieringa, S.E., J. Melvin and A. Pohlman (2019) *The International People's Tribunal for 1965 and the Indonesian Genocide*, Routledge, London.

Wijanarko, B. (2016) 'Menristek sebut LGBT tak dibolehkan masuk kampus', *CNN Indonesia*, 23 January.

Wijaya, C.A. (2016) 'Don't expel LGBT people from society: minister', *Jakarta Post*, 4 March.

Wilson, I. (1999) '*Reog* Ponorogo: spirituality, sexuality and power in a Javanese performance tradition', *Intersections: Gender History and Culture in the Asian Context*, Issue 2. http://intersections.anu.edu.au/issue2/Warok.html

Yosephine, L. (2016) 'Komnas HAM slams vilification of LGBT by officials', *Jakarta Post*, 5 February.

8 Localising queer identities: queer activisms and national belonging in Indonesia

Hendri Yulius Wijaya

In 2016, lesbian, gay, bisexual and transgender (LGBT) issues attracted national attention. Between January and May of that year, government ministers, senior officials, politicians, civil society organisations and religious leaders publicly condemned homosexuality, associating it primarily with potential threats to the nation-state because of its supposed immorality, its 'sins against nature' and its subversion of Indonesian culture. Some went so far as to say that LGBT people were mentally ill, while others accused homosexuals of being part of a 'proxy war' against Indonesia by Western countries (Wijaya 2017a). In one bizarre case, homosexual tendencies were even declared to be the result of overconsumption of instant noodles (TribunJogja 2016). While such pronouncements might cause laughter, it has also become obvious that non-heterosexual Indonesians are increasingly being excluded from the national identity and being vilified solely on the basis of their sexual non-normativities.

The outcomes of this anti-LGBT panic are twofold. First, as the term 'LGBT' has circulated with unprecedented frequency in the Indonesian press, it has become part of the everyday vernacular of Indonesians, usually with strongly negative connotations. Second, among the costs of this increased visibility of LGBT issues in the public sphere are the attempts of socially conservative Islamic groups to criminalise consensual same-sex relations and extramarital sex under the guise of protecting the morality of the younger generation. In 2016, for example, an Islamic organisation called the Family Love Alliance (Aliansi Cinta Keluarga, AILA) took a case to the Constitutional Court seeking to amend the Criminal Code to outlaw homosexuality (see Chapter 3 by Lindsey and Chapter 4 by Butt).

Although the Constitutional Court rejected that proposal, significant challenges and threats to LGBT communities remain. At the time of writing, one of them was a proposed amendment to the broadcasting law that would ban 'LGBT behaviour' from the media (Wijaya 2017b). Some queer activists are convinced that politicians are deliberately exploiting LGBT issues in order to shore up their public support. Indeed, the very term 'LGBT' has been framed negatively to perpetuate the idea that LGBT people and ideas are foreign to Indonesia and politically and morally threatening. Such politicisation is not exclusive to LGBT issues; rather, as several chapters in this volume attest, various other religious, ethnic and ideological minorities have also been constructed discursively as a menace to the nation-state.

Nevertheless, something important is missing here, and that is the question of Indonesia's queer activisms themselves. Here, the term 'queer activisms' refers to the continuous and organised articulation of Indonesian queer activists' desires, concerns and efforts to eradicate stigma and discrimination through diverse forms of advocacy. I use the plural form to indicate the multiple yet interconnected focuses, strategies and goals of queer activists; and I deliberately use the term 'queer' to express the diversity and sheer number of non-normative genders and sexual identities (gay, LGBT, SOGIE minorities and so on), which, as this chapter will show, shift across time. Some queer activists conduct media advocacy while others aim to change specific policies or laws. One of the main goals of activists is to create a link between queer identities and claims to national belonging. The focus of this chapter is on the strategies activists have used to shape public thinking and how those strategies have changed over time.

Of course, strategies to claim a place in the nation are not the preserve of queer activists alone; they are also central to other minorities, including the Chinese and Orang Rimba communities (see Chapter 11 of this volume by Setijadi and Chapter 13 by Manurung). What has been particular to Indonesia's queer discursive strategies, however, is the refashioning and localisation of transnational sexuality discourses to create a claim to national belonging. In other words, queer activists have adopted transnational notions of sexual and gender identities, but altered them to fit local contexts. In the process, they have had to balance developments in global discourses against the challenges and contingencies of daily life in Indonesia. Recently, for example, queer activists have been using the global discourse of sexual orientation, gender identity and gender expression (SOGIE) to promote a broader view of sexual and gender plurality in Indonesia, and to avoid the term 'LGBT', which has negative connotations in the public mind.

Drawing on historical archives and my own personal engagement with local queer activisms,[1] this chapter will trace the emergence of sexual and gender identities in Indonesia, from gay, to LGBT, to SOGIE minorities.[2] A study of the adoption and reshaping of those identities reveals the strategies of queer activisms and the nature of their encounters with transnational discourses. I will argue that LGBT and, later, SOGIE discourses are inextricably linked to claims of national belonging, and are deployed to forge a sense of community and political allegiance among Indonesian sexual minorities to resist heteronormativity. As Wieringa points out in Chapter 7 of this book, Indonesia has always been a heteronormative society that refuses to recognise people with same-sex desires.

The chapter is divided into three sections, coinciding with shifts in the country's gender and sexual politics. The first section deals with Indonesian gay identity and national belonging in the New Order era (early 1980s to early 1990s); the second covers the HIV/AIDS epidemic, the role of international assistance and the proliferation of sexual identities (early 1990s to early 2000s); and the third discusses the rise of religious conservatism and the construction of a discourse on SOGIE minorities and diversity since the mid-2000s. This division is also informed by the shifts that have taken place in transnational sexuality discourses, which have contributed significantly to the tactics employed by queer activists in each historical period.

GAY IDENTITY AND NATIONAL BELONGING IN THE NEW ORDER PERIOD (1982 TO EARLY 1990s)

A distinct gay identity first emerged in Indonesian public discourse during the New Order era. Although homosexuality was not usually perceived as a threat to the nation at this time, the state's heteronormative family principle and the view that homosexuality was irreconcilable with local cultures were major challenges for gay activists. In response, Indonesia's pioneering gay activists strategically undertook a mission to 'localise' homosexuality by drawing a discursively imagined continuity between indigenous homosexual and transgender practices, on the one hand, and modern gay identity on the other.

---

1 I worked for the United Nations Development Programme's 'Being LGBTI in Indonesia' program from May 2015 to May 2016.
2 In this chapter, I focus mainly on male homosexuality and gay identity. However, as I shall describe, the arrival of the term 'LGBT' in Indonesia in the early 2000s has to some degree enabled activists to speak on behalf of a common LGBT identity, rather than just their own 'gay' identity.

Proliferation of discourses on homosexuality in the public sphere

Non-normative sexualities and genders can readily be located in various indigenous Indonesian cultural practices, but modern gay and lesbian identities appeared in the public discourse only in the late 1970s and early 1980s (Boellstorff 2005). Through occasional reports of homosexuality in the media, Indonesians with same-sex desires began to learn of the possibility of naming and channelling their desires into a solidified identity. One particularly notable event took place in 1981, when national media coverage of a lesbian 'marriage' in Jakarta led to widespread public discussion of gay and lesbian sexuality in Indonesia (Boellstorff 2005: 73).

Such discussions initially focused on stories of unrequited love among 'lower-class' lesbian couples but attention later shifted to middle- and upper-class homosexual men. This kicked off a flourishing debate on gay and lesbian subjects in the media (Boellstorff 2005: 73). Some of the prevailing discourses portrayed homosexuality as an inborn trait that demanded acceptance from society, while others linked homosexuality to psychological problems, particularly dysfunctional family structures, hormonal imbalances and psychological conflicts.[3] A prominent theme was the ways in which homosexuality was understood to result from 'failed sociality'. This terminology pointed to the claim that homosexuality was primarily due to the influence of socialisation processes on a person's sexual development. For instance, same-sex dormitories and all-male Islamic boarding schools (*pesantren*) were said to provide a fertile breeding ground for the development of homosexuality. Unsurprisingly, the view that homosexuality was a result of failed sociality was connected to the understanding of the self in Indonesian society (Howard 1996: 331). Indonesians traditionally understood their individuality to be a divinely inspired destiny to fulfil (heterosexual) familial obligations; therefore, reproductive heterosexuality was widely deemed to be the default setting of an Indonesian person. For this reason, homosexuality was perceived as a social aberration.

Amidst the proliferation of negative views on homosexuality, there were also some more positive narratives of homosexuality in the media. Citing the stories in ancient Greek mythology about supposedly homosexual gods, the reports of homosexuality in the animal world and, equally importantly, Alfred J. Kinsey's highly influential sexology publications, some argued that the phenomenon of homosexuality was as old as civilisation itself (Sybylla Press 1984: 35–41). What was evident in such articles

---

3　For a collection of reports and mentions of homosexuality in the Indonesian press in the early 1980s, see Sybylla Press (1984).

was the strong influence of transnational sexuality discourses from the Western world.

The emergence of discourses around homosexuality produced multiple and contradictory views, signalling what Foucault (1978) termed 'the will to knowledge'. Although homosexuality was still widely perceived as abnormal, with the arrival of a distinct gay identity, individuals with same-sex desires began to find a language to describe their modes of sexual attraction, and to identify themselves as gay or lesbian.

The state's heteronormative family ideology and heterosexually married gay men

Although the coverage of homosexuality in the press enabled Indonesians with same-sex desires to embrace a gay identity, many of them still saw their sexuality as irreconcilable with local cultures and did not seek to defend their rights and identities in the public sphere (Boellstorff 2005). In many cases Indonesian homosexual men led double lives, as both gay and heterosexually married men. Through heterosexual marriage, both gay and lesbian Indonesians could fulfil normative societal ideals while at the same time pursuing private homosexual relationships. In this sense, it could be said that gay and lesbian individuals adopted a Western gay and lesbian identity, but reinterpreted it for an Indonesian socio-cultural context, which was strongly influenced by the state's heteronormative family principle.[4]

The New Order regime came to power in 1966 after a violent purge of members of the Indonesian Communist Party (Partai Komunis Indonesia, PKI) and other left-wing activists and sympathisers. Subsequently, anti-communism became a hallmark of the regime and its ideology, even extending to the fabrication of a myth about sexuality that was used to justify legislation of the state's heteronormative 'family principle' (*asas kekeluargaan*) (Suryakusuma 1996: 102). This myth was based on the assertion that 'communist-affiliated women activists' who engaged in lesbian practices had authorised the torture and mutilation of military generals during the attempted coup of 30 September 1965.[5] Women's sexuality that crossed the boundaries of traditional gender norms was deemed to imperil the nation, leading to the state's discursive construction of the ideal woman as 'wife and mother'. Simultaneously, President Suharto

---

4 Boellstorff (2005: 58–88) introduces the term 'dubbing culture' to refer to the ways in which gay and lesbian Indonesians made sense of, and reconciled, their sexual and national identities.

5 For a discussion of the attempted coup of 30 September 1965 and New Order sexual politics, see Wieringa (2002) and Chapter 7 by Wieringa in this book.

positioned himself as the 'father' of the nation. Rhetorically, the state was governed as a family institution through the deployment of the family principle.

Through the perpetuation of such ideology, the New Order regime attempted to establish the heterosexual family as the basis of the nation-state. In the regime's early years, the state put greater emphasis on policing women's sexuality than on regulating male homosexuality. Women who deviated from the role of wife and mother, as well as unmarried individuals who were sexually active, were deemed to breach national norms based on heterosexual family principles. No wonder, then, that belonging to a heterosexual family became the hallmark of a successful adult citizen. The fact that the globalisation of sexual rights and citizenship had not yet reached Indonesia may also have contributed to the government paying little attention to issues of homosexuality. At this historical juncture, then, the New Order should be perceived as heterosexist rather than homophobic (Wijaya and Davies, forthcoming).

The arrival of a transnational gay identity, in parallel with the deployment of the state's family principle, affected the ways in which gay Indonesians understood their sexuality and citizenship. Many saw their homosexual desires as illness or abnormality, and entered into heterosexual marriages as a way of gaining recognition as successful citizens. There was little to no interest in defending gay rights. As Boell-storff (2005) reminds us, in Indonesia the term 'gay' has become entangled with notions of national identity and other socio-cultural factors, and as such should be understood as an Indonesian term (*gay*), different from the English/American word 'gay' from which it is derived. That is why so many Indonesian gay men enter into heterosexual marriages or live double lives—conducting discreet same-sex relationships while being married to a woman.

Constructing an 'Indonesian' gay identity

As a gay identity carried Western connotations, and pressure to pursue heterosexual marriage was felt keenly by gay Indonesians, local activists strategically attempted to Indonesian-ise gay identity, while encouraging gay men to confidently embrace their homosexuality. The first gay organisation in Indonesia, Lambda Indonesia, was formed in Solo, Central Java, in 1982 by a group of well-educated homosexual men from middle- and upper-class backgrounds. They were committed to increasing social acceptance of homosexuality, reaching out to other homosexual men and, equally importantly, creating political solidarity with transnational gay activisms. Indeed, their connection to Western gay activisms enabled these men to adopt transnational sexuality discourses and refashion them so that they could be reconciled with local cultures, while resisting the pressure to enter heterosexual marriage.

Strongly influenced by the gay liberation movement in the United States, and especially Kinsey's theory that sexuality was marked by plurality and degrees of sexual orientation, one of the founders of Lambda Indonesia, Dede Oetomo, argued that homosexuality was a 'normal activity' that 'must not be made complicated' (Oetomo 1984: 37). As this attempt to normalise homosexuality in Indonesia did not significantly detach it from its Western connotations, Oetomo began the process of localising gay and homosexual identity. This was achieved by drawing a discursive continuity between 'indigenous local homosexual and transgenderism practices' and modern gay identity (Oetomo 1984: 37–8). The male same-sex relations observed in the Reog dance in Ponorogo, East Java, for example, or the cross-dressed performers found in local dances in other parts of Indonesia could be deployed to claim that homosexuality had long been an inherent element of local culture and was therefore compatible with it. Even today, Indonesian activists often deploy this argument to counter rising homophobia, the opponents of which conflate gay identity with decadent Western influence.

This tactical move has proven problematic, however. From an anthropological perspective, Boellstorff (2005: 45) argues that such indigenous practices were more accurately understood as 'ethnolocalised homosexual and transvestite professional subject positions' that could only be found in specific ethnic groups and geographical locations and were usually performed for ritual purposes. He notes, in addition, that these institutionalised practices 'did not [always] absolve the persons [...] from "heterosexual" marriage'.

Despite this incongruence, the imaginary connections between indigenous homosexual and transgender practices and the modern gay subject reveal the ways in which the understanding of local and global is always discursively entangled, and how each is understood in relation to the other. The discursive link between modern homosexuality and indigenous practices produced the argument that 'authentic' Indonesian cultures were actually tolerant towards homosexuality. As a consequence, it could be argued that negative attitudes towards homosexuality were a result of contamination of indigenous cultures by foreign entities, for example, monotheistic religions and bourgeois values (Oetomo-Oen 1982: 16).

Whether this was the truth need not be our focus. What is more important is to understand how a nostalgic fantasy, resulting from the entanglement of the local and the global, was able to generate a productive 'agency' for local activists to foster an attachment between gay identity and national belonging. Echoing such tactical combinations, Oetomo came up with a resolution for Indonesian gay movements: they should restore the traditions of same-sex compassion that were respected in ancient Indonesia, and combine them with the new ideas on gay liberation coming from the West (Oetomo 1982: 8).

HIV/AIDS AND THE CONSTRUCTION OF A 'HEALTHY' GAY IDENTITY (EARLY 1990s TO EARLY 2000s)

From the early 1990s, international humanitarian organisations channelled both technical and financial support to Indonesian gay organisations to help them deal with the sexual and reproductive health issues that were seriously affecting the health and well-being of gay men. The flow of aid and ideas had at least two consequences. First, it spread awareness of the distinctions between gay men, men who have sex with men (MSM) and bisexual men, creating new, clear-cut identities based on sexual desires and practices. Second, based on the rhetoric of public health, gay activists began to draw a correlation between health and self-acceptance of one's homosexual identity.

HIV/AIDS and sexual and reproductive health as international development concerns

Internationally, sexual and reproductive health issues have formed a significant part of population and development programs since the late 1960s. When the AIDS epidemic became a matter of global concern in the 1980s, international organisations active in the area of sexual health began to place greater emphasis on the language of empowerment and participation, and to pressure donor countries to increase their support for efforts to stem the spread of the epidemic (Altman 2001: 73).

The 1994 International Conference on Population and Development in Cairo marked a step forward in making sexuality and reproductive health a focus of global humanitarian attention. As a result, international aid organisations increasingly channelled technical support into such causes, treating sexuality as an important part of human well-being and welfare. It was through such health development programs that Western sexuality discourses were transmitted to non-Western nations, underpinned by notions of sexuality as an inherent aspect of human life, which contributed in turn to the classification of sexual practices and desires according to an individual's sexual identity (Pigg and Adams 2005).[6] Central to this

---

6 Pigg and Adams (2005: 18) argue that health development programs are 'based on taken-for-granted assumptions about bodies being biologically

new trajectory were the ways in which the programs' public health and epidemiological frameworks mapped sexual contacts in relation to specific identities, for example, through 'the use of development models of heterosexual sex and homosexual sex' (Pigg and Adams 2005: 18; see also Patton 2002). Building on this, HIV/AIDS programs in Indonesia made use of labels such as 'sex worker', 'gay' and 'MSM' to identify and target specific groups (Altman 2001: 74). Over time, the number of classifications categorising people according to their sexual practices and desires, and the number of HIV/AIDS organisations catering to those rigidly defined groups, escalated.

In Western countries, the HIV/AIDS epidemic of the 1980s and 1990s brought about a strong collective response and consolidated the identity of gay men. In Indonesia, however, the situation was vastly different, with no significant, solid 'gay community' coming into existence (McNally, Grierson and Hidayana 2015: 204). The first recorded 'HIV incidents' in Indonesia involved 30 *waria* (inadequately translated as 'transgender women') in Jakarta in 1983, while the first official diagnosis of AIDS was made four years later, from an autopsy on a Dutch tourist who had died while visiting Bali (Boellstorff 2009: 356). In these early years, HIV/AIDS was treated as a 'foreign' and 'distant' disease linked to Western countries.[7]

From the 1990s, Indonesian gay organisations began to receive 'transnational funding, generally linked to HIV/AIDS treatment and prevention', albeit on a limited scale (Boellstorff 2005: 143). They used this funding to reach out to gay men and deepen their knowledge of HIV/AIDS and sexuality. The scale of foreign funding rose significantly in the mid-2000s (Alicias-Garen and Jahja 2015: 7–8), leading to a burgeoning number of gay, MSM and *waria* organisations addressing HIV/AIDS issues. Most of the Indonesian government programs established to raise HIV/AIDS awareness were conducted through its family planning campaigns, leaving civil society organisations with little choice but to seek external funding to engage directly with sexuality issues (Blackburn 2004: 160). These organisations worked to provide a range of services, from sex education and reproductive health clinics for adolescents to outreach work among individuals vulnerable to the transmission of HIV and other sexually transmitted diseases. Under the new circumstances, gay organisations

---

sexual; individuals having sexual natures; and certain actions classified as sexual relations'.

7 For a thorough discussion of the HIV/AIDS epidemic as it affected gays in Indonesia, see Oetomo (2001: 169–205). Oetomo shares his experience of attempting to bring awareness of HIV/AIDS into the mainstream in the 1980s. He did not receive a good response from many people, including academics, who still saw AIDS as a 'distant' threat to Indonesians.

recognised the importance of HIV prevention work and saw the strategic use of health as a modality to achieve the broader goals of increasing identity awareness and self-acceptance among gays.

Constructing a 'healthy' gay identity

The classification of sexual practices was deemed a necessary part of attempts to measure HIV transmission risk. This led to a set of sexual acts acquiring a concrete identity, and produced a range of new sexual and gender identities. These included men who like men (*lelaki suka lelaki,* LSL)—the equivalent of men who have sex with men (MSM); men who have sex with *waria* (*lelaki yang berhubungan seks dengan waria*); and bisexual men (*biseksualitas/lelaki biseks*), that is, men who may be heterosexually married and in danger of contracting HIV from their male partners and transmitting it to their wives (Oetomo 2001: 195).

With the introduction of these terms, the choice of sexual partner became the basis for the construction of identities. The introduction of the category of bisexuality, for example, delineated distinct boundaries between 'gay' and 'bisexual' men. This meant that a homosexual male in a heterosexual marriage now fell into the category of bisexuality. He was no longer 'gay'. Put differently, a new identity boundary had been created. However, the category of bisexuality was also fraught with ambivalence, because many gay men entered into heterosexual relations or marriage simply due to societal pressures (Oetomo 2001: 81–91, 191–9). In this respect, the meaning of bisexuality in Indonesia was not as clear-cut as in dominant narratives of sexuality in Western countries, where bisexuality referred to a mixture of heterosexuality and homosexuality in one's sexual orientation and identity.[8]

While the focus on HIV issues thus led to a proliferation of sexual identities, Indonesian activists also linked self-acceptance of homosexuality with individual well-being. This was likely influenced by public health discourses that drew a connection between self-empowerment and well-being. Dede Oetomo captured this notion of public health priorities when he asserted in 1994:

> If a gay man, for example, does not feel himself worthy, his motivation to look after his well-being and his awareness of the risk of HIV transmission will not be high [...] Writing about gays and LSL [...] should not always be about their relation to HIV/AIDS, but also about community development, *increased visibility, and objective education about homosexuality and other alternative sexualities as normal,* which can be expected to empower those living around and among us [emphasis added] (reprinted in Oetomo 2001: 197).

---

8   For a critical discussion of bisexuality see, among others, Storr (1999).

The italicised section of this quotation draws attention to the perceived importance of visibility, acceptance and public recognition of non-normative sexualities. Closeted gay men were considered more vulnerable to HIV infection because it was difficult for activists and health workers to locate them and to educate them on matters of sexual health. Self-confidence was perceived as crucial if individuals were to properly manage their well-being and so reduce the rate of HIV transmission. Information about diverse sexual identities and the importance of social and self-acceptance was often included in training materials for HIV/AIDS outreach workers and gay/HIV activists, allowing knowledge about the existence of diverse sexual identities to circulate even more broadly.

After Lambda Indonesia disbanded in 1986, some of its former members formed GAYa Nusantara, now Indonesia's oldest gay organisation. Through the publication of gay *zines* (bulletins) and other avenues, GAYa Nusantara promoted the concept of a separate and distinct *gay* identity. As part of an effort to detach this identity from heterosexual marriage, and in response to continuing pressure on *gay* men to enter into heterosexual marriages, GAYa Nusantara activists demarcated clear boundaries between homosexuality and heterosexuality.

A 1994 article in the GAYa Nusantara bulletin by 'Dr Sm', for example, classified the varying degrees of homosexual (and perhaps bisexual) desire into three categories: 100 per cent heterosexual; 100 per cent homosexual; and bisexual. The author further divided bisexuality into four categories: 90 per cent hetero and 10 per cent homo; 80 per cent hetero and 20 per cent homo; 70 per cent hetero and 30 per cent homo; and 10 per cent hetero and 90 per cent homo ('Dr Sm' 1994). The use in this article of the terms 'homo' and 'hetero' (and, to some extent, 'bisexual') established concrete lines of distinction between sexual subjects based on an individual's choice of sexual object. With this classification of sexual orientations into clear-cut, unalterable sexual identities, entering into a heterosexual marriage would not release a gay individual from his homosexual desires. In other words, *gay will always be gay*.

THE EMERGING DISCOURSE ON SOGIE MINORITIES AND DIVERSITY (MID-2000s TO THE PRESENT)

The collapse of the New Order regime in 1998 signalled the start of democratisation in Indonesia. The transition to democracy was accompanied by efforts to address past human rights abuses, but it also opened avenues for religious conservatism, or political Islam and other socially conservative Islamic groups, to mobilise publicly and acquire more power. Political Islam has generated moral panic and staged protests against non-normative sexualities. At the same time, however, LGBT identities and rights have become an important concern of the international human rights community, contributing to the further circulation of LGBT rights discourses in Indonesia. In an unexpected development, the globalisation of the LGBT rights discourse has only given Indonesian conservatives *more* political capital to incite moral panic and antipathy towards the LGBT community. Activists have responded to the rapid rise in anti-LGBT sentiment by adopting the discourse of sexual orientation, gender identity and gender expression (SOGIE) and avoiding use of the term 'LGBT' altogether.

Democratisation and its discontents

The New Order regime began to cultivate Islamic groups from the mid-1980s, after systematically repressing them during its first two decades in power (Robinson 2015: 53; Wichelen 2010). In the post-Suharto period, conservative political Islam further expanded its activities and power: explicit Islamic signifiers began to proliferate in the public sphere; the number of Islamic-oriented programs on national television expanded; funding for Islamic schools rose: and the requirements in schools and workplaces for women and girls to remove their head coverings were removed (Wichelen 2010).

While the political reforms of the late 1990s and early 2000s seemed to promise greater freedom and protection of human rights, the reality on the ground was different. During *reformasi,* public support for political Islam grew. Robinson (2015: 53) argues that the rise of political Islam at this time was driven by the nostalgic ambitions of Islamic groups to establish Indonesia as an Islamic state, a goal that had been supressed by the New Order. Merging conservative Islamic discourse with nationalist sentiment, these groups spread moral panic around issues of non-normative sexuality, positioning themselves as saviours of national moral integrity. They launched repeated violent assaults on queer events in the name of protecting Muslims and the nation from corrupting Western influences. In the provinces, they succeeded in having new regulations enacted to police non-normative sexualities, to curb 'immoral' behaviour such as gambling and alcohol consumption, and to enforce female dress codes (UNDP and USAID 2014: 21–4).

Some local ordinances—for example, Regulation No. 13/2002 on the Eradication of Immoral Behaviour in the province of South Sumatra and Regulation No. 2/2004 on the Eradication of Prostitution in the city of Palembang, the capital of South Sumatra province—penalised male homosexual acts on the grounds that they were immoral and an abnormality. These conservative Islamic-based regulations were at first mainly enforced by male vigilante groups, a development made possible by the advent of decentralisation in the democratic era (Robinson 2015: 58). At the national level as well, homosexuality is at increasing threat of being criminalised (Wijaya, Tang and Offord 2018). In 2008 the Indonesian parliament passed Law No. 44/2008 on Pornography, which explicitly classifies homosexuality as a form of deviant behaviour. In 2016, the Islamic, pro-family group AILA proposed an amendment to the Criminal Code that would have made consensual same-sex and extramarital relations a criminal offence (see Chapter 4 of this volume by Butt). Although the Constitutional Court rejected this initiative in December 2016, the proposal was not abandoned; it is now in the hands of the parliament.

Efforts to criminalise LGBT individuals usually begin with non-state actors, particularly religious conservatives, then move to state institutions such as courts or legislatures, where they are championed by Muslim politicians not only from overtly Islamic parties but also, increasingly, from centrist parties.

The globalisation of LGBT identities and rights

The rise of anti-LGBT attitudes in Indonesia has coincided with increased international attention to LGBT issues, pushing them to the forefront of human rights concerns. The current prominence of LGBT rights as an international human rights concern can be traced back to the formulation in November 2006 of the Yogyakarta Principles, which became the basis for the articulation of, and demands for, sexual rights by queer activists.

The Yogyakarta Principles were intended to be 'a universal guide to human rights which affirm binding international legal standards with which all States must comply' (https://yogyakartaprinciples.org/). They were formulated during a meeting of international human rights experts in the Indonesian city of Yogyakarta to elucidate the human rights of people with diverse gender identities and sexual orientations. Under the Yogyakarta Principles, intimate characteristics such as sexual orientation and gender identity are explicitly recognised as rights of citizens that must be recognised and protected by the state. In June 2016, the United Nations Human Rights Council announced that it would appoint an independent expert on sexual orientation and gender identity; this is a further example of the ways in which LGBT identities and sexual and gender-based rights are increasingly being acknowledged and treated according to international norms on human rights (Human Rights Watch 2016).

International humanitarian organisations have also played a significant role in supporting LGBT activisms. Since 2004, the Dutch humanitarian organisation Hivos has channelled support to 25 local LGBT organisations in 18 provinces in order 'to create a safe, vibrant, strong and sustainable

LGBT movement in the region' (Alicias-Garen and Jahja 2015: 2). In 2007, the Indonesian government began to receive funding from the Global Fund against AIDS, Tuberculosis and Malaria (GFATM), which targeted gay men, MSM and *waria*. It helped to increase the circulation of knowledge about sexual identity in discourses on sexual health and led to an increase in the number of LGBT organisations, particularly for gay men, MSM and *waria* (Alicias-Garen and Jahja 2015: 8). Between 2015 and 2016, the United Nations Development Programme (UNDP) also channelled technical and funding support to Indonesian LGBT activists through its 'Being LGBTI in Indonesia' program.[9]

During this period, new terminology continued to make its way into the vocabulary of the Indonesian activists. From the early 2010s they began to popularise 'SOGIE' as an alternative to 'LGBT', in particular to counter the increasing politicisation of LGBT issues by conservative forces. The term 'LGBTIQ' arrived in Indonesia in 2010 with the formation of Forum LGBTIQ Indonesia, the first national umbrella group for LGBTIQ organisations in Indonesia. Although the forum itself was short-lived, the entrenchment of this term in the local landscape marked another step towards the unification of diverse genders and sexual identities into a single movement.

The discourse on SOGIE minorities and diversity

In their attempts to figure out who and what LGBT refers to, anti-LGBT groups appear to have decided that the term encompasses anyone with a gender expression that does not align to the dominant social norms—for example, men with feminine mannerisms or women with a hyper-masculine appearance. Thus, rather than being a catch-all for diverse groups of people with non-normative genders and sexual identities (Wijaya, Tang and Offord 2018), it has become a designation for any individual with an explicit and visible non-conforming gender expression. This has allowed conservatives to expand their attacks beyond people who identify themselves as LGBT to target local and indigenous practices associated with non-normative genders. In 2017, for example, pressure from religious conservatives led the South Sulawesi police to disband a planned arts and sports week for *waria* and *bissu*[10] in the district of Soppeng.

---

9   The program was halted by the Indonesian government in March 2016 during a national meltdown over LGBT issues (Jakarta Post 2018).

10   *Bissu* is a gender category among the Bugis people of South Sulawesi that combines both masculine and feminine elements. Individuals belonging to the *bissu* community are assigned a special status in Bugis society because of the belief that a god can only be incarnated in a gender-free body. For a comprehensive discussion of *bissu*, see Davies (2007).

Queer activists are now able to fight this misconception through the language of SOGIE, a discourse that distinguishes between sexual orientation and gender expression, and hence provides a basis for arguing that gender expression does not determine a person's sexuality. In this context, Indonesian queer activists often turn to the 'Genderbread Person' concept, which makes it easy to understand the ideas behind the SOGIE model. The Genderbread Person is a user-friendly and visually interesting graphic in Sam Killerman's best-selling *A Guide to Gender: The Social Justice Advocate's Handbook*, which was first published in 2013 (Killerman 2017 [2013]). The Genderbread Person is described as being open to change and capable of attuning itself to shifting quotidian practices among diverse groups of people with non-normative genders and sexualities. It has been revised several times, the most recent version being version 4 (Figure 8.1). Like activists and academics around the world, Indonesian queer activists see the Genderbread Person as a convenient way of understanding and providing basic information about the distinct differences between sexual orientation, gender identity and expression, and hence the complexities of diverse genders and sexualities.

The concept that sexual orientation, gender identity and gender expression are discrete elements of an individual's personality has given activists the means to counter conservative narratives that conflate sexual orientation with gender expression. They have moved quickly to disseminate the SOGIE model to tertiary education institutions, local human rights organisations and the media. It would be fair to say that the activists' thorough understanding of SOGIE issues, together with their heart-felt experiences as people with a non-heterosexual orientation, has increased their legitimacy as 'experts' on sexual and gender plurality in many public spheres.

Indonesian activists have also coined the term 'SOGIE/sexual and gender diversity' (*sogie/keragaman gender dan seksualitas*) to establish a claim to the recognition of diversity promised by Indonesia's official national motto, 'Unity in Diversity' (*Bhinneka Tunggal Ika*). Central to this slogan is the nation's claim to diversity as a component of its unitary identity. As a nation with numerous ethnicities, languages and faiths, Indonesia celebrates diversity, while also emphasising the unity of its peoples. In brief, differences are seen as legitimate components of Indonesian nationhood, not as a source of conflict. When SOGIE is associated with the notion of diversity, it not only becomes a successful example of the localisation of discourses of sexuality, but it also situates non-normative sexualities and genders as an intrinsic part of the nationhood project.

Finally, queer activists have begun to use the term 'SOGIE minorities' (*minoritas sogie*) to denote a new category encompassing diverse sexual and gender identities beyond LGBT, which can be imagined and understood

Figure 8.1   The Genderbread Person, version 4

The Genderbread Person

it's pronounced METRO sexual

Gender is one of those things everyone thinks they under-stand, but most people don't. Gender isn't binary. It's not either/or. In many cases it's both/and. A bit of this, a dash of that. This tasty little guide is meant to be an appetizer for gender understanding. It's okay if you're hungry for more after reading it. In fact, that's the idea.

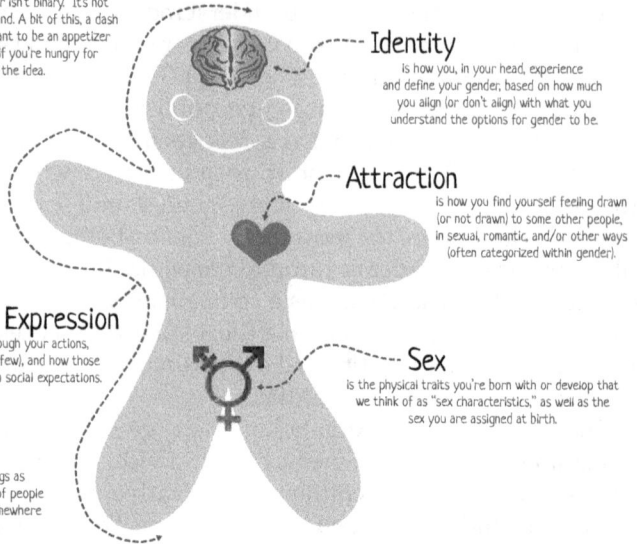

Identity
is how you, in your head, experience and define your gender; based on how much you align (or don't align) with what you understand the options for gender to be.

Attraction
is how you find yourself feeling drawn (or not drawn) to some other people, in sexual, romantic, and/or other ways (often categorized within gender).

Expression
is how you present gender (through your actions, clothing, and demeanor, to name a few), and how those presentations are viewed based on social expectations.

Sex
is the physical traits you're born with or develop that we think of as "sex characteristics," as well as the sex you are assigned at birth.

We can think about all these things as existing on continuums, where a lot of people might see themselves as existing somewhere between 0 and 100 on each

⊘ means a lack of what's on the right side

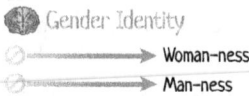

🧠 Gender Identity
⊘·········➤ Woman-ness
⊘·········➤ Man-ness

personality traits, jobs, hobbies, likes, dislikes, roles, expectations

common GENDER IDENTITY things

🧍 Gender Expression
⊘·········➤ Femininity
⊘·········➤ Masculinity

style, grooming, clothing, mannerisms, affect, appearance, hair, make-up

common GENDER EXPRESSION things

⚧ Anatomical Sex
⊘·········➤ Female-ness
⊘·········➤ Male-ness

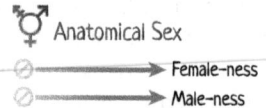

body hair, chest, hips, shoulders, hormones penis, vulva, chromosomes, voice pitch

common ANATOMICAL SEX things

Identity ≠ Expression ≠ Sex
Gender ≠ Sexual Orientation

Sex Assigned At Birth
☐ Female ☐ Intersex ☐ Male

Typically based solely on external genitalia present at birth (ignoring internal anatomy, biology and change throughout life), Sex Assigned At Birth (SAAB) is key for distinguishing between the terms "cisgender" (when SAAB aligns with gender identity) and "transgender" (when it doesn't).

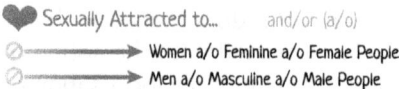

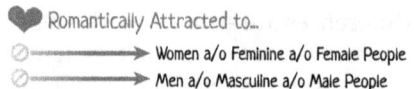

♥ Sexually Attracted to...   and/or (a/o)
⊘·········➤ Women a/o Feminine a/o Female People
⊘·········➤ Men a/o Masculine a/o Male People

♥ Romantically Attracted to...
⊘·········➤ Women a/o Feminine a/o Female People
⊘·········➤ Men a/o Masculine a/o Male People

Genderbread Person Version 4 created and uncopyrighted 2017 by Sam Killermann   For a bigger bite, read more at www.genderbread.org

in terms of a shared solidarity. Through this imagined alliance, activists hope to broaden their political constituency beyond LGBT individuals to include other identities that do not fit easily into the LGBT category, while also avoiding some of the negative connotations attached to the term 'LGBT' in recent media and public discourses. It is worth noting that Indonesian feminist groups are also increasingly using the SOGIE discourse, marking not only a shared solidarity with queer activism, but also a discursive means for feminists to speak about the marginalisation of women (including *waria*) based on genders and sexualities.

CONCLUSION

As this chapter has highlighted, homosexuality and other forms of non-heterosexuality have often been perceived as contrary to Indonesian culture, leading activists to counter this alienating discourse by seeking to link their queer identities with claims of national belonging. Through their encounters with transnational sexuality discourses, Indonesian activists have been able to adopt and refashion specific identities and discourses to address prevailing local challenges in the form of state heteronormative ideology and the rise of religious conservatism.

The refashioning of transnational sexuality discourses by activists shifts attention away from efforts to find the 'truth' about sexuality, to the question of how sexuality is constructed through a series of political negotiations. For example, to detach gay identity from its Western connotations, activists have argued that there is a continuity between indigenous homosexual practices and modern manifestations of homosexuality. Regardless of whether or not they have been successful, they have managed to demonstrate that there is no universal truth attached to notions of sexuality. Rather, discourses of sexuality are subject to continual revision and negotiation, particularly as activists strive to align queer identities with national belonging.

Like anyone else, Indonesian queers and other minorities, through various means, seek social acceptance and recognition within the nation-state, and hence link their sexual and/or gender identities with the national identity. As we learn more about the challenges faced by Indonesian minorities, we discover more about their survival strategies, particularly their attempts to claim a place within the nation. National belonging matters, not only because minority groups view their identities as inherent parts of the nation-state, but also because the discourse of national belonging and identity is subject to refashioning and modification, including by queer identities with valid claims to Indonesian-ness.

REFERENCES

Alicias-Garen, M.D., and R. Jahja (2015) 'Hivos Rosea LGBT program external evaluation report', unpublished report, Hivos Regional Office South East Asia, South Jakarta.

Altman, D. (2001) *Global Sex*, University of Chicago Press, Chicago IL.

Blackburn, S. (2004) *Women and the State in Modern Indonesia*, Cambridge University Press, Cambridge.

Boellstorff, T. (2005) *The Gay Archipelago: Sexuality and Nation in Indonesia*, Princeton University Press, Princeton and Oxford.

Boellstorff, T. (2009) 'Nuri's testimony: HIVAIDS in Indonesia and bare knowledge', *American Ethnologist* 36(2): 351–63.

Davies, S.G. (2007) *Challenging Gender Norms: Five Genders among Bugis in Indonesia*, Thomson Wadsworth, Belmont CA.

'Dr Sm' (1994) 'Asal-usul orientasi seks', *GAYa Nusantara*, No. 27 (March), GAYa Nusantara, Surabaya: 19–22.

Foucault, M. (1978) *The History of Sexuality. Volume 1: An Introduction*, Pantheon Books, New York NY.

Howard, R.S. (1996) 'Falling into the gay world: manhood, marriage, and family in Indonesia', PhD thesis, University of Illinois at Urbana-Champaign, Illinois IL.

Human Rights Watch (2016) 'UN makes history on sexual orientation, gender identity', *Human Rights Watch*, 30 June. https://www.hrw.org/news/2016/06/30/un-makes-history-sexual-orientation-gender-identity

Jakarta Post (2018) 'Kalla requests UNDP to not fund LGBT groups', *Jakarta Post*, 15 February. https://www.thejakartapost.com/news/2016/02/15/kalla-requests-undp-not-fund-lgbt-groups.html

Killerman, S. (2017) *A Guide to Gender: The Social Justice Advocate's Handbook*, second edition, Impetus Books, Austin TX.

McNally, S., J. Grierson and I.M. Hidayana (2015) 'Belonging, community and identity: gay men in Indonesia', in L.R. Bennett and S.G. Davies (eds) *Sex and Sexualities in Contemporary Indonesia*, Routledge, London and New York: 203–19.

Oetomo, D. (1982) 'Homoseks: siapa dia?', *G: Gaya Hidup Ceria*, No. 1 (August), Solo: 7–8.

Oetomo, D. (1984) 'Homosexuality from a different angle', in Sybylla Press (ed.) *Gays in Indonesia*, Sybylla Press, Fitzroy: 37–8.

Oetomo, D. (2001) *Memberi Suara pada Yang Bisu*, Pustaka Marwa, Yogyakarta.

Oetomo-Oen, D.T. (1982) 'Charting gay politics in Indonesia', unpublished manuscript.

Patton, C. (2002) *Globalizing AIDS*, University of Minnesota Press, Minneapolis and London.

Pigg, S.L., and V. Adams (2005) 'Introduction: the moral object of sex', in V. Adams and S.L. Pigg (eds) *Sex in Development*, Duke University Press, Durham: 1–38.

Robinson, K. (2015) 'Masculinity, sexuality, and Islam', in L.R. Bennett and S.G. Davies (eds) *Sex and Sexualities in Contemporary Indonesia*, Routledge, London and New York: 51–68.

Storr, M. (ed.) (1999) *Bisexuality: A Critical Reader*, Routledge, London and New York.

Suryakusuma, J. (1996) 'The state and sexuality in New Order Indonesia', in L.J. Sears (ed.) *Fantasizing the Feminine*, Duke University Press, Durham: 92–119.

Sybylla Press (ed.) (1984) *Gays in Indonesia*, Sybylla Press, Fitzroy.

TribunJogja (2016) 'Walikota Tangerang klaim mie instan jadi pemicu LGBT', *TribunJogja.com*, 27 February. http://jogja.tribunnews.com/2016/02/27/walikota-tangerang-klaim-mie-instan-jadi-pemicu-lgbt

UNDP and USAID (United Nations Development Programme and United States Agency for International Development) (2014) 'Being LGBT in Asia: Indonesia country report', UNDP and USAID, Bangkok.

Wichelen, S. (2010) *Religion, Politics and Gender in Indonesia: Disputing the Muslim Body*, Routledge, London and New York.

Wieringa, S. (2002) *Sexual Politics in Indonesia*, Palgrave Macmillan, London.

Wijaya, H.Y. (2017a) 'Moral panic and the reinvention of LGBT', *Indonesia at Melbourne*, 17 May.

Wijaya, H.Y. (2017b) 'Constitutional Court ruling a reminder that the state is not uniform', *Indonesia at Melbourne*, 19 December.

Wijaya, H.Y., and S.G. Davies (forthcoming) 'Lesbian and gay activism and Indonesia's unfulfilled promise of democracy', in M. Ford and T. Dibley (eds) *Activists in Transition*, Cornell University Press, Ithaca NY.

Wijaya, H.Y., S. Tang and B. Offord (2018) 'The globalization of LGBT identity and same-sex marriage as a catalyst of neo-institutional values: Singapore and Indonesia in focus', in B. Winter, M. Forest and R. Senac (eds) *Global Perspectives on Same-sex Marriage: A Neo-institutional Approach*, Palgrave Macmillan, New York NY: 171–96.

PART 4

Religion and Ethnicity

9 The mobilisation of intolerance and its trajectories: Indonesian Muslims' views of religious minorities and ethnic Chinese

Marcus Mietzner and Burhanuddin Muhtadi

The political demise of the former Christian-Chinese governor of Jakarta, Basuki Tjahaja Purnama (known as Ahok), has attracted much political commentary, both in Indonesia and abroad. Accused of blasphemy, Ahok faced unprecedented mass protests by Islamists during his re-election campaign in late 2016 and early 2017. Following his electoral defeat and subsequent imprisonment, debate about the relationship between Indonesia's ethno-religious minorities and the Muslim majority intensified (Setijadi 2017). These complex discussions centred on a number of key questions. For instance, were the sentiments of the anti-Ahok protesters—often middle-class Muslims accompanied by their children—representative of religiously and racially prejudiced views held by the majority of Indonesian Muslims (Assyaukanie 2017), or were they part of a pious movement in defence of Islam (Fealy 2016; Weng 2016)? What was the relationship between Islamist world views and the protests? Did the former cause the latter (Lindsey 2016), or have the demonstrations hardened exclusivist attitudes (Scherpen 2017)? And finally, what are the socio-economic profiles of those who hold such views (Chaplin 2016)? These questions have since dominated the scholarly and broader discourse on Indonesian politics and society, with passionate disagreements among participants about how best to research the problem and how to interpret the findings.

In our own work on the subject (Mietzner and Muhtadi 2018; Mietzner, Muhtadi and Halida 2018), we have taken the view that in order to explore the attitudes of Indonesian Muslims, there is no better way than conducting scientifically solid opinion surveys. We believe that such an approach is, in this specific case, superior to ethnographic or other qualitative approaches that necessarily focus on a much smaller number of actors in limited locations. By contrast, nationwide surveys based on multi-stage random sampling (Marsden and Wright 2010) can provide a reliable snapshot of Indonesian Muslim attitudes. Moreover, as we have access to a database containing multi-year data series, we are able to track changes in attitudes with much more precision than exclusively qualitative research could. In this contribution, we thus address the questions mentioned above based on a survey we conducted in August 2018, and identify long-term trends by comparing its data to similar surveys we and other researchers have carried out in the past.

The discussion below is divided into three main parts. First, we explore the level of intolerance among Indonesian Muslims towards religious and ethnic minorities (in the latter case, ethnic Chinese) and assess whether this level is high by international standards. Second, we examine changes in these intolerance levels over time, looking at data points before, during and after the Ahok protests. We show that the protests have left a significant legacy of higher intolerance among Indonesian Muslims. Based on our data, it is evident that while the protests initially drove up only Muslim opposition towards religious minorities holding political office, this sentiment later intensified to include the religio-cultural activities of non-Muslims as well. At the same time, however, the ferocity of anti-Chinese sentiment declined in the aftermath of the Ahok crisis, suggesting that heightened religio-political intolerance is consolidating as a long-term phenomenon, while the spike in racial resentment was more situationally tied to the rejection of Ahok personally and hence declined after his demise. The third section analyses the socio-economic backgrounds of those Muslims holding religio-racial prejudices and explains how these patterns evolved during the course of the anti-Ahok mobilisation. In the conclusion, we offer some reflections on what these findings mean for Indonesia's politics and the future of its democracy.

MUSLIM INTOLERANCE TOWARDS MINORITIES

Our first task is to establish the current level of Indonesian Muslims' intolerance *vis-à-vis* religious minorities and ethnic Chinese. We do this based on a survey we conducted with the Indonesian Survey Institute (Lembaga Survei Indonesia, LSI) in August 2018. This nationwide, multi-stage random sampling survey involved 1,520 respondents, which is a very reliable sample size; the American pollster Gallup, for example, uses a similar number of respondents for its polls, despite the United States having a larger population than Indonesia. For the analysis of the results below, we focused only on Muslim respondents.

In the 2018 survey, we measured the level of Muslim intolerance towards non-Muslims by using an index created from six major questions. These questions assessed the objections of Muslims towards: (a) the holding of religious events by non-Muslims in the neighbourhood; (b) the building of non-Muslim places of worship in the neighbourhood; (c) non-Muslims as mayors or district heads; (d) non-Muslims as governors; (e) non-Muslims as vice-president; and (f) non-Muslims as president. In the index developed from the answers to these questions, a score of between 75 and 100 (that is, a respondent answering all or almost all questions in the affirmative) led to a classification of 'very intolerant'; a score of 50–75 (meaning the respondent answered more than half the questions positively) to a classification of 'intolerant'; a score of 25–50 to a classification of 'tolerant' and a score of 0–25 to a classification of 'very tolerant'. Based on this classification scheme, 30.7 per cent of Muslim Indonesians were very intolerant, 17.1 per cent were intolerant, 20 per cent were tolerant and 32.2 per cent were very tolerant. Overall, then, the percentage of Indonesian Muslims holding strongly or fairly intolerant views towards non-Muslims in 2018 stood at 47.8 per cent.

If we further disaggregate the index into a religio-cultural intolerance index (consisting of the two questions on objections towards non-Muslim events or places of worship) and a political intolerance index (consisting of the four questions on opposition to non-Muslims holding political office), we note some significant differences. In these partial indexes, 38.7 per cent of Muslims could be described as religio-culturally intolerant, while 54.2 per cent were politically intolerant. The significance of this differentiation will be elaborated on in subsequent sections.

While the numbers above indicate the percentage of Indonesian Muslims who in August 2018 broadly subscribed to Islamist concepts of politico-cultural discrimination against non-Muslims, we also applied a separate radicalism index. 'Islamism' is defined here as the belief that Qur'anic scripture needs to be fully applied in the political sphere and that, therefore, Islamic teachings need to take precedence over modern state law. We define radicalism, on the other hand, as the pursuit of, or willingness to fight for, an Islamist religio-ideological agenda through involvement in organised (including violent) action. In this context, our 2018 poll asked Muslim respondents whether they had participated or were willing to participate in (a) donating to an organisation committed to the implementation of Islamic law; (b) convincing friends or relatives to join the fight for the implementation of Islamic law; (c) planning or taking part in raids on places deemed in violation of Islamic law, such as discotheques, brothels or gambling dens; (d) demonstrating against groups seen as insulting or threatening Islam; and (e) conducting attacks on non-Muslim places of worship. Based on a score system similar to the one applied in the intolerance index, 0.3 per cent of respondents were classified as radical; 11 per cent as willing to be radical; 21.5 per cent as neutral; and 67.3 per cent as unwilling to be radical. In combination, then, 11.3 per cent of Indonesian Muslims were radical or willing to be radical in the sense that they were committed to engaging actively in the struggle for an Islamist program.

In order to further gauge the support of Indonesian Muslims for exclusivist, anti-minority ideas, we asked Muslim respondents about their awareness and approval of the Islamic Defenders Front (Front Pembela Islam, FPI). FPI and its leader, Habib Rizieq Shihab, were at the forefront of the anti-Ahok protests. Since the organisation's foundation in 1998, FPI has made a name for itself by campaigning ferociously against Muslim minority sects, the building of non-Muslim houses of worship in Islamic neighbourhoods and what it views as vices, such as drinking alcohol or eating during the daytime in the fasting month (Wilson 2014). Rizieq used the Islamist mobilisation against Ahok to boost his own status, having himself declared the Great Leader (Imam Besar) of the Indonesian Muslim community in December 2017. Given the fame of both FPI and Rizieq, it can safely be assumed that respondents declaring support for the organisation do so in full knowledge of its ideals. In our 2018 survey, 55 per cent of Indonesian Muslims declared that they had heard of FPI, and 41 per cent of that group supported its agenda. This means that a total of 22.6 per cent of Muslim respondents expressed their approval of FPI and the ideas it represented.

While many Islamist campaigns target non-Muslims in general, some of these mobilisations have an explicit anti-Chinese connotation. Hence, it is necessary to explore to what extent resentment of non-Muslims is different from, or congruent with, anti-Chinese prejudices. In order to measure Muslims' general anti-Chinese sentiments, we asked a number of questions that were first applied in a 2017 survey conducted by the ISEAS–Yusof Ishak Institute and LSI (Fossati, Hui and Negara 2017; Setijadi 2017). Among other things, our 2018 results showed that 36 per cent of Muslims believed that Chinese only cared about their own kind; 33 per cent thought that Chinese possessed a culture that was incompatible with that of Indonesia; 32 per cent were convinced that Indonesian Chinese were still loyal to the People's Republic of China (PRC); and 35 per cent opined that Chinese were too greedy and ambitious. Overall, it is clear that about one-third of Indonesian Muslims in 2018 held strong socio-racial prejudices against ethnic Chinese. But rather counterintuitively, we found that antipathy towards non-Muslims and antipathy towards Chinese were not significantly related. Applying the Pearson correlation, we discovered that Muslims were more likely to hold anti-Chinese sentiments than non-Muslims, but that Muslims who were tolerant of non-Muslims were just as likely to endorse anti-Chinese views as Muslims who were more welcoming of religious minorities.[1] Thus, the two categories (of intolerance towards non-Muslims and intolerance towards Chinese) need to be treated as distinct. In later sections, we will demonstrate how this finding is borne out in the different trajectories the two trends have taken since the Ahok protests ended.

While the data are complex, they allow us to answer one of the main questions in the current debate, that is, whether the religiously and racially charged messages of some anti-Ahok protest leaders were shared by many demonstrators and the Muslim population at large, or whether the protests were more indicative of piety than exclusivism and racism. The data presented above clearly show that the kinds of sentiments propagated by some anti-Ahok campaigners—whether advocating the exclusion of non-Muslims from political leadership positions or echoing deeply seated prejudices against Chinese—are shared by large segments of the Muslim community. In our 2018 poll, 52.3 per cent of Muslim respondents across Indonesia rejected the election of non-Muslims as governors, supporting the main theme of the anti-Ahok campaign. That theme centred on the accusation that Ahok had made a blasphemous remark about the Qur'anic verse Al-Ma'idah 51, which—according to Islamist interpretations—precludes non-Muslims from holding political office (Menchik 2016). Our data show that not only did many demonstrators believe that Ahok had been guilty of blasphemy, but they also endorsed the content of the verse. They believed, in other words, that Ahok—as a non-Muslim—should never have been governor in the first place. Indeed, with half of Indonesian Muslims sharing this view, the group of Muslims who were intolerant of non-Muslims in political office went well beyond those participating in, or actively supporting, the protests.

But does this mean that Indonesia has extraordinarily high levels of intolerance towards minorities? A look at comparable surveys in other countries is instructive, especially if we turn to the reverse constellation— that is, surveys of intolerance towards Muslims in majority-Christian countries. For example, a Pew Research Center (2017) poll found that 69 per cent of Italians, 66 per cent of Greeks and Poles, 72 per cent of Hungarians and 50 per cent of Spaniards held negative views of Muslims in

---

1   For further discussion of anti-Chinese attitudes, see Chapter 11 of this book by Setijadi.

that year. In Western Europe, the numbers were lower but still significant, with 35 per cent of Swedes, 29 per cent of Germans and 28 per cent of Britons admitting to anti-Muslim views. In a 2015 Gallup poll, 38 per cent of American respondents stated that they would not vote for a Muslim presidential candidate, making Islam the least popular religion of nominees in the eyes of the electorate (Gallup 2015).

When we compare the level of intolerance towards non-Muslims in Indonesia to that in fellow Muslim-majority countries, the results again pour cold water on the idea of Indonesian exceptionalism. While a survey by the Pew Research Center (2013: 124) suggested that Indonesia had the lowest levels of tolerance in the Muslim world towards offspring marrying a Christian (6 per cent, as opposed to 30 per cent in Tunisia), other areas showed Indonesian Muslims to be more liberal than their African or Arab counterparts. For instance, 58 per cent of Indonesians considered polygamy—which is allowed by the Qur'an—to be morally wrong (Pew Research Center 2013: 84). This was the highest percentage in Asia, and it was significantly higher than in most African countries. A similar picture emerges in relation to radicalism—measured by the percentage of respondents who considered attacks against civilians in defence of Islam to be sometimes or often justified (Pew Research Center 2013: 70). That number was 7 per cent in Indonesia (similar to the numbers in our 2018 radicalism measurements), but much higher in other Muslim-majority countries. For example, it was 26 per cent in Bangladesh. Overall, then, the number of citizens endorsing discriminatory views of religious and specific racial minorities is high in Indonesia—but it is equally significant in other countries, including Western democracies.

INTOLERANCE AND ITS TRAJECTORIES

While the data presented above establish the current level of religious and racial intolerance among Indonesian Muslims, they tell us little about how these trends have developed over time, and how they have been influenced by key events in Indonesian politics and society. For this, we need to compare the 2018 data with previous datasets on the same or similar measures. For most of the measures used in the 2018 survey, our LSI dataset reaches back to 2010, allowing us to clearly identify fluctuations and relate them to particular timelines.

Given their socio-political magnitude and ideological framing, the anti-Ahok demonstrations are the most relevant incident to examine in terms of their interaction with data on intolerance. In this context, it is necessary to recap some of that event's main episodes. Previously the deputy governor to Joko Widodo (Jokowi), Ahok became the capital's governor when Jokowi was sworn in as president in October 2014. From the beginning, Islamist groups protested against Ahok's succession, pointing to Al-Ma'idah 51. But the initial demonstrations were small, and Ahok proceeded to acquire approval ratings of about 70 per cent (Mietzner and Muhtadi 2017). In September 2016, as the campaign for the February 2017 gubernatorial elections began, Ahok made a dismissive remark about Al-Ma'idah 51—the trigger for the blasphemy accusation and the subsequent series of mass demonstrations. After the first major protest, in November 2016, the police formally charged Ahok with blasphemy. This was followed by an even bigger demonstration in December calling for Ahok's immediate arrest. The embattled governor was put on trial shortly afterwards, further eroding his already weakened poll numbers. He failed to win an absolute majority in the first round of voting in February 2017; in the second round, held in April 2017, he lost in a landslide to the candidate backed by the Islamist movement, Anies Baswedan. A month later, Ahok was sentenced to two years in prison for blasphemy.

Our database allows us to trace the trajectory of intolerance among Indonesian Muslims as it developed before, during and after the events described above. We have three surveys on intolerance taken before the onset of the Ahok crisis, all carried out by LSI using the same methodology as the 2018 poll. These three surveys took place in 2010, 2011 and April 2016[2]—the last of these just a few months before the Islamist protests began. For the immediate effect of the crisis, we can refer to a survey we did in August 2017, shortly after Ahok's defeat and imprisonment. The medium- to long-term impact of the Islamist mobilisation, finally, is best measured by our 2018 poll.

Let us begin by analysing how the political dimension of Muslim intolerance towards non-Muslims evolved during the anti-Ahok campaign. Recall that we disaggregated our intolerance index into a political and a religio-cultural subindex, with the former consisting of measures that assessed objections to non-Muslims holding political positions. We do not have data points in 2010 and 2011 for this subindex, but in 2016, just before the anti-Ahok campaign, the average rate of objection of Muslims to non-Muslims holding political office stood at 42.3 per cent; this was the average taken from measures on non-Muslims becoming district head or mayor, governor, vice-president and president.[3] In 2017, just after Ahok's imprisonment, this average shot up to 49.6 per cent. We have argued elsewhere that this showed how strongly the central theme of

---

2 The 2016 survey was commissioned by the Wahid Institute.
3 As in previous surveys, the objection rate increased with the level of office: the rate was lowest for non-Muslim mayors or district heads (52.3 per cent) and highest for non-Muslim presidents (59.1 per cent).

Table 9.1   Share of Muslims objecting to non-Muslims occupying elected positions (%)

Position	2016	2017	2018
District head/mayor	39.3	47.4	52.3
Governor	40.3	48.2	52.3
Vice-president	41.4	49.6	54.7
President	47.9	53.2	59.1
Objection index (average)	42.3	49.6	54.6

the anti-Ahok campaign—that is, the Qur'an's putatative requirement that non-Muslims be excluded from political leadership—resonated with the Muslim community (Mietzner, Muhtadi and Halida 2018). The data suggest that Muslims who had previously been more pluralist were persuaded to endorse key notions of an Islamist agenda, especially those related to the demand that top positions in the state should be reserved for Muslims. Furthermore, our 2018 survey removes any speculation that this spike in political intolerance was only temporary in nature and likely to fade. Quite to the contrary, the level of objection to non-Muslims holding political office again rose sharply between 2017 and 2018, reaching a record level of 54.6 per cent (Table 9.1).

The indications that the anti-Ahok campaign drove up intolerance—rather than being caused by it—are further strengthened when examining the trends in the religio-cultural subindex. This subindex contains two measures. The first enquires about objections to non-Muslims holding religious events in the neighbourhood; and the second assesses opposition to non-Muslim places of worship being built in the neighbourhood. For these measures, we have 2010 and 2011 data points. They show that, before the anti-Ahok protests, the level of religio-cultural intolerance had been declining dramatically, with objections to non-Muslim houses of worship in the neighbourhood falling from 63.8 per cent in 2010 to 60.6 per cent in 2011, then to 52 per cent in 2016 (Figure 9.1). This demonstrates that a rise in religio-cultural intolerance towards non-Muslims could *not* have been responsible for the anti-Ahok protests (Mietzner and Muhtadi 2018); indeed, the levels of intolerance were consistently declining. This decrease continued even during the Ahok crisis, with the percentage of Muslims objecting to non-Muslim places of worship dropping to a low of 48.2 per cent in 2017. We have explained this phenomenon by the fact that the organisers of the anti-Ahok protests had promoted the notion that rejecting non-Muslims as political leaders did not mean opposing their

Figure 9.1   Religio-cultural intolerance: share of Muslims objecting to non-Muslim ceremonies and places of worship (%)

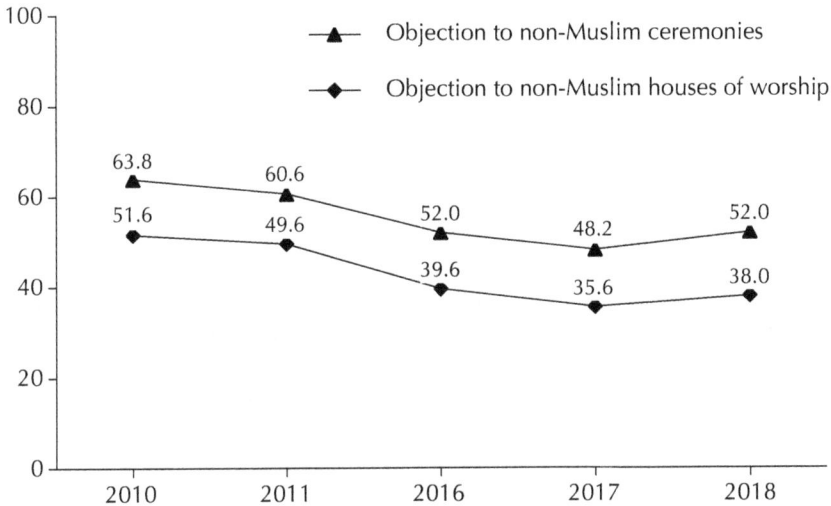

religio-cultural activities (Mietzner, Muhtadi and Halida 2018). Thus, in line with the prescriptions of protest leaders, Muslims were consolidating their opposition to non-Muslims holding political office while—in 2017—continuing to soften their views on religio-cultural expressions of non-Muslim life.

But the 2018 data show that, for the first time in a decade, religio-cultural intolerance has again begun to rise. The measures assessing both non-Muslim events and non-Muslim places of worship recorded increases in 2018, returning roughly to 2016 levels (Figure 9.1). Hence, while the two intolerance subindexes diverged during the anti-Ahok demonstrations—with political intolerance rising and religio-cultural intolerance falling, both corresponding to the instructions of the protest leaders—the post-2018 patterns exhibit a single upward trend. This suggests that, rather than waning in their impact (as some had predicted or hoped), the events of late 2016 and early 2017 left a long-term legacy of rising intolerance in all aspects of religio-political life. In this solidifying trend, the spike in political intolerance ultimately infected and undermined tolerance towards the spiritual and cultural dimensions of non-Muslim society as well. Consequently, the share of 'very intolerant' Muslims in the integrated intolerance index rose from 27.2 per cent in 2017 to 30.7 per cent in 2018, and that of the 'intolerant' Muslims from 15.0 per cent to 17.1 per cent. Trends in two other measures confirm this finding. First, in our radicalism index, the percentage of those 'willing to be radical' rose from

7.7 per cent in 2016 to 9.3 per cent in 2017, and to 11.0 per cent in 2018. And second, support levels for FPI have consolidated at a high level. In the 2016 survey, support for FPI stood at 15.6 per cent; it shot up to 23.6 per cent in 2017 and held steady at 22.6 per cent in 2018.

There is a striking difference, however, between the trends in cultural intolerance towards non-Muslims and towards Chinese. Recall that in 2018, about a third of Indonesian Muslims held prejudicial views towards ethnic Chinese. While this was a significant level, it was much lower than in 2017—that is, in the immediate aftermath of the anti-Ahok mobilisation (Figure 9.2). The average from the four measures on socio-cultural anti-Chinese prejudices (belief that Chinese only care about their own kind, that their culture is incompatible with that of Indonesia, that they are still loyal to the PRC and that they are greedy and ambitious) stood at 34.0 per cent in 2018—but it had been 41.3 per cent in 2017. Thus, there had been a considerable decline in anti-Chinese sentiment within a year of the Ahok crisis. This suggests that resentment towards non-Muslims has consolidated much more strongly than intolerance towards ethnic Chinese as a result of the anti-Ahok mobilisation. The latter, it seems, was driven by a rejection of Ahok personally, and softened considerably once he was imprisoned. The former, by contrast, has taken root more firmly in the mindset of Indonesian Muslims, as indicated by the post-crisis rise in religio-cultural intolerance towards non-Muslims described above.

This softening in socio-cultural anti-Chinese sentiment does not extend to the political sphere, however. In fact, the level of rejection of Chinese in political leadership positions increased further in 2018, in concert with opposition to non-Muslims holding such office. Between 2017 and 2018, the percentage of Muslims objecting to ethnic Chinese mayors or district heads rose from 51.7 per cent to 56.3 per cent—4 per cent higher than the share objecting to non-Muslims holding such positions. We propose that this is because of three factors. First, it was due to the success of the very specific campaign by the protest leaders to implement Al-Ma'idah 51—and with Chinese being almost exclusively non-Muslim, many Muslims automatically apply this Qur'anic verse to them. Second, as we have shown earlier, the constituencies holding anti-Chinese sentiments and reservations about non-Muslims are not entirely congruent; thus, there is an additional reservoir of objections to Chinese in politics among Muslims who hold no particular resentment towards non-Muslims. Third, the gap between socio-cultural resentment of Chinese and political objections to them is similar to the differences between religio-cultural and political intolerance towards non-Muslims—the protest leaders discouraged the former (at least in public) while openly encouraging the latter.

Overall, our analysis of the trajectory of intolerance in contemporary Indonesia supports general theories of Islamist sentiments being

Figure 9.2 Rates of Muslim prejudice towards ethnic Chinese (%)

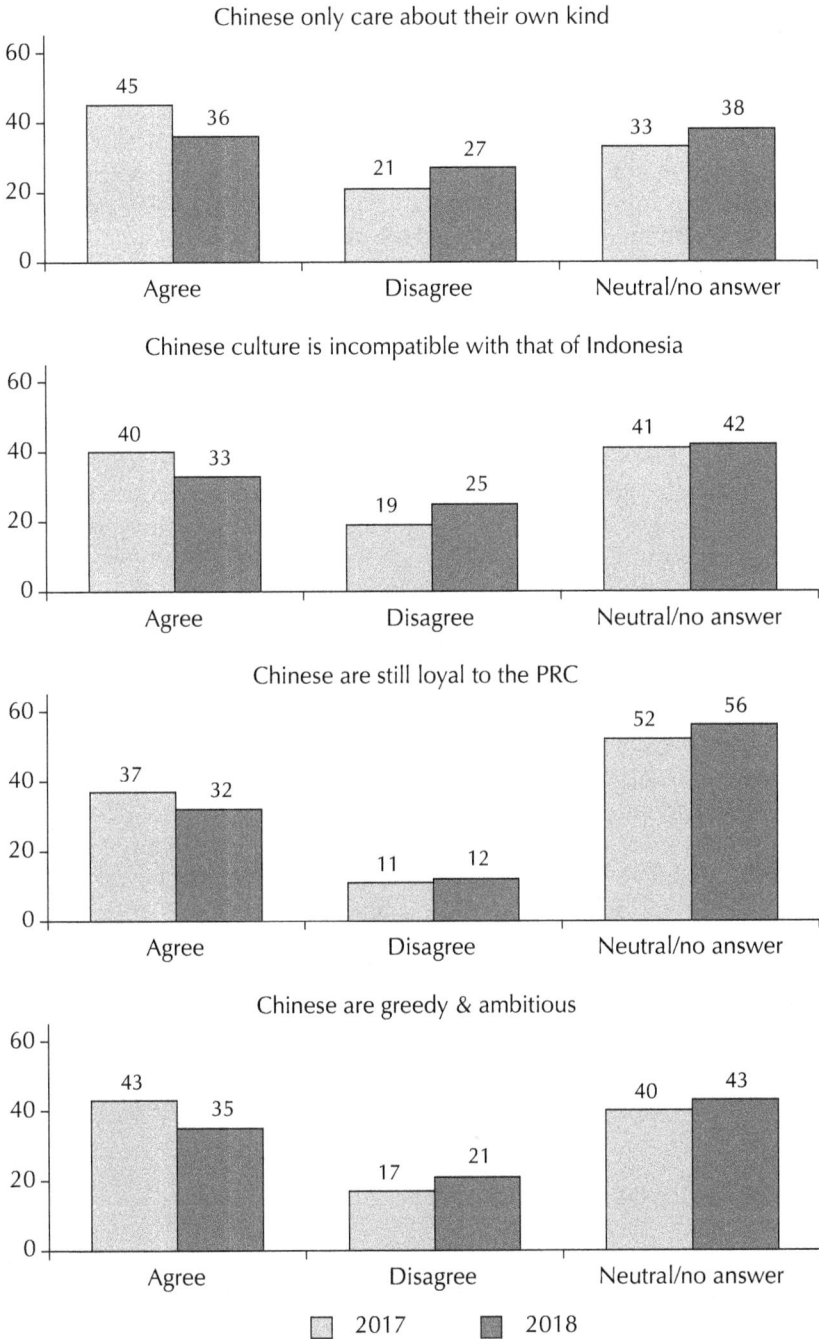

Chinese only care about their own kind

Chinese culture is incompatible with that of Indonesia

Chinese are still loyal to the PRC

Chinese are greedy & ambitious

engineered by religio-political entrepreneurs (that is, political actors with an interest in pursuing an Islamist agenda) rather than being driven by broader social change (Mecham 2017). The discussion above showed that the anti-Ahok campaign occurred against a background of declining religio-cultural intolerance, highlighting the mobilisational capacity of the protest leaders to overcome longer-term societal trends. The data also demonstrated that Muslims were drawn in great numbers to the key messages of the protest organisers—chief among them the exclusion of non-Muslims from political leadership positions, which the protesters defended with their claim to protect the sanctity of Al-Ma'idah 51. In this field of political intolerance, Muslim resentment escalated during and after the crisis, and continued to increase even two years after the onset of the Islamist mobilisation against Ahok. Another key theme of the protest leaders was the claim that Muslims were economically worse off than non-Muslims. Support for this statement also grew during the anti-Ahok campaign, rising from 31 per cent in 2016 to 35 per cent in 2017 and 38 per cent in 2018. Prior to 2017, the percentage of Muslims who felt economically disadvantaged *vis-à-vis* non-Muslims had declined consistently; it was 43 per cent in 2010 and 38 per cent in 2011. The anti-Ahok campaign clearly turned this trend around, increasing the long-term polarisation between Muslims and non-Muslims in post-Suharto Indonesia.

The data also show, however, that religio-political entrepreneurs cannot fully control the way their messaging is processed by the wider population. While the protest leaders had insisted that rejection of non-Muslims in leadership posts was consistent with tolerance towards the non-political aspects of non-Muslim life, this guidance was heeded only temporarily. In 2017, in the immediate aftermath of the Ahok crisis, religio-cultural intolerance continued to decline, but then it increased—for the first time since 2010—in 2018. This proves, in our view, that the political and religio-cultural aspects of intolerance ultimately can't be separated. While the protest leaders may have intended to escalate the former and contain the latter, this approach succeeded only briefly. Once the dust from the Ahok crisis had well and truly settled in 2018, the increased political intolerance dragged up religio-cultural resentment towards non-Muslims as well. Only social anti-Chinese prejudices, which networks associated with the protests had hyped in 2017 through social media messaging in particular, moderated considerably after the crisis.

THE PROFILE OF INTOLERANCE

Having established the level of Muslim intolerance towards religio-racial minorities, and having explained how intolerance levels have changed over time, we can now turn to the last remaining cluster of questions we set out to address. What is the socio-economic profile of those Muslims who hold intolerant views towards minorities, and how did these patterns evolve before, during and after the Islamist mobilisation against Ahok in 2016 and 2017?

Elsewhere, we have explored the changes in socio-demographic profiles between 2010 and 2017, covering the pre-mobilisation period and its immediate aftermath (Mietzner and Muhtadi 2018; Mietzner, Muhtadi and Halida 2018). Hence, those pre-2018 studies require only a brief summary here. In 2010 and 2011, several years before the anti-Ahok campaign, surveys showed a clear pattern of intolerance rising with declining income and educational attainment. In other words, the higher the income and level of education, the lower the level of intolerance towards minorities—confirming a long-held view among modernisation scholars that increasing prosperity and knowledge reduce sectarian views. But in the 2016 survey, taken shortly before the onset of the protests, that relationship disappeared. Indeed, detailed cross-tabulation analysis showed that in some key measures of intolerance, the rich and highly educated were now more intolerant than the poor and lowly educated. Based on these data, in combination with the overall declining trend in religio-cultural intolerance at the time, we proposed that the main cause of the 2016 Islamist mobilisation was not rising religious conservatism, but the growing organisational capacity of Islamist conservatives, as expressed in their penetration of the upper socio-economic and professional strata. That expanded capacity for mobilisation had been groomed under the presidency of Susilo Bambang Yudhoyono, and was brought to bear when Jokowi provoked the conservatives by openly supporting non-Muslim figures such as Ahok (Scherpen 2017).

In the immediate aftermath of the anti-Ahok campaign, in mid-2017, our survey showed further changes in the socio-economic profile of intolerant Muslims. While regressions still did not reveal an overall relationship between intolerance and income and educational levels, microanalyses of specific cross-tabulations demonstrated that the poor and lowly educated had been drawn more extensively to the messages of the protest leaders than the rich and tertiary educated. We argued that this showed the effectiveness of some of the protest movement's techniques specifically targeting lower-class Muslims, such as threatening that anyone voting for or supporting Ahok would not receive Muslim burial rites. Thus, the rise in political intolerance (that is, objection towards non-Muslims holding political office) between 2016 and 2017 was largely the result of lower-class Muslims being recruited to the anti-Ahok campaign, while richer and better-educated Muslims were less likely to endorse intolerant views if they didn't already do so before 2017.

Table 9.2   Share of Muslims objecting to non-Muslim governors, by
educational level (%)

Educational level	Share of sample*	Share of objections			Change		
		2016	2017	2018	2016–17	2017–18	2016–18
Primary school or less	45.8	39.0	47.8	53.7	8.8	5.9	14.7
Junior high school	19.7	40.7	52.4	49.8	11.7	−2.6	9.1
Senior high school	26.1	40.5	47.5	50.3	7.0	2.8	9.8
Tertiary education	8.4	43.9	43.2	55.8	−0.7	12.6	11.9

* These are averages taken from the 2016, 2017 and 2018 survey samples. There are slight differences between our data and those of the central statistics agency (Badan Pusat Statistik, BPS) because of differences in the age and education categories.

This pattern of lower-class Muslims being drawn heavily towards Islamist ideas after the anti-Ahok campaign was confirmed by our 2018 data. For the first time since the 2010 and 2011 surveys, our 2018 poll showed a statistically significant negative correlation between educational level and a wide range of measures assessing Islamist attitudes.[4] This means that—as in 2010 and 2011—the lower a respondent's education, the higher his or her level of intolerance and Islamist conviction. This highlights our earlier finding that the period between 2011 and 2016 was a phase of richer and more highly educated Indonesians becoming more prominent in intolerance activism, while the effect of the Ahok crisis was primarily to pull lower-class Muslims into anti-minority, Islamist thought.

But a close analysis of the 2018 cross-tabulations also shows changing trends in the small yet influential group of tertiary degree holders. Unlike the 2017 data, the 2018 poll indicates that the increase in political intolerance was driven by surges not only in the lowest educational stratum, but also in the highest group of educational achievers (Table 9.2). Overall, the percentage of Muslims objecting to non-Muslim governors grew from 48.2 per cent in 2017 to 52.3 per cent in 2018, an increase of 4.1 per cent. Among primary school graduates (or lower), the rise was 5.9 per cent, from 47.8 per cent to 53.7 per cent. But in the category of tertiary degree holders, the increase was a whopping 12.6 per cent, from 43.2 per cent to 55.8 per cent. In the two medium educational strata, junior and senior high

---

4 Our surveys also asked other questions, in addition to specific queries on attitudes towards non-Muslims. These questions focused on support for sharia regulations, objection to female presidents and similar themes. Our overall correlation analysis included those questions as well.

school graduates, the change was much less significant. Thus, the lowest and highest educational strata recorded the largest growth in intolerance, even though such sentiments had initially stagnated among tertiary degree holders in the immediate aftermath of the anti-Ahok campaign. It is important to keep in mind, however, that the lowest educational tier is numerically much larger than the highest (45.8 per cent versus 8.4 per cent), so it holds true that more poorly educated than highly educated citizens were added to the Islamist constituency after the 2016 protests. The numerical dominance of less educated Muslims makes the increase in intolerance in this group more significant than the increase among their tertiary-educated peers, explaining the result of the overall correlation mentioned above.

The growth in intolerance among the lowest and highest social strata shows that the government's attempts to curb the rise of intolerance both on campuses and among the wider population have been ineffective. Using a mixture of repression and accommodation (Mietzner 2018), in 2017 the Jokowi administration moved to ban the ultra-conservative group Hizbut Tahrir Indonesia (HTI). The government hoped that the ban would stop HTI's infiltration of campuses and discourage students and university graduates from endorsing intolerant views. The dramatic increase in political intolerance among tertiary degree holders in 2018 indicates the failure of that effort. Similarly, many of the accommodative policies directed towards lower-class citizens—promises of land reform, increased presidential visits to mosques and Islamic boarding schools, endorsement of conservative social policies—have not produced the expected results. In fact, it could be argued that key elements of this accommodation—such as Jokowi's selection of the conservative cleric Ma'ruf Amin as his running mate for the 2019 election—have made intolerant views not less, but more acceptable among many ordinary lower-class Muslims.

This pattern of growing intolerance among the lower and upper classes in the post-mobilisation period is also reflected in cross-tabulations on political intolerance and income levels. Whereas in 2017 the highest increase in political intolerance was among the lowest and the medium income earners (below Rp 1 million and Rp 1–2 million respectively), in 2018 the most significant spike was among high income earners (above Rp 2 million).[5] Between 2017 and 2018, the percentage of Indonesians opposing non-Muslim governors grew from 45.6 per cent to 46.3 per cent in the lowest income bracket, from 49 per cent to 52.7 per cent in the medium

---

5   Evidently, the categorisation of income over Rp 2 million as 'high' is outdated, and our newer surveys have a more disaggregated hierarchy of income strata. However, for purposes of comparison with pre-2017 surveys, we continue to use the three-level brackets.

*Table 9.3   Share of Muslims objecting to non-Muslim places of worship,
             by educational level (%)*

Educational level	Share of sample*	Share of objections			Change		
		2016	2017	2018	2016–17	2017–18	2016–18
Primary school or less	45.8	51.1	52.5	60.5	1.4	8.0	9.4
Junior high school	19.7	54.7	52.8	47.5	−1.9	−5.3	−7.3
Senior high school	26.1	50.0	40.6	42.9	−9.4	2.4	−7.1
Tertiary education	8.4	55.3	36.0	41.3	−19.2	5.3	−13.9

* These are averages taken from the 2016, 2017 and 2018 survey samples. There are slight differences between our data and those of the central statistics agency (Badan Pusat Statistik, BPS) because of differences in the age and education categories.

income category and from 48.9 per cent to 53.2 per cent in the high income class. Thus, while lower-income Muslims continue to be recruited into Islamist community networks and to support their ideas, higher-income citizens have been drawn in particularly strongly since 2017.

We stated earlier that for the first time since the LSI intolerance surveys began in 2010, an increase in religio-cultural intolerance (that is, objection to non-Muslim ceremonies and places of worship in the neighbourhood) was recorded in 2018. The socio-demographic characteristics of this increase also fit with the data presented above: the surge was pushed by massive increases in intolerance among lower-class Muslims, supported by significant growth among tertiary degree holders. Between 2017 and 2018, the overall rate of objection of Muslims to non-Muslim places of worship being built in the neighbourhood increased from 48.2 per cent to 52 per cent, a growth of 3.8 per cent. Among primary school graduates (or lower), however, it rose from 52.5 per cent to 60.5 per cent, more than double the average increase (Table 9.3). In the highest educational stratum, the increase was 5.3 per cent, slightly above the average. In the two medium strata, by contrast, there was much smaller growth or even some contraction. Thus, it was largely lower-class Muslims who, being affected by the impact of the anti-Ahok campaign, drove up religio-cultural intolerance after a decade of softening intolerance in this arena. However, Muslims with the highest educational attainment contributed to this turn as well.

But while intolerance towards non-Muslim minorities has spread chiefly among lower-class Muslims since the anti-Ahok campaign, FPI—the leading group in that campaign—is now supported mainly by affluent and highly educated Muslims. In an earlier publication, we had already begun to explore FPI's process of transformation from a thuggish youth group mainly interested in rent-seeking (Wilson 2014) into an organisation pooling anti-establishment views among conservative Islamic elites (Mietzner and Muhtadi 2018). Our 2018 survey shows that this transformation has progressed further, anchoring FPI firmly as an elite-level political actor. We found that 45.2 per cent of Muslim tertiary degree holders supported FPI in 2018, up from 18.7 per cent in 2016 and 34.3 per cent in 2017. The 2018 level of support was twice as large as the overall support for FPI among Muslims (22.6 per cent). High school graduates were also disproportionately drawn to FPI, at 34.1 per cent. By contrast, only 11.1 per cent of primary school graduates (or lower) approved of FPI's agenda, down from 15.3 per cent in 2018.

This concurrence of increasing intolerance and declining support for FPI among lower-class Muslims confirms our earlier hypothesis that the views of many ordinary Muslims were influenced by conservative preachers at neighbourhood mosques rather than by the intolerant groups directly (Mietzner, Muhtadi and Halida 2018). Those preachers, while sympathising with FPI, tended not to disclose their support for the organisation in their sermons, preferring to maximise their own authority as religious figures. Thus, lower-class Muslims absorbed the substance of these intolerant ideas without necessarily translating it into support for FPI. However, it is also important to recall that because of the large number of people with a primary school education or less, and the continued high levels of support for FPI, the representation of lower-class Muslims in that support structure remains significant. Indeed, in numerical terms, there are still more primary school graduates among Muslim FPI supporters than tertiary degree holders. In those total numbers, the largest contingent of FPI supporters are senior high school graduates.

Drawing from all our available datasets, then, the socio-economic profile of intolerant Muslims can be described as follows. After a period in the mid-2010s when lower-class Muslims were less prominent in the demographics of intolerance, they were recruited in large numbers into the intolerant pool after the Ahok crisis. Intolerant Muslims are also more likely to be older (but equally likely to be male or female), a trend driven by the increase in religio-cultural intolerance among citizens with no or low education. In regional terms, intolerant Muslims are more likely to be from Aceh, North and West Sumatra, Riau, West Java, North and South Kalimantan or West Nusa Tenggara.[6] Our microanalysis of survey data also showed, however, that *political* intolerance in particular (that

---

6   It is important to keep in mind that national surveys are not effective in measuring province-level attitudes, especially in smaller territories. Nevertheless, the data for the larger provinces—particularly West Java—are reliable.

is, objection to non-Muslims holding leadership positions) is very pronounced in the upper educational stratum as well. Tertiary degree holders are the most likely to support FPI, reflecting their key role in the organisation of the anti-Ahok campaign. Anti-Chinese sentiment, for its part, showed no particular demographic pattern, being spread evenly across all groups. In combination, the data tell us that the legacy of the 2016 Islamist events is strong; that it is a religious more than a racial one; and that Indonesia's conservative Muslim elite managed to plant ideas in the ordinary population that, two years after the initial Islamist mobilisation of 2016, seem set to persist.

CONCLUSION: INTOLERANCE AND POLITICS IN INDONESIA

At the beginning of this chapter, we set out to address three main questions arising from the debate on the Islamist mobilisation surrounding the Ahok affair in 2016 and 2017. First, were the protests indicative of deep-seated discriminatory sentiments in the broader Muslim community, or were they simply evidence of its non-political piety? Second, did exclusivist, anti-minority attitudes cause the onset of the anti-Ahok protests or, conversely, did the protests escalate intolerant views? Third, what were the socio-economic demographics of the intolerant Muslims and how did they change during the course of the Islamist protests and their aftermath?

Analysis of multi-year survey datasets allowed us to provide some answers to these questions. First, it is clear that a significant Islamist constituency with religio-racial sentiments exists in Indonesia. Roughly 30 per cent of Indonesian Muslims hold strongly intolerant views towards non-Muslims, and harbour deep anti-Chinese prejudices. While these numbers are similar to intolerance levels in other countries, they warn against dismissing the anti-Ahok campaign as a purely faith-based or political event without wider societal relevance. Second, the data showed that there was no increase in intolerance before the anti-Ahok campaign that could have caused the mobilisation; rather, that increase occurred *after* the Islamist protests, and consolidated further in their aftermath. In short, intolerance was mobilised, rather than being a mobilising factor. This highlights the role of religio-political entrepreneurs in using the existing baseline of intolerance to ignite the protests and to consolidate religious exclusivism further in their aftermath. The analysis of the 2018 data in particular suggests that any hope of religious intolerance declining after the Ahok crisis was misplaced—such a decline occurred only in socio-cultural anti-Chinese sentiments, while resentment towards non-Muslims increased further. And third, our data indicate that while rich and highly educated Muslims were the key drivers of intolerance before the anti-Ahok campaign, lower-class Muslims were the main recruits to the intolerance pool during the protests, and kept joining in its aftermath.

What, then, do these findings mean for Indonesian politics and the state of Indonesian democracy? Most importantly, they mean that anti-minority sentiments inherent in Islamist ideas of politics and society are becoming increasingly mainstream and thus a key element of the political agenda. President Jokowi, originally a religio-political pluralist, has acknowledged this reality by naming Ma'ruf Amin—a major advocate against religious and other social groups that do not conform to the Islamic mainstream—as his running mate for the 2019 presidential elections (albeit on the insistence of his coalition partners). This endorsement of anti-minority views by the political establishment has significant trickle-down effects throughout politics and society, and consistently harms Indonesia's democratic quality. Referring to the country's systematic anti-minority campaigns, the Economist Intelligence Unit's Democracy Index of 2018 relegated Indonesia by 20 ranks—the biggest drop of any country in that year (EIU 2018). Happily endorsing this trend, Muslim respondents in our 2018 survey picked the LGBT community as the 'least liked' social group in Indonesia, followed closely by communists. Marked by such mainstreaming of intolerance and other democratic defects, Indonesia is now arguably in the middle of a slow but perceptible process of democratic deconsolidation (Mietzner 2018). Our data provide very little evidence to suggest that this trend will come to an end any time soon.

REFERENCES

Assyaukanie, L. (2017) 'Unholy alliance: ultra-conservatism and political pragmatism in Indonesia', *Thinking ASEAN* 19, January.
Chaplin, C.J. (2016) 'Stuck in the immoderate middle,' *New Mandala*, 8 November.
EIU (Economist Intelligence Unit) (2018) 'Democracy Index 2017: free speech under attack', EIU, London.
Fealy, G. (2016) 'Bigger than Ahok: explaining the 2 December mass rally', *Indonesia at Melbourne*, 7 December.
Fossati, D., Y.-F. Hui and S.D. Negara (2017) 'The Indonesia National Survey Project: economy, society and politics', *Trends in Southeast Asia* 10, ISEAS–Yusof Ishak Institute, Singapore.
Gallup (2015) 'Six in 10 Americans would say "yes" to Muslim president', 22 September.
Lindsey, T. (2016) 'Blasphemy charge reveals real fault lines in Indonesian democracy', *Indonesia at Melbourne*, 25 November.
Marsden, P.V., and J.D. Wright (2010) *Handbook of Survey Research*, Emerald Group Publishing, Bingley.
Mecham, Q. (2017) *Institutional Origins of Islamist Political Mobilization*, Cambridge University Press, Cambridge.

Menchik, J. (2016) '"Do not take unbelievers as your leaders": the politics of translation in Indonesia', *Mizan*, 31 March.

Mietzner, M. (2018) 'Fighting illiberalism with illiberalism: Islamist populism and democratic deconsolidation in Indonesia', *Pacific Affairs* 91(2): 262–81.

Mietzner, M., and B. Muhtadi (2017) 'Ahok's satisfied non-voters: an anatomy', *New Mandala*, 5 May.

Mietzner, M., and B. Muhtadi (2018) 'Explaining the 2016 Islamist mobilisation in Indonesia: religious intolerance, militant groups and the politics of accommodation', *Asian Studies Review* 42(3): 479–97.

Mietzner, M., B. Muhtadi and R. Halida (2018) 'Entrepreneurs of grievance: drivers and effects of Indonesia's Islamist mobilization', *Bijdragen tot de Taal-, Land- en Volkenkunde* 174(2–3): 159–87.

Pew Research Center (2013) 'The world's Muslims: religion, politics and society', 30 April.

Pew Research Center (2017) 'Muslims and Islam: key findings in the U.S. and around the world', 9 August.

Scherpen, B. (2017) 'Is hardline Islam really rising in Indonesia?' *New Mandala*, 24 February.

Setijadi, C. (2017) 'Chinese Indonesians in the eyes of the *pribumi* public', Perspective No. 73, ISEAS–Yusof Ishak Institute, Singapore, 27 September.

Weng, H.W. (2016) 'Defending Islam and reclaiming diversity', *New Mandala*, 15 December.

Wilson, I. (2014) 'Morality racketeering: vigilantism and populist Islamic militancy in Indonesia', in K. Teik, V. Hadiz and Y. Nakanishi (eds) *Between Dissent and Power: The Transformation of Islamic Politics in the Middle East and Asia*, Palgrave Macmillan, Basingstoke: 248–74.

10 Disputes over places of worship in Indonesia: evaluating the role of the Interreligious Harmony Forum

Ihsan Ali-Fauzi

Disputes over places of worship (*rumah ibadat*) have become an increasingly common type of interreligious conflict in Indonesia in recent years, replacing the sectarian violence that racked areas such as Ambon (in Maluku) and Poso (in Central Sulawesi) during the early *reformasi* period (Panggabean, Alam and Ali-Fauzi 2010). Although conflict over sites of worship occurs mainly between Muslims and Christians, disputes within faith communities are also common, as when Sunni Muslim groups protested against the presence of Ahmadi mosques in West Java (Crouch 2014: 159). This type of conflict signifies the complexity of relationships between majority and minority religious groups in a plural and democratic Indonesia.

Statistics on disputes over places of worship can be found in the reports of institutions specialising in religious freedom, such as the Wahid Foundation (2017) and the Setara Institute (2018). Although these publications provide valuable data on violations of religious freedom, they seldom delve into how and why such incidents occur. In addition, their main focus is, understandably, on transgressions against religious freedom, such as attacks on houses of worship, rather than on incidents where religious tensions have been managed effectively and conflict has been avoided.

Departing radically from these reports, Ali-Fauzi et al. (2012) investigated the factors that gave rise to complex cases involving church

* The author would like to thank Greg Fealy, Ronit Ricci, Sidney Jones and colleagues at PUSAD Paramadina for their constructive comments on earlier drafts of this chapter.

construction in the greater Jakarta region. They analysed the variety of influences in different cases, paying particular attention to why some were successfully resolved, resulting in the building of the church, whereas others led to protracted legal, political and sometimes physical conflicts, some of which still continue. Panggabean and Ali-Fauzi (2015), meanwhile, located disputes over places of worship in the context of religious freedom and the role of the state, particularly the police, in protecting the rights of religious minorities. Both of these publications emphasised the need to improve police effectiveness and increase the role of religious leaders and civil society organisations in supporting state agencies to maintain freedom of religion.

Building on these previous publications, in this chapter I will look specifically at the role played by the Interreligious Harmony Forum (Forum Kerukunan Umat Beragama, FKUB) in managing conflict. These forums were established by a joint regulation issued by the ministries of religious affairs and home affairs in 2006. To date, there has been no systematic study assessing the effectiveness of the FKUB. Such a study is important not only to evaluate the forums' performance, but also because the most important policy-makers in the country, including President Joko Widodo, Minister of Home Affairs Tjahjo Kumolo, Minister of Religious Affairs Lukman Hakim Saifuddin and Indonesian National Police Chief Muhammad Tito Karnavian, want them to play a greater role in dispute resolution and have ordered an expansion of their mandate to enable this.

This chapter discusses the role of the FKUB in mediating disputes in two specific cases: the construction of a mosque in Kupang, East Nusa Tenggara, and the closure of a Christian church in Gunung Kidul, Yogyakarta. These two cases involved different religious minorities (Muslims in Kupang and Christians in Gunung Kidul) and had contrasting political, cultural and policy contexts. In each case, the course and final outcome of the dispute allowed me to study the role of the local FKUB in mediating disputes. Although the main sources of data for this chapter were interviews with the relevant parties and field observations, I have also incorporated pertinent information from the FKUB database now being set up by the Center for the Study of Religion and Democracy (Pusat Studi Agama dan Demokrasi, PUSAD Paramadina).[1]

In the following sections I will briefly discuss the origins of the FKUB, its mandate and its structure and activities, before moving to a detailed comparative discussion of the two case studies and how the local FKUBs

---

1   Under my leadership, PUSAD Paramadina has been compiling a database on the establishment and operations of the FKUBs. Since starting this work in early 2018, we have collected data on 105 provincial- and district/city-level FKUBs, or about a quarter of all FKUBs across the country.

performed as mediators in what proved to be complex religious disputes. I will close the chapter by offering some suggestions about the broader role of the FKUB in Indonesia and its relationship with local government and civil society organisations.

My examination of the two cases suggests that, in each instance, the FKUB was more of a contributor to the dispute than an institution for resolving it: in Gunung Kidul the local forum failed to fulfil its responsibility to act as a non-partisan interfaith organisation, while in Kupang the head of the local forum succumbed to political pressure from the mayor to recommend the construction of the mosque, without following due process. The cases also show that the forums' role in resolving the disputes was marginal in the sense that it was limited to issuing the recommendation that was necessary for the dispute to be resolved. But the fact that both disputes were finally settled, regardless of the peripheral role of the local FKUB, suggests some potential directions for change in the future relationship between the FKUB, local government and civil society organisations.

PBM 2006 AND THE INTERRELIGIOUS HARMONY FORUM

The FKUB was established by Joint Regulation of the Minister of Religious Affairs No. 9/2006 and Minister of Home Affairs No. 8/2006 (Peraturan Bersama Menteri 2006, or PBM 2006) on the Duties of Local Government Heads and Deputy Heads in Maintaining Interreligious Harmony, Empowering Interreligious Harmony Forums and Constructing Places of Worship. PBM 2006 replaced Joint Decree of the Minister of Religious Affairs and Minister of Home Affairs No. 1/1969 (Surat Keputusan Bersama 1969, or KBM 1969) on the Implementation of the Task of Government Officials to Ensure the Order and Undisturbed Implementation of Religious Development and Practices by Adherents. To grasp the intention of PBM 2006, it is important to understand the historical setting in which it was created.

KBM 1969 was enacted in response to rising levels of conflict between Muslims and Christians during the early New Order period (Mujiburrahman 2006). It did not focus specifically on regulating the construction of places of worship; rather, it dealt with the development and propagation of religion more generally. The only clause in KBM 1969 that addressed the construction of places of worship stated that the initiators of such projects had to secure permission from the local government head. In practice, a local government head would issue a permit only after obtaining the approval of the Special Territorial Administrator (Pelaksana Khusus Daerah, Laksusda). The Laksusda were the local security arms of the regime's primary security and intelligence organisation—Operational Command for the Restoration of Security and Order (Komando Operasi Pemulihan Keamanan dan Ketertiban, Kopkamtib)—and were thus an extension of Suharto's extensive machinery of political and social control. Despite the involvement of the security apparatus in the approval process, a significant number of churches were vandalised by irate Muslim groups during the early New Order. KBM 1969 remained in force throughout the Suharto period.

Attacks on houses of worship, particularly churches, intensified in the *reformasi* era (after 1998). The attackers often justifed their actions by claiming that these houses of worship had not secured construction permits and therefore did not comply with KBM 1969. Given the difficulty of obtaining a valid permit under this regulation if one belonged to a minority religion, advocates for religious rights called for KBM 1969 to be revoked and replaced with a new regulation.

After a lengthy period of consultation with religious leaders and much internal deliberation, the government enacted PBM 2006. It places responsibility for maintaining interreligious harmony on both the government (represented by the provincial governor or the district head/mayor) and religious communities (represented by the members of the local FKUB). The representation of each religion on the FKUB is to be proportional to the number of adherents each religion has in that area, with a minimum of one person for each religion. Only the six state-recognised religions (Islam, Catholicism, Protestantism, Hinduism, Buddhism and Confucianism) are entitled to representation.

PBM 2006 states that each forum at the provincial level is to have 21 members and each district/city-level forum is to have 17 members. Provincial forums have four main tasks: conducting dialogue with religious leaders and followers; accommodating the aspirations of religious community organisations and their members; formulating policy recommendations; and educating the community about regulations (*peraturan*) related to religious harmony. District-level forums have the same set of tasks, plus the additional responsibility of providing written recommendations on requests to build places of worship.

In addition to the technical requirements relating to construction, PBM 2006 states that the following must be obtained to build a place of worship: (1) a list of the names and identity cards (*kartu tanda penduduk*, KTP) of 90 people who intend to use the place of worship, confirmed by local government officials; (2) a list of the names and KTPs of 60 members of the local community who approve of the construction of the place of worship without necessarily intending to use it, confirmed by the village or subdistrict head; (3) a written recommendation from the city/district representative of the Ministry of Religious Affairs; and (4) a written recommendation from the city/district chapter of the FKUB. On the last point, the recommendation must be based on consensus and not on a majority vote of forum members.

PBM 2006 states that if support from the local community cannot be obtained, the government is obliged to find an alternative site for the proposed place of worship. In the interim, other buildings can be used as temporary premises for worship, but a permit must first be obtained from the district government. A permit will be granted if the local office of the Ministry of Religious Affairs and the local FKUB issue a letter of recommendation. Any disputes are to be resolved by seeking consensus within the local community. If consensus is not achieved, then the district government must facilitate a fair and unbiased mediation. If government mediation is unsuccessful, the matter may go to court.

By 2018—that is, 12 years after PBM 2006 was issued—FKUB chapters had been established in practically all provinces and cities/districts across the country. However, some districts in West Sumatra, such as Tanah Datar, consistently rejected efforts to establish an FKUB precisely because the dominant religious elite thought that it might recommend the construction of a place of worship for a religion to which the majority was opposed. The local government supported the elite in rejecting the establishment of an FKUB in Tanah Datar.[2] Sampang in Madura, East Java, was another district that refused to establish an FKUB. During the election campaign in 2012, the district head declared: 'As long as I am the district head of Sampang, the FKUB will not be established' (Panggabean and Ali-Fauzi 2015: 125–6).

The heavy dependence of the FKUB on local government can be problematic in regions where politicians dispute the very principles underpinning the forums' existence, despite the presence of a national ministerial decree (PBM 2006) on this matter. The closeness of the relationship between the FKUB and the local government is shown by the data now available through the PUSAD Paramadina database. The data show that all members of FKUBs at both the provincial and city/district levels receive their mandates from the provincial governor or the district head/mayor. While it is true that the local government is obliged to consult local religious councils before establishing a local FKUB chapter, the final decision on the composition of the forum rests with the local government. Moreover, the database shows that both provincial and city/district FKUBs are almost entirely dependent on the provincial or local government for their funding. This arrangement carries the risk that the FKUB may lack the independence to make decisions that are contrary to the wishes of the local government.

---

2 Interview with Ferimeldi, head of the Center for Interreligious Harmony (Pusat Kerukunan Umat Beragama, PKUB), Jakarta, 29 April 2018.

In practice, the forums are also vulnerable to manipulation by local political elites. This is particularly the case for city/district-level FKUBs, whose responsibilities include making recommendations on the construction of houses of worship—often a politically and religiously sensitive matter. Since Indonesia began holding direct elections for district heads and mayors in 2005, appointment to the local FKUB has often been offered as an inducement to religious leaders in exchange for them mobilising voter support for a particular candidate (Ali Fauzi et al. 2012: 142–3).

Another crucial issue related to the functioning of the FKUB concerns the selection of members to represent the region's various religious communities. Recall that PBM 2006 states that FKUB members have to come to a decision based on consensus rather than a majority vote. For this rule to function effectively, all FKUB members need to have a clear understanding that they are there to act as members of a non-partisan interfaith organisation, regardless of their own religious background. Although this has not been a problem in most parts of Indonesia, including Jakarta and Banjarmasin, it has proved to be a major stumbling block in other parts of the country, including Gunung Kidul, as discussed below.

NUR MUSAFIR MOSQUE, KUPANG

The first case study concerns the planned construction of the Nur Musafir Mosque by the Muslim community in the neighbourhood of Batuplat in Kupang, East Nusa Tenggara. This project encountered stiff opposition from local Christians, who form the majority in Batuplat. They accused the Muslims of failing to meet the requirements specified in PBM 2006. The dispute took more than a decade to be settled and the building of the mosque was able to begin only in 2016. Although the dispute generated considerable communal tension, physical violence was avoided, largely due to the role played by the new mayor elected in 2012, and the support provided by peace and interfaith organisations. During the course of the dispute resolution process, the local FKUB chapter acted as an instrument of political interests rather than playing a constructive role.

Chronology of the conflict

The dispute started in 2003 when about 30 Muslim families announced that they wanted to transform a makeshift house used for *tarawih* (special evening prayers during the holy month of Ramadan) into a mosque. This was justified on the grounds that the local Muslim population had grown significantly and there were no other mosques nearby. The plan drew immediate protests from local residents, who said that the building would be too close to their homes, where they bred pigs, and that the Muslim congregation did not have a valid construction permit. Until 2007 various efforts to find a compromise were to no avail.

The dispute was aggravated by the politics surrounding the 2007 local election. In 2007 Daniel Abdoe, a Christian candidate who was supported by two Islamic parties—the National Awakening Party (Partai Kebangkitan Bangsa, PKB) and the Prosperous Justice Party (Partai Keadilan Sejahtera, PKS)—was elected mayor of Kupang. His win showed that the Muslim community had considerable political influence despite constituting a minority in the area.

In an effort to resolve the dispute, Adoe held a meeting in September 2008 with the various stakeholders. They agreed that the mosque would be relocated to another site; that the issuance of a construction permit by the FKUB would be simplified because of the compromise agreement between the parties; and that the old site would still belong to the Muslim community, but would be converted to a multipurpose building. Nevertheless, the Christian community continued to oppose the construction of the mosque, regardless of its location, on the grounds that the Muslims had not met the requirement in PBM 2006 to collect the signatures of 60 members of the local community who were in favour of its construction. Although the construction committee had provided the requisite list of names, the mosque's opponents alleged that the signatures had been gained improperly while the Muslims were distributing food, without explaining that the purpose was to support the mosque's construction. The committee denied these accusations, saying that the requests for signatures were not tied to the distribution of food.

Tensions surrounding the planned mosque grew stronger in 2009. In May, the mosque's nameplate was destroyed and the house of a construction committee member was pelted with stones. Undeterred, the local government kept its promise to expedite the permit process. In April 2010, the mayor signed over the land title for the new mosque to the Nur Musafir Foundation and urged it to apply for a construction permit from the Kupang FKUB. Under pressure from the mayor, on 4 June 2010 the chair of the FKUB, Reverend Hendrik Malelak, signed the necessary letter of recommendation for the construction, but without consulting other FKUB members as required by the rules. This enabled the quick processing of the necessary permits on 15 June 2011 and the mosque's cornerstone was laid just 10 days later.

Protests by residents followed, this time attracting the attention of the provincial and central governments. On 10 August 2011, the East Nusa Tenggara branch of the FKUB held a meeting attended by representatives of the Agency for the Protection of National Unity and Politics (Badan Kesatuan Bangsa dan Politik, Kesbangpol), FKUB Kupang, and neighbourhood, subdistrict and other parties to the conflict. The provincial FKUB suggested the establishment of a fact-finding team to review the circumstances surrounding the controversy over the proposed mosque and suggest a way forward. Three days later, on 13–14 August 2011, a team from the Presidential Advisory Council (Dewan Pertimbangan Presiden, Wantimpres) that had been dispatched to Kupang by President Susilo Bambang Yudhoyono came up with the same recommendation.

In response to these recommendations, the Kupang mayor had little choice but to set up a fact-finding 'Team of Nine' on 19 August 2011. A few months later, the team announced its conclusions. It found that there had been defects in the application process, which did not comply with the provisions of PBM 2006. In particular, 10 of the 65 people who had been named as supporting the mosque's construction had subsequently withdrawn their support, and the letter of recommendation from the chair of the local FKUB was invalid. The team recommended the temporary suspension of construction while these problems were resolved, and asked the Kupang FKUB to issue a new permit based on the correct consultative procedure.

Tensions grew in the lead-up to the mayoral election of 1 May 2012, when the controversy surrounding the mosque's construction turned it into a major campaign issue. The incumbent mayor, Daniel Abdoe, was accused of supporting the mosque because he owed a political debt to the Muslim groups that had supported him in the 2007 and current elections. Abdoe's main opponent was Viktor Lerik, the chair of the East Nusa Tenggara provincial legislature. He had the backing of Karang Taruna Batuplat (Batuplat Youth), the most vocal opponent of the mosque. A third candidate, Jonas Salean, ran as an independent on a platform of peacefully resolving the dispute.

The new mayor and informal approaches by civil society organisations

The election results were unexpected. The incumbent, Daniel Abdoe, was defeated, and Viktor Lerik was declared ineligible after being dismissed from his own Golkar party for violating its code of conduct. This resulted in Jonas Salean being installed as mayor. He governed the city until 2017.

During his term in office, the new mayor played a key role in resolving the dispute over the proposed mosque. On 27 June 2013, he terminated the plan recommended by the Team of Nine but encouraged the mosque committee members to obtain the new signatures required to replace those declared invalid. The committee members responded positively to this call by working quietly to obtain the signatures while avoiding any confrontation with the mosque's opponents.

The new mayor's approach also won support at the grassroots level from civil society activists, who used informal approaches to ease community tensions and to promote communication between the disputing parties. The main civil society actors involved in this effort were two interfaith organisations—Kupang Peacemaker Community (Komunitas Peace Maker Kupang, Kompak) and Solidarity among Victims of Violations of Religious Freedom and Belief (Solidaritas Korban Pelanggaran Kebebasan Beragama dan Berkeyakinan, Sobat KBB)—but various other youth groups were also involved, including some that had previously fiercely resisted the mosque.

Kompak first became involved in the Batuplat case in 2012. It identified three main factors contributing to the conflict: (1) the approval process for the construction of the mosque was not in accordance with PBM 2006; (2) the attitudes of some Kupang Christians towards the mosque were influenced by perceived Muslim discrimination against Christians in Java; and (3) both sides had become stuck in their positions because they were too proud to admit their mistakes. In a 2015 report analysing the conflict, Kompak stated that 'this situation was detrimental to the feelings of local residents, who had earlier never looked at differences but had, rather, accepted each other, other religions, immigrants, everything. [At that time] there was no problem' (Kompak 2015: 4).

Kompak began the conflict mediation process by organising discussions between various groups. During the second round of the 2012 election, held in June, it brought the two mayoral candidates together to seek a joint commitment by them to resolve the conflict. In July 2013, Kompak invited the new mayor and other political and religious leaders in the area to share *iftar* (the evening meal with which Muslims end their daily Ramadan fast at sunset). Kompak also approached Batuplat residents who did not object to the construction of the mosque, but had not said so either out of a sense of solidarity with their fellow Christians or because they did not dare voice their opinions. Kompak asked them to testify to the Kupang FKUB that there were many residents who supported the mosque's construction and would agree to the old permit being used. Kompak also carried out interfaith training for young people in Batuplat in an attempt to balance the partisan views of the more vocal parties to the conflict.[3]

The second interfaith group, Sobat KBB, worked with Abdul Gaos, one of the members of the mosque construction committee, to advocate on behalf of tolerance and religious freedom. Abdul Gaos was acquainted with Reverend Palti Panjaitan, a victim of religious discrimination in Bekasi, West Java. Palti Panjaitan came to Kupang at the invitation of

---

3 Interview with Zarniel Woeleka, chair of Kompak, Kupang, 25 April 2018.

Sobat KBB to share his insights with the Christian community. In his speech, he urged the community to learn from the experience in West Java and do everything they could to avoid the type of religious conflict that was occurring there. 'Let peace come from the east to the west', he said.[4] Reverend Palti's moving testimony made people reflect on and reconsider their past behaviour.

A similar role was played by Reverend Emy Sahertian, the head of the advocacy and peace division of the Christian Evangelical Church in Timor (Gereja Masehi Injili di Timor, GMIT). She had worked with the Filadelfia and Yasmin churches in Bekasi and Bogor, both of which had suffered discrimination and intimidation for many years. When invited to speak at a Batuplat church seminar, she told her audience:

> Actually you are not victims [here]. I was a victim as a member of a minority there [in Java]. I was beaten with sticks [...] and I promised myself that if I ever became part of the majority, I would never treat friends in minorities that way. [...] And you don't have a right to disturb them [the Muslim minority in Kupang]. If it [the mosque] violates the law, you should report it to the police.[5]

Through such testimony and dialogue, the interfaith organisations gradually managed to shift community opinion on the mosque. They were aided in this task by the National Commission for Human Rights (Komisi Nasional Hak Asasi Manusia, Komnas HAM), representing the central government, and by the new mayor. In July 2015, Komnas HAM held a mediation session attended by the mosque construction committee, Batuplat youth leaders, Kupang city government officials, the head of Kesbangpol, members of the Kupang FKUB and representatives of the Kupang office of the Ministry of Religious Affairs. Those attending agreed that construction of the new mosque would be supported by all parties, as long as it was carried out in accordance with the provisions of PBM 2006. They accepted the validity of the signatures collected by the construction committee since 2012 and agreed to work together to obtain the additional signatures required (Komnas HAM 2015).

Thanks to this joint commitment, on 3 February 2016 the local government was finally able to issue a new permit. The end of the dispute was marked with a celebration and the laying of the first brick on 11 April 2016. The event was attended by Muslim and Christian leaders as well as senior political figures. A Christian youth choir and a Muslim tambourine group provided entertainment and the ceremony closed with a ritual animal sacrifice, in accordance with local tradition.

---

4 Interview with Abdul Gaos, member of the mosque construction committee, Kupang, 26 April 2018.

5 Interview with Emy Sahertian, Kupang, 25 April 2018.

Manipulation of the FKUB

Given the long tradition of interfaith cooperation in the area, the Nur Musafir Mosque should have been built much more quickly than turned out to be the case. In Batuplat, and indeed in Kupang more generally, interfaith cooperation between families is common. Interreligious marriages are entrenched in the local culture, and these marriages have created strong civil bonds through family gatherings involving relatives from both sides (Panggabean and Ali-Fauzi 2015: 236–7).

In the case of the dispute over the mosque, however, the long tradition of pluralism in Batuplat was undermined by local politicians who saw an opportunity to exploit a national regulation (PBM 2006), particularly the FKUB's authority to issue construction recommendations for houses of worship, to further their own political interests. At the same time, Kupang's Christian community was aware of the major obstacles, including physical threats, facing Christians who wanted to construct new churches in areas such as Bekasi and Bogor in West Java, and naturally wished to express solidarity with them. There was thus a range of factors contributing to the Christian majority's attitude towards the Muslim minority in Kupang.

Amidst this complexity, instead of leading the initiatives to resolve the conflict, the chair of the local FKUB aggravated a delicate situation by unilaterally approving the plan for the mosque and recommending a municipal permit. He did this after coming under political pressure from the mayor, who was keen to facilitate quick construction of the mosque in order to reward his Muslim supporters. In other words, the authority of the local FKUB was manipulated for political gain.

The catalyst for a breakthrough in the conflict came with the involvement of interfaith groups and peace activists. They not only calmed grassroot tensions and helped mend strained communal bonds, but also facilitated, even obliged, political and religious elites to participate in solving the problem. Their initiatives made it easier for the newly elected mayor to lead the conflict mediation.

CHRISTIAN CHURCH IN GUNUNG KIDUL, YOGYAKARTA

My second case study concerns the dispute over the closure of a Pentecostal Church of Indonesia (Gereja Pantekosta di Indonesia, GPdI) building in Tunggul Barat village, which is in Gunung Kidul district in Yogyakarta. In this instance, the local FKUB failed to function effectively because its members held different opinions about the issue, which had been divisive from the beginning. The dispute was finally resolved through mediation led by a competent local government bureaucrat. Also critical was the advocacy of civil society organisations, which provided practical advice to the church's congregation and brought the issue to the attention of local authorities.

Chronology of the dispute

The dispute began when the church hosted a community service program for students from the Semarang Theological School in October 2010. The students were involved in various church activities in the neighbourhood, including teaching primary school children. These lessons would begin and end with a Christian prayer. When the Muslim community learned about the prayers, fears of Christianisation arose. Protests against GPdI and its pastor started in early 2011 with Muslim groups not only seeking assurances that there would be no further prayer sessions but also raising questions about the legal status of the church, which had previously been used as a house. The protesters demanded the church's closure on the grounds that it lacked the necessary permit to be a place of worship under PBM 2006.

In response to the complaints, subdistrict authorities asked the church's pastor, Reverend Agustinus, to temporarily suspend religious services, which he agreed to do. Agustinus said he was also asked to vacate the building, which doubled as his residence, which he refused to do on the grounds that he had not breached any regulations. His refusal to leave hardened Muslim opposition to the church.

Tensions rose in mid-2012 after the caretaker of Tunggul Barat Mosque invited a speaker from the Islamic Jihad Front (Front Jihad Islam, FJI)—a Yogyakarta-based group well known for its agitation against perceived anti-Islamic activities—to speak at a rally opposing the church. The FJI speaker condemned GPdI's 'Christian missionising' and incited the audience to greater opposition. Matters came to a head in early 2013 when an angry group of 200 people descended on Agustinus's house, forcing him and his family to flee through a back door. A few days later, at a meeting with subdistrict authorities, the pastor was forced to sign an order to shut down the church and leave the house.[6]

In the midst of these escalating tensions, the members of the Gunung Kidul FKUB were unable to agree on a unified organisational stance because opinion within the forum was divided along religious lines. The partisanship of FKUB members exacerbated the problem rather than helping to solve it. This was acknowledged by no less than the chair of the local FKUB, H. Iskanto A.R., who said: 'While the church's opponents

---

6   Interview with Agustinus, GPdI pastor in Semanu, Gunung Kidul, 31 March 2018.

were mainly Muslim and would complain only to the Muslim representative, the members of GPdI would complain only to the Christian one'.[7] Iskanto was aware of the invitation to the FJI speaker but did nothing to prevent or counteract it.

Civil society advocacy and government mediation

The impetus to resolve the conflict started with advocacy for religious freedom by a Jakarta-based civil society organisation called the Unity in Diversity National Alliance (Aliansi Nasional Bhinneka Tunggal Ika, ANBTI). In November 2014, ANBTI invited Agustinus to take part in a workshop on religious freedom in Gunung Kidul, together with representatives of other churches and religions facing similar problems. The workshop resulted in a plan to investigate the cases raised by the participants, especially regarding documentation relating to the legal status of their places of worship. 'Since then I've been collecting [all the papers] so that it's easy [to locate them] when we need to seek justice', Agustinus said.[8]

Agustinus then approached the Gunung Kidul district administration seeking to reopen the GPdI church. On the advice of ANBTI activist Agnes Dwi Rusjiyati, he opted to act through non-legal channels: 'We wanted the government to help us meet the requirements regarding the church that were at issue, without us having to go to court. That is why we focused on strengthening the documentation aspect for all the churches that had [this] problem', Agnes said.[9] After listening attentively to Agustinus's request, the local government decided that it needed to address not only the issue of the church's closure and the expulsion of its pastor, but also the broader community concern about Christianisation. Hj. Badingah, the Gunung Kidul district head, entrusted this task to her most senior assistant, Tommy Harahap. A Muslim and a law graduate from the Islamic University of Indonesia in Yogyakarta, Harahap believed that religious conflict had the potential to damage community relationships and district development if not dealt with promptly and effectively.

Some detail is necessary in describing Harahap's work, as it reveals precisely how resolution of the problem was secured. He began by inviting all district-level stakeholders, including the local head of the Ministry

---

7 Interview with Iskanto, chair of FKUB Gunung Kidul, Gunung Kidul, 30 March 2018.
8 Interview with Agustinus, GPdI pastor in Semanu, Gunung Kidul, 31 March 2018.
9 Interview with Agnes Dwi Rusjiyati, ANBTI activist, Yogyakarta, 9 March 2018.

of Religious Affairs and the chair of the Gunung Kidul FKUB, to a meeting. 'I didn't want these two officials to issue any public statement about the case, unless they had discussed it with me and we had all reached agreement', Harahap said.[10] He suspected that both men held partisan views, having previously sided with the church's opponents. Second, he ensured that all government officials who were involved in handling the dispute, from the subdistrict to the village level, understood the case properly. All relevant officials were summoned individually and asked to explain their role in resolving the conflict and to provide detailed data supporting their decision-making.

After gathering the necessary data and discussing the problem separately with each major stakeholder, Harahap convened a final meeting at which a binding agreement on how to proceed would be reached. In his initial meetings with the protagonists, Harahap had asked about points of conflict and sought advice on how to resolve them. He stressed that advice that was in accord with the concepts of unity and tolerance, as stipulated in the Constitution, would be carefully noted but that he would suggest alternatives to any advice that fell outside that framework.

To reach a resolution in the case of GPdI, Harahap needed to find solutions to several core problems. First, the legal status of the church was uncertain: according to its opponents, the church had no building permit and was therefore illegal. Harahap tackled the problem in the following manner:

> I asked [the opponents]: 'If there is no construction permit, what should the government do?' Their representative said: 'Shut down the church and don't let it be used again'. Then I said: 'Fine, if that is your advice, we will close all places of worship that have no permits. Soon we will collect information on all of them in Gunung Kidul, regardless of their religion. All of them will be shut down'. They were shocked, because thousands of mosques, too, have no construction permits. They didn't want to see them closed.[11]

In the ensuing discussions, the stakeholders agreed to a compromise: all long-established places of worship that did not have building permits would be deemed legal. 'I welcomed this solution and prepared a draft decree for the district head to grant an amnesty for [illegal] places of worship', said Harahap. 'The district head signed it and the problem was solved. GPdI was legal based on that decree.'

The second challenge was the problem of Christianisation. This was a concern not only for Muslims but also some Christians. Reverend Adi,

10   Interview with Tommy Harahap, former first regional assistant to the district head, Gudung Kidul, 31 March 2018.
11   Interview with Tommy Harahap, former first regional assistant to the district head, Gudung Kidul, 31 March 2018.

a pastor at one of the mainstream Protestant churches in Gunung Kidul, said: 'It's actually our church that should be angry. Many members of GPdI in Gunung Kidul were recruited from [the congregation of] our church'.[12] Many established Christian churches in Indonesia were experiencing declining attendance as members of their congregations moved to evangelical churches, some of which proselytised intensively. The problem had become sufficiently acute that the churches in Gunung Kidul had banded together to address issues of interdenominational proselytism, forming the All Churches Cooperation Agency (Badan Kerjasama Seluruh Gereja, BKS Gereja). Nevertheless, interchurch grievances remained.

In seeking solutions to conversion-related tensions, Harahap again sought evidence that interfaith and interdenominational proselytism had taken place. He found none. When he asked GPdI's Agustinus about his outreach activities, the pastor told him that he was willing to preach to anyone but was not seeking conversions from other faiths. Harahap argued that all religious leaders, including non-Christian ones, had equal rights under the Constitution. Therefore, the government could not bar one pastor from preaching without barring all pastors from preaching. Moreover, such a ban would have to be extended to Muslim preachers. This resulted in a verbal agreement among the stakeholders that no party would attempt to convert the adherents of another religion.

Finally, on the matter of the expulsion of the pastor, Harahap could find no convincing reason to justify this. Agustinus had lived in Tunggul Barat for a long time, was registered as a resident and had documents confirming his ownership of the land and the house. Harahap decided there were no legal grounds preventing the return of the pastor to his house and he secured a commitment from all stakeholders that the church be allowed to resume its activities.

With mediation complete, the Gunung Kidul district government held a reconciliation feast for everyone involved in the dispute on 16 February 2015. During the event, Reverend Agustinus apologised for the noise caused by the church's rituals, although he refused to read a letter written for him by subdistrict officials, as he disagreed with the accusations it levelled against him.

Failure of the local FKUB

The Gunung Kidul case indicates that the local FKUB failed to fulfil its responsibility to act as a non-partisan interfaith organisation. From the beginning, FKUB members were divided along religious lines, and were unable to unite as a cohesive body committed to resolving the dispute.

---

12 Interview with Reverend Adi (pseudonym), Gunung Kidul, 30 March 2018.

Producing a recommendation was complicated not only by the strong objections of church opponents, but also by sharp disagreement among FKUB members themselves. Even worse, the Muslim chair of the Gunung Kidul FKUB failed to prevent the escalation of the dispute by seeking to stop a radical preacher from outside the district from inflaming Muslim sentiment regarding the church and Christianisation.

The case shows the importance of prompt and effective local government responses. In Gunung Kidul, a single Muslim official, Tommy Harahap, was pivotal to the peaceful resolution of this complex interfaith problem. With a clear mandate from his superior and a strong commitment to upholding the Indonesian Constitution, he acted firmly and impartially, without fear of being accused of being anti-Islam in a strongly Muslim neighbourhood. One factor contributing to his success was his decision to silence those members of the FKUB whom he deemed to be partisan and an obstacle to resolution if allowed a voice.

It is also notable that the Gunung Kidul district head who appointed Tommy Harahap only became aware of this conflict due to the activism of interfaith peace groups, which advocated for and empowered the most vulnerable stakeholders in the conflict, the GPdI minister and his congregation. The role of civil society activism was crucial in filling the void left by an ineffective and biased local FKUB.

CONCLUSION: LESSONS LEARNED

Below I will make some broad evaluations regarding the role of the FKUB in mediating disputes over places of worship. I will discuss them in light of some observations that have been made about the functioning of the FKUBs generally and their relationship with local government and civil society organisations.

First, in the two cases discussed in this chapter, the local FKUB was more of a contributor to the disputes than a solver of them. In Gunung Kidul, this was primarily due to the fact that the forum failed to operate as a non-partisan organisation focused on maintaining and strengthening interfaith harmony. This reminds us of the importance of FKUB cohesiveness and impartiality. If Indonesia's policy-makers really want to enhance the status of the FKUBs, then they need to ensure their non-partisanship. They could do so by revising the current mechanism in PBM 2006 for recruiting FKUB members: rather than consulting only local religious councils before forming a local FKUB, the local government should consult civil society organisations and other interested parties to ensure that the candidates have good standing as advocates for tolerance and harmony.

The Gunung Kidul case also indicates the risks of Muslims fearing Christianisation. Recall that similar communal and religious sentiment in Kupang—that is, the local Christians' feelings of solidarity towards their co-religionists in Java—fuelled opposition to the construction of a mosque. This issue of religious conversion and persecution has become a potent weapon in the hands of groups seeking to stop the construction of, or to destroy, places of worship (Ali-Fauzi et al. 2012; Crouch 2010).

The Kupang case illustrates the issue of excessive FKUB dependence on the local government. The chair of the local forum succumbed to political pressure from the mayor, who wanted to expedite mosque construction in order to win electoral favour from the Muslim community. It is unlikely that the dispute over the mosque would have occurred at all had there not been political interference in the internal affairs of the Kupang FKUB. But more than just undermining the legitimacy of FKUB processes, the mayor's manipulation of the forum soured a long tradition of interfaith cooperation in Kupang. This has also happened in other places in Indonesia, such as Ende, a district in another part of East Nusa Tenggara (Panggabean and Ali-Fauzi 2015: 265–88).

Yet the dispute resolutions in Kupang and Gunung Kidul also point to other, more promising directions in the FKUB's relationship with local government. Jonas Salean in Kupang and Tommy Harahap in Gunung Kidul did not interfere in local FKUB affairs or seek to gain political benefit from the FKUB's power to issue letters of recommendation. We have no reliable information on how many regional officials like Tommy Harahap or Jonas Salean there are in local administrations, because our existing reporting and research approaches usually focus on negative, rather than positive, cases—hence bad bureaucrats, rather than the good ones, get attention (Panggabean 2018: 5–7). But I believe the relationship between the FKUB and local government goes beyond the binary opposition of total dependence or total independence. Learning from the long experience of interfaith activists such as Syafi'i Mufid, chair of the Jakarta FKUB, we can see that the local FKUB can actually maintain a degree of autonomy from local government, dependent on its own commitment and capacity (Ali-Fauzi et al. 2012; Mulyartono 2017).

Lessons can also be drawn from the two cases examined above about the FKUB's role as a mediator. Although both disputes were finally resolved, in each case the local FKUB's role in the process of mediation was negligible. Indeed, analysis of the disputes suggests that both cases could have been resolved without involving the local FKUB at all. Local FKUBs are of course needed to issue construction permits, but if a dispute arises after this has happened, then they should be ready to act as mediators and to help solve the conflict. So, not only should FKUBs guard their impartiality, but they should also improve their mediation skills.

Some interfaith activists have called for the annulment of PBM 2006 and the dissolution of the FKUB as a national institution on the grounds that both are inherently flawed. Such a move would be counterproductive and could well result in worse tensions over places of worship. If functioning correctly, FKUBs have the capacity to fulfil their obligations effectively. Proper support from local government and civil society organisations is crucial for this. Local governments and FKUBs should focus less on the technical rules in PBM 2006 for the construction of houses of worship and place greater emphasis instead on the spirit of the document, which is about building cooperation between faith communities on the basis of mutual understanding and respect. In addition, local governments and FKUBs should address disputes over places of worship as early as possible, so that religious tensions do not spread to other areas.

Finally, as the cases in Gunung Kidul and Kupang indicate, support from civil society activists working on peace and pluralism issues can play a significant role in achieving reconciliation between communities. They can empower minority groups to defend their rights and negotiate long-term solutions to their grievances. Their role is similarly crucial in encouraging governments at the local, provincial and even national level to solve the conflicts fairly. In the future, civil society activists need to involve FKUB officials more often and as early as possible in their initiatives, so that these officials can strengthen their capacity in conflict resolution and be aware that support is available in fulfilling their responsibilities.

REFERENCES

Ali-Fauzi, I., S.R. Panggabean, N.G. Sumaktoyo, A.H. Tohari, H. Mubarak, Testriono and S. Nurhayati (2012) *Disputed Churches in Jakarta*, Asian Law Centre and Centre for Islamic Law and Society, University of Melbourne, Melbourne.

Crouch, M. (2010) 'Implementing the regulation on places of worship in Indonesia: new problems, local politics and court action', *Asian Studies Review* 34(4): 403–19.

Crouch, M. (2014) *Law and Religion in Indonesia: Conflict and the Courts in West Java*, Routledge, New York NY.

Komnas HAM (Komisi Nasional Hak Asasi Manusia) (2015) 'Laporan akhir tahun pelapor khusus kebebasan beragama dan berkeyakinan Komisi Nasional Hak Asasi Manusia Republik Indonesia 2015', Komnas HAM, Jakarta.

Kompak (Komunitas Peace Maker Kupang) (2015) 'Kabar dari Batuplat', unpublished report, Kompak, Kupang.

Mulyartono, S. (2017) 'Mengagungkan Tuhan, memuliakan manusia: kiprah Ahmad Syafi'i Mufid dalam Binadamai', in I. Ali-Fauzi and R. Panggabean (eds) *Pekerja Binadamai dari Tanah Pasundan*, Pusat Studi Agama dan Demokrasi (PUSAD), Yayasan Paramadina, Jakarta: 31–50.

Mujiburrahman (2006) *Feeling Threatened: Muslim–Christian Relations in Indonesia's New Order,* ISIM and Amsterdam University Press, Leiden and Amsterdam.

Panggabean, R. (2018) *Konflik dan Perdamaian Etnis di Indonesia: Menjelaskan Variasi,* Pusat Studi Agama dan Demokrasi (PUSAD), Yayasan Paramadina, Jakarta.

Panggabean, R., R.H. Alam and I. Ali-Fauzi (2010) 'The patterns of religious conflict in Indonesia (1990–2008)', *Studia Islamika* 17(3): 233–98.

Panggabean, R., and I. Ali-Fauzi (2015) *Policing Religious Conflicts in Indonesia,* Pusat Studi Agama dan Demokrasi (PUSAD), Yayasan Paramadina, Jakarta.

Setara Institute (2018) 'Ringkasan eksekutif laporan tengah tahun kondisi kebebasan beragama/berkeyakinan dan minoritas keagamaan di Indonesia 2018', Setara Institute, Jakarta.

Wahid Foundation (2017) 'Ringkasan eksekutif laporan tahunan kemerdekaan beragama berkeyakinan (KBB) di Indonesia tahun 2016', Wahid Foundation, Jakarta.

11 Anti-Chinese sentiment and the 'return' of the *pribumi* discourse

Charlotte Setijadi

Chinese Indonesians have received considerable public attention in recent times, mostly because of the blasphemy scandal involving the ethnic Chinese and Christian former governor of Jakarta, Basuki Tjahaja Purnama (known as Ahok). A popular governor with consistently high approval ratings, Ahok was widely tipped, before September 2016, to win the 2017 Jakarta gubernatorial election. Then, in late September, he made a campaign speech in Jakarta's Thousand Islands district referring to verse 51 of the Al-Ma'idah chapter of the Qur'an, which is generally interpreted as saying that Muslims should not have non-Muslim leaders. Ahok urged Muslim voters to make up their own minds about the interpretation of the verse and not simply to follow those who claimed that it was sinful to elect a non-Muslim leader like himself. Within weeks, a series of mass protests in central Jakarta organised by hardline Islamist groups such as the Islamic Defenders Front (Front Pembela Islam, FPI) were attracting hundreds of thousands of Muslim protesters from all over Indonesia.

What started as a religious issue soon also became a race and class issue. Very quickly, angry and hate-filled racist messages began to appear at the anti-Ahok demonstrations, directed not only towards the governor but also towards the ethnic Chinese as a group. The protesters cited Ahok's notoriously abrasive character as evidence of the arrogance and sense of superiority of Chinese Indonesians (Walden 2017).

Following the first mass demonstration on 4 November 2016, groups of protesters went to the exclusive north Jakarta residential estate where Ahok and his family lived. Most of the people living at the estate were affluent ethnic Chinese, and for them, the protesters' threats to torch their houses echoed the horrors of earlier riots in May 1998 targeting the Chinese. Although the protesters eventually left without creating much havoc, anti-Chinese rhetoric intensified in the months that followed, particularly on social media. For instance, rumours abounded that Ahok's political rise had been financed and engineered by Chinese Indonesian business tycoons who hoped to exert political influence on the governor and other politicians, including Ahok's close ally, President Joko Widodo (Jokowi). It was also claimed that Ahok's controversial Jakarta Bay land reclamation project was intended to house millions of new migrants from China, rather than providing low-cost housing for Indonesians.[1] Even senior government officials, such as the then head of the Armed Forces, General Gatot Nurmantyo, spoke of a 'Chinese proxy war' in which China sought to undermine the nation by infiltrating both government and non-government institutions (Allard and Kapoor 2017).

What happened next has been much written about: Ahok lost the election to the Islamists' candidate, Anies Baswedan, and shortly afterwards was found guilty of blasphemy and jailed for two years.

The rise of anti-Chinese narratives during the Jakarta election campaign and Ahok blasphemy trial has prompted questions about whether old stereotypes and prejudices about Indonesia's ethnic Chinese minority have persisted despite almost two decades of policy and social reforms. Was the Jakarta election an isolated moment, or has there been a sustained rise in anti-Chinese discourse and ethno-nationalist rhetoric in the post-Suharto era?

As 'essential outsiders' within the Indonesian nation (Reid 1997), the Chinese are the group that most readily springs to mind when discussing ethnic minorities in the country. Politically weak and widely loathed for their perceived economic dominance, the ethnic Chinese have always been easy victims of the racialised violence and riots that have flared up during episodes of political or economic instability in the colonial and post-independence eras. The most infamous recent incident occurred in May 1998, when Chinese individuals and property were attacked and ethnic Chinese women were raped. In the aftermath of these riots, successive *reformasi* governments began to dismantle the New Order's assimilation policy and other policies that discriminated against the Chinese, leading to a revival of Chinese identity politics and to significant improvements in the socio-political situation of Chinese Indonesians.

---

1   Social media reports that 10 million migrants from China had been allowed to enter Indonesia under Ahok's leadership in Jakarta and Jokowi's leadership at the national level were a prominent theme of the anti-Ahok protests. These claims were part of a broader political attack on Jokowi for supposedly allowing large numbers of low-skilled Chinese migrant workers to flood the Indonesian labour market. Even Indonesia's premier news weekly, *Tempo*, published a special issue criticising the influx of Chinese migrant workers under Jokowi's administration. For more on this topic, see Priyandita (2018).

I argue, however, that despite the post-Suharto reforms, anti-Chinese sentiment has never disappeared from the Indonesian national psyche, and that, as a result, the place of the Chinese in Indonesia continues to be contentious in nature.

In this chapter, I investigate the increase in anti-Chinese rhetoric surrounding the 2017 Jakarta election, as well as the re-emergence of the term *pribumi* (indigenous) in political and public discourse. I demonstrate that anti-Chinese narratives began to surface well before the Jakarta election and the Ahok trial, not at the time of those events as is often assumed. Sporadic incidents involving racialised attacks (both verbal and physical) on ethnic Chinese individuals and communities have taken place periodically since 1998. This indicates that anti-Chinese sentiment already lingered just below the surface, despite the outward appearance of greater societal acceptance of the Chinese.

In the discussion that follows, I include analysis of survey data on *pribumi* perceptions of the ethnic Chinese obtained from the Indonesia National Survey Project (INSP). This survey was conducted by the ISEAS–Yusof Ishak Institute in May 2017 while I was a visiting fellow there. I also analyse the potential implications of increased xenophobia and ethnonationalism for the upcoming 2019 presidential and legislative elections. I conclude that the belonging of ethnic Chinese in Indonesia will remain contested if Indonesia's national identity continues to be defined along nativist and ethno-religious lines.

THE ETHNIC CHINESE AS *CINA* AND *NON-PRIBUMI*

The social construction of Chinese Indonesians as *non-pribumi* began during the colonial period when the Dutch categorised them as Foreign Orientals (Vreemde Osterlingen) and accorded them higher status within the colonial hierarchy than the Native (Inlander) population. The fact that many Chinese served as middlemen for the Dutch in trade dealings with the non-Chinese perpetuated their negative image as opportunistic economic 'animals' who were profiting from the suffering of the indigenous population. As Reid (1997: 55) argues, during the independence struggle and the early days of the Indonesian republic, the position of the ethnic Chinese as 'foreigners within' made them 'one of the most important "Others" against which the new national identities defined themselves'.

Time and time again, scholars have pointed out the constructed and arbitrary nature of the *pribumi*–Chinese distinction in the Indonesian national imagination (Heryanto 2008; Suryadinata 2005; Tan 2008). In fact, Indonesia's supposedly unified and monolithic *pribumi* population is made up of diverse peoples from the many tribes, ethnicities and linguistic groups that exist across the archipelago. Before the national awakening of the twentieth century, the struggles against Dutch colonial occupation were localised and fought mainly by individual tribes, kingdoms and regions. It was not until the nationalist independence movement started to gain serious traction in the early 1900s that local leaders began to organise and to conceive of themselves as part of a unified national project. The ideological concept of *pribumi* as the original peoples of the Indonesian archipelago with identifiable homelands (comprising the Sundanese people from West Java, the Balinese from Bali and so on) was an important one in the context of the then imminent need for a unified anti-colonial struggle and nation-building. Although tribal and local identities remain important in Indonesia to this day, the *pribumi* construct as a marker of 'nativeness' provided common ground for Indonesians, who could now lay claim to a native homeland.

In the course of nation-building, however, modern Indonesian ethnonationalism never managed to successfully accommodate the Chinese. This situation allowed successive Indonesian governments to manipulate the vulnerability of the Chinese and use them as scapegoats in times of crisis. It is important to note that both the beginning and the end of President Suharto's New Order regime were marked by major episodes of anti-Chinese violence, encouraged at least in part by military-backed factions keen to demonstrate their power to 'save the day' by successfully handling the crisis (Purdey 2006). The fact that one of the New Order's first major acts of government was to introduce a policy of assimilation intended to erase all traces of Chinese-ness in Indonesia illustrates that it saw the ethnic Chinese—and by extension Chinese-ness—as a problem to be 'fixed' in the interests of national unity.

During the 32 years in which the assimilation policy was in force, the use of Chinese languages was banned, Chinese schools were closed, Chinese media and political organisations were disbanded and public expressions of Chinese culture were forbidden. In a decision issued in 1966 (Cabinet Presidium Decision No. 127/1966), Suharto's first cabinet suggested that ethnic Chinese families consider taking up new, Indonesian-sounding names; thus, the Chinese surname 'Tan' would become 'Tanuwijaya' or 'Tanumihardja', Lim would become 'Salim' and so on. It was not mandatory for ethnic Chinese to change their names, but they came under immense social and institutional pressure to do so in order to prove their loyalty to Indonesia and their commitment to becoming 'real' Indonesians. The implication was clear: Chinese-ness was ideologically suspect, and Chinese Indonesians who did not voluntarily erase their Chinese identities risked being accused of disloyalty or—worse—political subversion.

The policy of assimilation of Chinese Indonesians that prevailed throughout the New Order period was deeply problematic and paradoxical. On the one hand, the whole justification for the assimilation policy was to solve the 'Chinese problem' by absorbing Chinese Indonesians into the majority *pribumi* society. Yet the very fact that the ethnic Chinese were deemed to be the main group requiring assimilation singled them out as *the* problematic ethnic minority. Moreover, since careers in politics, the military and the civil service were effectively off-limits to ethnic Chinese, one of the few domains left for them to operate in was the world of business. Their visibility in commerce, combined with the corrupt system of patronage linking Suharto family members and associates with prominent Chinese tycoons such as Liem Sioe Liong (Sudono Salim), Ciputra and Bob Hasan, served only to reinforce the public image of Chinese Indonesians as what Amy Chua (2003: 6) has termed 'market-dominant minorities' and Ruth McVey (1992) has called 'pariah capitalists'.

During this period, language had much to do with the 'othering' of Chinese Indonesians at the everyday level. The importance of semantics was clearly something that the New Order government understood well. One of its first acts in 1967 was to issue a cabinet circular (No. SE-06/Pres. Kab/6/1967) instructing that the term *Cina* rather than *Tionghoa* be used to refer to the ethnic Chinese in official documents. This could be considered a deliberate insult to the Chinese considering the derogatory nature of this term. In addition, *Cina* implied ideological closeness to Communist China—thus carrying sinister overtones at a time when Indonesia–China relations were still frozen following accusations that China had been involved in the abortive communist coup of 30 September 1965.

Throughout the New Order, Chinese Indonesians were often called *non-pribumi* (non-native), or *non-pri* for short, in both official and everyday speech. The term *pribumi* itself has a long history that stretches back to an 1854 Dutch colonial law that categorised the inhabitants of the East Indies into three groups according to race, namely Europeans (Europeanen), Natives or indigenous Indonesians (Inlander) and Foreign Orientals (Vreemde Oosterlingen), the latter comprising Chinese, Arabs, Indians and other non-European foreigners. This racial division persisted even after independence, with the term *pribumi* by this time having acquired connotations of anti-colonial and anti-foreign native empowerment. While by definition the term *non-pribumi* theoretically describes anyone in Indonesia who does not belong to a tribe considered 'indigenous' to the country, in practice it is almost always used to refer, in a derogatory way, to ethnic Chinese (Hoon 2006a; Setijadi 2016). Indonesians of Indian or Arab/Hadhrami (Yemeni) descent, such as Jakarta governor Anies Baswedan or FPI leader Rizieq Shihab, are almost never referred to as *non-pribumi*. In other words, *pribumi* has become a politically charged term, laden with the historical baggage of decades of state-sanctioned discrimination against Chinese Indonesians.

POST-SUHARTO IMPROVEMENTS

Since the beginning of the *reformasi* period, Chinese Indonesians have generally become more optimistic about the state of their political situation and safety in Indonesia (Hoon 2006a; Purdey 2006). In the aftermath of the May 1998 riots, post-Suharto governments were only too eager to prove their commitment to human rights issues and their rejection of the harmful policies of the New Order by implementing new laws that recognised the rights of Chinese Indonesians. The Habibie government kicked off these reforms in 1999 by issuing a presidential instruction that proscribed the use of the terms *pribumi* and *non-pribumi* in official government documents. In 2000, President Abdurrahman Wahid revoked the bans on Chinese languages, religion and cultural expressions, allowing Chinese culture to be practised in public once more. President Megawati Sukarnoputri made Chinese New Year a national holiday in 2002 as an official gesture of recognition of both Chinese Indonesians and Confucianism (*Khonghucu*), which became Indonesia's sixth officially recognised religion.

Changes were also made in the realm of politics. The third amendment to the 1945 Constitution, in November 2001, replaced the constitutional requirement for an Indonesian president to be *asli* (indigenous) with a new requirement stating that both the president and the vice-president must be Indonesian citizens by birth and must never have voluntarily obtained the citizenship of another country. In 2006, parliament passed Citizenship Law No. 12/2006, which recognised all individuals born in Indonesia as *asli*. In combination, these two amendments gave Chinese Indonesians unprecedented political rights and, most importantly, the right to run for the presidency or vice-presidency.

Indeed, during the early years of *reformasi*, the improved treatment of ethnic Chinese became a marker for the 'progressive' policy-making of the post-Suharto period. For a few years, the belonging of Chinese Indonesians seemed a little less contested, and there was great hope that Indonesia's 'Chinese problem' could perhaps be solved as the nation adopted a more pluralist and accepting stance towards its ethnic Chinese minority.[2]

---

2 Ironically, while the situation improved considerably for the Chinese in the reform era, other minorities (most notably religious minorities such as the

A sense of rising confidence among the ethnic Chinese could be seen in their increased presence in mainstream politics, government and civil society. In politics, ethnic Chinese figures such as Ahok (governor of Jakarta), Sofyan Tan (member of parliament for Medan), Daniel Johan (member of parliament for West Kalimantan), Kwik Kian Gie (former economics and finance minister and former national development planning minister), Mari Elka Pangestu (former trade minister) and Enggartiasto Lukita (the current trade minister) forged successful careers as politicians (Setijadi 2014). Indeed, an increasing number of Chinese Indonesians have been contesting local, regional and national elections. In 2004, about 100 ethnic Chinese candidates participated in the legislative elections for the national parliament (Dewan Perwakilan Rakyat, DPR). This number doubled to approximately 200 in the 2009 elections and increased again to 315 in the 2014 elections. The vast majority of these candidates were backed by major political parties, with the Indonesian Democratic Party of Struggle (Partai Demokrasi Indonesia-Perjuangan, PDI-P), the National Democrats (Nasional Demokrat, NasDem) and the National Awakening Party (Partai Kebangkitan Bangsa, PKB) nominating the most ethnic Chinese candidates.

In the 2014 elections, a record 15 ethnic Chinese were elected to the DPR. As a share, this was 2.7 per cent of the 560 seats in parliament, or roughly the same as the share of ethnic Chinese in the total Indonesian population. Many more Chinese Indonesians are currently serving as senators, district heads and village heads. The number of ethnic Chinese who have served as government ministers or high officials in the post-Suharto era is in stark contrast to the New Order period, when only one ethnic Chinese—close Suharto business partner Bob Hasan—served as a cabinet minister, and even this came only at the very end of Suharto's rule.

A 'RETURN' OF ANTI-CHINESE SENTIMENT IN POST-SUHARTO INDONESIA?

Despite the euphoria over the re-emergence of Chinese culture and identity politics in the post-Suharto era, anti-Chinese sentiment never really went away. Minor incidents that had the potential to erupt into full-scale riots have occurred sporadically since 1998, almost all of them caused initially by small disputes or misunderstandings to do with money or religion (or both). For instance, a neighbourhood disagreement over alleged

---

Ahmadis and Christians) were subjected to greater oppression. See Hefner (2013) for more on this topic.

damage to a parked car led to the assault of an ethnic Chinese man in the Kalimantan city of Pontianak on 6 December 2007. This incident—called the 'Alleyway 17' incident after the name of the street where the dispute took place—quickly escalated into a small-scale riot in which ethnic Malays attacked a local Chinese temple and destroyed a number of Chinese-owned properties.

Much more seriously, in July 2016 a complaint by Meiliana, a 44-year-old Buddhist-Chinese woman, that the volume of a local mosque's call to prayer (*adzan*) was too loud led to riots, looting, attacks and the burning of several Buddhist and Chinese temples by a mob of hundreds in the North Sumatran town of Tanjung Balai (Tempo 2016). Meiliana was charged with blasphemy against Islam in early 2017. In August 2018, she was sentenced to 18 months in jail under the same law that had put Ahok behind bars: Law No. 1/PNPS/1965, better known as the Blasphemy Law.

In the political arena as well, anti-Chinese sentiment continued to linger. While the 2017 gubernatorial election and anti-Ahok protests brought anti-Chinese feeling to the fore, this was not the first time that Ahok had been targeted because of his ethnicity. During the 2012 Jakarta gubernatorial campaign, when Ahok ran as Jokowi's deputy, pro-*pribumi* Islamist groups such as FPI and the Betawi Brotherhood Forum (Forum Betawi Rempug, FBR) tried to turn Ahok's ethnicity and religion into an election issue.

During the 2014 presidential election, a campaign of misinformation against then presidential candidate Jokowi used viral memes to suggest that he 'looked Chinese' and was actually of Chinese descent. Jokowi's campaign team were quick to deny the allegations of Chinese ethnicity, but the very fact that they needed to do so is evidence of the negative political connotations still attached to Chinese-ness.

At the same time, anti-China sentiment has also risen, particularly since Jokowi took office as president in 2014. The view that Jokowi has been too reliant on Chinese foreign direct investment for his flagship infrastructure-building projects has fed fears about excessive Chinese political and economic influence in Indonesia (Herlijanto 2017). This indicates that, despite improvements in bilateral relations at the national level since Sino-Indonesian diplomatic relations resumed in 1990, undercurrents of distrust towards China still exist among the political elite and the general public.

Indonesians' perceptions of China almost inevitably feed into their perceptions of Chinese Indonesians. Historically viewed as China's 'fifth pillar', ethnic Chinese are still often seen as being agents for China, or at the very least as acting in China's interests in business and political dealings. In short, negative views of China heighten the risk of animosity towards Chinese Indonesians.

Contemporary expressions of anti-Chinese sentiment also have complex intersections with issues of class and religion, as Mietzner and Muhtadi point out in Chapter 9 of this volume. While religion features much more prominently now than it did in the past, class has always been an important element shaping how the non-Chinese public perceives Chinese Indonesians. Indeed, as analysts have pointed out, class was a key factor in the Ahok blasphemy case, with many Indonesians unable to separate the governor's supposedly blasphemous behaviour from policies of his that were viewed as harming the poor, such as the forced evictions of communities living along Jakarta's riverbanks and the disruption to fishers' livelihoods caused by the Jakarta Bay land reclamation project (Renaldi 2017). The overlap of issues of religion, class and ethno-nationalism in the recent rise in anti-Chinese sentiment is clear.

In an interview with *Reuters* journalists conducted shortly after Ahok was jailed, Bachtiar Nasir, an influential Islamist religious scholar (*ulama*) and key leader of the anti-Ahok protests, warned that the next target of the protesters would be ethnic Chinese wealth. Nasir advocated an affirmative action program for *pribumi* Indonesians in order to reduce economic inequality, an argument that has long historical roots in Indonesia. 'It seems they [Chinese Indonesians] do not become more generous, more fair', he said; 'That's the biggest problem' (Allard and Da Costa 2017).

It appears that even the language used to refer to Chinese Indonesians in the public domain is returning to the norms of the New Order era. Banners seen on the streets during the anti-Ahok demonstrations in Jakarta frequently referred to Ahok as *Cina* and never as *Tionghoa*. Senior politicians such as Amien Rais have publicly called Ahok *Cina*—and even 'that *kafir Cina*' (that Chinese infidel)—often also linking him to alleged involvement by China in Indonesian politics. While *Cina* has never entirely disappeared from everyday speech in post-Suharto Indonesia, its deliberate use in the public domain by senior, non-Chinese public figures carries the danger of once again normalising discriminatory terms and attitudes in the national imagination.

THE RESURFACING OF *PRIBUMI* NARRATIVES IN PUBLIC DISCOURSE

Alongside the rise in anti-Chinese sentiment in 2016–17, it was evident that the use of nativist, *pribumi*-based narratives by non-Chinese politicians and public figures was also increasing. In April 2017, right after Ahok's election defeat, Vice-President Jusuf Kalla made a statement implying that most of the rich people in Indonesia were of Chinese descent, and either Christian or Confucian, whereas most of the poor were *pribumi* and Muslim (Jakarta Globe 2017). In May 2017, the then commander of the Indonesian Armed Forces, General Gatot Nurmantyo, caused controversy when, during a speech to the Golkar Party National Leadership Conference, he recited a poem titled 'Tapi bukan kami punya' (But it is not ours), implying that Indonesia's wealth was not currently in the hands of *pribumi* Indonesians (Suryadinata 2017). Nurmantyo has become known for expressing rousing pro-*pribumi* sentiments in public speeches since at least 2016.

Many who had hoped that the new Jakarta governor, Anies Baswedan, would adopt a more conciliatory stance once he took office were deeply disappointed by his inauguration speech. In the speech, delivered on 16 October 2017, Baswedan invoked *pribumi*-ism, nationalist tropes, religiosity and fragments of New Order-era Pancasila ideology. Most controversial was his racially charged reference to *pribumi* in statements such as the following: 'In the past, we *pribumi* were the conquered. Now, it's time for us to be the hosts in our own land. We worked hard to get rid of colonialism and we must enjoy our freedom' (Ramadhani 2017).

The executive director of Amnesty International Indonesia, Usman Hamid, quickly criticised Baswedan's use of the term *pribumi*, calling it racist and inflammatory (Putri and Huda 2018). Many other commentators and members of the public were also aghast that Baswedan would express such sentiments so soon after such a tense election. He was accused of capitalising on the effectiveness of the anti-Ahok campaign; certainly, his rhetoric suggested that he intended to maintain the divisive, nativist stance that had helped him win the Jakarta election (Kapoor and Da Costa 2017).

Just as the resurfacing of anti-Chinese sentiment began before, not during, the Ahok case, the return of pro-*pribumi* narratives in public discourse was also apparent long before this case captured public attention. As early as 2006, while he was still vice-president to Susilo Bambang Yudhoyono, Jusuf Kalla received heavy criticism from civil society groups for a speech in which he referred to non-Chinese Indonesians as *pribumi* and urged the businesspeople in his Chinese Indonesian audience not to treat Indonesia like a 'hotel' that could be abandoned in times of crisis (Hoon 2006b: 273).

In August 2015, a group linked to the main opposition party in parliament, Gerindra, established a new party, the Pribumi Party (Partai Priboemi) (Antaranews 2015). With retired general Djoko Santoso—a well-connected politician and former army commander—on its advisory board, the new party declared its ambition to restrict the political and economic rights of people considered to be non-indigenous Indonesians. The party's platform was not explicitly anti-Chinese, but it was nevertheless clear that by 'non-indigenous Indonesians', the party really meant 'the Chinese'. While Partai Priboemi is still a very small and marginal party, the very existence of a political entity that publicly advocates a discriminatory (even oppressive) stance towards 'foreigners' shows the growth in xenophobic political mobilisation in Indonesia.

In September 2018, Santoso was appointed head of the 2019 presidential campaign team backing Prabowo Subianto and his running mate, Sandiaga Uno. Uno had been Baswedan's deputy in Jakarta and had resigned the vice-governorship to contest the presidential election. The candidates' decision to pick a man with such nativist sentiments to lead their campaign team strongly suggests that anti-foreign rhetoric will form a big part of their campaign strategy.

There has also been a backlash against the decision to extend the political rights of *non-pribumi* Indonesians. In October 2016, for instance, the chair of the United Development Party (Partai Persatuan Pembangunan, PPP), Muhammad Romahurmuziy, proposed restoring the original clause in the Constitution stating that the president of Indonesia must be an indigenous Indonesian (*orang Indonesia asli*), and said that the clause should apply to the vice-president as well (Fachrudin 2016).

It can be argued that pro-*pribumi* rhetoric and activity started to intensify following Ahok's political rise, first to become Jokowi's deputy in 2012 and then to become Jakarta governor in 2014. It appears that opposition politicians were worried that this popular politician might become Jokowi's vice-presidential running mate in the 2019 election. However, the resurgence of *pribumi* narratives in public discourse should not be attributed to the threat posed by Ahok's popularity alone; it should also be seen as evidence that, despite the policy reforms of the post-Suharto era, the view that ethnic Chinese are *non-pribumi* never disappeared from the national consciousness. As seen in the Ahok case, the terms *pribumi* and *non-pribumi* continue to be a convenient political tool for non-Chinese politicians bent on using ethno-nationalist narratives to their advantage.

PERCEPTIONS OF CHINESE INDONESIANS AFTER THE JAKARTA ELECTION

The impact of the racial and religious attacks on Ahok during the Jakarta election campaign was obvious enough in the final round of the election held in April 2017: Ahok lost to Anies Baswedan by 43 per cent to 57 per cent. Since then, the focus of researchers has shifted to trying to discern the longer-term effects of the rise in anti-Chinese sentiment. Would it quickly dissipate with Ahok's imprisonment in May 2017 or would it usher in a new period of intolerance?

One attempt to measure anti-Chinese sentiments in the immediate aftermath of the Jakarta election was the Indonesia National Survey Project (INSP) commissioned by the Singapore-based ISEAS–Yusof Ishak Institute (Fossati, Hui and Negara 2017). Administered by the Indonesian Survey Institute (Lembaga Survei Indonesia, LSI) across all 34 provinces of Indonesia and involving a randomly selected sample of 1,620 respondents, the INSP study sampled public opinion on a wide range of issues, including the economy, the state, politics, infrastructure, Islam, ethnicity and international relations.

Included in the interview questions were a series of statements reflecting longstanding prejudices about the ethnic Chinese. These statements were specifically designed to measure the degree to which non-Chinese Indonesians still held negative perceptions of Chinese Indonesians, so only the non-Chinese respondents were asked to answer these questions. The one-on-one interviews were conducted between 20 and 30 May 2017, less than six weeks after Ahok's defeat in Jakarta and just two weeks after he was sentenced to two years in jail for blasphemy. The survey data thus give us a snapshot of the public's views on the ethnic Chinese in the immediate aftermath of these events.

The statements were grouped according to three broad categories of potential prejudice towards ethnic Chinese: wealth and economic acumen, political and economic influence, and exclusivist behaviour. Later on in the survey, respondents were also asked specifically about whether it was permissible to have an ethnic Chinese as a political leader. Respondents were asked to rate their level of agreement or disagreement with each statement on a five-point scale.

In the case of wealth and economic acumen, the vast majority of respondents 'somewhat' or 'strongly' agreed that Chinese Indonesians were 'more likely to be wealthy' than *pribumi* Indonesians (59.8 per cent) and that they were 'usually at least middle class' (60.1 per cent) (Figure 11.1). It is therefore not surprising that nearly half agreed that life was 'easier for Chinese Indonesians' (48.0 per cent) and that Chinese had 'more opportunities in life' than *pribumi* Indonesians (48.7 per cent).

While these kinds of attitudes are not new, the strength of the agreement with these statements is surprising, considering that Chinese Indonesians are no longer visible only in the commercial sector as in the Suharto era. There appears to be an element of primordialism in these economic stereotypes, evident in the fact that one statement in particular— that 'Chinese Indonesians have a natural talent for making money'—drew by far the highest level of agreement among all the statements (68.1 per cent). This sense of primordialism, where Chinese Indonesians are seen as possessing certain characteristics that lead to irreconcilable differences

Figure 11.1   Respondents' views on whether Chinese Indonesians are economically privileged (%)

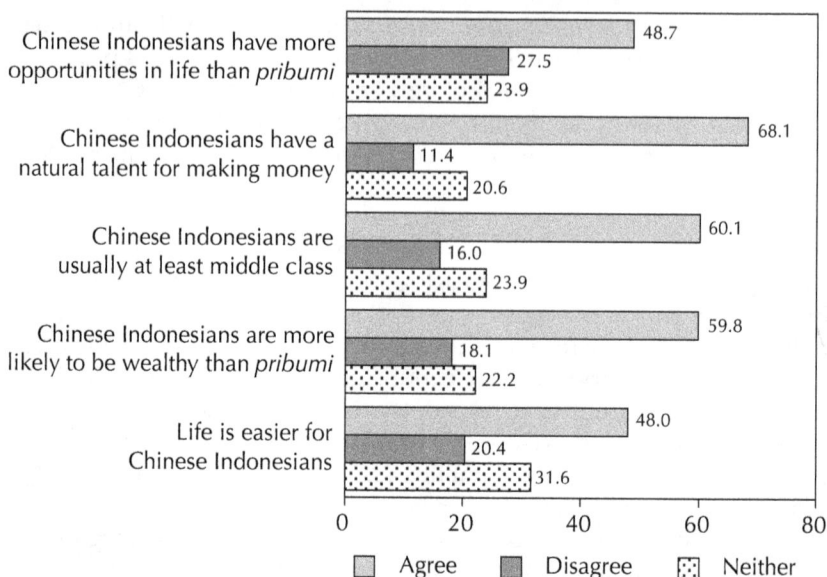

Chinese Indonesians have more opportunities in life than *pribumi* — 48.7 / 27.5 / 23.9

Chinese Indonesians have a natural talent for making money — 68.1 / 11.4 / 20.6

Chinese Indonesians are usually at least middle class — 60.1 / 16.0 / 23.9

Chinese Indonesians are more likely to be wealthy than *pribumi* — 59.8 / 18.1 / 22.2

Life is easier for Chinese Indonesians — 48.0 / 20.4 / 31.6

☐ Agree   ■ Disagree   ▦ Neither

Source: Indonesia National Survey Project (INSP).

between them and other Indonesians, is also reflected in some of the other responses concerning religion and culture.

As seen in Figure 11.2, the majority of respondents felt that the religion (42.4 per cent) and culture (42.6 per cent) of Chinese Indonesians did not fit well with Indonesian values. Most respondents blamed the Chinese themselves for their inability to integrate into Indonesian society, with 48.4 per cent agreeing that Chinese Indonesians 'only care about their own kind' and 46.3 per cent believing they were 'too greedy and ambitious'.

Interestingly, while 44.1 per cent of respondents agreed that essential differences in culture, character and religion meant that it was 'hard to be close friends with a Chinese Indonesian', only 33.7 per cent believed that marriage between ethnic Chinese and non-Chinese was inappropriate. This could be the historical legacy of centuries of intermarriage between Chinese and *pribumi*, which has often been seen as providing advantages for both sides. For the *pribumi* partner, taking a Chinese spouse could be economically advantageous. From the Chinese standpoint—particularly during the New Order—marriage into a *pribumi* family was seen as a good way to assimilate and show willingness to embrace 'local' culture, particularly if the Chinese partner converted to Islam.

Figure 11.2   Respondents' views on whether Chinese Indonesians are exclusive (%)

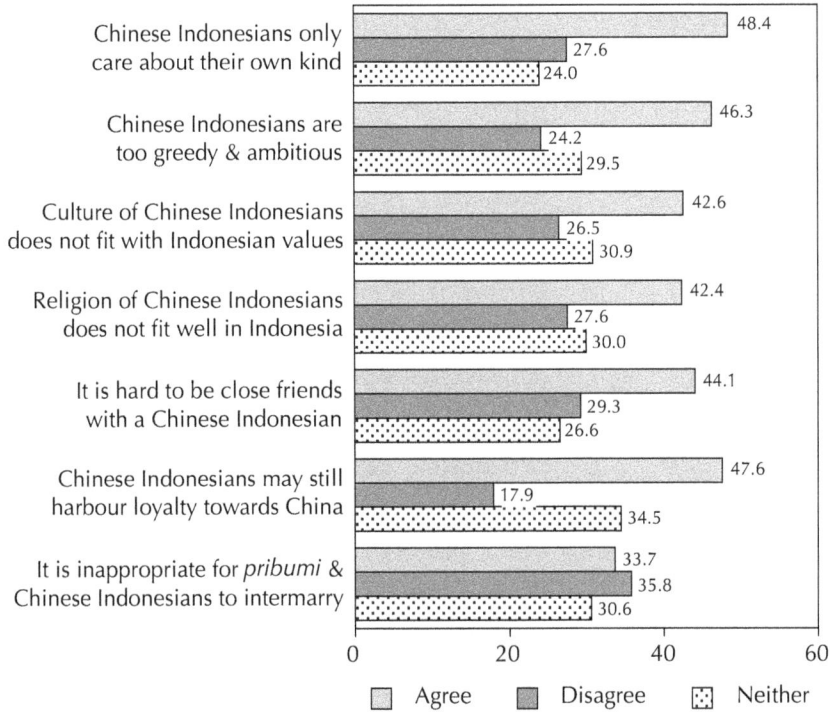

	Agree	Disagree	Neither
Chinese Indonesians only care about their own kind	48.4	27.6	24.0
Chinese Indonesians are too greedy & ambitious	46.3	24.2	29.5
Culture of Chinese Indonesians does not fit with Indonesian values	42.6	26.5	30.9
Religion of Chinese Indonesians does not fit well in Indonesia	42.4	27.6	30.0
It is hard to be close friends with a Chinese Indonesian	44.1	29.3	26.6
Chinese Indonesians may still harbour loyalty towards China	47.6	17.9	34.5
It is inappropriate for *pribumi* & Chinese Indonesians to intermarry	33.7	35.8	30.6

Source: Indonesia National Survey Project (INSP).

A fascinating pattern emerges if we sort the responses to the statement about intermarriage according to the religion of the respondents. As Figure 11.3 shows, Muslim respondents were more likely than non-Muslim respondents to 'somewhat' or 'strongly' agree with the statement that intermarriage was inappropriate (27.2 per cent), while non-Muslims were much more likely than Muslims to 'strongly' disagree with this sentiment (35.9 per cent). This suggests that the Muslim respondents regarded differences in religion as the main barrier to marriage between Chinese and *pribumi* Indonesians. Indeed, most Islamic authorities disapprove of, or even proscribe, marriage between Muslims and non-Muslims, although there are exceptions to this. It is surprising that Muslims have such strong views about interethnic marriage considering that it was encouraged during the New Order, when conversion to Islam through marriage to a Muslim was seen as an effective way for Chinese Indonesians to assimilate (Hew 2017).

Figure 11.3   Respondents' views on whether 'It is inappropriate for pribumi Indonesians to intermarry with Chinese Indonesians', by religious background (%)

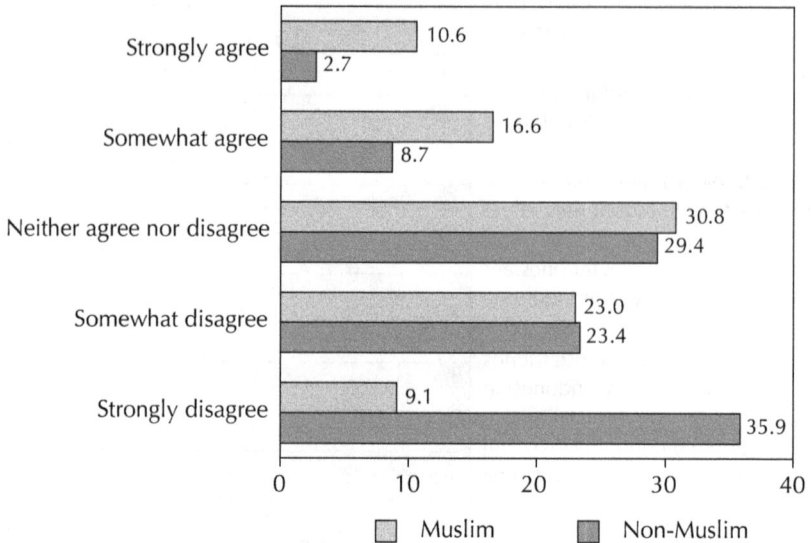

Differences between Muslim and non-Muslim respondents are also evident when we look at the religious backgrounds of those who agreed or disagreed with the statement that Chinese Indonesians had their own religion that did not fit well in Indonesia. As can be seen in Figure 11.4, non-Muslim respondents were overwhelmingly more likely to 'somewhat' or 'strongly' disagree with this statement (53.1 per cent), whereas Muslim respondents were vastly more likely to 'somewhat' or 'strongly' agree with it (46.0 per cent). What this means is that, for Muslim *pribumi* respondents in particular, religion is an important determinant of the perception that Chinese Indonesians differ from other Indonesians in essential ways and therefore do not fit well in Indonesia.

Referring back to Figure 11.2, it is worrying that almost half of the respondents (47.6 per cent) agreed with the statement that 'Chinese Indonesians may still harbour loyalty towards China', even though almost all ethnic Chinese in Indonesia today are Indonesian citizens (Fossati, Hui and Negara 2017).

It must be remembered that this perception exists within a very specific local and global context. China's rise as a regional and global power has resulted in the country having more direct investments and greater

Figure 11.4   Respondents' views on whether 'Chinese Indonesians have their own religion that does not fit well in Indonesia', by religious background (%)

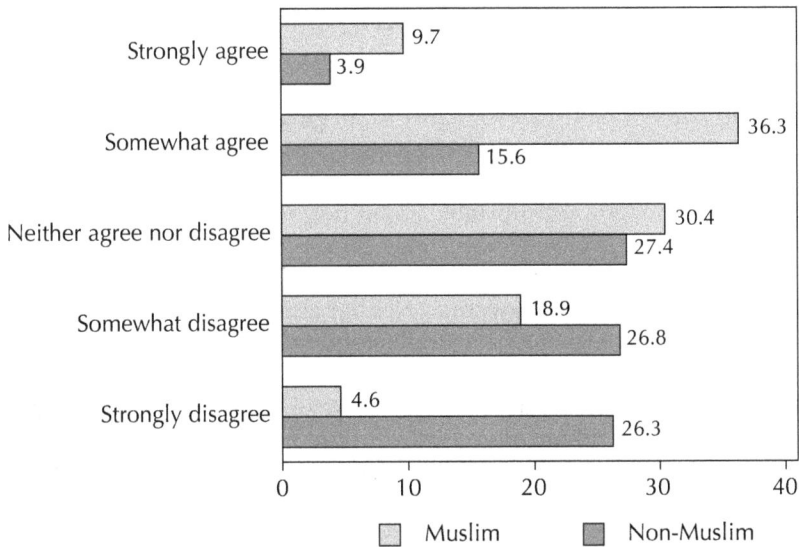

Source: Indonesia National Survey Project (INSP).

economic and strategic interests in Indonesia than ever before. The Indonesian government has mostly been happy to receive Chinese investment in order to fund Jokowi's many ambitious infrastructure projects. Domestically, however, there has been a backlash over what is seen as Jokowi's closeness to and reliance upon China. For instance, when his government awarded the construction contract for the proposed Jakarta–Bandung high-speed rail project to China rather than Japan after an opaque tender process, opposition politicians and the media quickly accused Jokowi of being a pawn of China (Negara and Salim 2016). Around the time of the Jakarta gubernatorial election, false news reports claiming that both Jokowi and Ahok were agents of the Chinese state were rampant on social media (Lim 2017). The perception that Chinese Indonesians may be loyal to China rather than Indonesia is dangerous for the ethnic Chinese, especially at a time of rising nationalist fervour among *pribumi* constituencies.

When respondents were asked whether they were comfortable with having a Chinese Indonesian in a position of political leadership, a large majority (64.4 per cent) said they were not (Setijadi 2017). While the timing of the survey (just two weeks after Ahok's sentencing) would undoubtedly have skewed public opinion on this issue, the size of this majority is worrying for Sino-Indonesians and those who espouse a pluralist Indonesia.

INTERPRETING THE SURVEY DATA

The INSP data reveal complex overlaps between religion, socio-economic class and perceptions of ethnic Chinese. In general, the data showed that Muslim respondents were more likely to regard ethnic Chinese as having unbridgeable differences with mainstream society and that they were more likely to feel uncomfortable about having an ethnic Chinese as a political leader.

It must be noted, however, that for each of the questions, a sizeable proportion of respondents answered: 'Neither agree nor disagree'. Some of these respondents may not have understood the question and others may have been undecided. Among the undecideds, some would have been leaning more towards a positive perspective of the ethnic Chinese, while others may have held negative views but did not want to reveal them to the interviewers. Either way, views about Chinese Indonesians are likely to be even more polarised than is suggested by the survey results.

It should also be remembered that the survey data were heavily influenced by the extraordinary events that had just taken place. In the aftermath of the Jakarta election, the Ahok blasphemy case and the return of nativist narratives, it should not be too much of a surprise to see heightened negativity towards Chinese Indonesians. The Ahok case was in many ways unique, in no small part owing to the fact that Ahok himself was a singular politician whose character and actions aroused deep divisions, both about him personally and also about the wisdom of having Chinese Indonesians in key political and social roles.

Surveys such as the INSP provide a useful tool for gauging public sentiment about Chinese Indonesians, particularly during pivotal times in Indonesia's political history. In the past, studies on Chinese Indonesians have not included large-scale survey data, so the existence of such surveys today has given scholars an additional analytical tool to track changes in attitudes towards the ethnic Chinese and other minority groups.

While I have focused on the INSP data, there have been other post-election surveys seeking to chart changes in attitudes towards the Chinese and other minorities since the Jakarta election. One of the most recent ones is a nationwide survey based on multi-stage random sampling, conducted in August 2018. It revealed that anti-Chinese views had declined in the social sphere but not in the political sphere. In fact, the level of objection to ethnic Chinese in political leadership positions actually increased further in 2018.

The August 2018 survey is discussed in more detail by Mietzner and Muhtadi in Chapter 9 of this volume. The authors argue persuasively that the increase in negative attitudes towards Chinese Indonesians as political leaders can be attributed to the success of Ahok's opponents in channelling public anger towards the political sphere as part of a strategy to consolidate their own power. They argue further that the anti-minority attitudes inherent in Islamist ideas of politics and society are becoming increasingly mainstream in Indonesia.

CONCLUDING REMARKS: ANTI-CHINESE SENTIMENT IN CONTEMPORARY INDONESIA

The relatively quick decline in negative societal attitudes towards the Chinese after the Ahok case demonstrates that anti-Chinese sentiment can die down just as quickly as it arose. Ultimately, the speed with which anti-Chinese sentiment flared up during the Jakarta election indicates that nothing much has really changed in terms of how ethnic Chinese are perceived in Indonesia, despite the reforms of the past two decades. The Chinese are still convenient scapegoats in times of political and economic instability. Rising Islamic conservatism and socio-economic inequality have only heightened old notions of the essential difference between Chinese and other Indonesians, making Chinese Indonesians, once again, the obvious targets of mob anger and frustration.

Making matters worse is the return of xenophobic pro-*pribumi* narratives in public discourse, and the public's seeming antipathy towards China. In the lead-up to the 2019 presidential election, Jokowi's opponents can be expected to continue to accuse his administration of overdependence on Chinese investment and of encouraging excessive inflows of Chinese migrant workers. A rise in negative public perceptions of China almost always results in increased suspicion of and hostility towards local ethnic Chinese—especially very wealthy Chinese with business and political interests.

A marker of the longer-term impact of the Ahok case will be how many Chinese run as candidates in the 2019 legislative elections. As noted earlier, the number of ethnic Chinese candidates has increased with each round of legislative elections since 2004. Now, many are wondering whether aspiring ethnic Chinese politicians have been discouraged by what happened to Ahok. The number of ethnic Chinese candidates in the upcoming elections will therefore be a useful indicator of the mood and level of confidence among Chinese Indonesians.

The re-emergence of anti-Chinese sentiment during and immediately after the Ahok case in Jakarta serves as a reminder that, in many ways, the issue of the contentious belonging of Chinese Indonesians was not 'solved' by policy changes during the early *reformasi* period, despite public opinion to the contrary. It should also remind the government and civil society organisations more broadly that dealing with the 'Chinese problem'—and maintaining interethnic and interreligious harmony more broadly—will require continuous hard work as part of nation-building efforts in Indonesia. Both Jokowi's government and Indonesia's liberals must show that they are committed to protecting the safety and rights not only of ethnic Chinese, but of all minority groups.

REFERENCES

Allard, T., and A. Da Costa (2017) 'Exclusive—Indonesian Islamist leader says ethnic Chinese wealth is next target', *Reuters*, 13 May.

Allard, T., and K. Kapoor (2017) 'Indonesia's president moves to rein in "out of control" military chief', *Reuters*, 9 January.

Antaranews (2015) 'Deklarasi Partai Priboemi', *Antaranews.com*, 18 August.

Chua, A. (2003) *World on Fire: How Exporting Free Market Democracy Breeds Ethnic Hatred and Global Instability*, Doubleday, New York NY.

Fachrudin, F. (2016) 'PPP desak amandemen UUD 1945, kembalikan frasa "presiden ialah orang Indonesia asli"', *Tribunnews.com*, 4 October.

Fossati, D., Y.-F. Hui and S.D. Negara (2017) 'The Indonesia National Survey Project: economy, society and politics', *Trends in Southeast Asia* 10, ISEAS–Yusof Ishak Institute, Singapore.

Hefner, R.W. (2013) 'The study of religious freedom in Indonesia', *Review of Faith & International Affairs* 11(2): 18–27.

Herlijanto, J. (2017) 'How the Indonesian elite regards relations with China', *Perspective* 8, ISEAS–Yusof Ishak Institute, Singapore, 10 February.

Heryanto, A. (2008) 'Citizenship and Indonesian ethnic Chinese in post-1998 films', in A. Heryanto (ed.) *Popular Culture in Indonesia: Fluid Identities in Post-authoritarian Politics*, Routledge, London: 70–91.

Hew, W.W. (2017) *Chinese Ways of Being Muslim: Negotiating Ethnicity and Religiosity in Indonesia*, NIAS Press, Copenhagen.

Hoon, C.-Y. (2006a) 'Assimilation, multiculturalism, hybridity: the dilemmas of the ethnic Chinese in post-Suharto Indonesia', *Asian Ethnicity* 7(2): 149–66.

Hoon, C.-Y. (2006b) 'Reconceptualising ethnic Chinese identity in post-Suharto Indonesia', PhD thesis, School of Social Sciences, University of Western Australia, Perth.

Jakarta Globe (2017) 'Kalla defends comment about Chinese wealth after criticism', *Jakarta Globe*, 3 May.

Kapoor, K., and A. Da Costa (2017) 'New Jakarta governor faces backlash for racially tinged speech', *Reuters*, 17 October.

Lim, M. (2017) 'Freedom to hate: social media, algorithmic enclaves, and the rise of tribal nationalism in Indonesia', *Critical Asian Studies* 49(3): 411–27.

McVey, R.T. (1992) 'The materialization of the Southeast Asian entrepreneur', in R.T. McVey (ed.) *Southeast Asian Capitalists*, SEAP Publications, Ithaca NY: 7–34.

Negara, S.D., and W. Salim (2016) 'Why is the high-speed rail project so important to Indonesia?', *Perspective* 16, ISEAS–Yusof Ishak Institute, Singapore, 7 April.

Priyandita, G. (2018) 'Chinese investment and workers in Indonesia's upcoming elections', *Asia Pacific Bulletin*, East-West Center, Washington DC.

Purdey, J. (2006) *Anti-Chinese Violence in Indonesia, 1996–1999*, University of Hawai'i Press, Honolulu.

Putri, B.U., and L. Huda (2018) '3 reasons why Anies Baswedan should've avoided mentioning pribumi', *Tempo*, 18 October.

Ramadhani, N.F. (2017) 'Anies's "pribumi" speech sparks debate, "racist" comments on social media', *Jakarta Post*, 17 October.

Reid, A. (1997) 'Entrepreneurial minorities, nationalism, and the state', in D. Chirot and A. Reid (eds) *Essential Outsiders: Chinese and Jews in the Modern Transformation of Southeast Asia and Central Europe*, University of Washington Press, Seattle WA: 33–71.

Renaldi, A. (2017) 'Land reclamation is more complicated than you ever imagined', *Vice*, 28 February.

Setijadi, C. (2014) 'Memories, spaces, identities: an ethnographic study of young ethnic Chinese in post-Suharto Indonesia', PhD thesis, School of Humanities and Social Sciences, La Trobe University, Melbourne.

Setijadi, C. (2016) 'Ethnic Chinese in contemporary Indonesia: changing identity politics and the paradox of sinification', *Perspective* 12, ISEAS–Yusof Ishak Institute, Singapore, 17 March.

Setijadi, C. (2017) 'Chinese Indonesians in the eyes of the *pribumi* public', *Perspective* 73, ISEAS–Yusof Ishak Institute, Singapore, 27 September.

Suryadinata, L. (2005) *Pribumi Indonesians, the Chinese Minority, and China: A Study of Perceptions and Policies*, Marshall Cavendish International, Singapore.

Suryadinata, L. (2017) 'General Gatot and the re-emergence of *pribumi*-ism in Indonesia', *Perspective* 49, ISEAS–Yusof Ishak Institute, Singapore, 7 July.

Tan, M.G. (2008) *Etnis Tionghoa di Indonesia*, Yayasan Obor, Jakarta.

Tempo (2016) 'Rusuh Tanjungbalai, jumlah tersangka bertambah', *Tempo*, 2 August.

Walden, M. (2017) 'It wasn't just religious hatred that cost Ahok the Jakarta vote', *Asian Correspondent*, 22 April.

12   Minority and advantage: the story of Sindhis in Indonesia

Maria Myutel

Most academic discussions on ethnic and religious minorities in Indonesia have focused either on the state's unilateral dominance over various minority groups or the resistance of those groups to state power. While revealing key aspects of ethno-religious conflict, such discourses can be misleading as they are based on two assumptions: first, that minority status equals disadvantage, and second, that in order to preserve their identities minorities have to actively confront the state. Although it is true that minorities do often find themselves in a vulnerable position *vis-à-vis* state power and/or an ethnic and religious majority, assuming that disadvantage is inherent to a minority status is erroneous. Moreover, an approach that focuses solely on active resistance, while ignoring other forms of identity negotiations, presents just a part of the story, albeit a very significant one.

I argue that minority status can signal an advantage, even privilege, over a majority of the country's population. I also argue that disregard of state power, often in the form of disregarding both obligations and rights, can be an effective way to preserve a distinct identity. The story of the Sindhis in Indonesia is precisely about advantage, and in some cases privilege, that has stemmed from ethnic minority status and global power dynamics. It is also a story of the generally neutral relations between the minority and the state when both had very few points of interaction and those rarely turned into pressure points. Overall, the relations between the Sindhi minority and the state do not fit into the commonly used frameworks of forced assimilation or targeted discrimination and marginalisation.

So who are the Sindhis in Indonesia? Originally from Sindh, the former territory of British India and currently part of the Islamic Republic of Pakistan, Sindhis claim Indian, rather than Pakistani, identity and maintain an exclusionist, endogamous way of life.[1] They see business as the core of life, practise a form of Hinduism that is heavily influenced by Buddhism, Sikhism and Sufism, and constitute one of the wealthiest and most well-connected trading communities in the world, the Sindhayat (Markovits 2000). There are approximately 10,000 Sindhis in Indonesia, making them a tiny minority in a population of around 260 million. With very few conversions to Christianity or Islam, Hindu Sindhis are a 'double minority' in a largely Muslim population.

Despite its small size, the Sindhi community has played a significant role in the Indonesian economy, and in cultural production in particular. While most Indonesian Sindhis built their fortune in textile trading and manufacturing, several families carved a niche for themselves in Indonesia's media industries, first in cinema (since the 1950s) and later in national television (since the 1990s). Although Thapan's (2002: 44) assertion that 'should the Sindhis withdraw from the region completely, it would not impact on the national economies' may be true in the case of the textile business, the popular culture landscape would have looked very different without Sindhis.

Apart from reintroducing Indian films to the local market in the early 1950s, Sindhis contributed to the golden age of Indonesian popular cinema in the 1970s and early 1980s. Releasing up to a quarter of the annually produced titles, Sindhis were able to tune in to audience tastes and produce films that were highly popular among local movie-goers.[2] It is important to emphasise that Sindhi producers not only worked in the genres of teen romance, slapstick comedy and category B films as is often assumed, but also collaborated with such key figures of Indonesian cinema as Teguh Karya, Sjuman Djaya, Wim Umboh, Arifin Noer, Slamet Rahardjo, Christine Hakim, Jenny Rachman, Deddy Mizwar and Rano Karno. Moreover, the Sindhis' international ambitions resulted in the development of the Indonesian horror film as a distinct genre in world cinema.[3] Lastly, Sindhis reintroduced joint production with overseas crews and normalised

---

1 Throughout the chapter I use the spelling 'Sindh' for the Sindh region as per Sindh Law Amendment Bill 2012. The alternative spelling 'Sind' will be used only in citations.
2 Sindhi producers sponsored such highly popular films as *Romi dan Juli* (Romeo and Juliette, 1974) *Jaka Sembung* (The Warrior, 1981), *Catatan Si Boy* (Boy's Diary, 1987), *Makin Lama Makin Asyik* (The Longer, the Cooler, 1987) the *DKI Warkop* series (1979 – early 1990s) and *Petualangan Cinta Nyi Blorong* (Love Adventures of Nyi Blorong, 1986).
3 Whether an increase in the production of horror films was a positive or a negative development for the Indonesian film industry is another question that will not be addressed here.

the casting of Indos, Indonesians of European descent, in locally produced films.

As for commercial television, Sindhi businesspeople can be credited with the establishment and development of a separate, economically significant sector of the media industry, the production of commercial soap operas, or *sinetron*. By drawing on the international pool of funding, human capital and creative ideas, available through ethnic networks, Sindhis turned the random production of this popular television genre into a well-organised routine (Myutel 2016). By the early 2000s, *sinetron* production had grown into a full-fledged industry, with an estimated turnover of $100 million (Rakhmani 2014: 441). Apart from providing numerous employment opportunities, the *sinetron* industry defined the production culture and aesthetics of Indonesian commercial television up to the mid-2010s (Myutel 2017). For example, the subgenre of *sinetron Ramadhan* (soap opera aired during the holy fasting month), pioneered by the Sindhi-owned MultiVision in 1998, revolutionised the industry by introducing Islam (expressed through the narrative, emphasis on prayer and devotion, and aesthetic aspects) to prime-time television. The central role of the Islamic-themed programs on national television considerably speeded up the process of making Islam a significant part of Indonesian popular culture.[4] In sum, despite constituting less than 0.01 per cent of the total population, the Sindhi community has played a disproportionate role for its size in Indonesia's economy and cultural life.

Over the century-long history of Sindhis' presence in the archipelago, tensions between Sindhis and other Indonesian communities or the state have been negligible, with the few episodes of anti-Indian violence being triggered by international, not local, conflicts. As the government of India's 'Report of the High Level Committee on the Indian diaspora' concluded, Indians residing in Indonesia 'do not seem to have any major grievances as such' (Singhvi 2001: 256). While retaining close ties with the global community of Sindhayat and India as their spiritual and cultural centre, Indonesian Sindhis call Indonesia home, enjoying the placid and comfortable lifestyles available to them in the country.

The overall positive, conflict-free experience of the Sindhi community within the nation does not mean, however, that ethno-racial tensions have been settled. On the contrary, the Sindhi story serves as further proof that ethnicity continues to define the distribution of political, economic and social power in Indonesia. Sindhis, citizens of Indonesia for over 50 years, are seen by other Indonesians first and foremost as an ethno-racial rather than cultural group, and importantly also as foreigners, being mostly

---

4   For an elaborate argument on the Sindhi community's effect on television production culture, see Myutel (2017).

referred to as *orang India* (Indian people) or *orang sana* (people from there, or foreigners). Despite the laws introduced during the *reformasi* period to abolish the distinctions between indigenous Indonesians (*pribumi*) and Indonesians of foreign descent (*Warga Negara Indonesia keturunan asing*), the division into 'us' and 'them', or locals and foreigners, persists in the public discourse.[5] Ethnicity as a category of social classification, a product of the colonial past, created to justify political, social and economic inequalities, retains its position as a 'powerful fiction' (Heryanto 2014: 163).

A BRIEF HISTORY OF SINDHIS IN INDONESIA

The story of Sindhi traders in Indonesia can be traced back to the late nineteenth century. Most Sindhis who established trading connections with Java in the 1870s were from Hyderabad and belonged to the Bhaiband, literally 'Brothers', a subcaste of Hindu Sindhis from a lower social stratum, concentrated in the commercial sector. The success of the first Sindhi companies in Java is still reflected in the Sindhi language: the verb *java* means 'spending very lavishly' (*java tho karain*) (Thapan 2002: 25). By the 1930s the Sindhi merchants had well-established trading contacts with all the main cities of the Dutch East Indies: Surabaya, Semarang, Malang and Batavia (later known as Jakarta). With constant growth of their businesses Sindhi merchants spent most of their time in Java; visits home to their families in Hyderabad were usually embarked on only once a year. Despite that, the Sindhi mode of living could best be described as circulation rather than migration, as people, goods and finances were in constant motion between Hyderabad, the network's centre, and other parts of the world (Markovits 2000: 5). Sindhi traders had no intention of migrating to Indonesia on a permanent basis.

The Dutch colonial administration classified Sindhi traders as Indians (and thus part of a larger group known as Foreign Orientals), together with other settlers from the Indian subcontinent who had very different economic, social and cultural backgrounds. Although the colonial administration did not make any formal distinction between the indentured labourers and free traders from the Indian subcontinent, in practice the Dutch patronised the Sindhis, a wealthy community that supplied the elites with textiles and luxury goods such as carpets, embroidery, and wooden and ivory carvings. In the prominent trading centre of Surabaya, for example, the Sindhis' leader was assigned the title of *Hoofd der Indiers* (Head of the Indians) and given authority to issue visas to newcomers.

---

5 For a discussion of this theme, see Chapter 11 of this volume by Setijadi.

Their prosperity and global connections secured Sindhis a higher status in colonial Indonesia.

As Foreign Orientals and new arrivals, Sindhis were similar to the so-called Totok Chinese, literally 'full-blooded' Chinese. Unlike Peranakan Chinese, a 'mestizo Malay-speaking group' whose descendants came to Indonesia centuries ago, Totok Chinese started arriving in Indonesia in the late nineteenth century and 'tended to maintain a more exclusively Chinese milieu, often bringing wives from China rather than intermarrying with local women' (Strassler 2008: 401). But this resemblance is in fact illusory; differences in migration patterns and class distinguished Sindhis from the Chinese migrants of the late nineteenth and early twentieth centuries. Although Sindhis spent most of their time engaged in overseas trade, their families and homes were in Hyderabad, so they were only temporary sojourners. As such, they focused almost entirely on business and did not seek positions in the colonial administration. Also, unlike migrants from China, more or less the *entire* Sindhi community was well connected to the colonial elite through business. Overall, during Dutch colonial times the relationships of the Sindhis with colonial elites were mutually beneficial: the Sindhi traders supplied the elites with exquisite goods and showed no signs of attempting to influence or challenge the established political and social order.

The arrival of the Japanese in the Indonesian archipelago in 1942, the reorientation of business towards war activities, new regulations on exports and rapidly rising inflation caused major disruptions to the trading activities of the Sindhis. The anti-Western sentiments and policies of the Japanese, including a ban on the use of English (which meant that the Sindhi-run community schools had to close), forced most Sindhis to leave Indonesia for good, or so they thought at the time.

Some, however, stayed and even became involved in the revolutionary struggle that followed the departure of the Japanese (Mani 1945–49). In Surabaya, T.D. Kundan, a Sindhi community leader in the 1930s and 1940s, acted as an intermediary and interpreter between the local revolutionary forces and the British commanders of Indian troops, who were sent to Surabaya to evacuate internees and pave the way for the returning Dutch after Indonesia proclaimed its independence in August 1945. The Indian reporter P.R.S. Mani called Kundan 'the main ambassador between us [Indians] and the local leaders, with whom he is extremely popular' (Mani 1945–49). Kundan's role was particularly difficult because the sympathies of many Indian soldiers lay with the Indonesian independence fighters rather than with their colonial masters, the British, who were allied with the Dutch. As well as supporting Indonesian republican youth, Kundan tried to keep Indian troops from fighting against the Indonesian nationalists. Although his involvement did not prevent one of the most violent battles of the revolutionary period (the Battle of Surabaya), the government of independent Indonesia highly appreciated Kundan's role in the negotiations that followed and bestowed honours on him posthumously (Mani 1993a: 102).

Sindhis who returned to Hyderabad soon discovered that their homeland had become a dangerous place. The decision of the British and Indian elites to split the territory of British India along religious lines caused unprecedented violence, which struck many regions of the subcontinent. In Sindh brutal riots broke out in January 1948, forcing Hindu Sindhis to flee Hyderabad *en masse*. Approximately '1,200,000 non-Muslim refugees from Sind and Baluchistan had entered India' (Markovits 2000: 278), with only a quarter of them being non-Sindhis. While most settled in India, a large percentage relocated to places where they had previously traded. In Southeast Asia, Hong Kong, the Philippines and Singapore attracted most of the fleeing Hindu Sindhis.

The exact number of Sindhis who entered Indonesia between 1948 and 1953 is unknown but was probably around 3,500 (Markovits 2000: 278). In 1953 Indonesia officially announced the end of the 'open-door' migration policy of the Dutch era and established a limit for prospective immigrants, with applicants from India, Pakistan, Burma and Ceylon being allocated a quota of 1,000 per annum, including wives and children (Thompson and Adloff 1955: 123). As priority was given to people who had previously resided in Indonesia, it is likely that Sindhi families continued to arrive in Indonesia after 1953. In the late 1950s the Sindhi community numbered approximately 8,000.

The (re)settlement of Sindhis in Indonesia went smoothly. India strongly encouraged the new migrants to settle outside the country as it struggled to accommodate the enormous number of Hindu refugees. Having amicable relations with India until the late 1950s, Indonesia welcomed post-Partition migrants, granting them permanent resident status and even allowing them to send remittances to India—which was banned for foreign Chinese residing in Indonesia (Willmott 1961: 74).[6] Overall, Indonesia welcomed Indian migrants without imposing pressure on them to assimilate into Indonesian society.

From the early years of permanent residence, Sindhis, who mostly settled in Jakarta, worked to preserve their cultural identity by forming associations and institutions. In 1949 Sindhi elders established the Bombay Merchant Association (BMA), defining its membership very

---

6   Apart from strong lobbying from India, Thompson and Adloff (1955: 69) suggest that the easing of restrictions on remittances was due to the fact that Indians, unlike Chinese residing in Indonesia, were free from suspicion of being disloyal to the country.

bluntly: 'BMA is exclusively for people of Sindhi descent, not anyone else'.[7] One of BMA's major goals was to provide 'the best possible education to the children of the community' (Sindhishaan 2010a). Indeed, the establishment of the Gandhi Memorial School, a community school open strictly to those of Sindhi descent alone, followed soon afterwards.

This is not to say that Sindhis walled themselves off from the wider, non-Sindhi community. Through business they were in constant interaction with all kinds of people. Pasar Baru, the district where most Sindhis settled in Jakarta, was well known as an Indian market offering textiles for all tastes. In the late 1950s Sindhis established connections with local elites such as politicians and foreign diplomats, mostly Soviets, through 'mail order' businesses. As the economic situation in the country was deteriorating, many goods were in short supply. Although Western diplomats could procure such goods in Singapore, Soviet diplomats did not have that option (Thapan 2002: 32). By mobilising their ethnic connections, Sindhis were able to find and purchase the items requested by the Soviets in Singapore, Hong Kong and Manila and send them to Indonesia using the diplomatic mail. Apart from this 'mail order' business, Sindhis also used film importation, distribution and production to (re)connect with local elites (Myutel 2016).

Importantly, during the first decade of permanent migration, children born to the Sindhi community were exposed to a wider social circle than their parents. The Gandhi Memorial School only offered primary schooling, so Sindhi children attended non-Sindhi, English-medium schools for their secondary education, mingling with children from very different backgrounds, including the children of foreign and local businesspeople, academics and diplomats.[8] The situation started to change only after the proclamation of the Emergency (1957), which led the government to severely limit the number of foreign-language schools (Willmott 1961).

It was during the Guided Democracy period that Sindhis experienced the greatest instability of settlement, triggered largely by worsening relations between Indonesia and India as a result of the Cold War. In 1962 a dispute between India and China over the Himalayan border turned into a military conflict, the Sino-Indian War. Sukarno was aligning Indonesia ever more closely with the Communist Bloc, and especially China, as part

---

7 The name of the organisation reflected the deep affection of Sindhis for Bombay as the quintessence of Indianness. The central importance of Bombay is explained by the administrative history of the region (from 1843 to 1936 Sindh was part of the Bombay presidency, or province) and the commercial importance of this city in India.

8 Many private schools established during the colonial period continued to operate after independence. The only novelty was the introduction of the term 'alien' for schools that used a medium of instruction other than Indonesian (Suryadinata 1978: 23).

of his campaign against the 'neo-imperialist' West. This led to staged anti-Indian demonstrations. The first of these, usually referred to as the Sondhi Affair, involved young nationalists marching in protest against India in the streets of Jakarta, and culminated in an attack on the Indian embassy in 1962 (Brewster 2011: 223–4). After the demonstrations, traders from Pasar Baru closed their shops and removed the word 'India' from their signboards (Lubis 2008: 98).

In September 1965 Sukarno instigated another series of anti-India rallies. This time the protests took place not only in Jakarta, where an angry mob attacked the Indian embassy and dozens of Indian shops, but also in other major cities, including Semarang, Surabaya and Surakarta. The government also froze monetary transactions of Indian businesspeople and appropriated their property (Arora 1982: 124; Mani 1993a: 109). Only its close connections with the Indonesian military helped protect the community from physical harm. These later protests were sparked by the Indo-Pakistani war and Sukarno's strongly pro-Pakistan stance. The president's hostility towards India had intensified after India endorsed the creation of Malaysia in 1963 (which Indonesia strenuously opposed) and advocated a continuing security role for Great Britain in the region (Brewster 2011). The presence of British power in Southeast Asia was denounced by Sukarno as both a neocolonial legacy and a threat to Indonesian independence.

Amidst mounting 'economic chaos' (Dick et al. 2002: 191), unresolved social issues inherited from colonial times and the 'unprecedented national prominence' of the Indonesian Communist Party (Cribb and Ford 2010), Sukarno's Guided Democracy teetered on the brink of collapse for much of 1965. An abortive coup by leftists on 30 September 1965 led to the demise of the regime, accompanied by massacres and the incarceration of hundreds of thousands of suspected communists throughout late 1965 and early 1966. The military-based New Order regime led by Major-General Suharto took power in March 1966, ushering in three decades of authoritarianism and state terrorism (Heryanto 2006).

For Sindhis, Suharto's regime, in contrast to that of Sukarno, was a time of prosperity for both individuals and the community. The growing wealth and well-being of Sindhis under the New Order can be attributed to the overall improvement in the Indonesian economic climate due to the privatisation and liberalisation of the economy and the oil boom, which significantly increased consumer purchasing power. The laws of the late 1960s reversed Sukarno's hostile policies towards foreign investors and private enterprises and introduced incentives for the development of private businesses (Dick et al. 2002: 206). For the Sindhi community—which, in Falzon's (2004: 189) words, was 'synonymous with business'—the favourable economic conditions were among the main factors fostering community well-being. The 1970s were a period in which many Sindhis, seeing great potential in the local economy, applied for and were granted Indonesian citizenship. Although the process did take a number of years, acquiring citizenship status was not a major ordeal for Sindhis. Those who retained their foreign passports were also able to continue to do business in Indonesia by moving from trade to textile manufacturing, which had been opened to private, particularly foreign, investors in order to encourage exports (Dick et al. 2002).

The restoration of amicable India–Indonesia relations in the late 1960s played a significant role in enhancing and securing the well-being of Sindhis during Suharto's rule. On a practical level, Sindhis became the main facilitators of Indian aid to Indonesia, which began flowing immediately after the change of regime in 1966. The aid was in the form of a substantial multi-year loan ($100 million), given in the form of Indian commodities such as paper, chemicals, steel and bicycle parts. Indonesian officials did not know what to do with some of these goods and asked Sindhi businesspeople, well known in Jakartan elite circles for their trading skills, for help (Sindhishaan 2010b). As a result, Sindhis became the key contacts for Indian businesspeople who wished to explore investment opportunities in the Southeast Asian region. By the early 1980s Indian companies had invested more than $200 million in Indonesia (Mani 1993a: 113).

The strategic position of India between two major powers, the United States and the USSR, during the Cold War, also favoured stability for Sindhis (and other Indian migrants) in Indonesia. The USSR and the United States saw India as an important player in the Cold War (Mastny 2010: 65) and it was in Indonesia's interests to maintain good relations with India, which like Indonesia was a member of the Non-Aligned Movement. In the 1970s, when India's political ideology and economic policies drew it closer to the Soviet Union, Suharto, who relied heavily on Western economic assistance, chose not to escalate frictions with India. In general, the 'model of mutually beneficial realpolitik' (Mastny 2010: 50) that India and Indonesia created during the Cold War served Sindhis and the broader Indian community in the archipelago well.

As the economic position of Sindhis strengthened, so did the educational, social and religious institutions established and patronised by the Sindhis. This was in stark contrast to Indonesian Chinese, whose expression of cultural and religious heritage during the New Order was increasingly circumscribed: the government shut down Mandarin-medium schools, banned the use of Chinese names, language and script, and significantly restricted cultural celebrations (Aguilar 2001).[9]

---

9   Curiously, during the New Order several Indian cultural festivals were banned in Sumatra. A ban on Thaiputsam, a Hindu festival celebrated by the Tamil community, was imposed in Medan in 1973. According to Mani

Meanwhile, the English-medium community-run schools in Jakarta and other cities in Java not only remained open but grew significantly, with enrolments exceeding 1,500 by 1978. In 1973, to cater for the vibrant cultural life of the community, BMA acquired a new hall in the centre of Jakarta, calling it Graha Sindhu (Sindhu House). Although community events were not open to the public, the closed nature of cultural celebrations had more to do with the Sindhis' desire to remain exclusive than with government policies (Myutel and Sandkuehler 2017). Overall, Indonesian Sindhis managed to preserve and perpetuate the lifestyle of pre-Partition Sindh to such an extent that Sindhis from other parts of the world regarded the Jakarta Sindhis as overly conservative, inward-looking, even 'backward' (Thapan 2002: 84).

The absence of discriminatory state policies targeting Sindhis, and more broadly Indians, in Indonesia did not mean that Indonesian Sindhis felt no repercussions from policies targeting other minority groups, in particular Indonesian Chinese. In the public imagination, fuelled by the government's rhetoric, *non-pribumi* largely meant foreign, and thus potentially threatening to the nation. In everyday encounters Sindhis were constantly reminded of their differences through the 'foreignising gaze'. 'Here [in Indonesia] it's automatic—when people look at you, they look at you as if you are a foreigner' (Reena, Indonesian Sindhi, personal communication, 6 March 2013).[10]

Those Sindhis who had gone into local film production and made a significant contribution to the industry in the 1970s and 1980s felt these repercussions more acutely. The New Order ideologists presented cinema historiography as *film nasional* (national cinema), which for all intents and purposes meant '*pribumi*, idealist and nationalist' (Barker 2011: 39). Such a version of history had no place for the 'inauthentic' Indonesians who, 'by virtue of their race', were 'feature-less financiers' with no artistic taste (Said 1982: 100–102) and an insatiable hunger for money (Biran 2001: 220). During the New Order the names of Sindhi filmmakers were almost entirely expunged from Indonesian historiography.[11]

Thus, the relations established between the Sindhis, the wider Indonesian community and the state during the New Order were highly ambivalent. On the one hand, Indonesia was a friendly and accepting

---

(1993b), however, the ban was not initiated by the state but was requested by Hindu temple leaders who supported total integration of local Tamils into Indonesian society.

10 All interviewee names are pseudonyms.

11 The film catalogue published by Kristanto et al. (1995) included the names of only two Sindhi producers. The second edition of the catalogue, published in the *reformasi* period (Kristanto and Ardan 2007), has entries on eight Sindhi personalities but the list is still far from exhaustive.

place, full of opportunity for economic and social prosperity. Foreign minority status often enhanced one's business prospects and offered an enriched cultural life. On the other hand, Indonesia's acceptance had limits. Regardless of their actual citizenship status, Sindhis were seen by other Indonesians only as foreigners, not fellow compatriots:

> I'm not a foreigner, I'm a citizen by naturalisation. [...] I had to give up my Indian passport. But here people still have different thinking. In America, if you have an American passport, whether you are of German or Polish origins, you are American. But here there is still this *pribumi* [matter] (Kumar, Indonesian Sindhi, personal communication, 18 February 2013).

Such treatment was, however, not very concerning for Sindhis, who invested heavily in maintaining their differences from the mainstream. In other words, mutual disregard was as much the result of the Sindhi community's efforts to preserve its cultural distinctiveness as it was the outcome of a continuing racialisation of Indonesian society.

The downfall of Suharto in 1998 and the outbreak of state-sponsored violence, which explicitly targeted Indonesian Chinese (Bertrand 2004: 67; Budianta 2000: 119), caused anxiety among minorities, including Indonesian Sindhis. Many waited out the turbulent days in neighbouring countries. Those who stayed were 'not sure where they stood' or whether the rioters would consider them to be 'the representatives of Chinese'. To protect themselves, women left notes written in Sindhi script on their house doors and men stood outside the shut gates with golf sticks and cricket bats. Several Sindhi families who were staying in a residential complex in the centre of Jakarta (near Gambir) managed to get a land tank to guard the gates for the duration of the social unrest. Although the Sindhis clearly felt vulnerable due to their ethnic and economic differences, they soon concluded that 'there were no orders to target Indians'. This reassured them that they were not identified with Indonesian Chinese in the minds of the power-holders. Overall, the Sindhi community was neither reshaped nor severely traumatised by the dramatic events of May 1998.

Among the reforms introduced during the post-Suharto era, the changes to the education system had the most impact on the community. In 2003 President Megawati Sukarnoputri's government issued Law No. 20/2003 on the National Education System, which lifted the ban on Indonesian citizens and residents enrolling in international schools. The law stripped Sindhis of their privileged access to an English-medium education in the country. Moreover, as high-quality education in English became accessible outside the community-run schools, for the first time since the late 1950s young Sindhis were again exposed to a non-Sindhi Indonesian community. The exposure weakened community ties and resulted in the production of ever more complex identities in a rapidly transforming Indonesia.

SCHOOL MATTERS

The Gandhi Memorial School (GMS) was established in Jakarta by BMA in the late 1940s to cater only to the needs of the Sindhi community. GMS used English as the medium of instruction, followed the Indian curriculum, and offered Sindhi and Hindi as extracurricular subjects. Recruitment of the school principal and teachers was done in India. After Sukarno proclaimed a state of emergency in 1957, the continued existence of the school came under threat. To prevent its closure BMA transferred authority for the school to the Indian embassy and turned the school into an all-level educational institution. Thus, since 1958 GMS has had the ambiguous status of an embassy school that is funded and managed by a local trust, the Gandhi Memorial Foundation, established by BMA specifically to finance the school.

Not only was the school's standing ambiguous, but its enrolment process was illegal. Government Regulation No. 48/1960 banned both Indonesian citizens and permanent residents from attending 'alien' schools (schools with a medium of instruction other than Indonesian). As by 1960 most school-age children born to Indonesian Sindhis were either permanent residents or Indonesian citizens by birth, they were not eligible for enrolment in GMS. State officials, however, turned a blind eye to the school's existence and enrolment practices.

Having the Indian embassy's protection for GMS for more than 30 years had a tremendous impact on the community's self-awareness and its relations with Indonesian society. First, admission to the school, which was based on ethnicity rather than citizenship, clearly put Sindhi ethnicity above Indonesian citizenship. Sindhi-ness, a 'foreign' ethnicity, therefore became a marker of distinction, not of discrimination or marginalisation. It ensured privileged access to a high-quality, English-medium education in Indonesia, not overseas, an opportunity not available to other Indonesian citizens.

Proficiency in English, a marker of the educated classes in the postcolonial world, reinforced the privileged position of Sindhis in Indonesia. Importantly, whereas for most Indonesians Bahasa Indonesia was a language for acquiring knowledge, for Sindhis, especially females, Bahasa Indonesia was mainly reduced to a means of communication with people of lower social rank (maids, drivers, gardeners). Many Sindhis across several generations grew up speaking only rudimentary Indonesian or none at all. For example, when I attended the Miss India Indonesia Pageant

2013, a popular community event aimed at demonstrating 'the perfect blend of two cultures', I found that the proficiency in Bahasa Indonesia of young Sindhi women was glaringly low. Although the participants were relatively successful in blending India and Indonesia during the first two rounds of the beauty pageant, their performance during the Q&A session was a total fiasco.[12] To the obvious disappointment of the judges, the contestants, all born and brought up in Indonesia, were unable to understand and answer questions in the Indonesian language.

Last but not least, as a foreign embassy school, GMS was excluded from the national education system. This meant there was no obligation on GMS to create 'good Indonesian citizens', that is, individuals with 'knowledge of the symbols, structures and form of the Indonesian state', 'respect for authority and an acceptance of state hierarchy and imposed discipline' (Parker 2002: 33). Moreover, it meant freedom from indoctrination with the state ideology of Pancasila. In sum, the exclusion of GMS from the national system further minimised the points of contact between the community and the state.

The early 1990s marked the end of the 30-year-long exclusive access of Sindhis to a privileged education. The end of the era was due not to state regulations, but to the prolonged internal conflict among school board members. The power struggles, which resulted in a fall in the quality of education, forced Sindhi families to explore other educational options, such as overseas education or schooling at one of the newly established private Christian schools. To keep the enrolment numbers up, in the mid-1990s GMS introduced the Indonesian curriculum and Bahasa Indonesia as the language of instruction, and opened up enrolment to non-Sindhi Indonesians.

Law No. 20/2003 made it possible for BMA (known since the 1990s as Gandhi Seva Loka) to bring Sindhi youth back to the community-run educational system. At the same time, after 2003 access to quality education was increasingly based on class, and not solely on ethnic heritage. BMA established two separate schools: Gandhi Memorial International School (GMIS) and Mahatma Gandhi School (MGS). As an international school, GMIS mainly targets upper-middle-class Sindhis and foreigners from South and East Asia. Following the Indian, British and International Baccalaureate curriculums and offering Hindi, French, Indonesian or Mandarin as a second language, GMIS is in the business of producing global citizens, for whom Indian-ness is a significant component of

---

12 The most successful performance was by a young woman who sang the famous Indonesian song *Sampoerna* while accompanying herself on an Indian harmonium.

identity. Meanwhile, MGS targets middle-class Indonesians, Sindhi and non-Sindhi alike. In 2013, for example, Sindhi community members constituted less than 40 per cent of the enrolled students, with the majority being Indonesian Chinese.

Although the educational reforms did not trigger the gradual weakening of community ties, they have contributed to it. After 2003 Sindhis could choose from a wide range of options, depending on cultural preferences and financial capability. When selecting a school, Indonesian Sindhis currently have more identities to choose from: Indonesian Sindhi (MGS), global Indian (GMIS or other Indian schools throughout the world) or global/Westernised (Jakarta International School or similar schools).[13]

It is difficult to overstate the role that Gandhi Memorial School played in community life for more than 30 years. It was the core community institution where children born to Indonesian Sindhi families became conscious of their distinct identity and the privileges associated with it in Indonesia—especially access to an exclusive education that opened opportunities worldwide. The efforts of the community to maintain its identity and the state's laxity in enforcing restrictions on 'alien' education produced several generations of local and global citizens who felt at ease in Indonesia while remaining close to India, who belonged without feeling obliged.

DISREGARD, BELONGING AND THE GROWING NATIONALISM IN ASIA

By and large, the relations between the Sindhi minority and the Indonesian state can best be described as mutual disregard. While not insisting on their rights, Sindhis have also often disregarded their obligations by evading laws and regulations and refraining from paying taxes.[14] Belonging to one of the world's wealthiest and best-connected networks, Sindhis have been very self-sufficient, requiring minimum support from the state. As for the state, it let the Sindhis run their own affairs as long as the community did not get involved in activities that directly affected the nation-building process. There was no pressure on Sindhis to assimilate, to actively confirm their citizenship by carrying special identity cards (as

13   In 2014 all international schools in Indonesia were renamed as 'intercultural' schools, so JIS now stands for Jakarta Intercultural School.
14   See, for example, an article in the *Jakarta Globe* by Bisara, Latul and Wibisono (2010), which names Gandhi Memorial International School as one of Indonesia's worst tax dodgers.

required for Indonesian Chinese) or to give up their cultural identity by changing their names to Indonesian-sounding ones.[15]

The denial of their place in the national cultural history has not been a major concern for Sindhis; the concept of nation as the ultimate locus of belonging remains rather alien to a community that is 'translocal, adaptive, and cosmopolitan' (Falzon 2004: 64). For Sindhis, it is among the Sindhayat, the global community of traders, that they ultimately belong. But although the nation-state may be illusory for Sindhis, home and homeland are very real. India is their homeland, and the site of their cultural roots and heritage, but Indonesia is home, and home, as Ignatieff (2001) has pointed out, is about feeling safe. India is where Sindhis aspire to be, but in fact never decide to stay. During regular trips to India for family, business or spiritual purposes, they blend in with the crowd, something that is impossible in Indonesia. But looking the same does not make them feel the same; mannerisms, slang, likes and interests constantly remind Indonesian Sindhis that they do not fit in seamlessly in India either. Indonesia is, however, a place to return to after periods of travel or years of studying or working abroad, a place that is safe, comfortable and familiar: 'I'm very used to living in Indonesia. I think I'm more Indian [than Indonesian] but Indonesia is family, it's home' (Sheeja, third-generation Indonesian Sindhi, personal communication, 6 March 2013). Such sentiments are shared by older and younger generations alike. The presence of a real and imaginary India in everyday life does not make Sindhis less connected to Indonesia; what closer connection can one develop with a place than to call it home? In sum, the story of Sindhis in Indonesia, who, in their own words, 'take the best of both countries', is largely about uncontentious but nonetheless multifaceted belonging.

The rise of India's political and economic power, and the upsurge of Hindu nationalism led by Indian prime minister Narendra Modi, has presented an option for Indonesian Sindhis to consider the rather simplistic identity of pan-Indian Hindus. In May 2018, driven by the increased presence of China in the region, Modi paid his first ever official visit to Indonesia.[16] During his two-and-a-half-day stay in Jakarta, Modi dedicated three hours of his time to a community gathering. Organised by the Indian embassy, the India Club Jakarta and several prominent Sindhi families, the event attracted more than 3,500 people from 'the Indian Diaspora and friends of India' (Sagar 2018). Modi's speech, delivered in Hindi to an excited crowd, was met with a standing ovation and chants

---

15 For the politics of naming among Chinese Indonesians, see Bailey and Lie (2013).

16 The visit to Indonesia was part of a five-day, three-nation visit to Southeast Asia that included official visits to Malaysia and Singapore.

of 'Har Har Modi'.[17] The ecstatic reception of the Indian prime minister, well known for his harsh nationalistic policies and intolerance towards religious minorities, including Muslims, shows that Indonesian Indians maintain a strong and affectionate connection to, and endorsement of, India as a Hindu state.

Given historical precedent, I presume that the resurgence of *pro-pribumi* rhetoric and the growing xenophobia in Indonesia, triggered by the race for power, will not have a negative effect on the Sindhi minority, even if Hindu nationalism takes deep root in the community.[18] For more than a century, the position of this minority has been defined by the relations between two countries and the presence of a common threat in the Indo-Pacific region, and not by domestic power struggles. As long as India and Indonesia continue to strengthen their relationship to contain the growing power of China, the Sindhi, and more generally the Indian minority in Indonesia, will retain the comfortable and often advantageous position of 'local foreigners'.

REFERENCES

Aguilar, F.V. (2001) 'Citizenship, inheritance, and the indigenizing of "Orang Chinese" in Indonesia', *Positions: East Asia Cultures Critique* 9(3): 501–33.

Arora, B.D. (1982) 'Indians in Indonesia', in L.J.B. Singh (ed.) *Indians in Southeast Asia*, Sterling Publishers Private Ltd, New Delhi: 119–29.

Bailey, B., and S. Lie (2013) 'The politics of names among Chinese Indonesians in Java', *Journal of Linguistic Anthropology* 23(1): 21–40.

Barker, T. (2011) 'A cultural economy of the contemporary Indonesian film industry', PhD thesis, National University of Singapore, Singapore.

Bertrand, J. (2004) *Nationalism and Ethnic Conflict in Indonesia*, Cambridge University Press, New York.

Biran, M.Y. (2001) 'The history of Indonesian cinema at a glance', in D. Hanan (ed.) *Film in South East Asia: Views from the Region*, SEAPAVAA, Hanoi: 211–53.

Bisara, D., J. Latul and A. Wibisono (2010) 'Officials name the 100 worst tax-dodgers', *Jakarta Globe*, 29 January 2010. https://jakartaglobe.id/archive/officials-name-the-100-worst-tax-dodgers/

Brewster, D. (2011) 'The relationship between India and Indonesia', *Asian Survey* 51(2): 221–44.

Budianta, M. (2000) 'Discourse of cultural identity in Indonesia during the 1997–1998 monetary crisis', *Inter-Asia Cultural Studies* 1(1): 109–28.

Cribb, R., and M. Ford (2010) 'The killings of 1965–66', *Inside Indonesia* 99 (January–March).

---

17 'Har Har Modi' is a slogan used by Modi's party, Bharatiya Janata Party (BJP). It virtually equates Modi with God, through its allusion to the original line, 'Har Har Mahadev', meaning 'Everyone is Lord Shiva'.

18 Whether any mistreatment of Muslims in India could challenge the status quo remains to be seen.

Dick, H.W, V.J.H. Houben, J.T. Lindblad and T.K. Wie (eds) (2002) *The Emergence of a National Economy: An Economic History of Indonesia, 1800–2000*, University of Hawai'i Press, Honolulu.

Falzon, M.-A. (2004) *Cosmopolitan Connections: The Sindhi Diaspora, 1860–2000*, Brill, Leiden.

Heryanto, A. (2006) *State Terrorism and Political Identity in Indonesia: Fatally Belonging*, Routledge, London and New York.

Heryanto, A. (2014) *Identity and Pleasure: The Politics of Indonesian Screen Culture*, National University of Singapore Press, Singapore.

Ignatieff, M. (2001) *Human Rights as Politics and Idolatry*, Princeton University Press, Princeton NJ.

Kristanto, J.B., and S.M. Ardan (2007) *Katalog Film Indonesia, 1926–2007*, Penerbit Nalar, Jakarta.

Kristanto, J.B., S.M. Ardan, H. Suwardi and H. Jauhari (1995) *Katalog Film Indonesia, 1926–1995*, Penerbit PT Grafiasri Mukti, Jakarta.

Lubis, F. (2008) *Jakarta 1960-an: Kenangan Semasa Mahasiswa*, Masup Jakarta, Depok.

Mani, A. (1993a) 'Indians in Jakarta', in K.S. Sandhu and A. Mani (eds) *Indian Communities in Southeast Asia*, ISEAS and Times Academic Press, Singapore: 98–130.

Mani, A. (1993b) 'Indians in North Sumatra', in K.S. Sandhu and A. Mani (eds) *Indian Communities in Southeast Asia*, ISEAS and Times Academic Press, Singapore: 46–97.

Mani, P.R.S. (1945–49) 'P.R.S. Mani collection. Conflicted dispatches: the writings of P.R.S. Mani, Indian journalist, nationalist and British army officer in Indonesia, 1945–1949', Open Publications of UTS Scholars (OPUS). https://epress.lib.uts.edu.au/research/handle/10453/28084

Markovits, C. (2000) *The Global World of Indian Merchants, 1750–1947: Traders of Sind from Bukhara to Panama*, Cambridge University Press, Cambridge.

Mastny, V. (2010) 'The Soviet Union's partnership with India', *Journal of Cold War Studies* 12(3): 50–90.

Myutel, M. (2016) 'Indians and national television in Indonesia: behind the *seen*', PhD thesis, Australian National University, Canberra.

Myutel, M. (2017) 'Ethnicity and social relations in Indonesian television production houses', *Journal of Southeast Asian Studies* 48(2): 219–36.

Myutel, M., and E. Sandkuehler (2017) '(In)visible ethnicity: celebrating Chinese and Indian descent in Indonesia', Occasional Paper No. 36, Southeast Asian Studies at the University of Freiburg, Freiburg, June.

Parker, L. (2002) 'The subjectification of citizenship: student interpretations of school teachings in Bali', *Asian Studies Review* 26(1): 3–37.

Rakhmani, I. (2014) 'Mainstream Islam: television industry practice and trends in Indonesian sinetron', *Asian Journal of Social Sciences* 42: 435–66.

Sagar, P. (2018) 'Home away from home: Indians in Indonesia', *IndoIndians*, 30 May. https://www.indoindians.com/home-away-from-home-indians-in-indonesia.

Said, S. (1982) *Profil Dunia Film Indonesia*, Grafitipers, Jakarta.

Sindhishaan (2010a) 'Gandhi Seva Loka', *Sindhishaan* 9(2). http://www.sindhishaan.com/article/personalities/pers_09_02.html

Sindhishaan (2010b) 'Sindhi business tycoons in Indonesia', *Sindhishaan* 9(2). http://www.sindhishaan.com/article/personalities/pers_09_02a.html

Singhvi, L.M. (2001) 'Report of the High Level Committee on the Indian diaspora', Non-Resident Indian and Persons of Indian Origin Division, Ministry of External Affairs, Government of India, New Dehli.

Strassler, K. (2008) 'Cosmopolitan visions: ethnic Chinese and the photographic imagining of Indonesia in the late colonial and early postcolonial periods', *Journal of Asian Studies* 67(02): 395–432.

Suryadinata, L. (1978) *The Chinese Minority in Indonesia: Seven Papers,* Chopmen Enterprises, Singapore.

Thapan, A.R. (2002) *Sindhi Diaspora in Manila, Hong Kong, and Jakarta,* Ateneo de Manila University Press, Quezon City.

Thompson, V., and R. Adloff (eds) (1955) *Minority Problems in Southeast Asia,* Stanford University Press, Stanford CA.

Willmott, D.E. (1961) *The National Status of the Chinese in Indonesia, 1900–1958,* Cornell Southeast Asia Program Publications, Ithaca NY.

13 'Normalising' the Orang Rimba: between mainstreaming, marginalising and respecting indigenous culture

Butet Manurung

The Orang Rimba (literally, 'People of the Jungle') are one of many indigenous communities in Indonesia. They are described as 'indigenous' (*asli*) not so much in the international sense of being the 'original inhabitants' or 'first peoples' of a particular region whose presence predates that of the main or subsequently dominant communities, but rather because they are isolated from, or peripheral to, mainstream Indonesian society. The Orang Rimba live predominantly in heavily forested and remote parts of Jambi province, Sumatra, where they have carefully guarded their distinctive traditional beliefs and way of life and deliberately limited their contact with the surrounding society and the state.

Over the past few decades, the Orang Rimba have come under increasing pressure from the national government and local governments, as well as from outside civil society groups, to integrate into Jambi society. This has included efforts to convert them to one of Indonesia's six state-recognised religions, especially Islam, to change the way they dress and to persuade them to allow access to state health and education services as well as housing and agricultural projects. State schooling is particularly controversial, with some fearing that it will detach Orang Rimba students from their traditional systems of knowledge and land use and create identity conflicts. Moreover, changes to the state's management of national parks and conservation zones have impacted heavily on the mobility and lifestyles of the Orang Rimba.

The place of, and policies towards, the Orang Rimba and other indigenous communities raises important and difficult issues for government and broader society. Indonesia prides itself on having an ethos of 'Unity in Diversity' (*Bhinneka Tunggal Ika*) and on valuing and accommodating the immense cultural differences that exist across the archipelago. But indigenous communities test the limits of this putative embracing of diversity more severely than most of the other minorities discussed in this volume, such as the Chinese, Indians and Arabs. There are two reasons for this. First, the Orang Rimba do not seek to be part of mainstream society, and self-consciously assert their separateness. In this sense, their sense of 'belonging' to Indonesia is markedly different from that of most other minorities. They have little or no knowledge of the Constitution, the national ideology of Pancasila or the nation's political and social history—all of which most Indonesians would regard as basic requirements of citizenship. To be Indonesian is to know such things because they are considered to define the nation. So how should the state and the rest of society deal with a community that has little interest in such features of nationhood? Second, most Indonesians hold a vision of their country as a rapidly developing and modern nation and welcome predictions that Indonesia will become one of the top ten or even top five economic powers in the world within the next few decades. In this context, the Orang Rimba, who cherish their centuries-old traditions and culture, who vigorously resist change and who have little grasp of, let alone interest in, the notion of modernity, stand in contradiction to this generally held view of Indonesia's inexorable advancement.

Should officialdom and society make an exception for indigenous peoples like the Orang Rimba and allow them to be separate and starkly different, or should they seek to bring them into mainstream society so that these 'People of the Forest' can enjoy the benefits of 'progress' that all citizens should have access to? Should the Orang Rimba be permitted to live by different rules than those governing most Indonesians? Does the notion of 'Unity in Diversity' extend as far as allowing certain communities to remain distinct and largely disengaged from the majority? These are not simple questions to answer and they involve fundamental matters of principle.

I will argue in this chapter that the Orang Rimba suffer systematic marginalisation as a result of the actions of the national government and local governments, as well as broader Indonesian society. This marginalisation is closely tied to efforts to integrate this indigenous community into national life, a process commonly referred to as 'mainstreaming'. Officials tend to regard the 'normalisation' of indigenous communities as a desirable objective, but I believe it is causing great disruption and harm to traditional communities. I will contend that greater awareness of and sensitivity towards Orang Rimba culture and aspirations are necessary if this particular indigenous community is to find true acceptance on its own terms within a diverse Indonesia.

I am writing this chapter not as an independent researcher or academic but rather as an activist and advocate for the Orang Rimba. I will draw on my 20 years' experience working directly with their communities, especially to provide contextual education that is tailored to the needs of each community and its particular geographical and cultural setting. On average, I have spent more than half of each year living among the Orang Rimba, seeking to deepen my understanding of their norms and way of life. In recent years, I have also been engaging increasingly with government in order to raise awareness of the plight and aspirations of the Orang Rimba and to argue for policies that are more respectful of the wishes of indigenous communities.

CULTURE, BELIEFS AND LIFESTYLE OF THE ORANG RIMBA

The Orang Rimba are nomadic hunter-gatherers who live in the jungles of four provinces in central Sumatra: South Sumatra, West Sumatra, Jambi and Riau.[1] According to a local NGO, the Indonesian Conservation Community (Komunitas Konservasi Indonesia (KKI) Warsi), the total population of Orang Rimba in 2018 was 5,235 (KKI Warsi 2018b). The majority live in Jambi, mainly in two national parks—Bukit Duabelas and Bukit Tigapuluh—and along the Trans-Sumatran Highway. Some 2,546 Orang Rimba occupy 60,500 hectares of lowland rainforest in Bukit Duabelas and another 474 live in Bukit Tigapuluh. Around 1,300 live near the Trans-Sumatran Highway in an area known as Singkut; this was the name of a nearby forested region from which they were displaced by plantation developments and transmigration projects some decades ago (KKI Warsi 2018a).

The communities have a clan-based structure, with each of the 16 clans (*rombongan*) headed by a chief (*tumenggung*), who is assisted by various intermediate-level leaders who fulfil a range of specific tasks within the clan. The size of the clans varies from about 70 to as large as several hundred. Contact between clans is limited and regulated by custom; until relatively recently there was little sense of an overall Orang Rimba community, as each clan's focus was largely internal. Marriage is usually endogamous to the clan but marrying across clan lines or even outside the Orang Rimba is occasionally permitted. Clan culture is matrilocal in

---

1   The best scholarly reference work on the Orang Rimba is Steven Sager's doctoral thesis, 'The sky is our roof, the earth our floor' (Sager 2008).

that husbands usually reside with the wife's extended family; couples prefer to have daughters rather than sons.

All Orang Rimba clans have their own system of zones within the forest, with specific areas set aside for living, birthing, farming, burial sites, religious rituals and good and bad spirits. Contiguous clans are aware of each other's zones and if members from one *rombongan* want to access another clan's zones, they will seek permission from that clan by emitting a series of loud calls or cries (*besasalung*), which echo through the forest. In recent years, several clans have been forced to relocate from one forest to another, usually due to the intrusion of mining or agricultural industries. This has required special ceremonies by the local tribes to accept the presence of the incoming Orang Rimba clan and agree upon the areas in which they will resettle.

Religious beliefs play a big role in the Orang Rimba's lives and in zoning. Their religion is usually described as animism but polytheism is a more accurate descriptor. They believe that many gods are present in the forest and that these exert a powerful influence on their lives. Gods may be benign or malevolent but many Orang Rimba regard their gods with fearful respect, believing that most misfortune occurs because their easily angered gods have been displeased. Particular areas are designated the preserve of the gods and Orang Rimba will not live or establish plantations in any godly zone. They also believe that rivers and creeks are the means by which gods move about the forest and they thus place great emphasis on the cleanliness of waterways. Only a shaman (*dukun godong*) has the power to intercede with the gods, and to dispense natural remedies or mantras to cure illness or counteract evil spirits.

The Orang Rimba are completely self-sufficient in the jungle. They hunt and eat almost all forest animals, including snakes, bears, wild boars, bats, lizards and birds. The only exceptions are tame animals that have been caught to keep as pets and animals regarded as belonging to a god, such as tigers and Hornbill birds. Men wear traditional loincloths; married women are bare-chested with a sarong covering the lower part of the body; and unmarried women wear a sarong that covers both the upper and lower parts of the body.

Although the Orang Rimba prefer to limit their contact with outsiders, they have developed systems to deal with such interactions. The *temenggung* has primary responsibility for communicating with the outside world and usually does so through a patron (*waris jenang*) who lives in a nearby village or city. Traditionally, the Orang Rimba sold goods and sometimes labour to the patron. Over the past 50 years, intrusions onto their land have become increasingly common, whether it be by government officials, doctors and nurses, teachers or NGO activists, or by miners, loggers, surveyors and illegal hunters. The Orang Rimba complain that outsiders have an objectionable odour from the soap, deodorant and perfumes they use, which drives away the gods and spirits. Over the past decade, growing awareness of and respect for indigenous culture has generally meant more sensitive engagement of outsiders with Orang Rimba communities.

LABELLING THE ORANG RIMBA

The very idea of an 'indigenous people' or 'indigenous community' is a colonial construct. Edward Said (1978: 10) described it as a Western discourse about the 'Other' that is reinforced by 'institutions, vocabulary, scholarship, imagery, doctrines, even colonial bureaucracies and colonial styles'. Linda Tuhiwai Smith (1999) considered the term problematic because it generalised the complexity and diversity of populations that encountered and perceived colonialism in different ways. Despite criticism of the assumptions that underlie its use, the term 'indigenous people' has gained wide international and domestic currency in describing communities that are native to a location and in identifying the challenges they face. These challenges include responding to environmental devastation, dealing with pressure for cultural change and negotiating a place within increasingly intrusive state systems. The story of many indigenous peoples across the world is one of adversity and tenacious survival.

In Indonesia, indigenous communities are usually called *masyarakat adat* (traditional or customary communities), or sometimes *masyarakat hukum adat* (customary law communities) or *masyarakat terasing* (isolated communities). The main umbrella organisation for such communities is the Alliance of Archipelagic Indigenous Peoples (Aliansi Masyarakat Adat Nusantara, AMAN). It defines indigenous communities as those:

> whose lives are based on customary rights to certain lands which have been handed down through generations and exert sovereignty over those lands and natural resources. Their societies and cultures are governed by customary laws and customary institutions which sustain the continuity of their communities (AMAN 2018).

AMAN calculates that there are 2,332 indigenous communities across Indonesia, and the Ministry of National Development Planning estimates the total number of people in those communities to be 40–50 million (Bappenas 2014). Some observers believe this figure is too high, but much depends on how one chooses to define an 'indigenous' community.

Mainstream society has a variety of perceptions of indigenous communities, ranging from sympathetic and supportive to paternalistic and antipathetic. These latter views find expression in such terms as *masyarakat perambah hutan* (forest encroachers) and *orang primitif* (primitive people). Often such perceptions are shaped by the degree of exposure to *masyarakat adat* and the ways in which indigenous communities either engage with or distance themselves from broader social and cultural life.

In Indonesia, the terms that indigenous communities use for themselves vary markedly from those used by the general community, including academics and government officials. Exploring these differences reveals much about attitudes to indigenous peoples, including the Orang Rimba.

There are at least three commonly used names for the Orang Rimba: Orang Rimba, which is the term preferred by the community itself; Kubu; and Suku Anak Dalam (SAD). 'Kubu' is the term used by the surrounding non-indigenous communities and 'Suku Anak Dalam' is the term used by the Indonesian government. The first publication using the term 'Kubu' for the Orang Rimba was a report by the Dutch scholar and resident of Palembang, G.J. van Dongen, in 1910. He appropriated a common Malay word (*kubu*) to describe the mobile, animist peoples who lived in the lowland forests of southeast Sumatra (Van Dongen 1910). In Malay, the word *kubu* can mean a defensive fortification, an entrenchment or a place of refuge, but in this case it was used as a metaphor for how the majority Malays saw forest-dwelling communities as resisting inclusion in the dominant Muslim society. Influenced by the prevailing Malay view, Van Dongen and other Europeans divided the Kubu into two categories: 'tame' or 'civilised' Kubu, who were predominantly swidden farmers; and 'wild' Kubu, who lived deep in the forests and avoided close contact with the outside world. Over time, 'Kubu' has come to have pejorative connotations, and is popularly associated with such qualities as being 'primitive', 'dirty', 'stupid', 'smelly' and 'irreligious'. Indeed, local non-indigenous people will often use the word 'Kubu' when referring with distaste to the Orang Rimba practice of eating forest creatures.

The term 'Suku Anak Dalam', meaning 'People from the Deep Jungle', is a more neutral term created by the Ministry of Social Affairs during the New Order period (1966–98). It refers to all indigenous people living in Jambi province and those residing on the border of West Sumatra and Riau provinces, including the Orang Rimba, Orang Bathin, Orang Singkut and Talang Mamak. In total, these communities are estimated to contain some 200,000 people (Rokhdian 2012). All Suku Anak Dalam were seen as primitive peoples who needed, for their own sake and for the good of the nation, to be brought into modern civilisation through government intervention. From the 1980s, the main program for achieving this was the Resettlement of Isolated Peoples program (Pemukiman Kembali Masyarakat Terasing, PKMT) (Taufik n.d.).

Since the 1990s, non-government organisations have campaigned, with some success, to make 'Orang Rimba' the only term used by government, the media and academia to describe this community. Nonetheless, the Ministry of Social Affairs continues to use 'Suku Anak Dalam' in its official documentation and public statements.

COMMUNITY ATTITUDES TOWARDS THE ORANG RIMBA

In general, the mainstream community in Jambi views the Orang Rimba in a highly negative light, often using derogatory language to describe them, and perpetuating unflattering stereotypes about their culture, intelligence and intentions. The term 'Kubu' is used widely, with all its connotations of primitiveness, lack of hygiene, ignorance, immorality and absence of faith. Local communities relate stories that underscore their suspicion or dislike of the Orang Rimba. They say, for example, that the Orang Rimba use black magic to lure business clients, seduce potential lovers and cause or heal sickness. Among the many popular sayings are: 'If you spit in front of an Orang Rimba, you will follow them into the jungle and never return'. It is also common to hear the word 'Kubu' being used to imply stupidity or dirtiness. If a person does not know how to complete a task, their friends or colleagues will call them a Kubu, and if children return home smelly or grubby, their parents may exclaim: 'Look at you! You're like a Kubu!' The presence of growing numbers of indigent Orang Rimba in Jambi's cities and towns or near the Trans-Sumatran Highway, often begging for money and food or selling forest goods such as animal skins, has added to communal disquiet. It is one thing for the Orang Rimba to live out of sight deep in the forest but it is another matter entirely for them to be highly visible as vagrants or disruptors of urban life.

Having said this, many in Jambi society and Indonesia in general would like the Orang Rimba and other indigenous peoples to play a greater role in the nation. They believe that the state would be failing the Orang Rimba if it did not seek to educate, house, provide employment for and bring religious enlightenment to them. As will be described in further detail below, the few examples of Orang Rimba who have succeeded in obtaining a formal education and gaining bureaucratic or political office have been welcomed with genuine enthusiasm by the populace. Often such cases are seen as providing an example for other Orang Rimba to follow.

STATE POLICIES TOWARDS THE ORANG RIMBA

In the colonial period, the Dutch displayed a somewhat disdainful, indeed Orientalist, stance towards the Orang Rimba and other indigenous peoples, having been strongly influenced by the prevailing Malay attitude.

They sought neither to intervene heavily in the lives of forest peoples nor to protect them, as did the British for indigenous peoples in their Malay Peninsula colony. From the 1920s, transmigration programs that brought settlers from overcrowded regions of Java and relocated them to forested areas in Sumatra severely affected the Orang Rimba and other indigenous communities. The accompanying deforestation and development of plantation and extractive industries saw the first widespread displacement of indigenous peoples on the island (Sager 2008: 309).

For most of the post-independence period (that is, since 1945), the Indonesian state has officially designated minorities living outside urban and village areas as 'isolated communities'—*masyarakat tertinggal*, which literally means 'left-behind communities' but is often translated more kindly as 'underdeveloped communities'. The state considers isolation or underdevelopment to be a justification for intervening to bring 'progress' and socio-economic advancement to indigenous groups. Although successive governments have regarded the 'normalisation' of indigenous communities as a meritorious element in the broader national development program, in reality their interventions have usually ended up being counterproductive and have actually worsened the socio-cultural and economic marginalisation of these communities. One of the key reasons for this is that state development programs are not based on consultation with target communities but rather involve the unilateral imposition of policies without indigenous consent. Both the national government and local governments believe they know what is best for the *masyarakat adat* and, until recently, have paid little heed to the wishes of the communities concerned. This is a problem across the region, not just in Indonesia. As Duncan (2008: 1) has noted:

> Most Southeast Asian governments have development programs, at times entire ministries, aimed specifically at developing indigenous minorities and incorporating them into the nation-state. These programs ostensibly seek to make these minorities conform to the norms of the ruling majority in the country.

The New Order regime under President Suharto was the first post-independence government to have a major impact on the lives of the Orang Rimba. It did not recognise specific groups of indigenous peoples in Indonesia, as all citizens were regarded as being, in one way or another, indigenous. Indeed, it saw protection of indigenous rights as an obstacle to accelerated national development, resulting in widespread disregard for the wishes of indigenous communities. Seizure of traditional lands was rampant, particularly for the development of forestry, agriculture and mining, often leading to the forced relocation of indigenous communities. One of the chief statutory means to achieve this was Law No. 1/1967 on Foreign Investment, which was frequently used as an instrument for the takeover of *adat* land, including that of the Orang Rimba. The regime regarded forests as a valuable economic asset and saw indigenous groups as an obstacle to exploiting the full potential of this resource. During the 32 years of the New Order, Indonesia lost 40–50 million hectares of forest, mainly due to logging, mining, infrastructure projects, transmigration programs and conversion to agricultural land or oil palm plantations (Sager 2008: 28–31).

Another New Order policy that had serious consequences for the Orang Rimba was the nationwide standardisation of village administration, which led to the abolition of traditional leadership models and the loss of consensual methods of community consultation and deliberation. They were replaced with a Javanese-style, hierarchical structure of local governance and decision-making. Law No. 5/1974 on Village Government and Law No. 5/1979 on Regional Governance swept away *adat* structures and installed new administrative systems that required certain levels of literacy and formal educational attainment in order to hold state-recognised positions in the community. This effectively excluded Orang Rimba from playing any role in state structures and deprived *adat*-based notions of clans or *rombongan* of any official status in decision-making processes. As a result, Orang Rimba communities were systematically disempowered *vis-à-vis* the state during the New Order.

The post-1998 *reformasi* period has been a time of mixed fortunes for indigenous communities. On the one hand, some legislation and government regulations have perpetuated the New Order policies allowing exploitation of forest areas and state intervention in *adat* areas, leading to continuing pressure on Orang Rimba communities. On the other hand, there now appears to be growing awareness of the rights and cultural richness of the Orang Rimba, accompanied by government attempts to better protect them.

One of the major policy reforms in the post-Suharto era was the devolution of substantial political and economic power to district-level administrations under Law No. 22/1999 on Regional Government and Law No. 25/1999 on the Fiscal Balance between the Central Government and the Regions. Although widely applauded for dismantling the highly centralised structure of the New Order, these decentralisation laws proved detrimental to indigenous communities because they allowed local businesspeople and political elites much freer access to natural resources with little or no scrutiny by national authorities. Indeed, the national revenue arrangements incentivised the exploitation of local resources, because the greater the income generated by a district, the greater the amount the central government was required to return to that district. Thus, devolution left the Orang Rimba much more vulnerable to the economic predations of the so-called 'lesser kings' (*raja kecil*), locally powerful figures who exploited the weaknesses in the new decentralised system to accumulate wealth.

Changes to forest management laws during *reformasi* also had significant consequences for the Orang Rimba. In 2000, after concerted advocacy by conservation groups, the Bukit Duabelas region was converted into a national park. Since 2002, the Natural Resource Conservation Agency (Balai Konservasi Sumber Daya Alam, BKSDA) in the Ministry of Environment and Forestry has been advising the government on how to regulate the national park. BKSDA meetings involve various stakeholders, including local governments, national park experts hired from the United States and NGOs that work with the Orang Rimba. Although BKSDA was welcomed as a means to pool information and discuss policies, it refused to invite Orang Rimba leaders to meetings, seemingly because officials were worried that they would not understand Indonesian. The largest NGO working with the Orang Rimba, the Sokola Institute, of which I am a co-founder, initially participated in the meetings, but was later excluded after querying the absence of Orang Rimba representatives.[2]

The national park regulations were introduced progressively from 2004 but immediately caused problems for the Orang Rimba. The main problem was the park's zoning system, which heavily restricted human movement and activities in specific areas. The regulations clustered areas into two broad types: core zones (or sanctuaries) that were unavailable for human use; and religious zones where all Orang Rimba were supposed to live (Rotich 2012: 175–8). Although the management regulations were supposed to recognise areas that contained sacred trees and plants, such as Sialang honey trees and Sentubung and Songoris trees,[3] in general the official zones did not correspond to the Orang Rimba's own customary zones. These competing zoning practices soon led to clashes between the

---

2 Established in 2003, the Sokola Institute is a not-for-profit organisation that provides educational opportunities for indigenous people and teaches them advocacy skills. Its vision is for indigenous peoples 'to have the ability to determine their own destiny and be sovereign over their territory and natural resources through learning processes'. It specialises in providing non-state schooling to the Orang Rimba that is sensitive to their culture and tailored to their specific needs. Sokola is the largest non-government provider of educational services to the Orang Rimba, through its Sokola Rimba schools. For more information, see Manurung (2012).

3 Every Orang Rimba has their own Sentubung tree and Songoris (or Senggaris) tree. After a baby is born, its umbilical cord is buried and a Sentubung tree is planted on top. To decide the name of the baby, the shaman uses the bark of the Songoris tree. Sentubung and Songoris trees are protected because the Orang Rimba believe that if these trees are harmed, their 'owner' will also suffer harm.

Orang Rimba and forest rangers. For example, rangers cut down all the trees planted by the Orang Rimba in a core zone where humans were prohibited from entering, and shot and injured an Orang Rimba man who was planting trees in that zone. The rangers' actions triggered large and angry protests from the Orang Rimba community, especially its young, literate students.

Since 2010, Orang Rimba in the Makekal Hulu clan (one of 12 clans in Bukit Duabelas) have employed a number of different strategies to have the forest regulations changed. In 2016, they independently mapped their own traditional territory in Jambi under the supervision of the CAPPA Foundation. For several months, each family contributed Rp 50,000 per month to cover the cost of the mapping. In 2017, the mapping project was completed and submitted for registration with the Ancestral Domain Registration Agency (Badan Registrasi Wilayah Adat, BRWA), a body founded by five non-government organisations, including AMAN, in 2010 to document and protect indigenous lands (BRWA 2019). This map has become an important resource for BKSDA in revising its management regulations.

In September 2018, the Orang Rimba, NGOs and the Ministry of Environment and Forestry (represented by BKSDA) reached agreement on amended management guidelines. All stakeholders signed a pledge declaring that the national park would acknowledge and incorporate the traditions of the Orang Rimba in the park regulations. This was a considerable relief to all sides after years of tensions over zoning.

Of all the post-Suharto governments, that of President Joko Widodo (Jokowi) has been the most sympathetic to indigenous peoples, including the Orang Rimba. Before the 2014 presidential election, Jokowi issued a statement—commonly known as the Nawacita (Nine Development Goals)—setting out his policy program for the country if he became president. One of the objectives was 'Strengthening the spirit of diversity and social reform through policies to improve diversity in education and create dialogue between citizens'. More specifically, this would mean 'revising and adapting all regulations and legislation relating to the recognition, dignity, protection and advancement of the rights of *masyarakat adat*' (Kompas 2014). The candidate further promised to set up an independent commission to manage disputes relating to indigenous rights. Unfortunately, Jokowi has yet to create a commission for *adat* communities, but he did establish, in early 2018, a special committee within the Executive Office of the President (Kantor Staf Presiden, KSP) with responsibility for indigenous matters. This committee has consulted with AMAN, other NGOs and some indigenous communities, including representatives of the Orang Rimba. In 2015, Jokowi became the first president to meet an Orang Rimba community in Jambi, during a visit to Air Hitam on the edge of an Orang Rimba forest (KSP 2015).

GOVERNMENT PROGRAMS FOR THE ORANG RIMBA

To get a better sense of how various policies have affected the Orang Rimba, it is necessary to examine the details of the main programs run by various government ministries within their communities.

Housing

The key ministry for the implementation of policies on indigenous peoples is the Ministry of Social Affairs. For more than four decades it has pursued a largely unchanged approach to indigenous peoples as part of its broader 'modernisation program', much of which has been focused on resettlement projects. These projects have had a variety of names over the years but they all share the same objective: 'civilising the margins'. The ministry provides housing in areas where forest land has been or is being converted to either a conservation or 'productive' use, such as plantations, mining or farming-related transmigration projects. Indigenous peoples who are relocated to the new housing projects are expected to adopt modern lifestyles and attributes, including learning new farming techniques, taking advantage of state health and educational services, dressing according to broader community standards (such as covering the torso if they are adults or wearing school uniform if they are children) and converting to one of the six state-endorsed religions. This model is applied extensively to indigenous peoples throughout almost all of Indonesia.

Religious identity

Religion has long been a priority of the national government in seeking to 'civilise' indigenous peoples. The Ministry of Religious Affairs has been pivotal to these efforts, especially in encouraging indigenes to become Muslims. This process began in the early New Order period, when citizens were pressured to join one of the major faith communities, such as Islam or Christianity, rather than adhere to local beliefs, including syncretic practices and tribal animism. Having a religion was not only morally desirable but also a constitutional requirement for all Indonesian citizens. Moreover, being religious was regarded as a means to combat communism, which the regime banned in 1966.

The New Order and, indeed, subsequent governments drew a distinction between 'beliefs' (*kepercayaan*) and 'religions' (*agama*), with only certain religions being recognised by the state and thus gaining funding and administrative support from the Ministry of Religious Affairs. Nearly all indigenous religions are classified as 'beliefs' and are supposedly under the purview of the Ministry of Education and Culture, but in reality the state provides no support for or formal acknowledgement of indigenous belief systems. In effect, millions of indigenous Indonesian citizens face discrimination because they do not subscribe to the narrow religious regulations set out by the state.

Mainstream Jambi citizens have long called the Orang Rimba 'infidels' (*kafir*). Many government officials hold a similar view, even if it is expressed in less blunt terms. In fact, the Orang Rimba have a very rich spiritual life and set of beliefs connected to their forest environment, something that is poorly understood by most outsiders. For many decades, officials have urged them to convert to a recognised religion, most commonly Islam, and Muslim and Christian missionary activity is common in their areas.

Pressure to convert has become far more intense in recent years, perhaps as a result of the growing pietism in Indonesian society. News of this attracted local and even international media attention in 2017, when it was reported that about 200 Orang Rimba in Batanghari district had converted to Islam in order to receive services and resources from the government. Before their conversion, they had been experiencing growing hardship after being forced off their land by palm oil and coal-mining interests. Unable to continue their traditional lifestyle in the forest, they had, in desperation, turned to the government for assistance. To be eligible to obtain state services, however, they first needed to obtain identity cards (*kartu tanda penduduk*, KTP). And in order to get an identity card, they needed to nominate a religion.[4] At a meeting to discuss which of the six official religions they would choose, the Batanghari Orang Rimba decided that Islam would be the most strategically sound choice. Government officials were quoted in the media as saying that they warmly approved of this decision, not only because it would make it easier for the state to provide welfare to the Orang Rimba, but also because it would help them to settle down and give up their nomadic lifestyles (Henschke 2017).

Obtaining a KTP also presents other problems for the Orang Rimba, especially women. According to customary law, it is forbidden to take photos of women or to mention their names to people outside their communities, particularly men. A similar ban on images and names applies to children under the age of five. This creates an obvious difficulty considering that ID cards always carry a person's name and photograph. In the case of the national census, the Orang Rimba circumvent the need to provide names by using generic terms that describe the relationships between various family members. Thus, fathers or husbands are referred to as *betangkay* and sons are called *bekilat*. Wives are listed as '*betangkay*

---

4 The requirement to list a religion when applying for a KTP is discussed in more detail by Butt in Chapter 4 of this book.

wife' and daughters as 'betangkay daughter 1', 'betangkay daughter 2' and so on. With the exception of those who have converted to one of the state-recognised religions, usually Islam, almost no Orang Rimba have KTPs.

Education

The provision of educational services has proven to be one of the most vexed issues for both the Orang Rimba and government. For many years, the preference of government officials has been to provide standard schooling to Orang Rimba children based on the national curriculum. The focus has been on literacy, numeracy and education in national history and principles. But most Orang Rimba are sceptical about the benefits of formal state schooling and seek an education for their children that is more closely aligned with community needs and traditions of learning. A good example of the Orang Rimba view of education comes from a class I was teaching in the forest in 2000. Our class was interrupted by the distant growl of chainsaws and the eerie sound of falling trees. A child stared at me and asked: 'Ibu, once we master reading and writing, we can then stop the logging, right?' In effect, the child was asking what use an education was if it could not prevent the destruction of the forest that was so precious to the Orang Rimba. It was indeed a difficult question to answer, as it raised questions about the essential purpose of education.

Among indigenous peoples, state schooling has been somewhat ruefully labelled sekolah untuk pergi (school for leaving), capturing the apprehension that going to state schools prises students away from their traditional lands and communities. The experience of the Orang Rimba over many years has been that the children who attend state schools are far more likely to leave their homelands, and the higher their level of education, the more likely they are to depart. The Orang Rimba contend that the national curriculum was created in Jakarta for students who live and work in cities and towns, not for jungle dwellers like themselves. It does not teach their children the skills they need to live in the forest, such as how to climb honey trees, how to hunt for wild boar, how to treat scorpion bites, how to look after the rivers and gods, and how to prevent deforestation and forest fires. These are the skills that the Orang Rimba regard as important.

CONTRASTING STORIES OF 'SUCCESSFUL' ORANG RIMBA

The sharply differing aspirations that Orang Rimba and Indonesian society in general have for their children can be illuminated by the cases of two students: Besudut and Pengendum Tampung. They are friends but have followed very different career paths. Besudut has become well known nationally as a 'successful' Orang Rimba by virtue of his education and job, but is regarded with pity by many in his home community. Pengendum enjoys high standing among the Orang Rimba but is far less well known outside his community. I have had the privilege to teach both students.

Besudut

What does success in education mean for the Orang Rimba? According to the late clan chief Temenggung Mirak, success is when a student is able to be of benefit to their community—it is not just about individual academic achievement. He also stressed the importance of successful students appreciating their cultural tradition whatever modern skills they may have mastered.

One remarkable Orang Rimba boy named Besudut provides an enlightening case study of this. He was one of my first students when I started teaching in 2000. I gave him intensive tuition for about four months until he mastered basic literacy and numeracy. I then lost contact with him when I moved to another part of the jungle to teach new students. He and his Bedinding Besi clan had a high level of interaction with the outside world, including selling permits to loggers to fell trees. Besudut always longed to get a modern schooling of the type he could not obtain in the forest. He gained his wish when a rattan merchant from the village of Tanagaro, Raman Kayak, adopted him and sent him to elementary school starting at grade 3. Besudut converted to Islam and changed his name to Irman Jalil.

People in the village and at his new school enthusiastically assisted Besudut, so keen were they to prove to the world that an Orang Rimba could be 'successful'. They wanted him to go to university and become a public servant in order to provide a model for what other Orang Rimba might achieve. In primary and secondary school, his teachers, the principal and other educational authorities gave him special attention, perhaps more than was wise. He was assisted to pass his examinations, even though he did not always attend class or perform well at school.

When Besudut graduated from high school, the government enrolled him in a primary-school teaching degree at the University of Jambi, making him the first Orang Rimba to attend university. Metro TV interviewed him on the high-rating talk show *Kick Andy*, during which the minister of education appeared to present him with a scholarship and commend his example to others.[5] The local district head also gave him a

---

5   See https://www.youtube.com/watch?v=R7UIWdqiBhU.

scholarship and the non-government organisation KKI Warsi provided him with additional financial support. Thus, Besudut became a 'poster boy' for the Orang Rimba.

Unfortunately, despite the generous funding, Besudut did not complete his studies. He dropped out in the second year of his course and turned up at a Sokola Rimba base camp, saying: 'I can't do this [university] any more' (*Akeh hopi endok lagi*). Soon after he was offered an honorary position as a public servant in the Ministry of Social Affairs. He remained there for about two years doing menial tasks such as photocopying and preparing coffee for guests. He was then given another honorary administrative position, this time in the office of the local subdistrict head, performing similar work. He soon left that job because he was bored. Now in his mid-thirties, Besudut has recently been nominated to stand for the local Jambi legislature (Dewan Perwakilan Rakyat Daerah, DPRD). If elected, he will be the first Orang Rimba to be a legislator.

Besudut is viewed as a success by the mainstream media and by many in the general public who have followed his career.[6] People often congratulate me personally for assisting with his achievements, even though I try to tell them that his situation is more complex, and less positive, than they realise. For the Orang Rimba community, on the other hand, Besudut is a failure. For them, his story proves that formal schooling takes Orang Rimba away from their land and alienates them from their traditions.

This case shows the marked contrast between the aspirations of the Orang Rimba and those of Indonesian society in general. The things that most Indonesians think are important and would like indigenous people to achieve are not those that the Orang Rimba themselves value. Formal education, salaried government jobs, recognition in the media—these are all matters of little moment to the Orang Rimba, however much they may be markers of success for the wider society and officialdom. In some ways, Besudut also sees himself as a failure, because he cannot be himself and is tired of trying to meet the expectations of others, particularly those outside the Orang Rimba. He may yet become a successful politician or official but it is unlikely that his community will praise his achievement.

Pengendum Tampung

Pengendum Tampung, who is now in his late twenties, began his schooling at Sokola Rimba in 2001.[7] He did so against the wishes of his parents,

---

6   For an example of the media coverage of Besudut, see the article in the *Jakarta Post* by Afrizal (2013).

7   A YouTube video on the Orang Rimba narrated by Pengendum Tampung is available at https://www.youtube.com/watch?v=DTe_8c_oYps.

who believed that reading and writing would make him evil because they involved the use of pencils, which they regarded as wicked. He was one of only two children from his family of six siblings to attend the school and he was the only one to complete his education. Although he disliked maths and science intensely, he was drawn to studying words and the law, saying that he wanted to become literate so that he could be of use to himself and his people. He would often ask about legal matters and rights, particularly when there was a difference between customary law (*adat*) and Indonesian civil law. As he got older and gained a better command of Indonesian, he began to study legal texts and to travel to the Legal Aid Office (Lembaga Bantuan Hukum, LBH) in Padang to learn more about human rights, especially relating to *adat*. He was also a gifted public speaker and debater and quickly developed a reputation in indigenous circles for his articulate advocacy on behalf of the Orang Rimba. Over the last decade, he has appeared several times on local and national television to speak about indigenous issues. He has given expert evidence to parliamentary committees and the Constitutional Court on the *adat* and rights of the Orang Rimba, and spoke at an international conference for indigenous peoples in Canada in 2017. All of this was achieved without any formal schooling.

Pengendum also went against his parents' advice in marrying an outsider, a Jambi woman of Javanese descent with whom he now has children. He moves easily between the world of the Orang Rimba and mainstream society. He and his family have a house in the district capital of Bangko, about two hours from his clan's traditional land, but he divides his time evenly between living in the city and living in the forest. He has produced and appeared in documentary films on *adat* communities, one of which won an award at the Melbourne Film Festival. In addition to his cultural activities, Pengendum has been successful in business. Like many Orang Rimba, when the forest management guidelines for the national park were announced, he claimed an area of land as a plantation lot. He now has a sizeable number of rubber trees—which can be planted in the forest without causing much harm to the existing flora and fauna—and has developed a lucrative rattan-farming business.

Pengendum represents a different kind of 'success' to Besudut. He remains an integral part of his clan and is equally at home living within his own culture or residing in mainstream Indonesian society. He has been able to engage with the outside world and advocate on behalf of his community without abandoning his identity as an Orang Rimba. Indeed, at every point in his career, he has made decisions on his own terms and has not succumbed to pressure to become something other than what he wants to be. He is much admired by Orang Rimba communities as someone who has not 'lost his soul' or his dignity, despite spending part of his time in the city and despite being feted by state institutions and the media. Interestingly, he and Besudut are good friends and the latter often expresses admiration for how Pengendum has managed his life.

CONCLUSION

This chapter's primary aim has been to examine the contemporary challenges faced by the Orang Rimba as an indigenous community. Their concerns are markedly different from those of most other minority groups, be they ethnic, religious or sexual. My focus has been on two main issues: the mainstreaming or normalisation of the Orang Rimba; and their marginalisation. This has raised questions about what should be regarded as 'normal' or 'valuable'. A great many non-indigenous Indonesians look down on the Orang Rimba because they lack the things that modern Indonesian life can bestow upon them: a good education, a well-paying job, adherence to one of the major religions and a sense of identification with a successful democratic nation ruled by law. They are mystified by the Orang Rimba's rejection of such benefits.

But the Orang Rimba view mainstream Indonesian life very differently. Let me list some examples based on what Orang Rimba have said to me.

- People living in city apartments or cramped houses are like birds trapped in small cages. It is much better to have a spacious and fascinating forest to live in.
- Drinking tap water is like drinking urine. The water from free-flowing rivers is far more palatable and abundant.
- The toilets in cities are disgusting because large numbers of people use the same pit for a long period of time. It is much cleaner to go to the toilet in the forest where each person can dig a hole in many different locations.
- Eating domesticated animals is unethical and a betrayal of nature's laws. It is much more humane to hunt and kill animals that roam freely in the forest.
- City people are obsessed with their possessions and have far too many of them. It is far better to share nature's bounty in the forest and be satisfied with having very few possessions.
- Being forced to study at school for years and then sit in an office working for the rest of one's life is pathetic. It is better just to learn what one needs to know to survive and be a good community member living freely in the forest.
- Schools teach people to look after themselves rather than share with the surrounding community. That is cruel to the less advantaged people in one's social group.

In short, the Orang Rimba love living in the forest where there is an abundance of food, natural resources and free time, as well as the opportunity to share in and support a rich community life. In this regard, the Orang Rimba see themselves as the lucky ones and mainstream society as lamentable.

The issue of marginalisation is also complex. One might ask how a community that prefers an isolated existence in the forest can complain about marginalisation. The answer is that the Indonesian state and the general public are placing increasing pressure on the customary lifestyle of the Orang Rimba in the forests of central Sumatra. Many of them have been forced off their traditional lands and exist on the margins of mainstream society where they are subjected to execration and ridicule, and where they struggle to be accepted unless they adopt the norms and aspirations of the majority.

In this chapter, I have argued passionately for greater awareness of and sympathy for the predicament faced by the Orang Rimba. Government policies should be flexible and sensitive when seeking to provide for indigenous communities. A one-size-fits-all approach will lead only to further dislocation and disruption for the Orang Rimba. If Indonesia truly is a nation that embraces 'Unity in Diversity', then it should learn from and value the very different culture and lifestyle practised by the Orang Rimba. This has not been the experience of the past century, when the 'belonging' of the Orang Rimba in Indonesia has been very much contested.

REFERENCES

Afrizal, J. (2013) 'First Orang Rimba graduates from senior high school', *Jakarta Post*, 28 May.

AMAN (Aliansi Masyarakat Asli Nusantara) (2018) 'Profile Aliansi Masyarakat Asli Nusantara (AMAN)'. http://www.aman.or.id/profil-aliansi-masyarakat-adat-nusantara/

Bappenas (Badan Perencanaan Pembangunan Nasional) (2014) 'Masyarakat adat di Indonesia: menuju perlindungan social yang inklusif', Bappenas, Jakarta. https://www.bappenas.go.id/files/7014/2889/4255/Masyarakat_Adat_di_Indonesia-Menuju_Perlindungan_Sosial_yang_Inklusif.pdf

BRWA (Badan Registrasi Wilayah Adat) (2019), 'Profil', BRWA, Bogor. http://brwa.or.id/pages/about

Duncan, C.R. (2008) 'Legislating modernity among the marginalized', in C.R. Duncan (ed.) *Civilizing the Margins: Southeast Asian Government Policies for the Development of Minorities*, National University of Singapore Press, Singapore: 1–23.

Henschke, R. (2017) 'Indonesia's Orang Rimba: forced to renounce their faith', *BBC News*, 17 November. https://www.bbc.com/news/world-asia-41981430

KKI Warsi (Komunitas Konservasi Indonesia Warsi) (2018a) 'Orang Rimba, Kubu dan Suku Anak Dalam', 24 April. http://warsi.or.id/content/showing/55/content

KKI Warsi (Komunitas Konservasi Indonesia Warsi) (2018b) 'Insisting an integrity towards natural resources management', 17 December. http://warsi.or.id/eng/content/release/360

Kompas (2014) '"Nawa Cita", 9 agenda prioritas Jokowi-JK', *Kompas.kom*, 21 May. https://nasional.kompas.com/read/2014/05/21/0754454/.Nawa.Cita.9.Agenda.Prioritas.Jokowi-JK

KSP (Kantor Staf Presiden Republik Indonesia) (2015) 'Memaknai blusukan Jokowi menemui Orang Rimba di Sarolangun, Jambi', KSP, Jakarta, 4 November. http://ksp.go.id/memaknai-blusukan-jokowi-menemui-orang-rimba-di-jambi/

Manurung, B. (2012) *Sokola Rimba*, Penerbit Buku Kompas, Jakarta.

Rokhdian, D. (2012) 'Alim Rajo disembah, Piado Alim Rajo disanggah ragam bentuk perlawanan Orang Rimba Makekal Hulu terhadap kebijakan zonasi Taman Nasional Bukit Duabelas, Jambi', unpublished thesis, University of Indonesia, Depok.

Rotich, D. (2012) 'Concept of zoning management in protected areas', *Journal of Environment and Earth Science* 2(10): 173–83. http://citeseerx.ist.psu.edu/viewdoc/download?doi=10.1.1.850.5207&rep=rep1&type=pdf

Sager, S. (2008) 'The sky is our roof, the earth our floor', PhD thesis, College of Asia and the Pacific, Australian National University, Canberra.

Said, E. (1978) *Orientalism*, Pantheon Books, New York NY.

Taufik, R.K. (n.d.) 'Orang Rimba: masyarakat terasing yang semakin termarjinalisasi', blog. https://wa-iki.blogspot.com/2010/10/orang-rimba-masyarakat-terasing-yang.html

Tuhiwai Smith, L. (1999) *Decolonizing Methodologies: Research and Indigenous Peoples*, Zed Books, London and New York, and University of Otago Press, Dunedin.

Van Dongen, D.J. (1910) 'De Koeboes in de onderafdeeling Koeboestreken der residentie Palembang', *Bijdragen tot de Taal-, Land- en Volkenkunde* 63(2): 187–335.

PART 5

Reflections

14 Manipulating minorities and majorities: reflections on 'contentious belonging'

Sidney Jones

The theme of this volume, 'contentious belonging', posits two possibilities: the inclusiveness that is expressed in the official national motto, *Bhinneka Tunggal Ika*, or 'Unity in Diversity', and the exclusiveness in the form of Muslim majoritarianism that generates pressure to conform to an increasingly conservative set of norms and values. The spectre of the latter as it affects religious and sexual minorities has been an important theme of the chapters in this book, but if we shift the focus away from the national to the local level, and we look at islands other than Java, then several other dimensions of minority status, also contentious, emerge. One is the tension between indigenous and migrant communities. Another is the transformation of ethnic minorities into majorities through *pemekaran*—a byproduct of decentralisation that has allowed the partitioning of administrative regions to create new provinces, districts and subdistricts. A third is racial identity, especially along Melanesian versus Malay lines.

MIGRATION

Any discussion of minorities and contentiousness cannot ignore migration. In many areas of Indonesia outside Java, the tensions are not primarily between Muslim and non-Muslim but between indigenous and migrant, and the line between the two is constantly changing. One can be from an ethnic majority at home (Javanese, Balinese, Madurese, Bugis), become part of a minority community as a migrant and then, through family networks, see one's ethnic group grow to the point of demographically and often economically displacing the indigenous population.

One example is the Butonese in West Ceram, Maluku province, who now constitute a majority in at least three subdistricts but who have no right to own land in those subdistricts owing to discriminatory local regulations. In one village, they actually constitute 90 per cent of the population but the indigenous lobby has had the village declared a customary village (*desa adat*) and the Butonese have been excluded from representation on the village council. At the same time, the redrawing of electoral districts in 2014 produced two out of five districts in which Butonese were the majority, enabling them to win seats in the regional parliament (Dewan Perwakilan Rakyat Daerah, DPRD) (Brauchler 2017).

Another example is the Balinese in South Lampung district, who were originally resettled on some 15,000 hectares of local customary land after the eruption of the Gunung Agung volcano in 1962 (Ariestha 2013: 72). By 2012, the third generation of Balinese dominated the subdistrict of Way Panji, with two villages that were almost exclusively Balinese and that were significantly better off than neighbouring Lampungese villages. As one scholar put it:

> The Balinese villages were the fortresses that protect Balinese culture in Lampung. These fortresses and many other enclaves throughout [...] Lampung are like islands in the midst of communities who mostly are Javanese and Muslims, just like the island of Bali, which is a basis of Hinduism in the midst of [mostly Muslim] Indonesia (Zulfa 2014: 266).

Conflicts between the two ethnic groups were common, over everything from Balinese motorcycle drag races during Muslim prayer times to Balinese letting their pigs wander onto Muslim land (Utami 2014). With support from some non-Balinese migrant groups, in October 2012 Lampungese attacked a Balinese village after two Muslim Lampungese girls fell off their motorcycle and rumours spread that they had been sexually harassed by Balinese youths. The violence led to 14 deaths, the destruction of hundreds of houses and massive displacement. If the short-term response was to flee, the longer-term response may have been to bring in reinforcements. According to the provincial bureau of statistics, the percentage of Hindus in South Lampung rose from 50,376 in 2010 (about 6 per cent of the population) before the conflict to 246,707 (about 21 per cent of the population) in 2015, three years later (BPS Provinsi Lampung 2011: 144; 2016: 96).[1] (It is such a dramatic jump that it is also possible that a data glitch of some sort was involved.)

---

1 The big jump in the Balinese population, not only in South Lampung but in other districts as well, appears to have occurred in 2014. This was an election year, meaning that in addition to whatever motivation the Balinese had for coming to Lampung, some candidates may have encouraged them to come because they would provide additional votes.

As one scholar notes, 'Mobility is a fundamental tenet of a liberal democratic society', but if one of the unstated premises of this volume is how to ensure justice and equality before the law for Indonesian citizens, how do you protect the rights of indigenous groups when they become minorities in their own territory, and how also do you ensure that migrants—including transmigrants—are not marginalised in the process (Bock 2012)?

The rise of the customary law (*adat*) movement can be seen as one way to provide restitution of minority rights, especially over land, as the Orang Rimba case makes clear (see Chapter 13 by Manurung). But it has also created new issues of justice, based on a romantic notion of *adat* that fails to recognise the realities of economic and political power in rural areas. This can lead to the creation of fake *adat* organisations; co-optation of *adat* leaders; competition among multiple *adat* organisations over the same land; and the disenfranchisement of migrants (McCarthy 2005). *Adat* claims can also be a way of reinvesting power in a dispossessed local aristocracy.

In 2013 in Mesuji, Lampung, a sharp rise in land values—the result of a boom in cassava production for biofuels—combined with the courts' sympathetic stance towards indigenous land claims, led to many dubious *adat* claims. In one case, a Jakarta-based group with close ties to the military facilitated the occupation of land that had been granted to an industrial tree plantation by thousands of squatters, in the name of reclaiming it as customary land. The group revived a long-inactive association, Persatuan Adat Megou Pak Tulang Bawang, and found a willing local to head it. The problem was that most of the squatters were not indigenous, so the group sold membership in the *adat* association to Javanese and Balinese migrants, recognising them as members of a local clan (*marga*) (IPAC 2013a).

In Jambi, migrants swelled the ranks of an indigenous group known as SAD 113. SAD was short for 'Suku Anak Dalam', or 'Tribes of the Interior'; the 113 referred to the number of claimants to a particular tract of customary land that they were trying to reclaim from a plantation concession. SAD 113 encouraged 'strategic marriages' between indigenous women and migrant men, producing children who under *adat* law had full rights to customary land. Both sides saw the marriages as beneficial. The migrant men saw the potential to acquire land if the claims were successful. Indigenous leaders saw the newcomers as strengthening their advocacy skills, since outsiders were thought to be more willing to challenge authority (IPAC 2014: 7).

Majority–minority dynamics can change when the dominant group risks being swamped or dispossessed by incoming migrants. Indonesian Papua is the most striking example. It has sometimes been compared to Tibet in terms of the indigenous population being overrun by the politically dominant majority, though in the Papuan case, much of the information circulating about the balance between indigenous Papuans and migrants is inaccurate or misleading.

The fact is that in several coastal cities in Papua and West Papua provinces, ethnic Papuans have become a minority compared to non-Papuan migrants. In both provinces, Papuans remained the majority in the 2010 census, though just barely in West Papua, where Javanese are now the largest single ethnic group. According to that census, the Javanese accounted for 15 per cent of the population in West Papua province, while all Papuan groups taken together accounted for 51.5 per cent. This will probably change in the migrants' favour by the next census in 2020 (Ananta et al. 2016). In Papua province, meanwhile, ethnic Papuans still accounted for close to 70 per cent of the population in 2010, notwithstanding the high proportion of other ethnicities in Merauke district, where Papuans accounted for only 37 per cent of the population.

At the same time, while political activists tend to see majority–minority issues solely in terms of non-Papuans versus Papuans, some of the worst outbreaks of ethnic violence have been between Papuan groups indigenous to a particular area and Papuan migrants from elsewhere in the province. The area around Timika, for example, has seen protracted conflict between the indigenous Amungme and Kamoro clans and migrants from the Damal, Dani and Mee populations from the central highlands. Much of the migration has been driven by the lucrative opportunities for illegal gold-panning in the tailings from the gigantic Freeport copper and gold mine (IPAC 2013b: 18).

PEMEKARAN

The process of subdividing administrative regions (*pemekaran*) provides another example of constantly changing majority–minority status at the local level. Through this process, Indonesia went from having 26 provinces and 293 districts and municipalities in 1999 to having 34 provinces and 508 districts and municipalities in 2016, when the Jokowi government imposed a moratorium on further subdivisions (Ratna Sari 2018). The redrawing of boundaries so that a particular ethnic group would dominate at the district level transformed ethnic minorities into majorities. The main reason for creating the province of West Sulawesi in 2004 was to permit the Mandars, hitherto largely excluded from local government in South Sulawesi, to become the new rulers. They are now estimated to constitute about 50 per cent of the population in West Sulawesi, followed by the Toraja, Buginese, Javanese, Makassarese and Balinese.

In Papua the subdivisions have been not just by ethnic group but also by clan. Jobs and spoils at the district level go to the clan that can win local elections, so there is an incentive to divide the district to ensure that one's own clan is in control—a different form of gerrymandering. This can be achieved in many cases by paying off the various bureaucrats whose approval is necessary for the subdivision, including the district head and the legislature of the 'mother' district and the members of Commission II of the national parliament, who must sign off on laws establishing the new units.[2] In this way an ethnic group or clan can secure majority status within a specific territory, with all the perquisites that go with it. In Papua, for example, the district of Lanny Jaya was carved out of Jayawijaya in 2008 so that the ethnic Lani—a minority within Jayawijaya—would become the largest ethnic group in the new district. Yahukimo, also carved out of Jayawijaya, is actually an acronym for the four clans that had been newly empowered: Yali, Hubla, Kimyal and Momuma (IPAC 2013b: 6).

RACE

Another dimension that needs greater attention is racism based on skin colour. Papuans experience it; so do West Africans, especially those who have the misfortune to become suspects in criminal cases; and so occasionally do black visitors. Because much of Indonesia shunned blackness, Melanesian identity became a critical marker for Papuan activists: it was what distinguished them from ethnic-Malay Indonesians. This identification led the independence group known as the United Liberation Movement for West Papua (ULMWP) to seek membership in the Melanesian Spearhead Group (MSG), a group of Pacific nations that also includes one non-state actor, the Kanak and Socialist National Liberation Front (Front de Libération Nationale Kanak et Socialiste, FLNKS) of New Caledonia.[3] As part of its effort both to undercut the Papuan claim to be different and to assert its own claim to membership of MSG, Indonesia in

---

2 Commission II is one of 11 commissions in the national parliament (Dewan Perwakilan Rakyat, DPR), and is responsible for home affairs, elections and the state secretariat. Other commissions cover foreign affairs and security, legal affairs and justice, health and so on. Groups campaigning for a new district or province often invite members of Commission II to visit, providing lavish entertainment in an effort to win their endorsement. Though a moratorium on *pemekaran* has been in effect since 2016, over 300 proposals for new districts and provinces were pending with the Ministry of Home Affairs in September 2018 (Ratna Sari 2018).

3 The other members are Papua New Guinea, Fiji, Solomon Islands and Vanuatu.

2015 created Melanesia Indonesia (Melindo), an organisation claiming to represent the Melanesian populations of five provinces of Indonesia—the two Papuan provinces, together with East Nusa Tenggara, Maluku and North Maluku—that together claimed a population of 11 million, more than the other MSG nations combined. A foreign ministry official claimed:

> We [Indonesia] are the biggest Melanesian country. So we will be the biggest elephant in the room if we're not part of the MSG (Chauvel 2015).

The claim was enough to secure Indonesia associate membership. The problem was that none of the ethnic groups outside Papua had self-identified as Melanesian, and certainly none had the political overtones that the Papuan independence movement had. But it was the first time that Indonesia had tried to co-opt Melanesian identity as a way of refuting Papuan political claims.

All this suggests that, especially in eastern Indonesia but elsewhere as well, the concept of 'ethnic minority' is both politically charged and infinitely malleable.

CONCLUSION: THE PLACE AND PROSPECTS OF MINORITIES

To close this discussion, let us return to the issue of majoritarianism as a political concept. It generally consists of two elements. First, there is the notion that 'a nation's political destiny should be determined by its religious or ethnic majority' (Kesavan 2018). Second, there is the idea that the majority's dominance is somehow under threat. As one scholar put it:

> Majoritarianism insists on different tiers of citizenship. Members of the majority faith and culture are viewed as the nation's true citizens. The rest are courtesy citizens, guests of the majority, expected to behave well and deferentially (Kesavan 2018).

The United States under President Donald Trump is an example:

> The underlying message of 'Make America Great Again' is to return the country to an age of majoritarian politics, when white people controlled everything on behalf of white people and when everyone else was accorded second-class citizenship (Kesavan 2018).

Buddhists in Myanmar take a classic majoritarian position towards the country's Muslims, and especially towards the Rohingya, who are not even recognised as citizens. Indonesian majoritarianism is not as dire, but the idea that only a Muslim can govern other Muslims is a majoritarian position that contradicts a basic premise of the Constitution that all citizens who believe in one God are equal under the law. The principle that only a Muslim should govern fellow Muslims was a central plank of the 212 Movement, a union of hardline Islamic groups intent on bringing down Jakarta's Christian-Chinese governor, Basuki Tjahaja Purnama (Ahok), in 2016–17; it was also used in the 2018 local election campaigns in West Kalimantan and North Sumatra.

In referring to majoritarians, I am not referring to most Indonesian Muslims but rather to those activists who very publicly adopt the political stance that they represent the majority—which, according to survey data presented by Mietzner and Muhtadi in Chapter 9 of this volume, is untrue—and that their views should therefore prevail.

Here are some classic majoritarian statements by 212 activists:

> The bigger goal is the same: how can Islam be honoured, respected, given its proportional place in Indonesia? What do we mean by proportional? If Muslims here constitute 90 per cent of the population, then that means their proportion of jobs in the government should also be 90 per cent. That means all policies of any kind—laws, local regulations and the like—should favour Muslims. If they [minorities] don't side with us, we should get angry. The most effective *dakwah* [religious outreach] is the *dakwah* of power. So the question is how to ensure that the legislative arm of government, and the executive as well, is controlled by Muslims.[4]

And another:

> We don't have a problem with NKRI [the Unitary State of the Republic of Indonesia], but we say our NKRI is better than yours. The majority has to rule, it's like that everywhere. It's not right that the majority is ruled by a minority. In certain areas, okay, but in matters of state, no way. And we have to have the biggest portion, don't just give us the small change.[5]

These statements are reminiscent of similar statements made by the Indonesian Association of Muslim Intellectuals (Ikatan Cendekiawan Muslimin Indonesia, ICMI) during the 1990s in an effort to control the Indonesian bureaucracy. At one point the founder and chair of ICMI, B.J. Habibie, said:

> The Muslim community as the majority in Indonesia should not have its affairs determined or directed by others, but, on the contrary, should determine and direct others. Because in democracies anywhere in the world, the majority should be the determiner, not the reverse (Aritonang 2004: 461).

Habibie, a respected former president who is now seen as having been a more effective reformer during his brief tenure than any other post-Suharto president, promoted the concept of 'proportional democracy'

---

4 Nava Nuraniyah, interview with Aminuddin, Presidium Alumni 212, Jakarta, 16 February 2018.
5 Nava Nuraniyah, interview with Lutfi Fathullah, Majelis Pelayan Jakarta, Jakarta, 3 November 2017.

during his ICMI days—the notion that the division of jobs in the government should be by religion, according to the proportion of followers in the population.

Where local elections have pitted Muslims against Christians or mixed slates, some Islamist groups have effectively suggested that Christians have no right to hold public office, at least in Muslim-majority areas. In West Kalimantan, for example, a sermon broadcast live over the RRI radio channel, with the Muslim candidate for governor in attendance, echoed all the anti-Ahok themes:

- Voting is obligatory for Muslims if, by failing to vote, leadership could fall to a non-Muslim.
- Islam absolutely forbids non-Muslim leaders.
- Muslims who choose non-Muslim leaders should be seen as apostates (IPAC 2018: 4).[6]

Majoritarians maintain not only that they have the right to determine the law but also that they have the right to reject laws and regulations that run counter to their interests or to their concepts of morality or orthodoxy. Hence the announcement by the district head of Luwu, South Sulawesi, followed by officials in other areas, that he would ignore the decree issued by the minister of religious affairs imposing limits on the use of loudspeakers in mosques (Nahimunkar 2018b). Even worse was the rejection, by several local councils of religious scholars (*ulama*), of the Ministry of Health's vaccination program against rubella and measles because the vaccines might contain traces of pork-related products.

The idea that the majority is under attack, a mainstay of majoritarianism, takes several forms. For the legally banned but still active Hizbut Tahrir Indonesia (HTI) and other groups that have bought into former Armed Forces commander Gatot Nurmantyo's 'proxy war' theory, it is the notion that the West (and now China) are out to weaken Indonesia and destroy Islam by stealing the country's resources, corrupting its youth and damaging its economy.

In one widely circulated tract, Nurmantyo wrote in 2017 that the National Resilience Institute (Lembaga Ketahanan Nasional Republik Indonesia, Lemhannas) and educational institutes of the Indonesian military had concluded that 'proxy war' could be undertaken by foreign interests in the following ways:

---

6 This suggestion follows from Al-Ma'idah 51, the same verse of the Qur'an that led to Ahok's downfall: 'O you who believe, do not take the Jews and the Christians as allies. They are allies of one another. And whoever is an ally to them among you, then he is one of them. Allah does not guide the wrongdoing people'.

a Make huge investments in Indonesia in order to exploit and control natural resources.

b Make trade agreements to put Indonesian products under pressure from diplomacy, alliances and interventions, and to make Indonesia a market for foreign goods.

c Spread black campaigns to weaken and destroy Indonesian commodity production.

d Control the making of policies and legislation through bribes to produce regulations or laws favouring foreign interests.

e Destroy the younger generation of Indonesians through various negative cultural approaches, such as consumer culture, online gambling, pornography sites and so on.

f Create domestic conflict to obstruct the wheels of the economy and wreck the government's concentration on building a national development program.

g Buy and control the mass media to shape public opinion, generate social engineering, rewrite history and create public grievances.

h Control strategic means of information and communication in order to monitor and wiretap the conversations of state officials.

i Create conflict between state institutions such as the military and the police through various means in order to create confusion and undermine national stability.

j Look for and create candidates for Indonesian leadership at all levels at the earliest stage possible so that they can side with and be controlled by foreign powers in the future.

k Create conflict between law enforcement institutions (the police and the Anti-Corruption Commission).

l Create conflict between and division within political parties.

m Create a negative image of Indonesia in international eyes through the issues of terrorism, human rights, democratisation, environment and other issues.

n Create conflict between state institutions to weaken their function and role in developing the nation.

o Turn Indonesia into a market for narcotics and forbidden drugs and destroy the younger generation through narcotics.

p Create euphoria on campuses so that students leave their studies, hold parties, join demonstrations and get into fights (Nurmantyo 2017).

For other Islamist majoritarians, the more immediate threat is Christianisation and, to a much lesser extent, Shi'ism. Natural disasters always bring allegations—sometimes true—that Christian groups are using the distribution of aid to attract converts; the Lombok earthquake is the latest example (Nahimunkar 2018a). But the fear of conversion is more widespread. A recent article on the Nahimunkar website warned that Gereja

Pasundan (the Sundanese Church) was converting Muslims in Cianjur (West Java) in droves through the strategy of ministers wearing *peci* (the traditional Indonesian fez) and sarongs and women wearing headscarves (Nahimunkar 2017). The notion of LGBT as an epidemic that can infect the young is another aspect of this fear-mongering, and part and parcel of the notion of a majority under threat from an influx of Western immorality.

What Indonesian majoritarians (and their counterparts in the West, such as Trump in America or Viktor Orban in Hungary) do not want to understand is that a fundamental principle of democracies is political equality and justice for all—and that means equal rights regardless of race, religion, ethnicity or sexual orientation. It does not mean simply that the majority can dictate the rules.

REFERENCES

Ananta, A., D.R. Willujeng, W. Utami and N.B. Handayandi (2016) 'Statistics on ethnic diversity in the land of Papua, Indonesia', *Asia & the Pacific Policy Studies* 3(3): 458–74.

Ariestha, B. (2013) 'Akar konflik kerusuhan antar etnik di Lampung Selatan', undergraduate thesis, Universitas Negeri Semarang, Semarang.

Aritonang, J. (2004) *Sejarah Perjumpaan Kristen dan Islam di Indonesia*, PT BPK Gunung Mulia, Jakarta.

Bock, M. (2012) 'Indigenous rights, rural migrants, and the informal divide', *Josef Korbel Journal of Advanced International Studies* 4(Summer): 48–73.

BPS (Badan Pusat Statistik) Provinsi Lampung (2011) 'Provinsi Lampung dalam angka 2011', BPS Provinsi Lampung, Bandar Lampung. https://lampung.bps.go.id/publication/2012/01/13/5c6ec87a5905679bb70e2cac/provinsi-lampung-dalam-angka-2011.html

BPS (Badan Pusat Statistik) Provinsi Lampung (2016) 'Provinsi Lampung dalam angka 2016', BPS Provinsi Lampung, Bandar Lampung. https://lampung.bps.go.id/publication/2016/07/15/f1a4eb2ab6d60d35e1f52d50/provinsi-lampung-dalam-angka-2016.html

Brauchler, B (2017) 'Changing patterns of mobility, citizenship and conflict in Indonesia', *Social Identities* 23(4): 446–61.

Chauvel, R. (2015) 'A Melanesian compromise opens the door for Jakarta–Papua dialogue', *Indonesia at Melbourne*, 14 July.

IPAC (Institute for Policy Analysis of Conflict) (2013a) 'Mesuji: anatomy of an Indonesian land conflict', Report No. 1, IPAC, 13 August.

IPAC (Institute for Policy Analysis of Conflict) (2013b) 'Carving up Papua: more districts, more problems', Report No. 3, IPAC, 9 October.

IPAC (Institute for Policy Analysis of Conflict) (2014) 'Indigenous rights vs agrarian reform in Indonesia: a case study from Jambi', Report No. 9, IPAC, 15 April.

IPAC (Institute for Policy Analysis of Conflict) (2018) 'Update on local election results in West Kalimantan and Papua', Report No. 50, IPAC, 16 August.

Kesavan, M. (2018) 'Murderous majorities', *New York Review of Books*, 18 January.

McCarthy, J.F. (2005) 'Between *adat* and state: institutional arrangements on Sumatra's forest frontier', *Human Ecology* 33(1): 57–82.

Nahimunkar (2017) 'Hampir 100% penduduknya pindah agama menjadi Kristen', *Nahimunkar.org*, 6 November.

Nahimunkar (2018a) 'Ini kata ketua MUI NTB soal dugaan pemurtadan di Lombok', *Nahimunkar.org*, 1 September.

Nahimunkar (2018b) 'Bupati Luwu: abaikan saja edaran menteri agama soal aturan pengeras suara di masjid', *Nahimunkar.org*, 5 September.

Nurmantyo, G. (2017) 'Memahami ancaman, menyadari jati diri sebagai modal membangun menuju Indonesia emas'. https://www.slideshare.net/arienugroho/memahami-ancaman-menyadari-jati-diri-sebagai-modal-membangun-menuju-indonesia-emas

Ratna Sari, D. (2018) 'Menyoal moratorium pemekaran daerah', Pusat Penelitian Politik, Lembaga Ilmu Pengetahuan Indonesia (LIPI), Jakarta, 17 September.

Utami, A. (2014) 'Resolusi konflik antar etnis Kabupaten Lampung Selatan', *Journal of Politic and Government Studies* 3(2). https://ejournal3.undip.ac.id/index.php/jpgs/article/view/4999/4832

Zulfa, E.A. (2014) 'Bali Nuraga-Lampung: identity conflict behind the policy', *Indonesian Journal of International Law* 11(2): 261–84.

Index

INDONESIA UPDATE SERIES

1989
Indonesia Assessment 1988 (Regional Development)
Edited by Hal Hill and Jamie Mackie

1990
Indonesia Assessment 1990 (Ownership)
Edited by Hal Hill and Terry Hull

1991
Indonesia Assessment 1991 (Education)
Edited by Hal Hill

1992
Indonesia Assessment 1992: Political Perspectives on the 1990s
Edited by Harold A. Crouch and Hal Hill

1993
Indonesia Assessment 1993: Labour: Sharing in the Benefits of Growth?
Edited by Chris Manning and Joan Hardjono

1994
Indonesia Assessment 1994: Finance as a Key Sector in Indonesia's Development
Edited by Ross McLeod

1996
Indonesia Assessment 1995: Development in Eastern Indonesia
Edited by Colin Barlow and Joan Hardjono

1997
Indonesia Assessment: Population and Human Resources
Edited by Gavin W. Jones and Terence H. Hull

1998
Indonesia's Technological Challenge
Edited by Hal Hill and Thee Kian Wie

1999
Post-Soeharto Indonesia: Renewal or Chaos?
Edited by Geoff Forrester

2000
Indonesia in Transition: Social Aspects of Reformasi and Crisis
Edited by Chris Manning and Peter van Diermen

2001
Indonesia Today: Challenges of History
Edited by Grayson J. Lloyd and Shannon L. Smith

2002
Women in Indonesia: Gender, Equity and Development
Edited by Kathryn Robinson and Sharon Bessell

2003
Local Power and Politics in Indonesia: Decentralisation and Democratisation
Edited by Edward Aspinall and Greg Fealy

2004
Business in Indonesia: New Challenges, Old Problems
Edited by M. Chatib Basri and Pierre van der Eng

www.ingramcontent.com/pod-product-compliance
Lightning Source LLC
Chambersburg PA
CBHW070910100426
42814CB00003B/120